AF505884

The Holocaust, Israel, and Canadian Protestant Churches

HAIM GENIZI

McGill-Queen's University Press
Montreal & Kingston · London · Ithaca

© McGill-Queen's University Press 2002
ISBN 0-7735-2401-0

Legal deposit fourth quarter 2002
Bibliothèque nationale du Québec

Printed in Canada on acid-free paper that is 100%
ancient forest free (100% post-consumer recycled),
processed chlorine free.

This book has been published with the help of a grant
from the Humanities and Social Sciences Federation of
Canada, using funds provided by the Social Sciences and
Humanities Research Council of Canada.

McGill-Queen's University Press acknowledges the
financial support of the Government of Canada through
the Book Publishing Industry Development Program
(BPIDP) for its publishing activities. We also
acknowledge the support of the Canada Council for the
Arts for our publishing program.

**National Library of Canada Cataloguing
in Publication Data**

Genizi, Haim
     The Holocaust, Israel, and Canadian Protestant churches
     (McGill-Queen's studies in the history of religion.
     Series two; no. 22)
     Includes bibliographical references and index.
     ISBN 0-7735-2401-0
     1. Protestant churches – Canada – History – 20th century.
     2. Christianity and other religions – Judaism.
     3. Judaism – Relations – Christianity. 4. Holocaust,
     Jewish (1939–1945). 5. Arab-Israeli conflict.
     6. Christianity and international affairs. I. Title.
     II. Series.
     BM535.G45 2002   261.2′6′0971   C2002-900408-X

This book was typeset by Dynagram Inc.
in 10/12 Baskerville.

Contents

Preface

The response of the Protestant churches in Canada to the Holocaust and to the State of Israel comprises two components of a single phenomenon, the Christian attitude to the Jews. The components were the relative silence of the Canadian churches during the Holocaust and their critical attitude to the emergence of a Jewish state in Palestine; both reactions stemmed, consciously or unconsciously, from deep-rooted anti-Jewish Christian theological teachings. After World War II the Christian churches were struggling with the difficult tension between various claims on the Christian conscience: first, guilt towards the Jews because of Christian tradition and Christian failures in Nazi times. For the conscientious, this sense of contrition produced sympathy for Jewish causes and for the Jewish state. Christians realized that the only guard against a repetition of mass destruction was a strong Israeli nation with secure borders. A second claim was a slowly mounting sympathy for the Arab Palestinians when they in turn were cast in the role of victims. Many maintained that the attempt to meet one refugee problem had created another, similar injustice. The result of the establishment of the State of Israel, they argued, was the creation of injustice to Arab refugees. Thus the shadow of the Holocaust hovered over the debate with regard to the attitude towards the State of Israel, and hence the need to discuss these two elements together.

How were (and are) these conflicting claims to be reconciled? Is it a question of either/or, or are there legitimate moral claims on both sides? How does one distinguish between legitimate criticism of Israel as a nation-state and ideological and antisemitic attacks on its legitimacy and right to exist? It is the purpose of this study to deal with the complications and ambiguities of the geopolitics of the Middle East and the dilemmas that these pose for both the Christian and the Jewish conscience. This book examines the struggle of Canadian Protestant churches with these moral dilemmas and the solutions they reached in the course of the five decades after the establishment of the State of Israel in 1948. Some individuals, such as Claris E. Silcox and Ernest Marshall Howse, supported Jewish refugees during the Holocaust but strongly opposed the Zionist idea and the State of Israel. This study will discuss these seemingly contradictory positions.

The United Church, the largest Protestant denomination in Canada, with its liberal and cosmopolitan outlook, promoted a policy of intervention in world affairs, including the Middle East. This involvement in the Israeli-Palestinian conflict, intensified by the constant anti-Israeli criticism of A.C. Forrest, the editor of the *United Church Observer,* led to a deep quarrel with the Canadian Jewish community. The debate was not only with Forrest but with the United Church, which supported his position. Although several authors have discussed the Forrest controversy, they have failed to use archival sources. Based on the vast body of material at the United Church Archives, including the files of the various United Church bodies and the papers of Forrest, Howse, and Silcox, we are now able to draw a clearer picture of the Jewish–United Church debate. Because of the great impact of the Forrest affair upon relations between the two communities, it was necessary to deal with the United Church in a more comprehensive manner than with other denominations.

Unlike the United Church, other groups with more conservative leanings, such as the Anglicans, the Presbyterians, and the Baptists, were more concerned with internal matters than with international affairs. The Baptists, in particular, were so busy with internal church problems that they hardly gave any attention to the Middle East crisis.

In the preparation of this study I am indebted to many people for their unfailing courtesy and helpfulness, among them the following librarians and archivists: Jean Dryden and Ruth Wilson of the United Church Archives; Janice Rosen of the National Archives of the Canadian Jewish Congress; Stephen A. Speisman and Howard Markus of the Ontario Jewish Archives; Janet MacPherson and Helen Leclerc of the Canadian Council of Churches; Dorothy Kealey of the Archives of the Anglican Church of Canada; Kim Arnold of the Archives of the Presbyterian Church in Canada; Carole Payne of the Holy Blossom Temple Archives; Judith Colwell of the Canadian Baptist Archives; and the archivist of the Evangelical Lutheran Church. I am particularly grateful to the following individuals, many of whom participated in aspects of the events described in this book, who devoted time to answer my questions in person or in writing: Irving Abella, Alan T. Davies, Michael J. Cohen, Roland de Corneille, John S. Conway, David Demson, Douglas duCharme, Shafik A. Farah, Raymond Hodgson, Joseph Kage, Ben G. Kayfetz, Angus J. MacQueen, N. Bruce McLeod, A.B.B. Moore, George Morrison, Marilyn F. Nefsky, W. Gunther Plaut, Brian Prideaux, David Rome, Lou Ronson, John H.B. Rye, Avrom Saltman, and Reuben Slonim. I also offer particular thanks to Professor Alan Davies of Victoria University, who read the entire manuscript and made important suggestions, and to Mrs Ruth Lockshin for her copy-editing. Special thanks go as well to York University in Toronto, where I spent my sabbatical as visiting professor, particularly to Professors Michael Brown and Martin Lockshin of the Centre of Judaic Studies. Thanks are also owing to Professor D.H. Akenson, editor of McGill-Queen's Studies in the History of Religion, and to Joan McGilvray, Kyla Madden, and Elizabeth Hulse, who saw the book through the Press with efficiency and skill. My deepest debt is to my wife, Elisheva, for her devotion and patience. Her technical assistance has made this book possible.

Abbreviations

CJCNA	Canadian Jewish Congress National Archives
CJDM	Christian Jewish Dialogue Montreal
CJN	*Canadian Jewish News* (CJC)
CJP	Commission on Justice and Peace (CCC)
CMEU	Canadians for Middle East Understanding
CNCR	Canadian National Committee on Refugees and Victims of Political Persecution
CSS	Council for Social Sevice (CEC)
CWC	Commission on World Concerns (CCC)
EMH	Ernest Marshall Howse Papers
EPS	"Ecumenical Press Service" (WCC)
GBW	General Board of World Missions (PCC)
GC	General Council (UC)
GS	General Synod (ACC)
IAU	International Affairs Unit (ACC)
JCRC	Jewish Community Relations Committee (CJC)
ME	Middle East
METF	Middle East Task Force
METG	Middle East Task Group (CCC)
MEWG	Middle East Working Group (CCC)
NCC	National Council of Churches (USA)
NTLC	National Tripartite Liaison Committee
OJA	Ontario Jewish Archives
PCC	Presbyterian Church in Canada
PCCA	Presbyterian Church in Canada Archives
PLO	Palestine Liberation Organization
SW	*Social Welfare* (Social Service of Canada)
UC	United Church of Canada
UCA	United Church Archives
UN	United Nations
UNRWA	United Nations Relief and Works Agency
WCC	World Council of Churches

The Protestant Councils
of Churches and
the State of Israel

1 The International Councils of Churches

Any discussion of the attitude of the Protestant churches to the Zionist movement and the establishment of the State of Israel should take into consideration Christian theology as it relates to the Jewish people and Judaism. The church traditionally believed that the destruction of the Second Temple in Jerusalem in 70 CE and the subsequent Jewish exile was a divine punishment for the crucifixion of Jesus and the refusal by the Jews to accept his redemption. Christians believed that the Jewish people were destined to wither away and be replaced by Christians. Even modern Protestant groups persistently upheld the theological doctrine of the disappearance of "Old Israel," the Jewish people, when "New Israel," the Christian church, came into being. The Jews lost not only their identity as Israel but also their divine right to Palestine, and Christians considered it theirs, calling it the Holy Land; the Jewish people had forfeited any claim of territorial ownership. Even after centuries of Muslim occupation, Christians never gave up their claim to the land. In the nineteenth century, Christian missionaries renewed interest among their co-religionists in the Holy Land, establishing settlements there and encouraging pilgrimages to the holy places. They were eager to preserve the country as it had been two thousand years earlier. "They fostered a desire to maintain Palestine as a purely historical museum, full of peasants, donkeys and vineyards. The terms Israel and Zion ... certainly did not relate to the contemporary Jewish population," John Conway, a historian at the University of British Columbia, remarked in 1998.[1]

This theological perception did not leave any room for the new phenomenon of a Jewish claim to a sovereign state and for the right of the

Jewish people to play, as a nation, a role in modern world history. The appearance of the dynamic Zionist movement in the late nineteenth century, with its claim to represent the renewal of the historical Jewish identity, along with the right to an independent state in Palestine – demands that Christians for centuries had denied – confronted the churches with a theological challenge. It contradicted the centuries-old Christian theological myth of Jewish national demise. Edward H. Flannery, a Catholic historian, has argued that Christian uneasiness about the restoration of Jews to Palestine and Jerusalem was the basis for Christian anti-Zionism and the cover for various "reasons" supplied for disfavouring the State of Israel. He maintains that the similarity of reaction in Christendom to the Holocaust and to the emergence of the State of Israel was symptomatic of "determinative unconscious forces, specifically, of an unrecognized antipathy [to] the Jewish people." The Holocaust and the State of Israel were at opposite poles in the existence of Jews: "One is nadir, the other, its zenith; Israel prostrate and Israel triumphant." Yet though the situations were opposite, the responses to them were identical: apathy and even hostility.[2] Even the fundamentalist Protestants who favoured the restoration of Israel as the forerunner of the Second Coming had no sympathy with the secular character of the Zionists and their socialistic leaning. They were afraid that the Zionists would introduce modernism, Marxism, and materialism. How could the Zionists build Zion without God?

The nationalistic character of the Zionist movement also prompted Christian antagonism. Jewish nationalism seemed to contradict the universalism of the prophets and of Jesus. When modern Jewish nationalists were juxtaposed to Jewish nationalists of the first century, traditional religious hostility towards Jews as "God killers" could now be directed to the "narrow Zionist nationalists" of the twentieth century, before Vatican II in 1965. The attitude of many Christians towards Jews as individuals stands in sharp contrast to their hostile response to the Jewish nation. While many Christians had friendly relations with their Jewish neighbours as individuals, they considered the contemporary Jewish people, as a collective body, to be responsible for the crucifixion of Jesus. The resurgence of Jewish nationalism was viewed as a repetition of the same fatal error that had led to the Jewish rejection of Jesus. "It is the focal point at which Christian opinion, in all brotherly love, should make clear and emphatic its disagreement with the dominant trend in contemporary Judaism," wrote Millar Burrows, professor of biblical theology at Yale University and president of the American School for Oriental Research in the Middle East, in an article in July 1948.[3] In the same vein, A.E. Prince, a historian at the University of Toronto, observed: "His own people, the

Jews, want to set up again a narrow Jewish political nationalism, against which He protested at the cost of His life."[4]

After World War II, a war that was fought against fascist nationalism, internationalism became a popular ideology in liberal circles. Its supporters opposed any movement that contradicted their democratic ideals. Therefore liberals who prided themselves on being open-minded saw nationalistic Zionism as a divisive factor and opposed the Jewish state. Jews were asked to give up their centuries-old prayer and dream for the sake of world peace.[5] Liberal church circles enthusiastically supported the process of decolonization and the national liberation movements in Asia and Africa, including that of the Palestinians. Yet the Jews were asked "for the sake of the peace of the world" to renounce their demand for a sovereign state, because it was "contrary to historic processes." This inconsistency probably resulted from traditional theological prejudices.

In addition to the aforesaid reasons for an unsympathetic approach to the Zionist idea, the Israeli-Palestinian conflict evoked the ethical demands of the Gospel to care for the poor, the persecuted, the refugees, and the uprooted. The emphasis on peace and justice led many Christians to sympathize with and support the struggle of the Palestinian people. Since the establishment of the State of Israel would be at the expense of the Palestinians, political and ethical considerations joined with theological ones to oppose any plan to reconstitute a Jewish state in Palestine.

On the other hand, many conservative Christians, the so-called Christian Zionists, supported Zionism, also for theological reasons. Thus the resurgence of Israel and the emergence of a Jewish state caused grave religious problems, leading many theologians and rank-and-file church members to oppose the Zionist movement and its purposes. Among the most outspoken and influential opponents were missionaries who were active in Arab countries, along with their families and the institutions affiliated with them. "Missionaries in the Arab world on the whole seem very sympathetic to the Arab cause. The majority of them have not been to the other side," reported the *Record of Proceedings of the General Council of the United Church of Canada* in 1958.[6] Naturally, these individuals wanted to protect the interests of their communities. Some of them believed that a Jewish state would be an obstacle to the missionary goal of the church.[7]

With the conclusion of World War II, however, when the mass murders and the cruelty committed by the Nazis became known, sympathy among church members for a haven for the persecuted Jews in their own homeland increased. This sympathy was stronger in western European countries, which had witnessed the annihilation of the Jews during the Holocaust.

THE WORLD COUNCIL OF CHURCHES

Insistence on peace, justice, and the integrity of Creation by the World Council of Churches (WCC) highlighted the ethical demands of the Gospel in a worldwide setting. The WCC, an umbrella organization for the major Protestant and Orthodox Christian denominations in the world, was established in September 1948.[8] The policies it adopted strongly influenced the Canadian Protestant churches that relied heavily on the international body, hence the importance of the WCC's Middle East position for this study.[9]

Since its establishment, the council has equivocated in its attitude to the Jewish people and their right to a state of their own. In addition to the deep-seated theological beliefs outlined above, the WCC, as an international organization, was committed to political and social causes, such as support for national liberation movements and the human rights of oppressed minorities. Consequently, it was exposed to influences and pressures from local religious and political groups in Asia and Africa. A combination of several powerful elements led to the gradual formulation of a pro-Arab policy on the Middle East. Among these were theologically anti-Jewish forces, the strong missionary groups operating in Arab countries, the Protestant churches in the Middle East, the miserable condition of Palestinian refugees and the suppression of their human rights, and finally, the fight by the Palestine Liberation Organization (PLO) for a just peace and for self-determination, that is, for an independent state.

The WCC's first assembly in Amsterdam in September 1948 considered the newly established State of Israel, but refused to pass judgment on the "rights" and "wrongs" of the Palestine question. It called upon nations to treat the problem, not as a political one, but "as a moral and spiritual question that touches a nerve center of the world's religions." This neutral position was the outcome of a compromise between the missionary groups, who were hostile to the Zionist idea, and the western European church representatives, who supported the need for a haven for the Jewish survivors of the Holocaust. Arab influence in Amsterdam was marginal.[10]

At the WCC's second assembly in Evanston, Illinois, in 1954, unlike at the Amsterdam assembly, a coalition of representatives from Arab and Asian countries, as well as from the United States, were able to prevent any reference to Israel as a political entity. A proposition that called for the evangelization of the Jews was rejected, however. The heated debate on Jewish nationalism showed how difficult it was for the Protestant world to face the theological consequences of a modern Jewish state.[11]

The gradual rise of Arab nationalism in the 1950s and American missionary influence on the WCC was evident when, in 1959, the council rejected Elfan Rees's program for the integration of the Palestinian refugees into Arab host countries. Dr Rees, an English clergyman and expert on refugees, had toured the Arab refugee camps, and he stated that the situation of the refugees was deplorable because the Arab host countries had refused to help them. Rees recommended the integration of the refugees into various Arab host countries with international financial backing. He maintained that integration into Muslim and Arabic-speaking countries would make absorption much easier than repatriation to Israel.[12] Thus the WCC preferred to emphasize the political aspect of the problem of the refugees and to press Israel to accept their repatriation; it put the humanitarian solution second.[13]

The Six Day War of 1967 was a turning point against Israel in certain church circles. The great victory of the Jews, the occupation of Jerusalem, the West Bank, and Gaza, and the significant growth in the refugee problem – which became an international, rather than a local, issue – turned many church members away from a sympathetic or even an apathetic approach and towards an anti-Israeli one. The speedy victory went against the Jewish image in the eyes of Christians; Israel had become a Goliath instead of a David.

Although the World Council of Churches in the late 1950s had been somewhat pro-Arab, after the Six Day War it became strongly anti-Israel. In the 1960s the WCC undertook to give voice to the voiceless by supporting national liberation movements. Partly to attract the support of the rising Third World, the WCC was determined to fight against racism and territorial occupation.[14] To be sure, the financial help given by the council to liberation movements to purchase weapons for armed struggle, such as support for the Rhodesian Patriotic Front, met with some criticism in church circles. Some groups argued that "the Council is controlled by radical, even revolutionary elements" of the Third World.[15]

On 23 August 1967, in Heraklion, Crete, the Central Committee of the WCC adopted a statement on the Middle East that called for "a just and durable peace." It deplored the annexation of the occupied territories, demanded the withdrawal of Israeli forces, and proposed effective international guarantees for "the political independence and territorial integrity" of all nations, including Israel and the Arab states. It also called for the repatriation of the refugees of the recent war. As well, the committee demanded free access to religious sites and advocated an end to the arms race. The great powers were held responsible for providing political and economic leadership for the welfare of the whole region.[16] Missing from the statement was any criticism of Egyptian president Abdel Nasser's provocative actions, which had led to the opening of hostilities, or of the Arab states' refusal to alleviate the situation of the refugees residing in their own countries. The statement stood in contrast to the silence of the churches both before and during the war.

In August 1969, in Canterbury, England, the Central Committee adopted a statement that marked a turning point in the WCC's policy on the Middle East. It was in fact the basis for all subsequent WCC Middle East policies. The Canterbury statement declared that, "in supporting the establishment of a Jewish State in Palestine, without recognizing the rights of the Palestinians to self-determination, the Great Powers have done injustice to the Palestinian Arabs, and this injustice should be redressed. No lasting peace is possible without respecting the legitimate rights of the Palestinian and Jewish people presently living in the area without effective international guarantee for the political independence and territorial integrity of all nations in the area, including Israel."[17] While the previous resolutions had regarded the Palestinians as "refugees" who should be helped and repatriated, the Canterbury statement emphasized the "legitimate rights" of the Palestinians to "self-determination" and "political independence." By adopting the Palestinian demand for an independent state, the WCC became a forerunner in supporting the Arab cause; it expected the Protestant churches throughout the world to follow its policy.

A rare exception to the WCC's nebulous Middle East position was its "unequivocal opposition" to the United Nations resolution that had equated Zionism with racism. Philip Potter, general secretary of the WCC, in November 1975 expressed his organization's "deep concern" about this resolution, stating, "Zionism has historically been a movement concerned with the liberation of the Jewish people from oppression, including racial oppression." He warned that the resolution which equated Zionism with racism "has the seriously damaging effect of exacerbating the already explosive situation in the Middle East." Potter therefore appealed to the General Assembly of the UN "to reconsider and rescind this resolution." To balance this pro-Zionist declaration, he also called upon the parties involved in the crisis to find ways "to enable the Palestinian people to achieve their legitimate rights to nationhood and statehood."[18] Criticism of the WCC's unbalanced position towards the Middle East conflict was expressed by the WCC's Committee on the Church and the Jewish People in its biennial consultation in June 1975. The committee declared that statements on the Arab-Israeli crisis made by various church organizations "were not always balanced as between Jews and Arab Palestinians, and it was urged that much greater care should be taken in future to achieve a fair representation of the conflicting views."[19]

This appeal for a more balanced approach does not seem to have changed the course of the WCC, however. The decisions on Jerusalem were a case in point. Israel's conquest of East Jerusalem in 1967 had roused strong resentment in Christian circles. It was not the fact that infidels ruled the Holy City which bothered Christians, since Jerusalem under Muslim control was acceptable to them. It was, rather, the great Jewish victory that antagonized church members. Using military force did not fit their image of the Jewish character; it "ruined Judaism," according to Christian perceptions. "Many Christians still had not made peace with a Jewish people who moved from the shadows of history into the sunlight and tasted the fruits of victory," Rabbi W. Gunther Plaut of Holy Blossom Temple in Toronto later observed.[20]

The Central Committee of the WCC in 1980 criticized the Israeli government's unilateral proclamation making Jerusalem the capital. It urged a dialogue between the three religions, hoping that this might lead to a "mutually acceptable agreement for sharing the city." In other words, a committee of three religions would decide the future of Jerusalem. The Central Committee regarded the Israeli move as "contrary to all pertinent UN resolutions"; it felt that the action undermined efforts towards a just peace in the region.[21] Canadian Jewish leaders angrily criticized the committee's resolution, saying that it was "wholly political in character and is flagrantly partisan, it disregards established facts and distorts reality." They also complained about the imbalanced information that the WCC relied on. While Arab Christians, as members of the Central Committee, were able to press their pro-Arab point of view, Jews had no direct voice in the WCC and their position was not represented. Christian members of the WCC dialogue recognized the need for better communication and offered "to seek further ways by which the voices of the Jewish community can be freely heard within the WCC."[22]

The political events in the Middle East during the decade of 1982–92 left their impact on the WCC position towards the region. The beginning of the decade saw the Israeli invasion of Lebanon and the continuing occupation of the southern part of that country, Arab terrorist activities and Israeli retaliations, and the emergence of the Palestine Liberation Organization as the representative of the Palestinians. In December 1987 the Intifada, the civil uprising by Palestinians, began, and Israeli measures to suppress it quickly followed. All these events sharpened the WCC's criticism of Israel's policies.

The sixth assembly of the WCC, held in Vancouver, issued a strong anti-Israel statement in August 1983. The Lebanese war and the continuing occupation of the West Bank and Gaza created a dangerous situation that "threatens the peace of the whole world"; hence the churches had a responsibility to intervene. The statement blamed Christians who "uncritically supported Israel" because of their guilt over the fate of Jews at the hands of Christians through the centuries, thereby "ignoring the plight of the Palestinians." It accused Israel of "flagrantly" violating the basic rights of the Palestinians by expelling, relocating, or imprisoning them, and it called upon the United Nations to revise Resolution 242 in light of the changes that had occurred since 1967, referring to the "the rights of the Palestinians to self determination including the right of establishing a sovereign Palestinian state." The statement also demanded the inclusion of the PLO in negotiations for a peaceful settlement. The WCC called upon churches to increase their awareness of the fate of the Palestinians, to encourage dialogue between Palestinians and Israelis, and to support peace movements in Israel.[23]

The Intifada, or "rebellion," according to Ghassan Rubeiz, secretary for the Middle East Commission on Inter-Church Aid, Refugee and World Service of the WCC, which began in December 1987 in Gaza and later spread to the West Bank, increased world sympathy for the plight of the Palestinians. Children throwing stones at armed soldiers were a "hot" item on television news. The uprising led to a change in the approach of the media: "terrorists" now became "fighters resisting occupation." Summarizing world opinion, Rubeiz wrote, "The psychology of today's events shows that the Palestinian question is more powerful when it portrays the Palestinians as militarily weak and morally strong. Rock throwing is very symbolic as a strategy of the victim facing colonials."[24]

Indeed, for five long years Israel confronted the difficult – almost impossible – task of handling the civil uprising. Its efforts to suppress the unrest by military means were far from successful, as well as attracting harsh criticism not only from abroad but also from within Israel itself. The WCC recognized the Intifada as "a genuine expression of the national aspiration of the Palestinian people," and it protested the violations of human rights and the closing of schools and colleges in the territories. Only a peaceful solution could stop bloodshed, and the WCC therefore strongly supported the idea of convening an international peace conference. The Central Committee expressed its solidarity with the Christian churches in the region, which were suffering, particularly in Jerusalem. It demanded that Israel dismantle Jewish settlements in the occupied territories and avoid establishing new ones.[25]

On 15 November 1988 the Palestine National Council, the umbrella body of the various Palestinian groups, issued a declaration of independence and a political statement, which emphasized the urgent need for the convening of an effective international peace conference under UN auspices. Emilio Castro, general secretary of the WCC, "welcomed" the declaration and expressed "appreciation for the positive spirit" it demonstrated. He pointed out that the political statement was "very much along the lines taken by the WCC." He regarded the occasion as "a decisive moment for the Middle East, offering a unique opportunity for peace-making."[26]

The presentation that the WCC made before the UN Commission on Human Rights in February 1989 could be considered a faithful summary of the council's position on the Middle East crisis. Ghassan Rubeiz opened his oral presentation by declaring that the WCC was "a friend of the peoples of Palestine and Israel," and that peace could be attained only by the recognition of their "legitimate aspirations." He reiterated the council's position that the Israeli occupation was "unlawful and must terminate to allow for the establishment of a Palestinian State neighboring to the State of Israel." The suppression of the civil uprising was "morally unacceptable and in contravention of the Geneva 1949 Conventions." The WCC welcomed Yasser Arafat's implicit recognition of Israel as a neighbouring state, regarding it "a new sign of the changing times." Rubeiz went on to say that "solutions based on greed, on simplistic understanding of history and on exclusive theology, have proven to receive decreasing support from the international community. This year ought to be the year of a major breakthrough in peace making. The Palestinians have made significant initiatives, which deserve positive reciprocation from the side of Israel." To Israel he advised an "exchange of land for peace"; to the Arabs he recommended "creative thinking." Israel was considered strong enough to take some risk in making peace. Rubeiz concluded the WCC presentation by calling for the convening of an international peace conference under UN auspices with PLO participation.[27] Although he insisted that the WCC was not pro-Palestinian, he understood why Jews felt differently.[28]

Thus we can see the long way the WCC had travelled, from a neutral position in 1948 regarding the aspirations of the Palestinians to supporting the demand for an independent state in the 1980s. Its support for Third World liberation movements, as well as the constant encouragement of the Middle East churches, influenced the WCC to take an umbalanced position on the Arab-Israeli conflict. As a result of its international stature and its well-informed structure, the World Council of Churches was frequently followed by national and local church groups. Both the Canadian Council of Churches (CCC) and major Canadian denominations were deeply influenced by the resolutions made by the various bodies of the WCC. It was easier for them to adopt pro-Arab statements when they could rely on the Geneva-based senior body – hence the important role that the WCC played in the uneven Middle East policy of Canadian churches.

THE MIDDLE EAST COUNCIL OF CHURCHES

The establishment of the Middle East Council of Churches (MECC) in 1974 was the outcome of a long process. The growing interest of Christian denominations in the Middle East in ecumenical cooperation, unity, and witness had begun in 1948 with the formation of the Near East Christian Council for Missionary Cooperation. This body, which was controlled by U.S. missionaries residing in the region, brought Protestant missionary churches together for cooperative purposes. It eventually became the Near East Christian Council and later the Near East Council of Churches (NECC). Despite its various names, it continued in its first decades to be dominated by Western missionaries. The NECC organized two councils in Beirut, in 1951 and 1956, in order to discuss the refugee problem.[29]

Growing Arab influence on the NECC gradually changed its character, however. By the mid-1960s, Arab clergy had taken over the leadership of this body. A clear sign of this change was the election of an Egyptian Coptic pastor as the first Arab executive of the council. While Western missionaries had been dealing with the humanitarian aspect of the refugee problem through the financing of various relief programs, the Arab leaders of the NECC openly insisted on a political solution.[30]

This trend of the Arabization in Middle Eastern churches, taking over their leadership from American and European missionaries, coincided with the rise of Arab nationalism in the area. Therefore the leaders of local church denominations tended to support the Palestinian cause. When the Oriental Orthodox and Eastern Orthodox churches joined the Protestant NECC in 1974, the Middle East Council of Churches was formed. It defined itself as "a meeting place for the churches, as a facilitator of their dialogue towards unity, and as an instrument of their cooperation in witness." Its three-point program was "unity, witness and service." Eventually, its member churches included twenty-four denominations from the four "families" of Oriental Orthodox, Eastern Orthodox, Protestant (evangelical and episcopal), and Catholic churches.[31]

Gabriel Habib, the energetic general secretary, made great efforts to interest Western churches in the Palestinian cause and tried to involve them in the Middle East crisis. As a summary of MECC activities stated,

"Since its establishment in 1974 the MECC has been deeply involved in the search for justice and peace in the Middle East. The MECC efforts include information and interpretation through publications and exchange of visits by and to the churches abroad, international discussions on the biblical and theological implications of the ongoing conflict in the region, promotion of international solidarity in support of human rights, and humanitarian assistance to the victims of conflict and oppression."[32] Habib's program to invite foreign church ministers to visit the Middle East and to send Arab church leaders to their countries, in addition to its ecumenical benefits, successfully involved Canadian churches in the Palestinian cause. The position of the MECC was also strengthened by the active support of the World Council of Churches, hence the importance of discussing the MECC in this study of Canadian Protestant churches.

The MECC, in cooperation with the WCC, held a conference on the Palestinian refugee problem in Nicosia in November 1979, which explicitly favoured the "recognition of the political rights of the Palestinian people and of the injustices inflicted on this people" over a relief program for the refugees. While Nicosia conference was called a "Consultation on Service to Palestine Refugees," the discussions and resolutions were focused on the political rights of the Palestinian people to statehood. The conference appealed to the world Christian community "to be more fully sensitive" to Palestinian rights and to spread this awareness not only within their churches but also among policy- and public-opinion-making circles. The most far-reaching resolution of the conference was its call upon the churches "to promote the idea that the PLO must be admitted as full partner into any deliberations dealing with the future of Palestine." The message directed to the world's churches was that there would not be a solution to the problem unless the Palestinians could be ensured "their exercise of self-determination and statehood."[33]

In January 1983 the MECC founded a travel agency called the Ecumenical Travel Office (ETO). Its aims were to expose Christians to the heritage and cultural traditions of the Middle Eastern countries and to connect local Christian groups with Western churches. The major reason for what was called "alternative tourism" seems to have been political – to compete with the Israeli government's subsidized tours for Christian ministers. While the latter showed the positive side of Israel, including visits to religious sites in Nazareth, the Sea of Galilee, Bethlehem, and Jerusalem, ETO seminars toured Arab countries and Palestinian refugee camps in the occupied territories. In addition to political education about the Palestinian cause, alternative tourism was a potential source of significant income for the MECC. The council therefore made a great effort to attract Canadian church members to its tourist program. The project, however, had only limited success.[34]

On another front, the MECC undertook to challenge fundamentalist support for Israel. Right-wing evangelical fundamentalists were Protestants who believed in the coming of the millennium. They rejoiced in the creation of the State of Israel, seeing it as the fulfillment of biblical prophecy, and the occupation of East Jerusalem in 1967 gave them "a renewed faith in the accuracy and validity of the Bible."[35] The fact that these right-wing Christians were enthusiastic supporters of Israel was considered by the MECC to be a "challenge to the church and [a threat] to the credibility of Christian witness." It feared that the backing of the Christian Zionist groups might cause some Christians to attribute divine support to Israel's handling of the Palestinian problem. Habib was particularly worried that, in some parts of the Third World, Christians might confuse biblical stories and prophecies about Israel's divine election with the idea that the modern State of Israel was the fulfillment of these prophecies or an eschatological entity. The MECC urged the CCC to ensure "that this response not go unchallenged by the Christian churches." The CCC responded positively: "This troublesome business of the 'right-wing fundamentalists' phenomenon is a subject which badly needs to be looked into," replied Tad Mitsui of the CCC to Leopoldo J. Niilus of the MECC.[36] A decade later, the polemic against the resurgence of Christian Zionism still continued. Yet fundamentalist support for Israel was unabated, as evidenced by the growing number of visits to Israel by its adherents.[37]

As we have seen, five years of the Intifada produced widespread suffering among the Palestinians. The MECC focused its activities on raising Christian solidarity worldwide. Gabriel Habib appealed to the general secretary of the CCC "to join us during this critical period in trying to alleviate the suffering of the population."[38] The heads of the churches in Jerusalem also voiced their concerns. In a unique announcement, the first joint statement since the Six Day War, in January 1988 they appealed to Christians in the Holy Land "to pray for justice and peace for our Land." The church leaders declared that they stood "with the suffering and the oppressed, we stand with the refugees and the deported, with the distressed and the victims of injustice," and they asked church members to dedicate a day "for fasting and self-denial, identifying ourselves with our brothers and sisters in the camps on the West Bank and in the Gaza Strip."[39] It is not clear whether the MECC initiated this statement by the heads of churches in Jerusalem, but it was widely circulated together with a letter of support from Gabriel Habib.[40]

Utilizing the great impact of the uprising on individuals and politicians around the world, the MECC pursued active ecumenical involvement towards promoting "a just solution" to the conflict. Accordingly, it organized a large ecumenical assembly in Cyprus for 20–9 January 1990, which was a real success for the council. Two hundred delegates and guests attended, including representatives of Pope John Paul II, the general secretary of the WCC, and heads of denominations and ecumenical councils. The assembly demonstrated the status that the MECC had achieved, and it was an affirmation of the Christian presence in the region. Given the participation of Catholics, it was a rare example of Christian unity. The assembly expressed its solidarity with the suffering of the Palestinians and emphasized Christian responsibility for them. It reiterated its support for Palestinian rights to an independent state and urged the governments of the world "to contribute effectively toward the implementation of those rights." The assembly also stressed the importance of Jerusalem to Christians. It called for a dialogue between the three monotheistic faiths and appealed to the churches to follow recent MECC initiatives for Christian solidarity in prayer and action for peace in Palestine.[41]

The Middle East Council of Churches, under Arab leadership and representing millions of Christians in Arab countries, quite naturally supported the Palestinians' struggle for independence. From its formation in 1974, the council had pursued the goal of bringing peace and justice to the Palestinians, and it never criticized Arab actions. The continuing efforts of the MECC to increase the awareness of churches around the world about the fate of Christians in the Middle East, particularly of the Palestinians, eventually bore fruit. With the growth of its authority, it succeeded in transferring its pro-Arab position to the World Council of Churches and later to the Canadian Council of Churches and church members in Canada. Thus the umbalanced position of the WCC and the MECC was an important influence on Canadian church leaders in their formulation of opinions on the Palestinian-Israeli conflict.

THE NATIONAL COUNCIL OF CHURCHES OF CHRIST IN THE U.S.A.

Another ecumenical council outside Canada, in addition to the World Council of Churches and the Middle East Council of Churches, which had some influence on the attitude of the Canadian churches towards Israel was the National Council of Churches of Christ in the U.S.A. (NCC). Leaders of the Canadian Council of Churches and the United Church of Canada, as well as individuals such as A.C. Forrest, showed interest in the position taken by the parallel body across the border.[42] Relying on declarations of the NCC on the Middle East, Canadian church officials found justification for their own nebulous position. There was close cooperation between Canadian and American pro-Arab, as well as pro-Israeli, groups through seminars, conferences, and public lectures. Therefore it is worthwhile briefly examining the NCC's attitude towards Israel.[43]

The National Council of Churches was an umbrella organization, representing thirty-four national Protestant denominations in America with forty-two million members. While such a large body obviously included different approaches, its statements of policy reflected the official position.[44] In the 1930s the NCC's predecessor, the Federal Council of Churches, had actively supported the Jewish cause. It condemned antisemitism in Germany and America, protested against Nazi persecution of the Jews, and supported the admission of refugees, Jewish and Christian, to the United States.[45] However, the Federal Council's attitude to the Zionist concept and the Jewish state was controversial and perplexing to some of the church leadership. There was a sharp division between supporters of the Zionist claim to a homeland for the Jewish people and those who strongly opposed it. While the former believed that, particularly after the Holocaust, Jews were entitled to a national home with secure borders, the latter, whose position was influenced by missionary groups and institutions operating in Arab countries, rejected the moral and historical rights of the Jews to an independent state. The *Christian Century*, an influential, independent, liberal Protestant weekly, consistently opposed, on theological grounds, the restoration of the Jewish people to Palestine.[46] Protestant liberals, who defended the principle of the melting pot in the United States, regarded Jewish nationalism as an ethnic refusal to assimilate. They were antagonistic to the Jewish struggle to uphold tradition because it preserved Jewish distinctiveness. Under the banner of liberalism, many Protestant circles expected the assimilation of ethnic groups in America. Jewish nationalism went contrary to this view. Furthermore, support for a Jewish state would create the danger of dual loyalties. As time went on, the interests of the Palestinians were raised as a cause for objecting to a Jewish state. Thus the anti-Jewish thrust was diverted from the theological to the political arena.[47] Hertzel Fishman, in his study of the attitudes of American Protestants to a Jewish state, concludes that "an analysis of American liberal Protestant policies regarding problems of the Near East discredits the pietistic Protestant belief that these policies have been based on purely objective, humanitarian, altruistic, or religious motivations. Like all large religious and secular groups, American liberal Protestantism has its own truths and biases. These attitudes are neither devoid of political considerations nor of power mongering."[48]

The Six Day War and the events that followed focused the NCC's attention on the Israeli-Palestinian conflict. The executive committee of the General Board of the NCC adopted a resolution on 7 July 1967 admitted the council's part in the "sin of neglect" with regard to the plight of the Palestinians. On the other hand, it also confessed to the churches' silence when Israel's existence was in danger. The statement opposed territorial expansion by the use of force, called upon the international community to accept the State of Israel, and asked Israel to let the new refugees return to their homes. As a long-term solution, it recommended repatriation or emigration to other countries. It also proposed an "international presence" in Jerusalem, disapproving of Israel's unilateral annexation of East Jerusalem, and free access to the Gulf of Aqaba and the Suez Canal. It advocated arms control and proposed the introduction of a new spirit of reconciliation and reconstruction.[49] The statement was a balanced one, giving equal weight to its various components. While Jews criticized the statement, the *Christian Century* commended the NCC's courage in speaking the truth without bending to pressure groups.[50]

After the war of 1967, criticism of Israel's expansionism and its treatment of Palestinians in the occupied territories grew. Following the resolutions of the World Council of Churches in Heraklion in 1967 and in Canterbury in 1969, the NCC's even-handed policy changed.[51] The atmosphere at the NCC's convention in 1975 clearly reflected this shift; as a participant reported, "There was a striking difference in this meeting and all the others I have attended heretofore in that no time was wasted on such issues as Israel's right to exist and American responsibility to support the Jewish people based on prophecy or history, etc. On the contrary, a great deal of time was spent considering the existence of the Palestinian people ... my point is that even among the Protestant churches in the United States an obvious change is taking place and I think this is wholesome."[52] From this time on in the NCC a pro-Arab approach prevailed, which supported the right of the Palestinians to self-determination and later recognized the PLO as the legitimate representative of the Palestinian people.[53]

2 The Canadian Council of Churches

Canadians suffered badly during the Great Depression of the 1930s, but the churches suffered even more. Ministers' salaries decreased, churches fell deeply into debt, and congregations were closed, particularly on the prairies. Hardship produced sometimes irrational or dangerous reactions. Disappointment in the existing political, social, and economic system led some people to look to Europe for radical solutions, and left- and right-wing social movements flirted with fascist or communist ideas.[1] Others lost their faith in Europe, developing nativist and isolationist tendencies instead. The outcome of these responses to the difficult situation was xenophobia, with its companions – racism and antisemitism. Strong anti-alien feelings led to restrictionist regulations and the closing of doors in Canada to refugees, especially to Jewish ones. Canadian antisemitism, nourished by traditional Christian anti-Jewish teachings, was meaningfully intensified during the Nazi era.[2]

The growth of such anti-Jewish sentiment among the Canadian public at large naturally influenced the attitude of the churches to the Holocaust and to Jewish refugees. Certain conservative church members believed that the Jews deserved Nazi persecution as a punishment for their rejection of Christ's redemption; anti-democratic and pro-fascist articles appeared occasionally in the church press. On the other hand, many individuals protested from their pulpits against Nazism and against the persecution of Jews. Some even called for the admission of Jewish refugees into Canada. "How silent were the churches?" ask Alan T. Davies and Marilyn F. Nefsky in their book on the attitude of Canadian Protestantism to the Jewish plight. The various denominations reacted differently. The United, Anglican, and Baptist clergy were the most outspoken on behalf of the Jewish victims. The Lutherans and the Salvationists said the least. The Presbyterians and the Mennonites, motivated by conservative religious doctrine compounded with defensiveness about the immigration issue or pro-Germanism, were not sympathetic to the Jewish cause. Summarizing their findings, Davies and Nefsky have written: "No sustained universal outcry on behalf of the beleaguered refugees ever erupted from either the Christian or the Protestant rank and file, unless the coast to coast post Kristallnacht rallies are regarded in this light. Neither Christian nor Protestant Canada spoke with a collective voice. But many Protestant pulpits were not silent, nor were many presbyteries, conferences and synods, nor were a sizable number of editorials, bishops and academics ... Were the churches then silent? Yes and no ... It is gray."[3]

The churches' response to the persecution of the Jews should be compared with the moral responsibility and compassion they later showed towards oppressed minorities such as the Palestinian refugees. Unlike the frequent anti-Israel resolutions adopted by the highest courts of national and interdenominational church organizations on behalf of the Palestinian refugees, anti-Nazi protests in favour of the persecuted European Jewry were few and vague.

After World War II there was a general expansion in the Canadian churches. Reacting against wartime dislocation, Christians searched for old traditions, and people returned to the churches. Religious education increased in colleges as well as in Sunday schools. The change was particularly evident in the well-to-do suburbs. The fear of the Cold War, as well as personal worries, also contributed to the growth of religion. Interdenominational organizations, such as the Canadian Council of Churches, lost influence in the eyes of conservative elements.

At the same time as the churches became crowded, however, Canadian society generally turned secular. The affluent society brought about a moral revolution in which many taboos were broken. Lay people who had joined the church after the war changed the patterns of moral behaviour, adopting secular ways of living outside the church.[4] By the 1960s the position of the church in Canadian society had changed significantly and in some ways diminished, observes John W. Grant, a historian of the Canadian churches. The easing of Cold War tensions and the end of McCarthyism in the United States led to a relief from tensions, and people no longer listened to the clergy. The churches, concerned that their programs were no longer relevant to their congregations, searched for new styles and new projects. A certain effort was made to modernize the church and adopt it to a secular Canada. But increasingly, secular individuals rejected the churches' attempts to keep the old emphasis in new forms. Grant maintains that in the 1960s, consumerist society led to the decline of Christendom. However, its demise did not mean the end of Christianity.[5]

In the following decade the churches took an increasing interest in public policy. They became aware of international problems, particularly in the area of human rights. The United Church and the Baptists had had a long history of interest in the social gospel, and other denominations now joined them in their call for justice. The churches came to believe that in order to make the world a safer, better, and more just place, they should make efforts to influence government policies, and they frequently sent representations to Ottawa. Thus the churches gradually shifted from being involved in the traditional Canadian way of life to a more assertive role of emphasizing Christian responsibility to take a stand on the major issues of the world.[6] This noticeable change in the Canadian churches was partly in response to the new program by the World Council of Churches to combat racism. Canadian churches decided to become part of a worldwide movement for human rights, for economic and social justice, and for peace. Accordingly, in the 1970s and 1980s they issued statements on internal and external problems, such as poverty, unemployment, and attitudes to Native Canadians, nuclear weapons, energy issues, immigration, refugees, and apartheid. In order to pool their resources, the churches established ad hoc coalitions to address certain problems. These alliances represented the ecumenical common ground on foreign policy. Through these joint church projects, a peculiarly Canadian technique, the churches were able to show an ecumenical consensus.[7]

How successful was the church lobby? What was the impact of church presentations, protests, and resolutions on the Canadian government? Robert O. Matthews, professor of political science at the University of Toronto and a representative of the CCC to the WCC's commission on international affairs, concluded in 1989, "With increasing vigor over the last two decades the mainstream Christian churches have campaigned publicly and have lobbied the federal government to ensure that Canada's foreign policy and programs better reflect a concern for human rights and social justice. Although they have become increasingly sophisticated and systematic in approaching this task, the churches have not had much direct impact on public policy ... While they have had reasonable success in gaining access to policy makers, their influence on actual government policy has been marginal."[8] Despite their limited success in changing governmental policy, the churches continued their efforts to preach Christian principles and to perform what Matthews termed "a prophetic role." Disregarding their relative ineffectiveness, they persisted in speaking out on behalf of the oppressed. At least it was a way to educate the rank-and-file church members about the moral principles of the churches.[9]

While the churches lost their influence on Canadian society, which proceeded "almost as if they did not exist," there were impressive ecumenical and egalitarian achievements in these decades: several churches united; the Catholic bishops joined the Canadian Council of Churches; equality became the goal of liberals; women were ordained ministers and even became moderators; Natives, lay people, and newcomers were nominated to various bodies; and gays and lesbians were recognized. Evangelists challenged these liberal reforms, however, causing alienation and polarization. Grant wonders whether, at the end of the twentieth century, the churches were capable of responding creatively to a secular, urbanized, and pluralistic society.[10]

A LOW PROFILE, 1944–1982

The establishment of the Canadian Council of Churches (ccc) in June 1944 was the outcome of long deliberations. At the end of 1942 an unofficial delegation of Canadian church leaders had asked the representative of the World Council of Churches to help them to establish a cooperative organization in Canada, following the example of the British and American church councils. Eventually, the first meeting of the ccc was held on 20 June two years later. The council "accepted the responsibility of serving as the agency of the ecumenical movement in Canada, and of pursuing the purposes and caring for the interests of the wcc" in Canada. It was to serve as an ecumenical voice for its Protestant members and their common Christian faith and mission within Canadian society.[11] One of the first major interests of the ccc was in helping people in wartorn Europe, particularly in England.[12] The council recommended the admission of 4,000 Polish veterans, 8,000 people of Baltic and Mennonite background, and "a token group" of 2,000 Jews. The ccc also called for a revision of Canadian immigration laws. In the following years it assisted with the admission of displaced persons, finding sponsors and shelters for them.[13]

In its formative years the council had no clear policy on the Arab-Israeli conflict. Despite the fact that Lester Pearson took an active role in the UN Partition Resolution of November 1947 and that, from 1956 on, Canada participated in the UN Emergency Force in the region, the Canadian government had little direct interest in the Middle East. Indeed, during the 1950s and early 1960s Canada had only a marginal role in and almost no influence on the Middle East peace process. The Canadian churches reflected this policy of non-involvement. They had no missionaries in the region and no strong contacts with Middle

Eastern churches. The lack of clarity in the churches' policy was because "traditional and emotional attachments to Arabs and Israelis, to Muslims, Jews and Eastern Christians, have translated the political conflict into one embedded in the conscience of the concerned Christian," stated the March 1978 report of a study group established by the Ecumenical Forum of Canada. The report concluded that "it is this internal debate that is reflected in the hesitations and ambiguities of the Churches' official documents."[14] The Canadian Council of Churches followed this pattern of lacking a decisive policy in this area, and between 1948 and 1967 almost no Middle East resolutions were adopted.[15]

Even the Heraklion statement of the World Council of Churches of August 1967 did not motivate the CCC to adopt a similar resolution. Unlike the United Church of Canada and its journal, the *Observer*, which after the Six Day War became critical of Israel, the council maintained its noncommittal position. A.C. Forrest, who strongly supported the Palestinian cause, maintained that the CCC was "not a very strong organization in Canada." However, he saw some value in being associated with it, because of its ability to bring some pressure to bear on Ottawa.[16] Accordingly, he made efforts to direct the council towards more involvement in the Middle East crisis. In October 1969 he suggested organizing a joint United Church–CCC delegation to the Middle East to learn about the situation first-hand. Unlike the Israeli-sponsored tours, his would visit the neighbouring Arab countries and the refugee camps in order to educate Canadian clergy about the Palestinian issue.[17]

The outcome of the three-week-long CCC Middle East study tour, which took place in September 1970, was the publication of a resource kit entitled *Search for Understanding: A Study Booklet on the Middle East*. Its objective was to achieve "a fuller and more helpful understanding" in Canada of the Middle East. The pamphlet pointed out that the UN partition plan proposed the establishment of two independent states, which the Arabs rejected. The hostilities in 1948 had broken out "because of Arab opposition." The pamphlet commended Israel's "remarkable material and cultural accomplishments." However, it emphasized the unjust and bitter situation of the Palestinians, who had been rejected by Israel "and even to a considerable extent by other Arab countries." In the section that discussed the injustice done to the Palestinians by the establishment of Israel, it added that "just compensation must be secured for Jewish refugees from Arab lands."[18] *Search for Understanding,* as one of the first – if not the first – official policy statement by the CCC on the Middle East situation, was a moderate, even-handed document.

In September 1970 Emil Fackenheim, the noted philosopher at the University of Toronto, strongly criticized the CCC for refusing to sign a telegram urging the governments to stand firm in insisting that Jewish hostages be released from a hijacked plane. The council's excuse for refraining from signing the telegram was that it had been studying its Middle East policy. "It was a clear-cut case of racism," responded Fackenheim, arguing that there was no connection between the Middle East conflict and the hijacking of an aircraft. Since Jews and not Israelis had been held as hostages, he regarded the council's evasive policy as "anti-Semitic."[19]

The CCC made a clear distinction between its careful attitude to the complicated Middle East problem and its effort to maintain friendly relations with Canadian Jewish leaders. It invited Rabbi Nesis to represent the Jewish community at its 1972 annual council. In light of an ongoing debate between the Jewish community and the United Church, Nesis suggested to W. Gunther Plaut that they initiate a dialogue with local Christian clergy "to educate them to some of the major concerns of the Jewish community and Israel."[20] Accordingly, a delegation from the Canadian Jewish Congress met with the leaders of the CCC to discuss the renewal of dialogue, which had been damaged by the quarrel with the United Church.[21] However, it seems that as a result of the deep involvement of Jewish leaders in the quarrel with the United church, as we will see later, they neglected their relationship with the CCC. Alan Rose of the Canadian Jewish Congress repeated the argument made by Rabbi Nesis: "I think we should give further consideration to our relationship with the Council."[22]

The attitude of the council to Israel in 1972 was not clear-cut. The CCC was reluctant to be led by the strongly anti-Israel mood of the United Church.[23] On 7 October 1973 Egypt and Syria launched an attack on Israel. The reaction of the churches to the Yom Kippur War was meaningfully different from their response to the Six Day War of 1967. Part of the difference was probably the result of the differing Jewish attitudes towards these two conflicts and towards the Christian community itself. In 1967 there had been a deep fear among Jews of a second Holocaust. The churches responded slowly, and the war ended with great speed before they were ready to publish their positions. Therefore it looked as if the silence of the churches during the Holocaust had been repeated. Jews were disappointed by the lack of response from the Christian community. With the Yom Kippur War, however, the situation was different. While the statements of church leaders did not satisfy the friends of Israel, there was an increased Christian sensitivity to and awareness of the conflict in the region. The survival of Israel had become a primary concern of the churches, but at the same time their support for the Palestinians became evident. Ronald de Corneille, an Anglican priest, warned Jews that they should understand that the structure of the churches prevented the issuing of quick statements.[24]

After the Yom Kippur War ended on 22 November 1973, the General Board of the CCC released a statement in which it commended the federal government for Canadian participation in the peacekeeping force and pressed for the convening of a peace conference. While Israel was entitled to "security and territorial integrity," the Palestinian people needed "a just settlement of the refugee problem," and their representatives should be involved in the negotiations. A new element now appeared – a call for the "protection of the rights of the Palestinian minority resident in Israel and the Jewish minorities resident in Arab lands."[25]

The council's policy of giving equal treatment to both sides in the Middle East found its expression in May 1974 when Palestinian terrorists murdered schoolchildren in Ma'alot, Israel, and when in retaliation for the Ma'alot attack, Israeli air strikes killed people in Lebanon. The CCC issued a statement on 16 May 1974 expressing its "shock and dismay at the act of wanton terrorism committed yesterday against defenceless school children in Ma'alot." On the next day the council issued another statement in which it expressed "our horror at this act of retaliation, which can only serve to exacerbate an already embittered situation." The CCC leaders called upon both parties to search for a solution at the negotiating table, rather than by "fruitless violence."[26]

In August 1975 Floyd Honey, as general secretary, clarified to Gunther Plaut the council's policy on the Middle East. "As you know, the Council has tried to maintain as balanced a position as possible on the complexities of the Middle East situation. It is two years since the Council has had anything to say by way of a resolution on the Middle East conflict. I felt, therefore, in view of all the intervening developments, that it was time for us to take another overall look at the situation … I hope you can understand that we are dealing with an extremely complicated situation in which it is almost impossible for us to be right."[27]

The relative silence of the council on the Middle East situation worried Forrest, who made a renewed effort to enlist its voice against "the continuing denial of human rights in the Occupied Territories." In 1975 he prepared "a proposal to the Canadian Council of Churches" which enumerated the points that the CCC should demand. "However, if such a statement is imbalanced," wrote Forrest to the council, then "it would be better to remain silent." But, he warned the CCC, a prolonged silence would be harmful, since the council was being heard on other issues.[28]

The Middle East Council of Churches organized a study tour to the Middle East in 1980, inviting several ecumenical bodies. The international affairs committee of the CCC decided against participation.[29] But while it did not send a delegation to the tour, contact with the Middle East was maintained by facilitating the participation of four CCC members in the Palestine refugee program. Through this program, the council channelled money to the refugees and became a partner in various consultations, which formulated ecumenical policy for the region.[30]

Although the CCC did not issue any official resolutions on the Middle East in the early 1980s, it organized seminars on Middle East settlement proposals and facilitated cross-Canada speech tours for Ghassan Rubeiz, of the WCC Middle East desk, and for Eugene Makhlouf, of the Red Crescent Society of Palestine. It also held a dialogue between church leaders and Palestinians, including members of the PLO.[31] Thus the CCC's Middle East position during the years 1944–82 was a low-profile one, as it tried to maintain an even-handed policy. In several instances the council refused to follow the anti-Israel initiatives of Forrest and the United Church.

GRADUAL INVOLVEMENT, 1982–1987

The early hesitations and moderate position of the Canadian Council of Churches on the Israeli-Palestinian conflict gradually disappeared as a result of two basic factors: the Israeli invasion of Lebanon in 1982 and the growing influence of the Middle East Council of Churches. The outcome was an increasing awareness of the Middle East situation. Leaders of nine Canadian denominations issued a strong statement condemning Israel's invasion of Lebanon and urging "immediate withdrawal" of the Israeli forces. The churches denounced terrorism and called upon the PLO and the Arab states "to accept the legitimacy and permanence of Israel." They stressed the need for "a negotiated settlement, which should include the re-establishment of a genuine independence for Lebanon and the achievement of an autonomous political entity ... for the Palestinians, which will not preclude the long-range possibility of a Palestinian state." The leaders appealed to church members to contribute morally and financially to the Middle Eastern churches.[32] After this statement appeared, the CCC was seen as "a repository of resources and a facilitator of ecumenical events on Middle East issues and churches," reported the council's Tad Mitsui. The Lebanese situation would be a constant concern for the CCC in the years to come.[33]

In the 1980s Canadian churches, particularly local ones, increasingly became involved in the Middle East.[34] As an initial response to growing awareness of the Palestinian-Israeli conflict, the CCC initiated a tripartite dialogue with the Jewish and Arab communities in Canada, hoping to narrow the gap between the groups. The Middle East Task Group (METG) of the Committee on International Affairs (CIA) of the CCC undertook in November 1983 to organize two multilateral conversations with the Canadian Jewish Congress (CJC) and the Canadian Arab Federation (CAF). Robert Matthews, chair of the Committee on International Affairs, explaining to his Christian colleagues the meaning of the WCC's 1982 statement, said that although the churches identified with the Palestinians, they "do not place blame on either side." The interest of Christians in the Middle East conflict was the outcome of their anxiety about the danger to peace. "The Christian churches wish to be peace-makers rather than judges," said Matthews.

The Canadian Arab Federation hesitated at first to come to the dialogue because it had not had previous relations with the CCC, but it eventually accepted the invitation.[35] To the council's disappointment, however, the Canadian Jewish Congress refused to participate in the dialogue with the Arabs. CCC members speculated that the reason for the CJC's refusal to join was its opposition to becoming involved "with a PLO dominated organization." Another explanation for the CJC's refusal was that the Jews did not trust the CCC outside the Christian-Jewish dialogue.[36]

The deliberations between the Christian group, which the Anglicans and the Presbyterians joined, and the Canadian Arab Federation continued for eight months. There was a consensus among the participants about the need to maintain constructive working relations between the CCC and the CAF, to which the Jews should be added. They also agreed upon the need to educate the churches about stereotypes and prejudices concerning Arabs held by Canadians. "It remains to determine the best channels for ensuring that this work is done, and that the contact which has been established is continued," concluded Douglas duCharme of the CCC in his report on the dialogue.[37] The most important outcome of the dialogue with the CAF was probably a better understanding on the part of the CCC about the Middle East situation and of the need to formulate a clear policy on this issue. While the hope for a dialogue with the Jews was not fulfilled, in June 1984 Rabbi Robert Sternberg, director of the religious affairs department of the Canadian Jewish Congress, joined a CCC delegation on a tour to Israel. "A considerable degree of goodwill and understanding resulted during this joint tour," reported a CCC source.[38]

At around the same time, in the autumn of 1984, Joe Clark, secretary of state for foreign affairs in the new federal government of Brian Mulroney, invited the public to participate in a review of Canadian foreign policy. Responding to Clark's call, the Canadian churches produced a carefully worded document entitled "Canada's International Relations: An Alternative View." This comprehensive paper offered a Christian ethical perspective on Canada's place in the global community.[39] The size of the Israeli-Palestinian section – three and half out of the ninety-six pages of the document – reflected the relatively marginal interest of the churches in this subject. The paper observed the change on the part of the Canadian government from an "uncritical pro-Israel position" to a recent "more even-handed position." The churches advised the government to "(a) display a greater sense of urgency concerning the creation of a Palestinian state; (b) participate in a strong sustained international effort to secure genuine Israeli-Palestinian negotiations; (c) be part of the international input into these negotiations, and part of the implementation and enforcement of their results."[40]

The growing involvement of the Canadian council in the Middle East in the mid-1980s was intensified by pressure from Gabriel Habib, of the MECC, who suggested in October 1985 that the CCC take measures to deepen the relationship between the two councils.[41] The church bodies decided to establish a working group of experts on the Middle East that would bring the various elements together and coordinate ecumenical solidarity. The Middle East Working Group was established in December with the following terms of reference: to watch events in the region, to draft statements to the media, to prepare briefs to the government, to develop relationships with Middle East countries, and to educate the Canadian churches on Middle East problems. The Committee on International Affairs had recommended the immediate formation of the group and specified that the term "Middle East" was to also include western Asia, Cyprus, and Egypt. While the Palestinian-Israeli conflict was "central to any study of the area," the MEWG proposed to take care of other issues as well.[42] On 3 October 1985 Marjorie Ross, associate secretary for world concerns, asked member denominations to send representatives to the new working group.[43]

At the first meeting on 16 December 1985, participants included representatives of the Anglican, United, Presbyterian, Greek Orthodox, Baptist, and Mennonite churches, along with Canadian Friends (Quakers) and the CCC. Later, other denominations joined the working group, including the Catholics.[44] The first months of the group were characterized by a moderate and cautious attitude. The proposed draft of "Canada's International Relations" seemed "provocative" to some members of the group, and they requested that "more 'neutral' language" be used. On another occasion, concerns were expressed about the deviation of the document from the cautious attitude of some churches regarding the Israeli-Arab crisis. Members were particularly worried about the fact that the MECC, with its pro-Arab approach, would represent Canadian church interests in the Middle East.[45]

These early hesitations soon disappeared, and the working group gradually took a pro-Arab position as a result of deepening connections with Gabriel Habib and the MECC. In October 1986 he visited Canada and participated in the CCC General Board meeting in Niagara Falls. As an outcome of his talks with council officials, he proposed to the CCC that it appoint a Canadian liaison with the MECC. "In view of the growing relationship between the churches of Canada and the Middle East, and the growing agenda, which that relationship implies, it seems to be an appropriate time to consider the placement of a qualified and committed person from Canada with the MECC. A significant part of this person's responsibilities would involve interpreting the life and work of the Middle Eastern churches within the complex political and ideological dynamics of that region to the Canadian churches. The emphasis would be on education and interpretation."[46]

When Habib suggested the appointment of a liaison officer, he had Douglas duCharme in mind.[47] DuCharme, a Presbyterian missionary, had served the Canadian churches in numerous areas of work related to foreign policy. From 1983 he was assigned to prepare reports for the CCC,[48] and in 1985–86 he spent a year in Beirut, partly affiliated with the MECC and partly as a teacher in the Near East School of Theology. His good contacts with local, as well as with Canadian, churches were appreciated by the MECC.[49] The appointment of duCharme as the representative of the CCC to the Middle East met some opposition because there was no precedent for such a position. Eventually, after long deliberations and various draft proposals for a staff position, the General Board approved the assignment on 21 September 1987, stipulating that various missionary groups should finance the position. The plan was for duCharme to spend three months in Cyprus at MECC's headquarters and three months in Canada. The purpose of the assignment was defined as follows: "To interpret the situations and events in the Middle East as well as the concerns of the MECC in order that the churches are encouraged to include the Middle East as an important issue of Justice and Peace in their programmes."[50]

DEEPER INVOLVEMENT:
SUPPORT OF THE ARAB CAUSE, 1987–1993

The mission of Douglas duCharme to the Middle East beginning in September 1987 signalled a new phase in the CCC's position on the

Israeli-Palestinian conflict. Although the appointment itself was the outcome of deepening relations with the MECC, duCharme's activities served as a catalyst to further strengthen those relations; it was thus both a cause and a result. Since duCharme was staying at the MECC's headquarters in Cyprus and closely following its policy, he facilitated the adoption by the CCC of a pro-Arab position. Earlier efforts at maintaining an even-handed policy gave way to total support for the Palestinian cause. "Our commitment to the MECC clearly compromised our efforts of balance," duCharme admitted later, adding, "It was a conscious option that we took."[51]

Since the CCC had no qualified staff in the region to verify Arab complaints, duCharme had to accept the reports of the MECC as fact and report accordingly to the MEWG. Contrary to its original terms of reference, the working group largely disregarded other Middle East countries such as Syria, Iraq, and Iran and concentrated almost solely on the Israeli-Palestinian problem. Israel was always criticized for violating the human rights of the Palestinians, but no comparable attention was paid to human rights violations in Syria, Iraq, or Iran. Regarding Iran, there was perhaps some excuse for non-intervention, because of the precarious situation of the Christian communities there. However, this situation did not prevail in the other countries of the region.[52]

As part of Habib's program to deepen the relationship between the CCC and the MECC, in October 1985 he invited the leadership of the Canadian council to visit the Middle East and learn about the situation first-hand. In October 1986 the CCC General Board reacted positively, deciding to send a delegation.[53] The council had already conducted two Middle East tours in 1970 and 1978. However, the 1987 tour, which comprised representatives of ten denominations, was more wide-ranging. It included the situation of the churches in the Middle East, the Palestinian-Israeli problem, and Canada's role in the region.[54] The aims of the visit were "to gain a solid grasp of the suffering and the injustice experienced by many in the Middle East including the Lebanese and the Palestinian peoples. On the other hand they will also be concerned to achieve a realistic appreciation of the struggle for peace and justice being undertaken by many in the region."[55]

Following the return of the delegation a statement was published that recommended an increase in donations to the Palestinian refugee program and the pursuit of "alternative approaches to tourism." It urged the World Council of Churches to convene a conference of church leaders to discuss the Middle East crisis. It suggested that moderate Jewish and Palestinian representatives be invited to the 1988 CCC triennial assembly and that dialogue with the Jewish and Arab communities in

Canada be encouraged. Finally, the statement suggested that the Canadian government should be requested to support UN resolutions concerning the Middle East, including the call for a peace conference on the Israeli-Palestinian issue.[56]

Douglas duCharme, who participated in the 1987 tour, was eager to launch a wide-ranging educational campaign on the Middle East situation in Canadian churches. He enlisted the help of members of the delegation, organizing public lectures for them across Canada.[57] As part of the public relations effort, the CCC published a pamphlet in April 1988 entitled *Old Patterns, New Possibilities*. It contained the impressions of the delegates on the tour and included pictures and cartoons.[58] Several United Church groups criticized the pamphlet for its unbalanced coverage. At the triennial assembly a complaint was made that "no story had been told from the Israeli perspective." John Berthrong of the United Church, a member of the MEWG, also felt that "some of the cartoons were a bit unfortunate." He suggested that "a carefully worded covering letter" be attached which would explain that the delegation was invited by church organizations and that it was "not a fact-finding mission" but a "church-to-church visitation."[59]

The active members of the MEWG came from varied backgrounds, but they generally had pro-Arab sympathies. Several members of the working group, including Marjorie Ross, the chair, Maxine Nunn of the Friends, Douglas duCharme, and Robert Assaly, participated in various pro-Arab conferences in the United States.[60] Assaly, an Anglican priest of Lebanese origin, organized student tours to the Middle East and published critical reports on Israeli treatment of the Palestinians.[61] Another active representative of the Anglican Church to the MEWG was Canon Shafik A. Farah, a Palestinian.[62] In addition, the working group enjoyed the help of Mubarak Ali as a volunteer.[63]

The MEWG invited people who supported the Palestinian cause to lecture to the group.[64] It gathered information on the conflict mainly from Arab organizations, and it also turned for information to Jewish anti-Israel groups, such as the New York – based International Jewish Peace Union, or to Professor Israel Shahak, an outspoken Israeli critic. However, when a distinguished Israeli dove, Professor J. Harkabi, a former general, was lecturing at the University of Toronto, the MEWG did not invite him to address the group.[65]

In 1988, after his first year in the Middle East liaison position, duCharme reported on the "mix of achievements and items needing more work," terming it "an experiment." For nine months of the year, he had worked in Nicosia with the communication department of the MECC, editing its monthly *MECC News Report* and its journal, *MECC Perspectives*, and coordinating international press relations. As a matter of fact, he served as the press officer for the council, editing everything that appeared in English. He also made several field trips in the region, to Jerusalem, the occupied territories, and Beirut.

DuCharme spent January–March 1988 in Canada, focusing on interpretation and education about the Middle East with the Canadian churches. He organized study seminars and publicized the findings of the study-tour delegation, including its report, and he lectured widely in churches on the Middle East and met with representatives of various Arab bodies, such as the Arab League, the Palestine Information Office in Ottawa, and the PLO. As coordinator of the work of the MECC ecumenical travel office in Nicosia, duCharme devoted the major part of his report to alternative tourism, rather than the tours organized by the Israelis. He emphasized the importance of choosing the MECC's tours, providing spiritual, theological, political, and economic reasons.[66]

DuCharme's first year of interpretive work among the Canadian churches could be regarded as a success. The interest of the churches in the Middle East grew. However, there was no effort to give an even-handed picture; his reports from Cyprus about the oppressive Israeli occupation clearly reflected the MECC's point of view.[67] This close relationship with the MECC and duCharme's active campaign in Canadian churches provoked some reservations in certain CCC circles. A re-evaluation of the goals of the Middle East Working Group in February 1988 recommended that the group "focus on Canadian and Middle East agencies in a balanced fashion." Donald Anderson, the general secretary, who said he was afraid that the Canadian council "might become the MECC-West," reflected the reluctance of the CCC to become merely a representative of the MECC in Canada.[68]

As a result of the report of the CCC delegation to the Middle East in the fall of 1987, the growing involvement of the council in the Israeli-Palestinian conflict, and pressure from Gabriel Habib and Douglas du-Charme, the MEWG decided to prepare a statement of policy on the Middle East. Since the CCC had not issued an authoritative statement on this subject for almost a decade, and since the council, as an inter-denominational agency, was dependent on its affiliated churches, the preparation of the "Statement on the Middle East" was carried out with great care and extensive consultation.[69] The MEWG, including representatives of the Canadian Conference of Catholic Bishops (CCCB), discussed in detail the first drafts, in whose preparation duCharme played a key role,[70] and sent the statement for comments to the CCC' members and to various Jewish and Arab agencies in Canada.

The statement warned that the dangerous situation in the Middle East was threatening the peace of the world; therefore attaining peace

was a continuing challenge. It emphasized the importance of recognizing the concerns of both parties: "The human and political rights of
the Palestinians cannot be fulfilled at the expense of the Jewish people, nor vice versa." The statement called for the withdrawal of Israeli
forces; recognized the rights of all states, including Israel, to live in secure borders; and called for the "implementation of the rights of the
Palestinians to self determination, including the right of establishing a
sovereign Palestinian state." The document strongly supported the
convening of an international peace conference, at which the PLO
would represent the Palestinians. It called upon the churches, as well
as the Canadian government, to demonstrate a greater awareness of
the urgency of the Palestinian problem. The statement declared that
the Israeli annexation of East Jerusalem was "a violation of international law and as such is null and void," and it called for greater awareness of the sufferings of the Christian community in the city. The
statement on the Middle East was presented to the CCC's triennial assembly in Montreal in May 1988, but because of many reservations
raised by various groups, the assembly refrained from approving the
document. Instead, it decided to send the statement "out to member
churches of the CCC for detailed consideration and reporting back to
the General Board by spring of 1989."[71]

The document, which, as Douglas duCharme admitted, accurately
represented the positions of Arab Christians, was criticized by Christians and Jews alike.[72] The Canadian Conference of Catholic Bishops,
after worldwide consultation, including with the Vatican, considered
that the position paper was "too ambitious and would cause more diffi-
culties than it is worth." Instead, CCCB suggested that "a strong clear
statement limited at this time to the defence of Palestinian human
rights would be much more timely and effective."[73] The House of Bishops of the Anglican Church of Canada insisted that the document be
amended. The Anglicans recommended the inclusion of additional
sections that would give a more balanced and comprehensive picture
of the Israeli-Palestinian conflict.[74]

The Canadian Christian-Jewish Consultation (CCJC), formerly known
as the National Tripartite Liaison Committee, strongly opposed the
statement. While the position paper accepted the Arab point of view,
members of the Consultation wondered, "Where is the Canadian critical reflection?" They also complained about the lack of a constructive
aim for the future. "I should like to strongly underline that these [com-
ments] were made by people from all participant groups," including
representatives of the CCCB, wrote Heather Johnston, chair of the
group.[75] "There was strong exception by Christian members of the

CCJC to the CCC statement, which was regarded as 'unbalanced,' " reported an Anglican source.[76]

Members of another group, the Christian-Jewish Dialogue in Montreal (CJDM), criticized the position paper for its factual errors. However, it was more disturbed by the document's "unhelpful tone," which might harm the continuation of a dialogue that had succeeded in building up "a great deal of openness and trust." The Christian members of the CJDM criticized the CCC delegation to the Middle East in 1987, whose members "could not have had much time to talk to representatives of the Jewish faith, yet judgments are being made in the Statement before a dialogue has occurred."[77]

The Christian-Jewish Dialogue in Toronto also considered the statement a biased, inaccurate document that could only make the continuation of relations more difficult, without having any influence on the Israeli scene. "The statement, in our view, overlooks key facts and is not objective in some of its analysis of the sources and the nature of a number of conflicts in the Middle East ... The statement is based on the perceptions of a group of people who consulted with Arab Christians, but who show no evidence of having consulted with Jews who live in and struggle with the conflict ... We don't believe that this statement adequately acknowledges the history, which lies behind the present situation."[78]

Alan Rose prepared the official response of the Canadian Jewish Congress. After deliberation, in a carefully worded document he pointed out that in the position paper "the situation in the Middle East is narrowly defined and does not provide a tour d'horizon of the current situation. There are significant factors, which are not subsumed in the statement. An important consideration for Canadians should be the plight of minorities in Arab countries, which are not traversed. We believe the statement does not advance dialogue and fraternity between Christians and Jews, nor does it exemplify the integrity spirit evidenced in Canada. Unfortunately it relegates the Arab-Israel conflict as the sole cause of tension in the Middle East." The CJC complained that the position paper had failed to mention the Iran-Iraq War or the treatment of minorities in Islamic states, including persecution of the Kurds in Iraq, the Baha'is in Iran, and the Jews in Syria. Rose wondered why a Middle East statement should concentrate on the Arab-Jewish conflict, rather than on violations of human rights in the whole region. "We believe that an appreciation of the regional conflict in the Middle East must be factual and balanced." [79]

The MEWG took the various comments and reservations seriously. The revised version of the statement included sections dealing with human rights abuses in Iran, Iraq, Syria, and Lebanon. The section on the Palestinian-Israeli crisis was expanded, and some implied subjects received clarification in the new version. On 13 October 1989 the General Board of the CCC approved the amended position paper, the culmination of more than two years of effort. To educate church communities, it decided to publish a study guide, which actually appeared in November 1990.[80]

Reactions to the revised version of the position paper were positive. The fact that the General Board had endorsed it without dissent indicates that the member churches were satisfied with the revised text. Dorris Sallah, general secretary of the YMCA in Jerusalem, responded enthusiastically to the position paper, saying that it served as a proof that "the Church is still alive and true to its calling for peace."[81] The Canadian Christian-Jewish Consultation and the Christian-Jewish Dialogue in Montreal pointed out that a number of suggestions made by members of the dialogues had been subsumed in the final statement, which they regarded as a "great improvement" over the original document.[82] The Canadian Conference of Catholic Bishops supported the CCC's statement concerning a sovereign Palestinian homeland, free access to Jerusalem, and peace in Lebanon.[83]

Jewish reaction was mixed. "We are going to say things in this statement that they [Jews] don't want to hear but we did consult with them," reported duCharme, adding that they would be surprised to learn of the changes made in the original position paper.[84] If the Beirut-based *Al Anwar* reported with satisfaction on the CCC's position paper,[85] it is not surprising that the Canadian Jewish Congress disagreed with some of its basic points. The congress was "pleased that you were good enough to consult with us and indeed a number of our suggestions to enhance the balance of your statement were subsumed." While the revised paper was "generally more balanced," a number of issues caused the CJC "great concern." It disagreed with fundamental perceptions of the CCC, such as the definition of the crisis, the character of the PLO, the exact meaning of UN Resolutions 242 and 338, the section on free access to religious sites in Jerusalem, the position on terrorism, and the importance of Christian-Jewish dialogue.[86] Rabbi J. Benjamin Friedberg of Beth Tzedec Synagogue in Toronto responded in a less diplomatic manner. While the first draft "was so blatantly biased against Israel that I wondered how the authors were not embarrassed to submit it, ... the present paper ... is a vast improvement and much more even handed." However, as a "paranoid Jew" – a term used by Robert B. McClure, the United Church moderator – he voiced his objection to the document's biased treatment of violations of human rights in Israel and Syria, his concern about the threat of a Palestinian state to the security of Israel, and his opposition to the section on Jerusalem.[87] Thus although the position paper on the Middle East was not balanced, as Douglas duCharme claimed it to be,[88] the MEWG had made a sincere effort "in soliciting comments from other groups that do not reflect our position."[89]

Joining in international criticism of the suppression of the civil uprising with military force, the CCC's Middle East Working Group decided in December 1988 to prepare a document on Israel's violations of human rights and submit it to the United Nations Commission on Human Rights and to the Department of External Affairs in Ottawa. The members of the working group were anxious that the document should present "indisputable facts." Furthermore, John Berthrong cautioned his colleagues that, "unless some balance is kept in such a statement to satisfy the many church people who are engaged in the dialogue with Jewish people, such a statement will not be endorsed by the churches."[90] The preamble to the brief that was submitted in January 1989 to the Department of External Affairs declared that the church had great interest in the subject because human rights were a "fundamental part" of its commitment to justice and peace. From the start of the Intifada, "blatant violations" had occurred in the occupied territories. The brief particularly criticized the excessive use of force, the transfer of prisoners to detention centres in Israel, the widespread use of torture and collective punishment, and the destruction of private homes. The MEWG called upon the Canadian government "to speak out vigorously against the comprehensive violations of basic human rights in the territories."[91]

Responding to the brief, Joe Clark reiterated his intention "to find ways to ensure that Canada can play an active and constructive role in the search for a just and lasting Middle East settlement." He further noted Canada's "deep concern" in regard to human rights violations and the serious situation in Gaza and the West Bank.[92] Jewish groups, such as B'nai Brith Canada (BB), however, strongly criticized the CCC's brief on human rights. Where were the churches when for generations Christians had violated the human rights of Jews? The B'nai Brith statement indicated that "the purpose of this response is not to deny these abuses. Rather, we seek to present a critique of these elements of the Working Group brief that lack balance and fairness, and that fail to meet accepted norms for accuracy in the reporting and judging of human rights violations." The BB response pointed out the brief's lack of objectivity and balance, and questioned its sources and terminology. "We find it saddening that a church body condones violence against the Jewish people in Israel, fails to take historical realities into account and projects a biased and ill-prepared brief for distribution to Canadian policy makers," concluded the BB document.[93]

Criticism by B'nai Brith did not change the MEWG's course of action. It annually submitted a brief to the Canadian government in preparation for the UN Commission on Human Rights. In the brief of 1990, after enumerating abuses of human rights, particularly since the outbreak of the uprising, it urged the Canadian government "to recognize the extensive violations ... and to pursue these concerns *diligently*." In 1991, during the Gulf War, although the MEWG was "aware of extensive violations of human rights in the region as a result of preparations for the Gulf War," mainly the occupation of Kuwait by Iraq, it still concentrated on Israel. It called upon the Canadian government "to speak strongly in favour of the need for respect for human rights, particularly in the occupied territories and South Lebanon."[94]

From the late 1980s on, the warm relationship between the CCC and the MECC had led the Canadian council to abandon almost any effort at an even-handed approach. A letter of commendation from Stuart E. Brown to Gabriel Habib in June 1989 clearly reflected the CCC's position: "I write to you ... to express our deep admiration for the fine work you and your colleagues are doing in very difficult circumstances ... We assure you of our constant prayer and solidarity with your team in Cyprus, Beirut and throughout this troubled land."[95] The participation of a high-ranking delegation that included Bishop Donald Sjoberg, president of the CCC, Archbishop Michael Peers, primate of the Anglican Church of Canada, and Harrold Morris, moderator of the Presbyterian Church, in the MECC's fifth assembly in January 1990 in Larnaca, Cyprus, was another sign of this special relationship. In his address to the assembly, Bishop Sjoberg pointed out the important contribution of the MECC to the "presence and witness of Christians in the region." "In view of our close ties," he extended an invitation to visit Canada to the leaders of the MECC, hoping that the visit "would strengthen the relationship between the two Councils."[96] Douglas duCharme gladly supported the invitation, saying that "it comes at a good time to deepen partnership and solidarity in the relationship." He emphasized the success of his own efforts in arousing the awareness of the Canadian churches about the Middle East.[97]

Not everyone in the CCC or even in the MEWG was happy with this close cooperation with the MECC. When, in 1990, the proposal of extending duCharme's appointment for an additional three years and widening his function was considered at the working group, there was some hesitation. Since the CCC had interests in various regions of the world, Stuart Brown was worried that "it could convey an incorrectly imbalanced impression to have a 'specialist' for one area only ... We really do not need a full-time regional liaison at this end."[98] But duCharme argued that a reliable first-hand contact was needed at the MECC headquarters in Cyprus. As a compromise, the working group agreed in November 1990 to extend the appointment for an additional three years, but it set up an advisory committee to act as a "watchdog" to the liaison officer.[99] Because of duCharme's success in establishing close contacts with the MECC, this position continued to function after his promotion to associate secretary for justice and peace of the CCC in May 1992. Robert Assaly from Ottawa, a member of MEWG, was appointed as his successor.[100]

The Gulf War in 1990–91 partially distracted the churches' attention from the Palestinian cause. The CCC issued several protests about the use of arms by the coalition forces, criticizing Canada for sending warships to the region without bringing the matter before Parliament.[101] A joint communiqué of the CCC delegation and the MECC called for the withdrawal of the Iraqis from Kuwait and of the coalition forces from the region. The document also called for an international peace conference to deal both with the "disastrous conflict" in the Gulf and with "the outstanding conflicts including Palestine, Lebanon and Cyprus."[102] While the Canadian churches unanimously opposed the use of arms in the Gulf conflict, only the CCC emphasized the linkage with the Palestinian crisis.[103] In its 1991 annual brief on violations of human rights in the Middle East, the MEWG could not disregard the new situation in the Gulf, yet it continued to focus on Israel.[104]

In conclusion, we can see that the response of the Canadian Council of Churches to the Israeli-Palestinian conflict went through three basic phases. From its foundation until 1982, it was not really involved in the Middle East, although it participated in several study tours and issued two policy statements. During the years of 1982–87, as a result of the Israeli occupation of Lebanon and the growing influence of the Middle East Council of Churches, early hesitations about supporting the Arab cause disappeared, and the CCC became more involved in Middle East affairs, as the establishment of the Middle East Working Group in 1986 attested. From the time of Douglas duCharme's nomination as the council's liaison with the MECC in September 1987, the MEWG was "in virtual 'communion' with the MECC, whose anti-Israel bias" was well established, as Alan Rose later observed.[105] Thus the close collaboration with the MECC, an obvious departure from the Canadian council's efforts at balance, led the latter to a clear pro-Arab position. From 1987 on, the CCC was the leading supporter of the Palestinian cause in the Canadian Protestant church circles.

The United Church,
the Holocaust,
and the State of Israel

3 The United Church of Canada and the Holocaust

The formation of the United Church of Canada on 10 June 1925, after decades of consultation and negotiation, was the first of its kind in modern Western society. Political, economic, and evangelical considerations led to this union of the Methodist, Presbyterian, and Congregational churches in Canada. It was a bold and unique action. A strong liberal point of view and an emphasis on the social gospel were characteristics of the new body, which became the largest Protestant denomination in Canada, in 1941 embracing 2,204,875 members and adherents.[1] The terms of union of the three different denominations did not require unanimous consent in decision-making, allowing dissenting minorities to have their own opinions. Hence the United Church, unlike other denominations, did not speak with one voice. Independent points of view, not only political and social but also theological, were not unacceptable in the church. Its membership and clergy ranged from the left, with its belief in social justice, to the right, with its fundamentalist and highly traditional point of view.[2] How this entity reacted to the Holocaust and to the admission of Jewish refugees into Canada would prove interesting.

The Great Depression of the 1930s influenced every aspect of Canadian life, personal as well as political. The rise of radical movements from the right and from the left created fear of a revolution. The revolution never materialized, but fear was a symptom of the era.[3] This atmosphere strengthened well-imbedded traditional Christian anti-semitism, as Davies and Nefsky, who have written on the issue in Canada, have pointed out: "in spite of the social gospel [the country] remained strongly imbued with older pietistic and evangelical assumptions concerning the alleged superiority of Christianity to Judaism and the necessity of converting Jews to the true religion. Moreover, as often in the past, these missionary aspirations frequently contained an implicit antisemitism."[4]

Because of centuries-old predominantly negative interpretations of Jews within Christendom, as in the New Testament, the United Church, struggling through modern liberalism to re-evaluate this anti-Jewish teaching, achieved only mixed results. The following antisemitic comment appeared in the *United Church of Canada Year Book* for 1927: "Wherever the Jew has settled in any part of the world he has created new problems, political, social, economic and religious ... The power these people wield among the nations is out of proportion to their numbers. They have attained positions ... enabling them to mold thought and public opinion and to influence the life and destiny of nations ... No democratic nation can survive unless its roots sink deep into the soil of moral religious truth. It is the task of the Church to teach these things unto the people and especially unto their children."[5]

The official bulletin of the United Church, the *New Outlook*, during the 1930s published articles with uncomplimentary comments on the Jews, calling them "a bigoted people" with a "narrow" and "selfish" religion.[6] In spite of the fact that most members of the church strongly supported democracy, a few individuals flirted with fascism, looking on Hitler as a genuine leader: "The Nazi leader is really more than a mere demagogue, he has notable gifts of leadership and [he is] the man God is looking for."[7] A few Germanophiles, such as the Reverend Harold B. Hendershot, who had been much impressed by the Nazi "idealism" when he studied in Germany, praised Hitler and the Nazi regime. Hendershot was not alone in this point of view. Frank Hoffman, a United Church missionary from Saskatchewan, and G.R. McKean of Nova Scotia represented a small but persistent minority in the United Church with pro-Nazi sympathies.[8] Although the editor of the *New Outlook* criticized this position, he did not refrain from printing comment supporting it time and again. Some groups in the church considered democracy a failure and supported the fascist regime. "There is a considerable feeling that democracy has failed to meet the present problems and the call is for someone strong and wise, who might bring order out of chaos ... There is such a thing as surrender of life to save the soul, and possibly the time has come for this," read an article in the church bulletin in 1938.[9]

Even when German totalitarianism was criticized and persecution of the Jews condemned, several writers "understood" the German drive against the Jews. "If she has vented her wrath on a race, never beloved under the best of circumstances, may that not be a natural and quite logical outcome of an irrepressible feeling of resentment against powers, beyond the reach of her wrath" read one comment.[10] The Reverend Burgess of Queen Street United Church in Toronto stated that Jews themselves, as deicides, were responsible for their suffering.[11] "The Jews' denial and crucifixion of Christ was the reason why God's curse rested on them and why they would continue to suffer even more," declared the Reverend John Insker of Knox Presbyterian Church. He complained that the Jews had been looking for the world's sympathy "instead of confessing their sins."[12] A strong antisemitic atmosphere in Canada quite naturally influenced a certain element of the United Church clergy. Faced with reports of Hitler's atrocities, some people refused to believe in what they termed "exaggerated horror stories." "It would be foolish to deny that antisemitic feelings existed in the United Church; even those who publicly decried events in Germany tacitly made this admission," maintain Davies and Nefsky.[13]

If such were the views of some people to what they called "the Jewish Race," we should not be surprised to learn of their negative attitude to the admission of Jewish refugees from Nazism. In addition to the economic reasons of unemployment and financial hardship, there was a feeling of self-righteousness among a WASPish group which was confident in its moral superiority and did not care about the suffering of a minority in a distant country. This sense of religious superiority was strengthened by the feelings of Anglo-Saxon racial superiority that dominated part of the United Church leadership. The outcome of these feelings was that the Jews "were not worth rescuing."[14] To be sure, only a minority of church members held that view, but it would be hard to determine how large and how influential that minority was.

Gradually, the United Church pulpit and press responded more sympathetically to the wave of persecutions in Germany. The British heritage of admiration for a democratic government rejected the Nazi totalitarian regime. Furthermore, the neo-paganism of the Nazis and their barbaric persecution not only of Jews but also of Protestant churches led church ministers and editors to condemn such acts. The liberal outlook and belief in social justice of rank-and-file church members made them sympathetic to the suffering of the Jewish people. The brutality and injustice inflicted upon the Jews called for protests and criticism of Germany.

As early as April 1933, the *New Outlook* reported on pogroms in Germany, which, "stripped of all exaggerations, [were] a systematic persecution of the Jews more inhuman and atrocious than any that has occurred in the Middle Ages." The editorial was still hopeful that, as a result of protests from around the world, Germany would stop its policy.[15] The Reverend Richard Roberts discussed what would happen if Jesus were to go to Germany: he would not be allowed to land and might be deported as an undesirable alien.[16] Claris E. Silcox, a clergyman and journalist though not a United Church minister, was one of the most outspoken members of the clergy to openly support the cause of Jewish refugees. Through lecture tours, sermons, and articles in church bulletins, as well as in the general news media, he tried to persuade the Christian community in Canada to condemn Nazi atrocities in Germany and help Jewish refugees.[17] In January 1936, after the introduction of the Nuremberg Aryan laws and the resignation of James G. McDonald, the League of Nations high commissioner for refugees, the *New Outlook* issued a strong protest, editorializing that "the anti-Jew policy has reached a pitch of brutality and injustice that can hardly be any longer tolerated by the world … That some millions of people are being deprived of all their legal and human rights and driven out of their country for the rest of the world to look after seems an injustice that cannot be endured without protest, even if protesting may be very dangerous work."[18]

Two months later, a group of thirty-one clergymen in Toronto issued a "Manifesto" that expressed "unqualified protest against the treatment which has been meted out to the Jews."[19] The pogrom of Kristallnacht in November 1938 brought widespread protests and demonstrations in Canada. The editorial in the *New Outlook* rightly saw in the events in Germany "a new phase. Something much more serious than anti-Semitism is involved."[20] As for antisemitism, the *New Outlook* was disturbed to learn that the German churches supported the Nazis and their antisemitic views: "The danger is that we have not adequately taught our people what Christianity really presupposes … we need a more constructive approach if we are to escape being swept away on a wave of anti-Semitism."[21]

Since these articles failed to change the attitude of the Christian community at large, the Committee on Jewish-Gentile Relations, headed by Claris Silcox and Rabbi Maurice N. Eisendrath of Holy Blossom Temple in Toronto invited the Reverend James Parkes from England to deliver a series of sermons on the theme "Christian Responsibility and Possibilities of Christian Action." In November and December 1938 Parkes preached in United and Anglican churches in Canada. He also delivered public lectures and radio talks, reaching thousands of listeners. He condemned Christian antisemitism and called the Canadian people to absorb a certain number of Jewish refugees.[22]

When war began and Canada joined Britain to fight the Axis Powers, the head of the Canadian Christian churches issued a statement of support for the war, which "is the cause of Christian civilization."[23]

With the advent of the war, patriotism grew and with it an anti-German attitude. There were no longer any reservations about criticizing Germany and the danger of fascism.[24] Preoccupation with the war, in which Canadian soldiers participated, turned public attention away from the plight of the Jews; but when detailed reports about mass murder in Auschwitz were published, sympathy for the victims increased. "In a day when terror has been spread around the world among the children of Abraham, … I pay this tribute to how much we owe them in the hope that it may add to the peace of our Jewish brethren," wrote the Reverend C.A. Lawson of Toronto.[25] In September 1944 the *United Church Observer*, from 1940 the successor of the *New Outlook* as the official organ of the United Church, admitted its past reluctance to believe reports of Jewish extermination: "For some time we were reluctant to accept at face value the accounts which occasionally leaked out of the atrocities perpetrated by the Nazis … The publication of those figures did not arouse the conscience of the world, perhaps because again we are defending ourselves against propaganda."[26] In a protest meeting organized by the Canadian Jewish Congress in Toronto in October 1944, Dr Slater conveyed the feelings of the United Church as follows:"The United Church would wish me to express in the strongest terms our amazement and our anger at what is being done to your people."[27]

In certain circles the world crisis of the 1930s and 1940s was considered as operating in favour of Christianity. The Jewish situation throughout the world, the refugee problem, and the rise of antisemitism created an "unparalleled opportunity" to work for Jewish redemption. "To do nothing for the Jews in a time like this is really to do something grave," maintained a Home Mission Council article. Friendship and kindness towards Jewish refugees would be the best way to attract them to the church. Dr Conrad Hoffmann, secretary of the Committee on the Christian Approach to the Jew, pleaded that local churches where there were Jews "should develop a helpful ministry to them."[28] Thus Christian denunciation of antisemitism and sympathy for Jewish refugees was not merely the outcome of disinterested humanitarianism and Christian charity, but was sometimes motivated by missionary zeal.[29] In United Church circles, together with sympathy for the Jews and an acknowledgment of the contribution of Judaism to Christianity, there was also a basic assumption about the superiority of Christianity. A good Jew was always considered a Christian one. As an editorial in the *New Outlook* remarked, "To be sure, the ultimate solution of the Jewish problem … must largely depend upon the reaction of the Jewish people themselves to the situation in our present world."[30] "In the context of the era," maintain Davies and

Nefsky, "such statements were intended to evoke Christian sympathy for Hitler's victims."[31]

Although it was not always easy to preach against antisemitism and to criticize German atrocities, a belief in social justice, well entrenched in the hearts of many members of the United Church, moved them to sympathize with the suffering of the Jewish people. But it was much more difficult to translate this sympathy into action by advocating the admission of Jewish refugees into Canada.[32] To fight against strong anti-alien and antisemitic sentiments was an unpopular task, which only a few church leaders had the courage to undertake. During the first years of the Nazi regime the refugee problem was almost disregarded. A few scattered reports appeared in the pages of the *New Outlook* in 1936–37 about a church campaign to collect money for Jewish refugees or an appeal to the League of Nations to take responsibility for them.[33] Reporting on the Evian Conference, which discussed the refugee problem, the *New Outlook*, probably for the first time, saw the issue as a Canadian one, stating that "the whole refugee question should be considered in relation to the wider issue of an intelligent immigration policy for this country."[34]

With the foundation of the Canadian National Committee on Refugees and Victims of Political Persecution (CNCR) in December 1938, a non-sectarian pressure group on behalf of the refugee cause was established.[35] Several leading United Church ministers participated in its activities, including E. Crossley Hunter, Ernest Marshall Howse, Stanley Russell, and James Bryce. They preached from the pulpits of churches and Jewish synagogues, wrote articles, and called upon the Canadian government to admit Jewish refugees. Hunter, as co-chair of the Canadian Conference, issued statements against Christian anti-semitism. "I believe that Christians who treat lightly this modern outbreak of anti-semitism have little idea of its implications for their own freedom and life. *But this thing is not only ugly and dangerous, it is wicked.* It is utterly and absolutely unchristian."[36] There were also UC ministers such as A.J. MacQueen, later moderator of the church, who spoke from their local pulpits against Germany and supported the admission of refugees, but did not receive any publicity. Therefore one may conclude that there were probably more individuals in the United Chuch who sympathized with the plight of Jewish refugees than were recorded.[37]

When we turn from individuals to official church statements, the picture is gloomier. The editorial in the *New Outlook* in February 1939 openly criticized the churches for their silence:

We live in a large but sparsely settled country; to deny a refuge to those in such terrible need would be unpardonable selfish ... To keep out others when our own house is largely empty is to be "guilty of a political immoralism as grave in its implications as the crude immoralism of the Nazis" ... We might expect the Churches of Canada to be courageous and humane, but on this subject there has been (officially at least) a disconcerting silence. In this respect the responsibility of the United Church is particularly heavy. We are the largest Protestant denomination in this country and we pride ourselves on being a progressive Church, with a sensitive social conscience ... Where the Church leads so haltingly, is it surprising that the government stumbles?[38]

The Board of Evangelism and Social Service (BESS) of the United Church was responsible for the area of the church and world order. Therefore institutional response to German atrocities and the refugee problem was in its purview. The BESS's decisions, its reports to the General Council of the church, and its recommendations to the approximately one hundred presbyteries represented the official policy of the United Church of Canada – hence the importance of the board's records.[39] The subject of European refugees, including Jewish ones, first appeared in the BESS annual report for 1937. It briefly mentioned that the board had recommended the approval of a letter which had been sent by Claris Silcox, who wanted the Canadian government to be urged to assume "responsibility of providing a haven for at least a reasonable number of selected refugees."[40] The first serious discussion of the refugee issue is recorded in the 1938 report, after the establishment of the CNCR, when it was decided that the United Church should officially join the CNCR and adopt its program. James R. Mutchmor, the secretary, represented the board on the CNCR. He raised the question "as to the part the UC should take in providing a haven for our share of these unfortunate people." The board was also asked "to state the position of the United Church" on the refugee problem. It was recommended that the board write directly to Thomas A. Crerar, the federal minister of mines and resources, who was responsible for immigration, stating that "we believed the UC would favor a slightly more 'open door' policy in the matter of immigration." The board joined other church organizations in appealing to the government to "do its utmost for refugees." As far as real action was concerned, the BESS decided that "in any plan considered for admitting refugees into Canada, provision be made for the reception of young children for legal adoption into Canadian families," and the United Church "will undertake its share in this connection." The board turned to its presbyteries to give the refugee issue "careful and constructive thought," in order to create a favourable public opinion.[41] This pattern of joining in other declarations and following the requests of other institutions, rather than formulating a policy for the

United Church itself as far as the issues of refugees and antisemitism were concerned, was repeated time and again. The sub-executive of the General Council of the church in November 1937 endorsed a statement issued by the Canadian National Council of the World Alliance for International Friendship, which "viewed with great sorrow the spread of Anti-Semitic propaganda in Canada … We call upon the leaders of our Christian Churches to urge their people to ignore such propaganda and … repudiate it as utterly unchristian."[42]

In September 1938, on the eve of the Jewish New Year, the General Council, the highest court of the United Church, had expressed its sympathy for the suffering of the Jews as follows: "We have learned with deep sorrow and mortification of the sufferings inflicted upon the Jewish people by many nations which profess to believe Him who was the Light of the Gentiles and the true glory of His people, Israel, as well as on many Christians … In your sufferings we suffer; and in any earnest and considered efforts to effect the appeasement of the lot of those who, for conscience's sake, or because of racial origin and enduring political persecution, we pledge our active and devoted co-operation."[43] From this first statement of the General Council on behalf of the persecuted Jews, which was issued after five years of Nazi anti-Jewish terror, we can trace the hesitation and irresolution of the leaders of the United Church in this matter. First of all, Germany was not mentioned and obviously was not criticized. There was no specific protest against Jewish persecution. Furthermore, as an expression of "sincere New Year's Greetings on the observance of the immemorial feast of Rosh Hashana," as the preamble indicated, the declaration showed a great measure of insensitivity by referring to Jesus as "the true glory of His people, Israel."

No new decisions were made in 1939. It seems that the church relied on the activities of the CNCR, reporting in detail the latter's resolutions. The annual report of the BESS repeated the decision that had been made the previous year that if the CNCR succeeded in bringing to Canada one hundred refugee children, "this Board will accept its share of responsibility in regard to this undertaking."[44] The board's earlier appeal to the church's presbyteries received some response. Several communities passed resolutions imploring the Canadian government to adopt a more lenient policy and admit "a selected number of refugees." The *United Church Year Book* for 1939 reported on "joint meetings of Christian churches and community organizations," where hospitality to refugees was recommended and urgent appeals to dominion and provincial governments had been sent "to take generous part in the world fellowship of welcome and help to the refugees."[45] Probably in order to avoid unnecessary opposition, the reports always referred simply to "refugees," refraining from mentioning Jewish refugees.

In 1940 the annual report again commended "the work of the CNCR and pledge our continued support." The board was asked for a written document concerning its previous commitment to take responsibility for a specified number of refugee children, a request with which it complied immediately. Since there were many legal obstacles, by 1941 only two children had arrived and an additional four were waiting for transportation from Europe.[46] The subcommittee of the General Council in 1940 appointed a special committee to investigate the refugee problem and relief to Protestant churches in Europe, though to be sure, this committee was set up to take care of Christian refugees and churches. Following this line of being interested only in Christian refugees, the subcommittee extended its sympathy to Jews who had converted to Christianity: "The Gospel … is the fulfillment of the Jewish hope. The Christian Church owes it, therefore, to the Jewish people to proclaim to it the fulfillment of the promises, which had been made to it. And it rejoices in maintaining fellowship with those of the Jewish race who have accepted that Gospel."[47] This evangelical outlook was frequently maintained, along with friendliness to Jewish refugees. In 1941 the BESS called on church members to oppose anti-Jewish hatred, but added that the church's attitude today would decide "the strength of the Christian Gospel message among Jewish people tomorrow."[48]

Two years later the board again repeated the CNCR's program, calling on the government "to offer the sanctuary of Canada to such refugees without regard to race, creed or condition, and in particular to take immediate steps to facilitate the entry of some of them (especially those stranded in Portugal) whose lives it is still possible to save."[49] Unfortunately, even among those who supported the refugee issue and opposed antisemitism, there were individuals who were not immune to anti-Jewish perceptions, such as James Mutchmor, the secretary of the board. He maintained that "organized Jewry is busy and … will need watching." Mutchmor admitted, "I am not opposed to the Hebrew people, but I do not regard myself as one of those who is very keen for them."[50]

The General Council struggled with the dilemma of choosing between the liberal ideology of its members and the security of the country during the war. When Japanese citizens were evacuated from the West Coast and interned in concentration camps, it commented, "The Church recognizes the need of such action by the Government as will adequately protect the country against subversive activity." However, it expressed its hope that the women and children would be soon transferred to camps with better conditions.[51]

With the advent of the war, the General Council had appointed a Commission on the Church, Nation and World Order, which was to consider "the deeper moral and spiritual issues of the war, and the peace following, and the call involved in the present world situation to a more Christian order."[52] The commission was in operation for three years, and its report went through nine drafts. Among other topics, it dealt with antisemitism. In an early draft it investigated "the growing anti-Semitism within the Church." The commission was pointed out that this reference was "not a charge against the Church but queries to guide inquiry to be taken to [determine whether] these conditions exist or not, and if they do what should the church do about them."[53] One of the last drafts of the commission's report, dating from January 1944, framed the problem of antisemitism as follows: "The Church recognizes with sorrow a growing tendency to anti-Semitism in Canada. That faults of our Jewish fellow countrymen contribute to this particular form of prejudice may be admitted, but those who are well informed in this field know that anti-Semitism does not require as its basis anything really deserving the name of evidence ... In combating this insidious and abominably unchristian antipathy ... the United Church has already aligned itself with other Christian bodies ... However, much more remains to be done."[54]

The final report of the commission, which was submitted to the eleventh General Council of 1944, read differently: "We rejoice in the strong stand taken by the Christian Church in this and other lands against anti-Semitism, no matter on how many grounds it might differ from Jewish faith and practice. We hope and pray that the victory over Nazism will also prove to be a victory over racial idolatry and racial arrogance wherever it exists ... In particular we deplore the bitter spirit of anti-Semitism, which is manifest in different parts of Canada and the exclusiveness and prejudice too often displayed toward non-Anglo-Saxon Canadians."[55] One may marvel that in a very rare statement of the General Council about antisemitism, which appeared as late as 1944, instead of an expression of repentance for not fighting the vice wholeheartedly, it "rejoice[d] in the strong stand taken by the Christian Church ... against anti-Semitism."

To sum up the period of 1933–45, how silent was the United Church about the plight of Jews during the Holocaust? Were its members apathetic to the fate of German Jews? Reflecting on these questions, one has to bear in mind the theological, economic, and political pressures of the era. Since members of the church did not speak with one voice, there were both harsh antisemitic and pro-Nazi expressions and protests against anti-Jewish persecution and support for the admission of Jewish refugees by proponents of social justice. Individual ministers delivered sermons from the pulpit, gave public lectures, and wrote editorials. However, statements by official church bodies were rare and vague. The General Council adopted very few resolutions that denounced persecution of the Jews in Germany and antisemitism in Canada. The Board of Evangelism and Social Service was the single church body that from 1938 on, openly supported, through the CNCR, the lobby for a more lenient immigration policy. Several of the church's presbyteries also joined the call for the admission of a certain number of selected refugees.

Was the United Church silent then? "Yes and no," argue Davies and Nefsky.[56] Irving Abella and Harold Troper, in their book *None Is Too Many*, are highly critical of the restrictionist policy of the Canadian government and the hostile atmosphere in the Christian community at large to the Jewish refugee issue. Yet they also point out that, although Canadian churches remained silent, "some organizations and highly placed members of religious groups, such as the Anglican and United Churches, actively campaigned on behalf of Jewish refugees."[57]

George Morrison, a former secretary of the United Church's General Council, admitted recently that in UC circles there was "limited or no awareness of the breadth and depth of the Holocaust."[58] Davies and Nefsky conclude that "as a religious community the United Church at large was silent, but not that silent. Institutionally, if editorials, letters, resolutions and sermons count for anything, and if speech is the opposite of silence, it was not silent at all. Far more was said than the post-mortems of our day have acknowledged."[59] Davies and Nefsky demonstrate their thesis that the church was not totally silent. However, if it was supposed to have served as the moral compass for its people, then the limited expressions of support for the Jews, particularly the mute attitude of the General Council and other major church bodies, can scarcely serve as more than a fig leaf to cover the bad conscience of the Christian community in Canada. One may agree with the comments of N. Bruce McLeod, a former United Church moderator, that "while many individuals stood out as exceptions, Canadian institutions, by and large, were silent in the face of what was happening to Jews in Europe. Sadly, the institutional United Church was probably part of this silence, as were most Canadian Churches."[60]

4 Claris E. Silcox, the Refugees, and the State of Israel

Claris E. Silcox (1888–1961), a renowned Canadian clergyman and journalist, campaigned extensively during the Nazi era for the lifting of immigration restrictions in order to allow the admission of refugees from Nazism. He was one of the most outspoken clergymen who openly supported the cause of Jewish refugees. In recognition of his pro-Jewish views, he was named director of the Canadian Conference of Christians and Jews, a position in which he served from 1940 to 1946. After World War II, however, Silcox became a strong anti-Zionist. He considered the Balfour Declaration (which promised the Jews a national homeland in Palestine) a "mistake" and described the UN partition plan of 1947 as "utterly stupid." The establishment of the Jewish state was aiming "to destroy the United Nations and invite the emergence of World War Three," he said, and it would bring about "a more bitter anti-semitism than this world has ever known." As late as 1960, a year before his death, Silcox still vehemently opposed the State of Israel. How can one reconcile these seemingly contradictory positions: love of Jews and help for Jewish refugees and, on the other hand, strong opposition to the Zionist idea and to the State of Israel? Was Silcox an antisemite, as some people have said? It is the aim of this chapter to deal with these questions.

Claris Edwin Silcox was born on 14 August 1888 in Embro, Ontario, to a well-known and distinguished family. His grandfather, who had emigrated from England, established the first Congregational church in northern Canada, and Claris's father was the editor of the *Canadian Congregationalist* for fifteen years. After graduation with honours from the University of Toronto, Claris completed his graduate studies at Brown University in Rhode Island. He then studied theology at Andover Seminary in Boston, where he was ordained as a minister. In spite of the fact that for eleven years he served as pastor in a number of Congregational churches in the United States, he was torn between the pulpit and academia:[1] "I have felt the contrast between the scientific temper ... and the propagandist attitude of the preacher ... You will thus see how weak-minded I am, and how much of a temptation it is for me to get up into a pulpit and try to appeal to men's emotions and ideals ... I am not sure that I can completely escape from the lure of the pulpit," wrote the young Silcox to the president of Brown University in 1928.[2] Although he abandoned the pulpit, choosing a scientific and journalistic career, the temptation "to appeal to men's emotions and ideals and sense of value" never left him.

In 1926 Silcox became a researcher at the Institute of Social and Religious Research. Here he was asked to investigate the church union movement after the establishment of the United Church of Canada in 1925. The outcome of this research was his book *Church Union in Canada: Its Causes and Consequences* (1933). Silcox continued the investigation of the relations between the various churches, and in 1934, with Galen H. Fisher, he published *Catholics, Jews and Protestants*. In these studies he advocated a unified body, and during the 1930s he appealed to the three major religions to join together. They "must seek a common ideology not in the dogmatic but in the dynamic sphere; and they must search for ... that dynamic in the whole of the Judaeo-Christian tradition."[3] During World War II Silcox intensified his appeal for unity among the three religions, calling for mutual understanding and sympathy: "The problem of religious peace in Canada is, therefore, one of our major national problems."[4]

Unity of the churches was not an end in itself for Silcox, but a means of unifying society. In the 1930s he was preoccupied with the problem of restoring unity to society. Since the basis for social unity was spiritual, Silcox believed that the Judeo-Christian ideal could lend true cohesion to the spiritual centre of society. The preservation of this spiritual centre became the primary aim of his involvement in practical social issues. Thus Silcox became a social reformer. It was to reach that goal that he took responsibility for the general secretariat of the Social Service Council of Canada, whose aim was to promote social welfare. For six years (1934–40) he led the social reform movement almost single-handed; he was leader, mediator, and spokesman for the council. But when, in spite of his appeals, lectures, and sermons, the churches refused to accept the importance of a common front on the social questions of the day, he resigned out of frustration in 1940.[5]

Silcox failed to unite Protestants on social issues because he did not offer a comprehensive plan for social reform and because he had no intellectual followers, either inside or outside the churches. As Mark van Stempvoort, who has studied Silcox's social unity thesis, observes, "his rhetoric of radical toryism was largely critical, not offering a comprehensive program for social change."[6]

Silcox's efforts to find a common denominator for the various religions had led to his involvement in 1929 in the reorganization of the Canadian branch of the Conference of Christians and Jews. He took a major part in the preparation of the syllabus used at a seminar at Columbia University where Catholic, Protestant, and Jewish lecturers discussed the social implications of their differences. In April 1934 Silcox prepared a program for a seminar on "Jewish-Gentile Relations ... for the purpose of the achievement of a better understanding between the two groups of persons who live and labor together."[7]

The rise of Nazism and the persecution of Jews in Germany evoked in Silcox a strong desire for justice and an urge to help the victims. As a liberal humanitarian, he wanted to assist minorities. Following the British tradition of fair play, he demanded fair treatment for refugees. Particularly strong and vocal was his support for the admission of Jewish refugees from Nazi Germany into Canada. In the unfriendly atmosphere that prevailed in Canada in the 1930s over the refugee issue, Silcox, in calling for the abandonment of the restrictionist immigration policy, embarked on an unpopular tack.

As early as August 1933, he had criticized Germany's racial policy and highlighted the loyalty of Jews to Germany in World War 1.[8] As we have seen in the previous chapter, after the publication of the "Letter of Resignation" written by James G. McDonald, the high commissioner for refugees, a group of thirty-one Christian clergymen in Toronto issued a "Manifesto" in March 1936. It expressed "unqualified protest against the treatment which has been meted out to the Jews, 'non Aryan Christians' and various Gentiles deemed 'undesirables' by the present government of Germany." After enumerating the reasons for earlier silence on the part of Christian leaders, they declared, "Now, however, further silence is impossible; it will only aggravate a condition which civilization should deem utterly 'intolerable.'" The manifesto appealed to the League of Nations, to the governments of the United States and Canada, and to Christians in those countries to urge the government of Germany to realize "the full weight of the moral indignation throughout the world which has been evoked by their treatment of Jews." Although it is not clear whether Silcox himself was the author of this document, he was deeply involved in its publication. The preamble of the manifesto appealed to prominent church leaders who identified with the content of the document to send their signatures to Claris Silcox,[9] and the document was published by the Social Service Council of Canada, of which he was director, in its official organ, *Social Welfare*, of which he was editor.

With the German annexation of Austria in March 1938, the number of refugees increased greatly. U.S. president Franklin D. Roosevelt therefore called for an international conference at Evian to discuss the refugee problem. When Canadian prime minister Mackenzie King was reluctant to send representatives to Evian, the Social Service Council, Silcox's organization, called for Canadian participation.[10] He continued his pressure on Ottawa through the World Alliance for International Friendship through the Churches. More effective was his cooperation with the Canadian Jewish Congress, along with Canon W.W. Judd of the Anglican church, on the Jewish refugee cause. They supported the congress's plan to form a non-sectarian pressure group on behalf of refugees and decided to activate the League of Nations Society in Canada, an organization with the aim of promoting world peace. In October 1938 the society resolved to devote its energy to the aid of Jewish refugees by appealing to the Canadian government to liberalize its immigration policy. After Kristallnacht, the momentum for the establishment of a non-sectarian pro-refugee organization grew. On 6 December 1938, partially as a result of Silcox's pressure, the Canadian National Committee on Refugees and Victims of Political Persecution was created, with Senator Cairine Wilson as president and Constance Hayward as executive secretary.[11]

In its initial stage, Silcox served for several months as the CNCR's chair. He was a member of a small delegation that met with Prime Minister King and members of the cabinet, to appeal for a humanitarian gesture that would admit refugees fleeing from Nazi persecution. He was also the author of several CNCR pamphlets and articles, such as "Should Canada Admit Refugees?" in which he outlined the arguments in favour of the admission of refugees. In this article, after analyzing the urgency of the situation in Europe, he pointed out the economic and cultural advantages for Canada of the admission of German refugees.[12]

In a radio broadcast entitled "Should Canada Provide Sanctuary for European Refugees?" Silcox criticized the Canadian government, saying that "to date [it is] extraordinarily hesitant to do anything" on behalf of refugees. To preserve the British way of life, Canada "primarily needs an influx of Anglo-Saxons." Since there was no real prospect of immigration from Britain, "German Jews could be a reasonable substitute ... What do we need most on this continent – the Anglo-Saxon blood or the Anglo-Saxon spirit? Is it not primarily the

Anglo-Saxon spirit, the love of freedom, the regard for fair play, the intellectual eagerness, the respect for capacity for cultural and scientific attainment ... Is it not this, which we most need in Canada." Silcox reminded his listeners of what Holland and England had gained from the expulsion of the Huguenots from France at the end of the seventeenth century. He concluded the broadcast by arguing that even if there were no motives of self-interest, "no truly Christian nation can look upon these victims of ruthless persecution and refuse the demands of humanity, especially when it is well within its power to help."[13]

In 1938–39 Silcox devoted his energy to the refugee cause, including combating antisemitism. "Anti-semitism is in essence anti-Christianity." Therefore, the church "must make the fight against anti-Semitism its own battle." He called those churchmen who toyed with antisemitism "traitors to the deepest things in their own faith."[14] In January 1939 Silcox was sent by the CNCR on a lecture tour to the west, financed by the Canadian Committee for Jewish Refugees. From Winnipeg to Edmonton, Calgary, and Vancouver, he delivered lectures, sermons, and interviews with newspapers and helped to organize local refugee committees, Jewish and non-sectarian. Although his main purpose was to persuade his audiences to take a more sympathetic approach to the refugee cause, he focused on the topic "The Challenge of Anti-Semitism to Democracy." As a "Britisher," Silcox called for fair play, which Jews were not receiving either in Canada or abroad. As a Canadian, he lamented the lack of toleration towards minorities – including Jews – which he felt put national unity at risk. As a Christian, he was conscious of the church's debt to Judaism: "The impending conflict is essentially one between spiritual ideals – between the Judaeo-Christian tradition of compassion and respect for personality which flowers naturally into democracy on the one hand, and the totalitarian idea that subordinates the individual to the mass-interest on the other." As a Gentile, he came to the help of the Jew because the Jew "cannot well make his own defence," since the Jewish problem "is a Gentile problem, created by Gentiles and to be solved only by Gentile action." "Anti-semitism is the spear-head of the totalitarian attack on democracy. If it succeeds, democracy will fail; if it fails, democracy stands a fair chance of weathering the storm." Therefore antisemitism constituted the great challenge of totalitarianism to democracy. What could be done? Silcox demanded the admission of a selected number of skilled and intellectual German refugees, such as Nobel Prize winners, who could contribute to the country.[15] His tour of the west was a great educational success, and his lectures were widely reported by the local and national press. But whether he succeeded in changing people's attitude to the refugee issue is questionable.[16]

Silcox also tried to create a more sympathetic attitude towards Jews by attempting to understand the way that they behaved. In a survey of Jewish-Christian relationships through the centuries, he pointed out the cruelty of Christian treatment – the persecution of the Jews, their removal from the structure of society, and the prohibition against Jewish landholding and many occupations, which left the Jews only the infamous outlet of usury. Thus Christians, not Jews, should be blamed for the fact that many Jews were bankers and moneylenders.[17] In an article entitled "What Do We Owe to the Jews," Silcox pointed out the fact that "Christianity was built on a Jewish foundation." Among the contributions of Judaism to civilization, he mentioned humility, ethical monotheism, social justice, and the challenge to subordinate creeds and dogmas to the practical problems of life. He concluded with a reminder that "Christians can never forget that the founder of the Christian Church was at least a non-Aryan."[18] In October 1939, after the outbreak of the war, Silcox defended Jews against the accusation that they would not enlist in the Canadian army and would therefore evade fighting.[19]

Silcox criticized not only the Canadian government for its refusal to admit refugees from Nazism but also the Christian church for its disregard of the refugee issue. Along with others, he wondered "why have the Churches done nothing?" After citing several church-related resolutions that protested against antisemitism, he concluded, "The churches may have done little, but they are the first organization to do anything." Yet he admitted that these actions by the churches had not changed the government's policy, and "no significant steps … were taken."[20] In a sermon at Knox United Church in Regina on 8 January 1939, Silcox criticized the church for its failure to support the persecuted Jews and lamented the absence of great church leadership in Canada during the difficult days of the 1930s.[21]

In recognition of his contribution to Jewish-Christian relations, Claris Silcox received an honorary doctorate of divinity from Queen's University in Kingston, Ontario, in 1939. A.B. Bennett, president of the Canadian Jewish Congress, conveyed to him the official message of felicitation on behalf of the cjc: "Your contribution to the cause of better understanding among the various groups … has been outstanding, and our organization feels itself deeply indebted to you for your wise counsel and inspiring co-operation."[22]

The Conference of Christians and Jews had operated since 1934 to promote "sympathy and understanding" between the two religions. With the menace of war it became more active, and in May 1940 it was reorganized, changed its name to the Canadian Conference of Christians and Jews (cccj), and enlarged its board to fifty prominent

Christians and Jews from various organizations. Its aims were "to promote justice, amity, understanding and co-operation among Catholics, Jews and Protestants." The selection of Silcox as director of the newly reorganized group was a natural one, particularly in light of his recent resignation from the directorship of the Social Service Council of Canada.[23]

Silcox accepted the appointment with some reluctance, because of criticism that he received from his friends and from Christian society at large:

There are times when I am sorely tempted to relax in my efforts towards Jewish-Gentile understanding. One gets little but criticism from the Gentiles who tend to look upon a "professional good-willer" as a queer and deluded fool – probably a tool of the Jews. Indeed, some anonymous letters received indicate just that ... I was told by one of my best friends that my interest in Jewish-Gentile relationships had closed the doors to certain things that I might now be doing for my country ... and a professional man told my wife that in his opinion it was a shame for a man of my experience to devote myself to such an unpopular cause as that of the Jews ... This is hard enough; but if Jewish leaders are going to be hypercritical, one might just as well throw in the sponge.[24]

At the end of 1941 Silcox admitted, "The organization is far from complete." Its board had met only once, and there was no constitution. After nineteenth months of operation Silcox still needed "to map out more clearly the scope and ultimate goals of our work."[25] For six years, 1940–46, he led the struggle against antisemitism, along with E. Crossley Hunter of the United Church and Rabbi Maurice N. Eisendrath of Toronto as co-chairs. Particularly during the war, Canadian unity was highly important; this unity could be better achieved if Jewish-Christian relations were improved. So the struggle against antisemitism was a war aim, maintained Silcox. It, however, should be attained through the education of young people and the churches, not through public and aggressive attack on antisemitism, because it "is rather futile and might only prove a boomerang."[26]

Thus we can see that Claris E. Silcox was one of the few Gentile friends of the Jews and of Jewish refugees. He closely cooperated with Jewish and non-sectarian organizations to campaign against antisemitism and on behalf of the admission of refugees into Canada. But relations between Silcox and the Jewish organizations were more complicated than they appear from this conclusion. In certain matters he took an opposite point of view from that of Jews and publicly confronted them. Religious education in Ontario public schools was a case in point.

In 1944 the Ontario government issued a regulation introducing the teaching of religion in public schools in the province as of September that year. It was clear to everyone that by the term "religious instruction," school officials meant "instruction in the tenets of the Christian faith." Jewish organizations, particularly the Canadian Jewish Congress, strongly opposed the introduction of religious education into public schools. "We have examined the textbooks used and find that what is proposed to be taught is Christian dogma, to which no Jewish child, in all conscience, should be exposed," wrote an official of the CJC to Jewish parents. "Please be assured that the Congress will use every means of developing a public sentiment which will ultimately cause the removal of this undemocratic element from the life of our society." A special committee was established consisting of rabbis and laymen, with rabbi Abraham L. Feinberg of Holy Blossom Temple in Toronto as chair.[27]

After long deliberation, the congress, in the name of the Jewish population of Canada, submitted an official protest to the government, declaring: "This age-old heritage of positive religious conviction impels the Canadian Jewish Congress to oppose religious instruction in the public schools. Religion ... cannot be taught effectively as a separate subject in an hour a week. The Public Schools should not be charged with a task that legitimately belongs to church and synagogue, and even more to the home." The congress regarded the introduction of Christian teaching into the schools as "anti-democratic, imperiling the principle of separation of Church and State, and leading to disunity in society."[28] Jewish leadership was preoccupied with this subject for many years. Between 1941 and the 1960s one can find sermons, pamphlets, declarations, and articles enumerating the reasons for Jewish opposition to religious instruction in public schools. (Interestingly, Orthodox Jews did not make much of this issue, since they hoped that dissatisfied parents would transfer their children to their own religious schools.)[29]

In complete contrast with the Jewish position, Claris Silcox was a strong and open supporter of the introduction of religious instruction into the curriculum of the public schools. To clarify the various opinions, he suggested that the CCCJ should organize a seminar on "Religious Education in Schools." But Rabbi A.L. Feinberg and Rabbi S. Sacks, who were leading figures in the Jewish community, opposed the idea of a seminar because "the subject is too hot." When two radio stations appealed to Silcox for a talk on the subject, he accepted the invitation despite the fact that, as he confessed to a friend, "I received a formal warning from the Canadian Jewish Congress here. But I felt that the Government was protecting 'dissenters' by a conscience clause, and the rights of the majority had to be protected as well as the rights of the minority. I knew that I was taking 'the bull by the horns' as it were, but that I had to put myself in the open on the matter and take the consequences. There was great praise from the Christian side of the house and grave opposition from the Jewish end. Since then, I have lost a measure of my enthusiasm for the Conference."[30]

In an article for the *United Church Observer* in 1952, Silcox stressed the important link between education and religion. "One simply cannot segregate religion from education," he wrote, refuting the argument of secular people who wanted to leave religion to the home and the church and exclude it from the school. To ignore the important relation between education and religion "is not only tragic, but if persisted in, will prove suicidal." Silcox denied the accusation that the inclusion of religion in the schools was an assault on religious freedom or that it might interfere with "private judgement." He also defended the Ontario government's action as bolstering majority rights, arguing that minority rights were secured by the permission granted to children who were not interested in the religious teaching to leave the classroom.[31] From 1944 until his death in 1961, Silcox continued to defend this issue in articles, radio talks, and pamphlets. He was convinced that the exclusion of religion from the school would leave "a disastrous moral vacuum." After his death some newspapers considered his fight for religious education as his major contribution to his era.[32]

Another area in which Silcox directly confronted the position taken by Jews, both in the Canadian Jewish Congress and in the Canadian Conference of Christians and Jews, was with regard to the Zionist concept, the Palestine problem, and, later on, the attitudes to Israel. In 1942 he participated in a meeting of the pro-Zionist Christian Council on Palestine in the United States and "was far from unsympathetic with the course proposed," as he recalled later. On his return to Canada, he initiated an educational campaign aimed at explaining the Palestine situation to Canadian audiences: "I tried to be neutral as between a pro-Zionist and a pro-Arab position." Gradually, however, he changed his position from neutrality to a pro-Arab one.

In 1917 Silcox has been "thrilled" by the Balfour Declaration, which promised Jews a "national home" in Palestine. At that time he did not take Arab protests seriously, and only the flow of Jewish refugees from Nazi terror led him to reconsider the situation in Palestine.[33] After 1943 he became increasingly anti-Zionist. The Palestine question troubled him, and he lectured and wrote articles on the subject quite frequently. In the January 1943 issue of *Fellowship*, the official bulletin of the Canadian Conference of Christians and Jews, he offered a solution based on the Christian image of the prophecy of Isaiah about the world to come: "The only solution is to make Palestine a kind of federal district of the world, a new Geneva ... in which a new and redeemed Israel based not on an alleged blood inheritance, but on the spiritual kinship of humanity, shall establish a new Jerusalem organically related to the deepest and most ancient traditions of an enlightened world."[34]

At an international conference of Christians and Jews at Oxford in 1946, Silcox warned that if the Zionists succeeded in establishing a Jewish state, "they would create not only a new focal centre of anti-Semitism in the world, but also a grave and all but insoluble international situation." His address shocked some of his listeners, who had come to discuss reconciliation between Jews and Christians.[35] When in January the following year the editors of the *University of Toronto Quarterly* asked for a contribution on the Palestine situation, Silcox hesitated at first, but after a week he agreed. "I decided that there were things that ought to be said, and I said them."[36]

Refuting the Zionist claim to Palestine, he stated his conclusion that it had no foundation historically, legally, or practically. As for the Balfour Declaration of 1917, British support of the Zionists during World War I was mainly a war tactic in the cause of the Entente. Britain believed that the Bolshevik revolution was backed by Jews, and it feared that the revolution would cause the crumbling of the eastern front in the war; it therefore promised a "national home" for the Jews in Palestine. It hoped in this way to discourage Russian Jewish support of the Bolsheviks and at the same time to attract the financial aid of world Jewry in support of the Entente. "Without this explanation, it is difficult to understand the reason for the Balfour Declaration," wrote Silcox.[37]

Repeating his accusation that a Jewish state would increase antisemitism in the world and alienate those Christians who sympathized with the Jews during the Holocaust, Silcox added sarcastically: "Let it not be said tomorrow that the Jews seem to have a positive genius for making enemies!" If Zionists would only rise above the present situation, they "might see on the far horizon the promise of the real fulfillment of the mission of Israel – peace on earth among men of goodwill." If Zionists refused to accept his advice, "the Holy Land will become unholy, will prove only a curse and an abomination; and the international Jew may begin his wandering again."[38] Arab groups in Canada and the United States were so enthusiastic about this article that they ordered 5,000 offprints[39]

In 1948, with the establishment of the State of Israel imminent, Silcox became more critical and issued warnings about the situation. Gradually, he reached the conclusion that the Balfour Declaration "was a terrible mistake and should never have been issued; that it was deliberately ambiguous and that out of that ambiguity most of our present troubles emerge; that the Zionist propaganda, immense as it has been, has failed and will fail, because it has been entirely one sided, and moreover it deliberately minimized the case of the Arabs; the present situation is all but hopeless and no solution is possible without a complete change of front of the Zionist side – and this is not likely to happen." In spite of British efforts to deal fairly with Jews, extreme Zionists and terrorist actions had alienated the sympathy of the British people. Even in Canada, no sympathy could be aroused for Jewish displaced persons because of the Zionist position.[40] When, because of the Zionists' uncompromising demands, he saw that his warnings were futile, Silcox threatened that "the Zionists may have to learn the hard way." Muslims and Christians would force them to wander the world once again.[41]

He also criticized the United Nations partition plan and called the UN General Assembly's decision of 29 November 1947 an "utterly stupid" one. The assembly had agreed upon the plan "without enthusiasm and with many adverse votes and abstentions"; Silcox therefore called for the postponement of the final decision in order to allow "for a more favourable atmosphere." Meanwhile, he suggested the establishment of a provisional international commission to govern Palestine. He warned that if "the ultra Zionists" forced the partition of Palestine, it could lead to the destruction of the United Nations "and invite the emergence of World War Three."[42]

Silcox did not abandon his anti-Zionist campaign, even after the establishment of Israel. In 1956 he publicly called for support of the Arab cause: "A better understanding of the Islamic world is the absolute imperative for the Western countries. For the Zionists to insist that the so-called Christian West ignore the Islamic world and support the dubious claims of their amour propre, Israel is really asking a bit too much."[43] Silcox, who had defended Jewish refugees during World War II, now transferred his humanitarian sympathy to the Arab refugees. Israel should not be a haven for Jewish refugees from Nazism because it would infringe on the rights of the Arabs. And he quoted the old proverb "Two wrongs never make a right."[44]

Thus Claris Silcox directly opposed Jewish opinion on two major issues: religious instruction in Ontario public schools and the Zionist solution for Palestine. At the same time he continued to serve as director of the Canadian Conference of Christians and Jews. His ideas were held to be unacceptable by many leading members of this organization. No wonder, then, that he felt himself an outsider and a stranger and lost "a measure of my enthusiasm" to continue his work in the conference. In a letter to a friend, who was a co-chair of the conference, he wholeheartedly confessed that "altogether, I have felt that I should at the first opportunity withdraw from the Conference." He maintained that the Jewish positions on religious education in public schools and the Palestine question "have made many Christian leaders feel that the Jews had themselves destroyed the possibility of 'fellowship'" – that is, destroyed the confidence of the church in cooperation with Jews. Silcox preached "a great ideological rapprochement," but he was skeptical about whether the Jews were prepared for such a move, particularly after the Holocaust, when their Jewishness and their "feeling for martyrdom" had been intensified.

After the war Silcox became tired of the Jewish question. He was convinced that the "great issue before Canada is steadily looming up, and it is the Protestant-Catholic issue ... And we are handicapped if we have to consider all the time the question of Jewish-Christian relations ... I am inclined to think now that the immediate challenge ... is to discover a better modus vivendi with the Roman Catholics and let the Jewish-Christian issue works itself out naturally. Meanwhile, if we press the latter, many of the Christian leaders will feel that the Jewish leaders only want to use the Christian forces for their own political purposes, and will not hesitate to fight their champions if any of their programs is rejected."[45]

Silcox was only waiting for an appropriate time to resign from the cccj. It was clear to him, as well as to the leaders of the conference, that the real reasons for his resignation should be concealed. As he wrote, "If I resign and walk off in the clear air, people will realize that the Jews have possibly forced an issue, and that will not help them very much."[46] A special committee was therefore established by the conference to formulate a statement concerning the resignation.[47] The official announcement obviously covered up the real reasons for Silcox's departure, pointing out that the purpose for which the conference had been organized in 1934, to combat antisemitism in Canada, "had been largely fulfilled." Furthermore, Silcox's interests "were presently engaged in other directions."[48] It seems that with his resignation as director of the conference in 1946, he gave up his efforts to improve relations between the Jewish and Christian communities.

Did Claris Silcox become an antisemite? Several members of the Canadian Jewish Congress strongly maintained that opinion.[49] Certainly, to be an anti-Zionist did not mean to be an antisemite, although not everyone was prepared to make the distinction. Silcox complained in 1956 that if anyone was critical of the behaviour of the Zionists, "he will invite the charge of being anti-Semitic."[50] There are, however, several factors that lead us to consider the charge seriously.

In February 1928 Silcox was invited to deliver a lecture at the ywha in Lawrence, Massachusetts, on the topic "Can Jews and Christians Live Peaceably Together?" According to a report by a Jewish participant, he went to Lawrence with the idea "that he was to convert Jewish people to Christianity." She considered Silcox a "narrow, bigoted fool" who utilized his opportunity "to expound his views before Jews and to try to convert them." The audience was outraged because "we did not send for a missionary." In a long and unconvincing letter, Silcox gave his own version of his lecture: he was supposed to speak on "a ministerial viewpoint on Judaism." But even he admitted that some members of the audience, who were recent arrivals from Europe, were "apparently supersensitive to anything that sounded like criticism." Furthermore, he admitted that he used silly comments, such as "if I were in an anti-Semitic mood I would say ..."[51] Probably this incident was misunderstood, as Silcox maintained, but on several occasions his attitude towards Jews could not be considered complimentary.

Silcox disliked what he considered to be typically Jewish pushy behaviour, writing that Jews "have pushed themselves unduly in Germany."[52] When he came to the defence of the Jews, he called for an understanding of their bad behaviour, which was a result of Christian oppression over the centuries. "I know that in large measure the unhappy and pathological condition of the Jews in many lands is not the result of any inherent inalienable racial characteristic, but the understandable reaction of the Jew to the kind of treatment which the Gentile world has meted out to him."[53] Some people heard him complaining that Jews "should learn some manners so they would be more acceptable."[54] Discussing the revival of antisemitism in 1960, he suggested that "the best way to fight it is not to make any form of criticism of Jewish behaviour," in spite of the fact that Jewish behaviour was different. He blamed Jews for the revival of antisemitism and neo-Nazism in the world, writing: "Why ... despite the high-powered propaganda emanating from Jewish and Zionist centres ... [do] they still have enemies, not only in West Germany and in Arab lands, but in many other countries. Are all the faults on the part of the Gentiles?"[55]

How should one categorize these comments? Perhaps an answer can be found in Silcox's character and beliefs. Several times he declared, "I am a Britisher."[56] He admired the British tradition and concept of fair play, and he strongly supported British interests in the Middle East. His devotion to the refugee cause was partly an outcome of this belief: he called for the admission of refugees from Germany because they had "Anglo-Saxon spirit." He encouraged a welcome for the British king, who was coming to visit Canada, as follows: "Let us show His Majesty that the spirit of British fair play is still alive in this Dominion, by our answer to the challenge of the refugees."[57] In the same way we can understand Silcox's support of religious education in the schools, since it was part of the curriculum in England. British education at the time included religious instruction, which was always Christian. What was good for the British obviously should be good for Canadians. Why not follow the British tradition?

Silcox was very proud of his British ancestry and considered himself part of the British elite in Canada. He looked down upon the Jews as newcomers who did not behave according to his standard. It was elitism and British snobbery, apparently, rather than antisemitism, which conditioned his attitude towards the Jews. As an admirer of the British Empire, Silcox supported the British mandate in Palestine, and quite naturally defended British interests in the Middle East, namely, the Arab cause. The Arabs were the majority in the area, they had oil, and they had political power in the United Nations. His support of British foreign policy was at odds with the Zionist aim of establishing a Jewish state in Palestine. Furthermore, his belief in cosmopolitan liberalism directly opposed the Zionists' "narrow-minded nationalism." He maintained that, "in the name of rising internationalism emerging in our world, it might also rebuke the rising nationalism of the Jews."[58] Silcox saw in Zionism a kind of tribalism that was totally different from the universal ideas of the prophets. As a humanitarian and champion of social justice, he helped the underdog and defended minority rights. While, during the Holocaust, Jewish refugees were the oppressed, after the war the Arabs became the victims of war and persecution; therefore he offered his help to the Arabs.[59]

In conclusion, although Claris E. Silcox had his blind spots, he was not an antisemite. His humanitarianism and quest for social justice led him to help both Jewish and Arabs refugees. His admiration for British tradition and British policy could explain both his support of religious education and his anti-Zionist approach. He shared with United Church clergy the universalist vision of world peace of the ancient Jewish prophets, which they felt contradicted the narrow nationalist idea of a Jewish state.

5 Ernest Marshall Howse, the Refugees, and the State of Israel

Claris E. Silcox was not alone among clergy and intellectuals who had actively supported the case of Jewish refugees during the Nazi era and who nevertheless opposed the Zionist idea. Americans such as the Reverend Harry Emerson Fosdick, minister of Riverside Drive Church in New York City, and Dorothy Thompson, the well-known journalist, also followed such a path. As well, in the United Church of Canada there were ministers who had helped Jewish refugees during the Holocaust but "were not sympathetic with Zionism, on historical or religious grounds," recalled Angus J. MacQueen, a former moderator.[1]

A characteristic United Church leader who had worked for the admission of Jewish refugees to Canada, on the one hand, and yet was highly critical of Israel, on the other, was Ernest Marshall Howse (1903–93). A native of Newfoundland and the son of a Methodist minister, Howse was an author, newspaper columnist, social activist, and outspoken radical. He regarded himself as "an unrepentant liberal." He was frank and said what he believed; he therefore became a controversial figure. He shocked many church members when, shortly after becoming moderator in 1964, he denied that Christ rose physically from the dead, though Howse believed in "spiritual resurrection." He opposed Canadian divorce laws and dismissed the birth control laws as "utterly without sanction." He served as minister of Westminster United Church in Winnipeg; after the war he moved to the prestigious Bloor Street United Church in Toronto.[2]

From 1939, when he established the Western branch of the Canadian National Committee on Refugees and Victims of Political Persecution in Winnipeg, until the 1960s Howse was a champion of refugees, Christian and Jewish. In articles, sermons, and public lectures, he espoused the refugee cause, calling upon the Canadian government to liberalize its draconian immigration regulations. In October 1942, in Winnipeg's Civic Auditorium, he delivered an important Christian message entitled "I Speak for the Jew." "Facing that abomination of obscenity and bestiality which, in the foul shadows of the swastika, has come into unnatural being ... Now the new suffering comes to the Jew first, and it comes most terribly. The scourge has fallen upon defenceless people, as perhaps earth has not seen at since the siege of Jerusalem ... So I speak for the Jew. But I speak, not as for someone different from myself. When I read the dark and bloody record of what, in these very days, ... is happening in Nazi lands, I think not of Jews and Jewesses: I think of men and women and children ... and when I plead for the Jew I plead for my own family and yours, and the families of all mankind."[3]

Howse delivered two sermons in Winnipeg on behalf of Jewish refugees. Since his audience in western Canada was far from sympathetic to the admission of refugees, particularly Jewish ones, he had to be careful. He called upon Canada to act: "Something then can be done – but what? We have to move wisely and carefully, but that does not mean that we must not move at all." And he set forth a program of action for people that included temporary relief, public education, and an appeal to the provincial and federal governments to admit refugees by establishing an emergency quota for them. "No truly Christian nation can look upon these victims of ruthless persecution and refuse demands of humanity especially when it is well within its power to help."[4]

Howse was also personally involved in bringing refugees to Canada, arranging their release from prisons or camps and helping with their resettlement. "What you have done for me, quick, efficient and planful [sic]. As it has been hardly anybody achieved of all my friends," wrote a refugee doctor to Howse.[5] He was also instrumental in the placement of British children who were brought to Canada during the war. For this work, he later received a hand-signed letter of commendation from Queen Elizabeth, which read: "I wish to mark by this personal message my gratitude for the help and kindness, which you have shown to the children who crossed the sea from the United Kingdom many months ago ... By your generous sympathy you have earned the true and lasting gratitude of those to whom you have given this hospitality, and by your understanding you have shown how strong is the bond uniting all those who cherish the same ideals. For all this goodwill towards the children of Great Britain, I send you my warmest and most grateful thanks."[6]

After the war Howse continued to serve the cause of displaced persons. He visited Germany and established connections with German Christian displaced persons, sending them money and packages.[7] Yet the decades-long efforts on behalf of refugees seem not to have substantially changed Canadian attitudes towards newcomers. In 1960, which was declared World Refugee Year, Howse lamented that "considering the wealth and resources of Church members in Canada I find it difficult to summon up any pride in the measure of our response." He also maintained that the government's role in the year had been "disappointing." He suggested that one thousand Palestinian refugees be admitted into Canada as a "symbolic gesture," along with a "symbolic number" of five hundred Jews who were escaping from behind the Iron Curtain.[8]

E.M. Howse's involvement with Jewish and Christian refugees led him to try to bridge the gap between the three major religions.[9] From 1942 until 1948 he was active in promoting efforts to break through ancient barriers and bridge deep divisions between Christianity and Judaism. In 1972, when he realized that the Muslims in Canada were unpopular and were being treated unfairly, he campaigned to expand the activities of the Canadian Council of Christians and Jews and rename it the Canadian Council of Religious Faiths.[10]

According to Reuben Slonim, who knew him first-hand, in spite of Howse's friendship with Jews, he lacked familiarity with the behaviour and sensitivities of Jewish people, and his knowledge of Jewish laws and philosophy, based as it was on the New Testament, was inaccurate.[11] For instance, he argued that Jewish refusal to allow marriage with a Gentile was motivated by an "incredible carry-over of animosity" to the Gentiles. This view shows an ignorance of Jewish sources on the subject. Another of his perceptions was that Zionism contradicted the teaching of the prophets and was therefore contrary to the Jewish religion; a better knowledge of those prophetic works could have led to the opposite conclusion.[12]

During the war years, Howse not only sympathized with the plight of Jewish refugees but also supported the Zionist claim that Jews had the right to settle in Palestine. A memorandum prepared by a group of Christian leaders, clergy, and lay people on behalf of Jewish immigration into Palestine, published in 1942 in *Fellowship*, the monthly bulletin of the Canadian Conference of Christians and Jews, stated that "to Palestine the Jews have an ancient moral claim, never relinquished in all their history. That claim has been recognized by international sanctions." The document, approved by Howse among others, went on to say that Arabs had "abundant opportunity for political self-determination in many lands, whereas the Jewish people have no such hope except in Palestine." The signatories of the memorandum therefore called for the opening of Palestine to settlement by Jewish refugees.[13] Thus there were United Church ministers, including Howse and E. Crossley Hunter, who before the end of the war felt that persecuted Jews were entitled to a haven. Since no other country was ready to accept them, Palestine offered the most practicable solution. The continuation of Jewish immigration would greatly increase Palestine's potential resources and be a blessing for both Jews and Arabs.[14]

In the mid-1950s Howse switched his interest from dialogue between Christians and Jews to that between Christians and Muslims. He became chair of the Conference of Muslim-Christian Cooperation, held in April 1954 in Bhamdoun, Lebanon. The American Friends of the Middle East, with Dorothy Thompson, an American pro-Arab committee member, organized the conference. Its purpose was to find common ground between the two religions and to face the danger of communist materialism.[15] For several years Howse dedicated his energy to developing "better understanding and fuller cooperation between the adherents of Islam and Christianity." As co-chair of the Continuing Committee on Muslim-Christian Cooperation, he organized conferences in Alexandria, Teheran, Bhamdoun, and New York, helping to establish local chapters of the association.[16] Through these annual conferences he visited Arab countries and developed close relations with Arab leaders.

In order to understand the problems of the Middle East, Howse also accumulated a vast amount of literature, mainly from Arab publications. Based on this material, he formulated his opinion about the Middle East crisis.[17] Soon in United Church circles he was considered an expert on the Arab-Israeli conflict, and as such, he was invited to serve as a member of the important UC Committee on the Church and International Affairs (CCIA), the body that was responsible for preparing reports and statements on international affairs for the General Council. In January 1956 Howse addressed the committee and led its discussion on the Middle East situation. The minutes of the CCIA summarized his talk as follows:

Dr. Howse … referred to the Arab awakening and the growing sense of indignation on the part of these people because of losses and injuries which they believe they have suffered due to the failure of the United Nations and particularly of the United States and the United Kingdom to rectify injustices resulting from the establishment of the state of Israel. Dr. Howse pointed out that the establishment of this state was the result of the strong Zionist movement. He referred to the very considerable sums of money raised by the Zionists, particularly in the United States. He pointed out that the Zionists were very powerful, particularly in that country and in many other nations of the world. On the other hand, he made it clear that the Arabs, though they numbered some 40 millions, have been unable to place their arguments effectively before the political leaders in the U.N. …

Dr. Howse spoke in detail about the border raids, the loss of life and property and the ever-increasing bitterness and hatred between Jews and Arabs. He stated that the refugee problem continued to become more serious.[18]

Howse implied that the establishment of the State of Israel was an act of injustice. He did not discuss the Arab refusal to accept the UN resolution calling for the foundation of two independent states, including a Palestinian one. The reference to the "very powerful" Zionist movement in Canada and "in many other nations of the world," which had raised "very considerable sums of money," smacks of old-fashioned antisemitism. Nor did Howse mention the flight of persecuted Jewish refugees from Arab countries, the refusal of those countries to absorb Palestinian refugees, or the Palestinian terrorism that had caused the Israeli border raids.[19] The committee was so impressed with his mastery of this complicated subject that he was asked to prepare a statement on the Middle East. Nevertheless, when he submitted his report five weeks later, members of the committee were not satisfied with it, demanding "that the section on the Middle East written by Dr. Howse be referred for re-drafting."[20] But eventually, his report on the Middle East was approved by the General Council in 1956.[21] Between that year and 1960 Howse played a major role in the formulation of the United Church official policy, changing the balance to favour the Arab cause.[22]

Howse, who met with Arab leaders such as King Hussein of Jordan and King Saud of Saudia Arabia, propagated the economic and social progress of Arab countries. Apparently forgetting his earlier comments, quoted above, that "to Palestine the Jews have an ancient moral claim, never relinquished in all their history," he criticized Israel's open-door immigration policy. He maintained that its purpose was "to create a plausible demand for more territory."[23] By 1957 Howse considered the country to be "already over-crowded"; he did not believe that Israel would be able subsequently to absorb more than five million immigrants. He compared the creation of Israel and the "ejection or subjection of the Arabs, with ousting the population of Quebec with the suggestion it settle in a Mexican desert." As was popular in the anti-communist atmosphere of the Cold War, Howse pointed out that no Muslim country had turned communist, while Israel was the only country in the Middle East that tolerated a communist party. In this regard, his attachment to Islam seems to have overcome his liberal and demo-

cratic principles. Howse also criticized the kidnapping of Adolf Eichmann by the government of Israel as "a blow to international law and
the good name of Israel." No criminal guilt, even as enormous as that
of Hitler, could justify national lawlessness, he maintained.[24]

After the Six Day War of 1967, Howse continued his criticism of Israel. He condemned the use of military power to solve international
problems, because local wars carried the danger of easily becoming
global and nuclear ones. "In the long run, Israel cannot remain militarily superior to its past enemies. In the long run its existence de-
pends upon the good will of the world." But he warned Israel not to
rely upon the automatic help of the Christian world: "it is unrealistic
and wrong for Jewish leaders to call on Christian leaders to do so." For
a lasting settlement, he called for genuine dialogue, since he realized
that there were "fundamental differences where rough edges grind
one another." But, he lamented, "a vacant chair hampered such a dialogue. The homeless Arab never speaks." Only "imagination of the
first order" would bring the embattled parties together, concluded
Howse.[25]

The Israeli conquest of Jerusalem in 1967 caused Howse to express
strong resentment. In an article called "Who Should Control Jerusalem?" he examined the history of the city and reached the conclusion
that "the Hebrews, in fact, never held more than a tenuous and inter-
mittent authority over certain scattered sections." With the exception
of the eras of David and Solomon and the "tragic interval of the Maca-
bees," Jews had had no sovereignty over the city, Palestinian Arabs,
however, "have guarded and protected" it for 1,300 years. Although
Jews had a "deep emotional attachment" to Jerusalem, "most of them
had no intention of returning." Howse implied that their fervent chant
of the verse "If I forget thee O Jerusalem let my right hand forget her
cunning" did not express a serious longing. He admitted that the
Christian period was "inglorious ... and the story of the Crusades reflects no credit on Christianity," but he accused Israel of taking the city
by force, like the crusaders. However, "the age of the Crusades is over.
By attempting to throw the cloak of holiness over the undisguised re-
conquest of a city sacred to all ... [Jews] make a mockery of the high
ideals of their own faith." The only just solution, according to Howse,
was "a free city under international guardianship."[26]

Rabbi Gunther Plaut vigorously objected to Howse's arguments: "It
was bad enough for Dr. Howse to say that the Jewish 'next year in Jerusalem' was insincere. This merely shows that Dr. Howse does not know
Jewish sentiment or the implications of this hallowed phrase and the
long centuries of exile. When he goes on to imply that for Israel a major enticement of Jerusalem is its high economic revenue, he descends

to the level of old-time Jew baiting which identifies Mammon as a Jewish God and money as an all-consuming goal for our people. I am saddened that a former Moderator of the United Church should believe this and shocked that he would consent to give it currency in print."[27]

Antisemitism was one of the subjects that Howse considered frequently during his career. Many of the issues he dealt with were, in one way or another, related to hatred of the Jews, such as the Jewish refugee question, dialogues with Jews and Muslims, support for the Palestinian cause, and criticism of Israel. He denied that German antisemitism had originated in New Testament teachings. In developing his thesis, he turned the argument of the Canadian Jewish Congress against itself, as had often been his tactic in debates. He maintained that Jewish rabbis could be put in jail for hatred of Gentiles. Jews were also responsible for the Middle East controversy. "The bitter animosities of the Middle East today have their subconscious origin in the historic teaching of the synagogue," he wrote. The Talmud, the Zionist press, and even Leon Uris's *Exodus* could be seen as hate literature. "If hatred itself is evil, we should recognize that the quality of evil is not determined by the persons against whom it is directed. We must recognize also the futility of trying to destroy hate with jail sentences." Howse's solution was education.[28]

Debating with Rabbi A.L. Feinberg of Toronto, who stated that, according to Christian belief, Jews must remain "rejected" and wander like Cain, Howse declared: "I am not … just the lingering unconscious of ancient prejudice … I am repulsed both by the butchery written in earlier Scripture, and the pogroms written in later history." He denied the accusation that devotion to Christ made him an antisemite or that the crucifixion of Jesus nineteen centuries ago made him hostile to Jews in Israel. Howse maintained that exploring unconscious Christian anti-Jewish attitudes was as much a distortion of the faith as was examining Jewish unconscious hatred of Christians.[29]

These positions of Howse's practically ensured his involvement in the heated debate that took place in the 1960s and 1970s between the Jewish community in Canada and A.C. Forrest.[30] Howse was one of several leading United Church ministers who defended Forrest. His support of his colleague brought a storm of charges of antisemitism against him. But like several other United Church leaders, he refused to recognize the uniqueness of the Christian-Jewish relationship; they did not want to consider that Jewish bitterness and suspiciousness might be the result of two millennia of degradation and persecution by Christians. Howse refused to admit any guilt for the Christian past: "As soon as you talk with me about anti-Semitism you are talking only about my failings … Just as there is a capacity in Christians to create anti-Semitism, so there is within Jews a possibility of creating hostility to Gentiles. Is not one as bad as the other?"[31]

To conclude, Ernest Marshall Howse sincerely believed that he was concerned equally with the welfare of Arabs and of Jews. He participated in dialogues with Jews as well as with Muslims. But in the over-sensitive atmosphere of the Jewish community in Canada after World War II, neutrality was almost impossible. Many Canadian Jews and Christians regarded him as an antisemite. His refusal to treat Israel with care and his disregard for the religious and historical meaning of the establishment of a Jewish state and particularly for the impact of the Holocaust made Jews feel that he was insensitive, while his public support of the controversial Forrest added to his unpopularity among friends of Israel.

Unlike Claris Silcox, who was a journalist, Howse played a leading role in the United Church. As a former moderator and a minister of Bloor Street United Church in Toronto, he had a following, which represented a segment of the rank-and-file members of the United Church. He took a major part in the pro-Arab decisions of the General Council during the years 1956–60. While Howse supported Jewish refugees during the Holocaust because they were the victims, later the Palestinian refugees, as the underdogs, received his sympathy. As a liberal, he opposed narrow Zionist nationalism, and as a Christian who refused "to wrestle with his own ideological past," to use Gregory Baum's phrase, Howse held a position in the Israeli-Arab conflict that was far from even-handed. The image of Forrest remains in the public mind as the most notable United Church leader who supported the Arab cause and strongly criticized Israel. While Forrest was the most outspoken, as we shall see in the following chapters, Howse not only essentially agreed with him, but he preceded Forrest in influencing the United Church to adopt an unbalanced policy. His opinions concerning the Jews and Israel shaped those of a great part of the membership of the church.

6 The Committee on the Church and International Affairs of the United Church

The attitude of the United Church to the Zionist ideal and to the establishment of the State of Israel was not clear-cut. While the approach of the great majority was negative, partially for theological reasons, there were also supporters, particularly after the Holocaust, who called for a haven for the Jewish people. A.E. Prince, a historian at the University of Toronto, argued in the *United Church Observer* that "Zionism is an unhappy and disastrous denial of the finest prophetic traditions of Judaism." The "aggressive" concept of Zionism, set in motion by Theodor Herzl, was like a "putting back of the clock many centuries to the earlier more primitive concept of a religious nationalism, based on the narrow-'racism' of a 'Chosen People.' " Zionism caused "ill-will" and was a "tragic obstacle to closer co-operation" between the three religions. "If the Jews would only relinquish their political ambitions to establish a separate state in Palestine, then the New Year of 1946 would indeed be an *Annus Mirabilis*" for the Jews, for the Arabs, for Britain, and for the whole world. The Promised Land "could then become the Holy Land of Promise for all peoples and all faiths," concluded Prince.[1]

Given the growing tension between Eastern and Western powers after the war years, an editorial in the *United Church Observer* of December 1947 asked Zionists to give up their demand for an independent state, in order to save humanity from the danger of another world war.[2] While the Zionists were blamed, on the one hand, for being secular, they were attacked for planning to establish a religious state, on the other. The editorial predicted that the future Jewish state would be a failure, since it would be based on religion. The record of the Vatican in politics taught that "it is hardly one that would give the student of history much hope for the future success of another religious-political state."[3]

A.J. Wilson, the editor-in-chief of the *Observer*, in a rare editorial on the subject of Palestine, expressed his opposition to the Jewish state one month before its establishment: "At a time when small nations are being absorbed into large national units, it seems contrary to historic processes that a new sovereign state should be set up for the Jews in Palestine. We have one politico-religious sovereign state in the world ... Another in Palestine is bound to increase national and racial tensions." The editor complimented the Jews for doing "a phenomenal job in Palestine, building up the waste places, and making the desert blossom as the rose." But why did they need a state? "If they would be satisfied to live and work, and to enjoy the prosperity they have wrested from the soil, without fanatically insisting on the status of a sovereign state, all would be well. For the sake of the peace of the world, the Jews should renounce their claims for an immediate sovereign state. Such a renunciation would do more than any other single act, to restore confidence in the essential goodness of human nature."[4]

Yet during the Nazi era certain United Church ministers had supported the idea of a Jewish state in light of the persecution of the Jews, the refugee problem, and growing antisemitism in Canada. Those members of the church who sympathized with the victims of Nazi terror in the 1930s and called for the admission of a certain number of Jewish refugees to Canada were also the ones who supported the Zionist desire to open Palestine to large-scale immigration of European Jews. When the Canadian Christian Council on Palestine was established in 1944, representing the Anglican, Baptist, and United churches, it issued a statement calling for the churches to support the entrance of Jewish refugees to Palestine. "With the utmost faith and confidence in British ideals, justice and fair play, the Jewish people have gone ahead with a tremendous project in the establishment of Palestine as a National Home. Now that the time has come in which they feel the need of using that home as a haven and refuge for the martyred people of their own race are they to be deprived of the precious privilege of offering sanctuary? ... The church has a tremendous influence and backed by a wholehearted membership should go far in following the lead offered by the Canadian Christian Council on Palestine towards righting, not only historic, but present-day injustice against the Jewish minorities."[5]

With the end of the war in Europe, when reports of mass murder and the cruelty of the Nazis became known, sympathy among members of the United Church for a haven for the persecuted Jews in their own homeland increased. "The horror of our people expressed itself in the support of the establishment of Israel. The only guard against a repeat of such mass destruction was a strong Israeli nation with secure borders," recalled A.B.B. Moore, a former secretary of the UC General Council.[6] One should be careful of evaluating the church's support of the idea of a Jewish state before 1948 on the basis of a personal recollection, however. Moore's memories probably reflect the private feelings of some of his colleagues. But as far as church policy was concerned, no official resolution was adopted, and the articles and editorials in the *United Church Observer* were rare and not sympathetic to the UN resolution concerning the partition of Palestine into two independent states, Jewish and Arab.

While these articles and editorials were the individual expressions of United Church members, the body that formulated official policy towards the State of Israel was the Committee on the Church and International Affairs (CCIA). Why did the church have a special committee on international affairs, in view of the fact that this was not an area of individual, but rather of government, concern? Why was the United Church, which was a Canadian communion, interested in foreign affairs, and why was it so involved in such matters? The liberal and cosmopolitan outlook of United Church members led the church to a policy of intervention in world politics. As we have seen, during the war years a Commission on the Church, Nation and World Order had been struck, which set out the biblical and theological basis for the church's concerns in the field of international affairs. Its final report, approved by the eleventh General Council in September 1944, represented the first real attempt to define a comprehensive role for the church. The report stated that since World War II was being fought "in defence of our Christian civilization," "It is incumbent upon the Church to declare what are the basic elements in a Christian civilization and to point out where we have failed to incorporate such elements in the body politic ... Furthermore, the crisis through which we are passing *is a judgment of God upon all nations.* It is not alone a national crisis; it is international ... Because of this faith and this experience in seeking redemption of the people of every race and country, it [the church] feels a solemn obligation to enunciate those spiritual and moral truths, which make for international understanding and an enduring peace."[7]

THE EARLY YEARS OF THE CCIA, 1947–1967

The Committee on the Church and International Affairs was organized in September 1947 as a standing committee of the Board of

Evangelism and Social Service, which had hitherto been responsible for foreign affairs. The terms of reference included the collection of material on international relations, providing leadership in clarifying and formulating policies on foreign affairs, organizing regional committees, reporting to the General Council and making recommendations on resolutions concerning foreign affairs, educating ministers and members in that field, and cooperating with other church bodies, in particular the World Council of Churches and the Canadian Council of Churches.

From the beginning, the CCIA had to justify its very existence. It was asked time and again why the church should be involved in international affairs. The answers were mainly theological.[8] Believing strongly in social justice, the CCIA took into consideration long-range objectives based on Christian principles, such as the teaching that the strong should help the weak and should provide equitable treatment and justice. "As Christians we want these decisions to be made not only from the viewpoint of economic, material or military advantage, but also from the viewpoint of our Christian moral duty," stated the chair of the CCIA.[9] The committee gradually became an active, powerful policy-making body in the United Church. It not only responded to world events but also instigated more than its share of action, such as a call for recognition of the People's Republic of China.

During its formative years (1947–48), the CCIA concentrated on relief to displaced persons in Europe and on immigration. Accordingly, a statement on immigration was prepared which included Canada's role in offering relief to displaced persons.[10] While the subjects of immigration, relief, nuclear disarmament, and communism were discussed frequently, the Palestinian problem was briefly mentioned on two occasions. As Canada had had an important role in the preparation of the UN partition plan for Palestine, the CCIA agreed to recommend that the Canadian government back the UN resolution, "even to the point of military support."[11] With the establishment of the State of Israel in May 1948, an authoritative statement from the United Church's General Council was expected. However, the one-year-old committee, which had no experts on the Middle East, was unable to produce an adequate policy recommendation; as the minutes of the CCIA reported, "It is realized that this complex and difficult subject cannot be presented adequately, and we are quite sure that the Committee would not favor any resolution." Therefore a neutral position was chosen.[12] Indeed, the *Record of Proceedings of the Thirteenth General Council* (1948) reported that "it would be unwise to prepare a statement on the Palestinian question." The council therefore printed the summaries of the official statements by the three parties involved without any commentary: those of

Moshe Shertok, the Israeli foreign minister, of Jamal el-Husseini, representing the Arab position, and of Arthur Creech-Jones, outlining position of the United Kingdom.[13]

When the Vancouver regional committee on international affairs in 1954 requested "that the United Church issue a statement concerning the injustice in the treatment of Arabs in the Middle East," the CCIA resumed dealing with the Arab-Israeli conflict. To avoid a partisan position, the major aspects of both sides were presented in its deliberations.[14] The final report that appeared in the *Record of Proceedings of the General Council* in 1954 was different in tone from the atmosphere that had dominated the committee's deliberations. It was prepared by R.B.Y. Scott of the United Theological College in Montreal. The report blamed the United States, Britain, and the United Nations for not acting to solve the crisis. The foundation of Israel was supported by Christians who sympathized with Jewish suffering during the Holocaust, but "an attempt to meet one refugee problem has created another of similar injustice." The result of Israel's establishment was the creation of one million refugees. The refusal of Arab countries to absorb their refugee kindred was mentioned, though not criticized. The historical survey went on to blame Israel's use of force, its retaliatory massacres, its expansionism, and its refusal to comply with UN resolutions, including the repatriation of Arab refugees and the internationalization of Jerusalem. The existence of Israel was considered to be "an unalterable fact of history, and a new, real political entity." Therefore the report called on Arabs to accept the existence of Israel "and learn to live with her as a neighbor." Israel should participate in the compensation of those Palestinians who could not return to their homes. As for Jerusalem, since its internationalization was impossible, the United Church would be satisfied with UN supervision and protection of the holy sites. The General Council turned to its members to contribute to relief projects for the Arab refugees, urged the government of Canada to help the United Nations to find a permanent peace, and requested the UN to supervise the holy sites.

In a curious resolution, the General Council requested the United Nations "to accept responsibility for reviewing its decisions on Palestine since 1947 in view of subsequent history, and see that a workable modification of them is actually enforced." The meaning of this statement was that the church preferred the nullification, or modification, of the partition resolution, because of injustice done to the Arabs and because of the turmoil that the establishment of Israel had created in the Middle East. Thus the General Council's 1954 statement of policy concerning the Arab-Israeli conflict was generally an effort at a balanced position. However, the resolution that called on the United Nations to reconsider its decision from 1947 was one-sided.[15]

The transformation of the Committee on Church and International Affairs from a neutral to a pro-Arab point of view took place in 1956, partly as a result of the addition of Ernest Marshall Howse to the committee. As we have seen, Howse prepared an unbalanced report. During the CCIA's deliberations, it was decided to give more attention to the neglected problems of the Arab refugees. As the first step in this direction, the committee recommended that the *United Church Observer* be asked to invite an article on the Middle East conflict from Claris Silcox, whose anti-Israeli opinions were well known.[16] In addition, reference was made to the need for wide publication of the fact that $800,000,000 of American money [had been] sent by the Zionists to Israel.[17]

The CCIA report to the General Council of 1956 emphasized the need for impartiality: "As a Church we must be careful not to take a partisan position. Our policy cannot be less than that of a 'just and impartial friendship' to *all* peoples in the Middle East. We are, however, aware that in Canada the case for Israel has been much more fully presented than the case for the Arabs. We believe that in justice we must take cognizance of all facts as they relate to both sides and to the rest of the world. Our statement, therefore, is an earnest attempt to bring a proper balance to conflicting pleas."[18]

Israel was held responsible for the outbreak of the war in 1948, since it had occupied large areas that had not been allotted to it by the United Nations. In the anti-communist atmosphere of the era, Israel's victory was regarded as the outcome of a massive shipment of arms from the Soviet Russia. Western countries were blamed for sacrificing the interests of Arab refugees "for partisan advantage in domestic politics." In spite of Western compassion for the survivors of the Holocaust, no country was ready to provide a haven for them. To soothe their conscience, the Western countries had sent the Jewish refugees to Palestine, thereby causing the Arab refugee problem."The Western world therefore has an inescapable share of responsibility for the Arab refugees, the Semites, who have become the ultimate victims of anti-Semitism," concluded the report.[19] In spite of the preamble, which declared the need for a more sympathetic attitude towards the Arab case, there was some effort at a balanced approach, such as a note about Soviet sales of arms to Egypt. Also, the report did not blame Israel for expelling the Arabs in the war of 1948, but pointed out that the Palestinians had left their country during that war in accordance with the advice of their own leaders. Unlike the report of 1954, that of 1956 contained no operative resolutions.

In September 1956 the committee, at Howse's instigation, decided to protest to the Canadian government about the sale of twenty-four fighter jet planes to Israel. Prime Minister Lester Pearson responded to the United Church appeal by saying that the government had reached its decision in favour of the Israeli request only "after long and careful consideration." He pointed out that Israel had promised to use the planes only as defensive weapons. Furthermore, to keep the balance of power in the Middle East, it desperately needed arms to offset recent massive Soviet shipments of arms to Egypt.[20] During the Suez crisis in October–November 1956, while the fighting was going on, the CCIA continued to protest against the selling of arms to Israel, sending a cable to Ottawa that read: "Deplores the amoral arguments of major powers supporting current aggression and urges Canadian Government to do utmost to improve relations with Arab states. Committee reinforced in belief that Canadian offer to ship 24 jet planes to Israel should not have been made and in present crisis planes should not be sent."[21]

Because of the Suez crisis, the government retreated from its earlier position and decided against the shipment of planes to Israel. The CCIA was jubilant; although the members realized that their pressure obviously was not a major factor in the cabinet's decision, "doubtless our expressed opinion had some influence."[22] "We had a share in determining the policy by which a UN emergency force was sent to the Middle East under a Canadian commander," boasted J.R. Mutchmor, the secretary of the CCIA.[23] The opposition of the United Church to the sale of arms to Israel was obviously harmful to that country 's defence, but the motive behind that policy was apparently not an anti-Israeli one, but rather a deep desire for disarmament. After World War II, disarmament was high on the United Church's foreign policy agenda.[24]

The frequent appeals of the church to the Canadian government were not confined to the Middle East. There was regular communication on international affairs, such as nuclear disarmament; the church and peace in the world; NATO; the new nationalism; human rights in South Africa, Korea, Angola, and Rhodesia; recognition of the People's Republic of China; and protest against American bombing in North Vietnam and against actions taken by dictators in South America. Involvement of church leaders in political matters was a tradition in Canada, and they knew their lobbying power.[25]

The CCIA report of 1958 to the General Council was probably the most sympathetic towards Israel that the United Church had ever adopted. During the Sinai campaign of 1956, Israel had occupied the Sinai Peninsula and reached the Suez Canal, but following American pressure and a UN resolution, its forces retreated from Sinai. Probably because of this fact, the church's report was complimentary to Israel: "No Jew and few Christians can help but thrill at what is being accomplished in Israel." The report enumerated Israel's achievements: one million Jewish refugees were resettled and helping to build the country; Jews had become farmers instead of merchants; the "kibbutz," the communal settlement, was highly regarded; religious differences did not divide the country; in democratic Israel, which was "the little bastion of western life," there were Arabs as members of the parliament.[26] However, even in a laudatory mood, members of the United Church were unable to grasp the meaning of the rebirth of Israel. Israelis, even the secular ones, considered Israel to be a nation as well as a religion, but church liberals, who opposed nationalism, accepted Judaism only as a religion. "It is recognized, however, that this is a national more than a religious movement," complained the report to the General Council.[27]

As for the Arab refugees, the report admitted that many refugees were not destitute and "probably that the majority of them are better fed and educated than they were before." In a fairly balanced survey of the refugee problem in the world, it mentioned not only the Arab refugees who had fled from Palestine but also the one million Jewish refugees who had sought sanctuary in the new state. Furthermore, 400,000 Jews had been forced to leave their homes in Arab countries. While previous reports had demanded that Israel repatriate the Arab refugees, this one clearly stated that repatriation was not practical. The only solution was "integration of refugees in host countries." With international assistance, Israel should compensate the refugees, and the Arab countries should provide land to resettle them.[28]

Then for almost a decade after this report, the Arab-Israeli conflict played no part in the deliberations of the CCIA and the General Council; the Middle East was entirely disregarded by United Church bodies. Thus to sum up, in the CCIA's first two decades of activity, 1947–67, the Middle East was not high on its agenda. Except in 1956, the committee did not devote much thought or discussion to this subject. The initial drive for a balanced position gradually gave way to an approach that tended to favour the Arabs. The General Council adopted the committee's reports, but there were almost no resolutions. The war of 1967 drastically changed this situation.

FROM THE SIX DAY WAR TO
THE YOM KIPPUR WAR, 1967–1973

In May 1967 President Abdel Nasser of Egypt closed the Strait of Tiran, cutting off Israel's southern access to shipping. His threat "to drown all Jews in the sea" created the fear of a second holocaust among Jews. Nevertheless, the churches in Canada were silent. It seemed to the Jews that the indifference of the churches during the Holocaust was being repeated. No official organ of the United Church issued any statement of support for the beleaguered nation during the weeks of anxiety preceding the outbreak of war. Rabbi Stuart E. Rosenberg of Beth Tzedec Synagogue in Toronto criticized Christians for "equivocation," comparing their failure to support Israel's right to exist with their silence during the Nazi era.[29]

To be sure, there were individuals such as N. Bruce McLeod, a minister in Hamilton who organized a petition signed by four hundred people of different denominations expressing concern for Israel's survival. However, no official support for Israel was expressed. On 6 June 1967 the United Church moderator joined with the heads of the Anglican Church and the Canadian Conference of Catholic Bishops in a statement that called upon church members to pray "for a just and honorable peace." But the statement made no reference to Israel's right to exist; nor did it offer consolation or support to the Jews in those difficult days.[30] In 1991 Angus J. MacQueen observed in retrospect: "After the Six Day War A. Forrest, and most of us, failed to speak up on behalf of Israel and her survival … We in the Christian world tended to underestimate Jewish fear and the depth of their identification as a People with Israel."[31] While there was no declaration of support for Israel's right to exist before or during the fighting, in the year that followed Israel's victory, various agencies of the United Church engaged in intensive discussion concerning an official church policy on the Arab-Israeli conflict. On 25 May 1967, during the days of anxiety preceding the war, the CCIA had appointed a subcommittee "to review the situation in the Middle East and to prepare a statement for the guidance of the United Church." The subcommittee, consisting of E.M. Howse, W.S. McCullogh, and Wilson Woodside, submitted a statement with recommendations for a detailed peace settlement, which the higher courts of the United Church rejected.[32]

In February 1968 the executive of the General Council, the highest body in the United Church when the General Council was not in session, issued a declaration that was based upon the Heraklion statement of the World Council of Churches[33] and upon the UN Security Council's Resolution 242 of 22 November 1967. The declaration reaffirmed the traditional position of the church that the Arab states should recognize that the State of Israel had the right "to live in peace, secure from threats." It demanded the withdrawal of Israeli forces, allowing "minor adjustments of boundaries," and urged Israel to permit the repatriation of "all displaced persons." The executive disregarded earlier recommendations concerning Israeli compensation of refugees and their resettlement in Arab countries. It praised Canadian relief to refugees and called on United Church members to contribute to overseas relief. It also appealed to the parties in the conflict to begin peace talks under UN auspices. The executive proposed that it initiate a dialogue between Christian, Jewish, and Arab communities in Canada to find some way "to contribute to peace, justice, and the settlement of the refugee problem." It expressed the church's deep fear that if the Arabs and Israel would not change their recent positions, "there will be a war again in the Middle East."

Turning from the Middle East to the home front, the statement read as follows: "We deplore suggestions that Christians who criticize Israeli policies are anti-Semitic and that those who criticize Arab policies are unsympathetic to the plight of the Arab people."[34] This resolution was a reference to the heated debate concerning A.C. Forrest's anti-Israeli position as editor of the *United Church Observer*, which was taking place in Toronto at the time.[35] The church executive, in resolution no. 6, was therefore supporting his argument about the right to criticize Israel without being accused of antisemitism. Forrest was glad to receive the executive's backing, and he published the entire statement in the *Observer*.[36] Reuben Slonim later maintained that the church's declaration was not identical with Forrest's position, but was an effort to take "a mid course between *Observer* supporters and opponents within the Church."[37]

The General Council appointed a committee to modify the executive's statement, and only after its "re-editing" was the council ready to adopt it. Unlike the reports and resolutions of former councils, this time it regarded the subject carefully, as the various editions attest. The General Council's statement was shorter than that produced by the executive and more balanced. While the latter demanded unconditional withdrawal of the Israeli forces, the former added that this act should be "part of a general settlement." The executive had demanded that Israel permit repatriation of all refugees, while the council gave the option of compensation instead of repatriation. The council statement added that the Arabs should give up their "threatening posture" (a recommendation that was missing from the executive's statement), and it omitted the reference to the Israelis' insistence that "Jerusalem is not negotiable." Thus one can see that the General Council made an effort to issue a balanced declaration.[38] It was decided that this resolution should be made known to the members of the United Church through the *Newsletter* and be sent to the World Council of Churches and the Canadian Council of Churches.[39]

Some elements in the United Church were not happy with the General Council's recognition of Israel's right to exist. "I have come to regard Zionism as so essentially evil that I am horrified by this evidence of recognition and approval of it by ... the highest authority of the United Church," wrote a church member.[40] Probably more meaningful and disturbing was the reaction of J.R. Mutchmor to this letter: "I can understand something of your fears concerning Zionism and probably if we were having some conversation I would share your point of view. I think it is fairly evident that the very wealthy Jewish community in the United States in particular uses its money power to get concessions in the Middle East and that in some instances those who receive these concessions are not entitled to them."[41]

After its intensive treatment of the Middle East in 1967–68, the CCIA now turned its interest to other areas. When the publication of a "study guide" on the Middle East was suggested in early 1969, the committee's secretary replied negatively, because it was busy preparing a program on Latin America.[42] Several individuals who wished to propel the United Church into deeper involvement in the Arab-Israeli crisis proposed a study tour of the area. Mennonite historian Frank H. Epp, who had conducted several "study seminars" to the Middle East for clergy, suggested that the CCIA follow his example. Epp toured Lebanon, Jordan, and Egypt. In Israel he visited refugee camps and met with critics of Israel's policies.[43]

Forrest also proposed the dispatch of a group of church leaders to the Middle East, so that they could get a better picture of the situation, with a view "to providing a strengthened base of informed Canadian opinion "in regard to the area.[44] When members of the committee questioned the effectiveness of such a program, Forrest stressed its "long term benefit." He emphasized that "this would be no tourist proposition," meaning that such a seminar would make a great impact on Canadians' understanding. He was convinced that the study group would be "a sort of mission of understanding" on the Arab-Israeli conflict, and he hoped that after returning to Canada, members of the group would make "some significant contribution to the understanding of the Middle East." Forrest's intention was, as he told Mohamed Chouiri, the Egyptian ambassador in Ottawa, to shift the pro-Israeli sympathy of many United Church leaders to the cause of the Palestinian refugees.[45] The committee's reason for sending the delegation was that the consistently anti-Israeli articles and editorials in the *Observer* increasingly bothered many United Church readers. Thus its basic mission was a fact-finding one, as N. Bruce McLeod later stated.[46]

E.M. Howse suggested that the group should consist of persons of top stature, in order that their findings would have greater influence.[47] Accordingly, the United Church delegation consisted of Robert B. McClure, McLeod, who was minister of Bloor Street United Church in

Toronto, and Donald V. Stirling, chair of the Toronto Conference International Affairs Committee. They toured the Middle East for three weeks (6–25 August 1970), visiting Egypt, Lebanon, Syria, Jordan, and Israel. They met high-ranking officials and members of academia, and visited refugee camps. Their report about the tour and their recommendations fulfilled Forrest's expectations. Stirling issued a separate statement, in which he attacked Israel, condemning its "traditional" aggression, but church members such as Charles M. Forsyth, secretary of the CCIA, and Maurice Whidden of Don Mills publicly dissociated themselves from Stirling's views, which deviated from official United Church policy.[48]

The delegation was impressed by the "renaissance of national identity" among the Palestinians, and it called upon the international community to support Palestinian national life. The delegates found "determined idealism and longing for peace." Canada could contribute to reconciliation by organizing an informal gathering of young people from both sides. The delegates pointed out the emergence of political dissent among Israelis, although Arabs in Israel did not dare to oppose the government publicly. They found in Israel some flexibility concerning Jerusalem and some voices supporting an independent Palestinian state. The attitude of the West to Israel was regarded as an outcome of its "inglorious record of anti-Jewish anti-Semitism, which can find its own form today beneath both blind criticism and blind support." Both the Arabs and the Israelis had made mistakes in the past, but the report appealed to both sides to ignore the past and look forward. The delegates promised to use their findings "to promote lasting reconciliation" in the Middle East.[49] Although the official report was balanced and moderate, some individual members of the group took more extremes stands. In an interview in the *Toronto Star*, McClure declared, "Al Fatah guerrillas have no hatred whatever for Israelis." He regarded them as "responsible ... social reformers."[50] McLeod also returned from the Middle East an Arab sympathizer.[51]

In September 1970 King Hussein of Jordan decided to disband the Palestinian armed forces in his country. Following a bloody civil war, PLO strength in Jordan was broken. The United Church and the Canadian branch of B'nai Brith issued a joint statement with regard to relief for the victims of the war in Jordan. Among members of the CCIA there was some hesitation as to a joint declaration with B'nai Brith, because of "possible misinterpretation of the motives of the church ... which might be interpreted either as slanted toward the propaganda interests of Israel, or reflecting a desire of the church to mend its fences with the Jewish community for less than worthy motives." After consultation with the Canadian Council of Churches and a revision of the text, the CCIA agreed to issue a joint statement with B'nai Brith on behalf "of the wounded victims of the civil war in Jordan." They appealed to the Canadian government and the Canadian Red Cross to send immediate aid to Jordan. The joint statement emphasized that "we make this appeal out of our humanitarian concern" for the victims in Jordan.[52]

The report of the CCIA's Middle East subcommittee, written by its chair, W.S. McCullough, a professor at the University of Toronto, was in certain respects different from previous reports. It mentioned the UN partition plan of 1947 calling for the establishment of two independent states, which the Arabs had rejected. It did not blame Israel for the war of 1948. Rather, it criticized the Arabs for ignoring traditional Jewish hopes for returning to Zion and for disregarding the "tremendous achievements" of the Jewish settlers in Palestine. The report also pointed out that Jewish determination to create a homeland after the Holocaust was "a kind of guarantee that such a catastrophe would never happen to them again." Al Fatah was considered a "disturbing element," since it called for the dissolution of Israel, and therefore "their goal appears to be a pipe dream." On the other hand, Israel was called on to display "considerable flexibility," particularly in light of its victory. It should provide assurance that it would give up the occupied territories "as part of the peace settlement" and acknowledge the right of the refugees to compensation.

The report did not ask Israel to accept mass repatriation; the great majority of the refugees should be settled outside the country. It admitted that "such a resettlement will be a hard proposition for most of the refugees to accept." Both sides would be required to make hard decisions. Israel was asked to accept the Palestinians' right "to determine their own political future," which meant an independent Palestinian state, and the Arabs were asked to acknowledge the existence of Israel, which involved "a complete *volta-face* in the traditional Arab policy." The Arab countries should contribute to the resettlement of refugees. Jewish refugees who had lived in Arab countries and resettled in Israel should be included among those who would be entitled to compensation. This was the first time that the United Church accepted Jewish demands for compensation for Jewish refugees coming from Arab states. However, McCullough, in a realistic tone, admitted that the chances of these proposals being achieved in the near future were "minimal." The report clearly expressed the views of moderates in the two camps.[53]

The CCIA report also called for the withdrawal of Israeli occupying forces, affirmed the right of Israel to freedom of navigation through international waterways, demanded solutions for the refugees, and recommended the establishment of demilitarized zones among the states in conflict. In line with statements of the World Council of Churches, it recommended that the United Church "urge the Government of Canada to back any action of the United Nations, that while guaranteeing the security of Israel, aims to secure justice and self-determination for the Palestinian Arabs."[54] A demand for the recognition of Palestinian "rights for self-determination" was a new element introduced by Forrest. While previous resolutions had discussed the problem of Palestinians as refugees, the church recommended changing their status by granting them the political right to an independent state. Through Forrest's intervention, the United Church thus became the first Canadian Christian denomination to support Al Fatah's claim to statehood.[55] His recommendation to urge the Canadian government to increase its support to the United Nations Relief and Works Agency was also accepted.[56]

From 1970 on, Forrest became a dominant force in the formulation of the CCIA's policy on the Middle East. As a member of its executive and its subcommittee on the Middle East, he initiated resolutions on various subjects, some of them concerning the refugee cause and some purely anti-Israeli measures. Because of his reputation for being familiar with the issues, as well as his many connections with Arab sources, his opinion was always seriously considered.

Forrest's friendship with the new secretary of the CCIA, W. Clarke MacDonald, also helped to advance his ideas. MacDonald had a great deal of compassion for the Palestinians, participating in such pro-Arab bodies as the World Conference of Christians for Palestine and the Commission for the Defence of Human Rights in Palestine. He understood Israel's retaining of the Golan Heights, because they commanded a position which, were it under enemy rule, "would be almost intolerable."However, Israel's treatment of the Palestinians had been "remiss." As for any special consideration for Israel because of the Holocaust, MacDonald was "deeply moved" by the tragedy that had befallen the Jews, but "what we need to do is simply acknowledge that fact, express profound contrition for it and move on."[57] Forrest fed MacDonald with pro-Arab publications, and he became a strong and influential ally of Forrest's.[58]

With the appointment of Deanna Skeoch as chair of the CCIA Middle East subcommittee, replacing W.S. McCullough, in October 1972, another pro-Arab element entered the committee. Skeoch's knowledge about the Arab-Israeli conflict was based on the year that she had spent in Tripoli, Syria. She served as the secretary of the pro-Arab group that Forrest had established, called "Canadians for Middle East Understanding."[59] In order to keep Skeoch well informed and up to date on Middle East events, after consulting with Forrest, MacDonald ordered pro-Arab and Jewish anti-Zionist publications;[60] there seems to have been no effort to obtain reliable information from all sides.

In the autumn of 1971, acting upon a motion by Forrest, the CCIA decided to ask the Canadian secretary of state for external affairs to inquire into the status of Israeli bonds. Israel issued long-term bonds to cover its expenses on the absorption of immigrants. Canadian Jews considered these bonds a contribution to Israel's well-being. MacDonald asked the government to investigate the amount of money, the way it left Canada, the use to which the money was put, and whether it was exempt from income tax, like charitable donations.[61] One may wonder how such an inquiry, which insulted the Canadian Jewish community and was intended to harm the income of the Jewish state, could possibly increase the well-being of Arab refugees or contribute to reconciliation.

Another measure that aimed to jeopardize Israel's economic development was a demand that the government cancel a Canadian loan to Israel. In January 1972 Canada and Israel had signed an agreement that the Canadian Export Development Corporation would lend up to $100 million to Israel to finance the sales of Canadian goods and services to Israel.[62] Forrest succeeded in passing a resolution through the CCIA to ask the Canadian government: "Whether the granting of loans up to $100 million to Israel seems in keeping with Canada's declared support of the Security Council Resolution 242, and Israel's refusal to abide by UN resolutions in respect to the annexation of Arab Jerusalem, the return of refugees, who fled in 1967, and the continued violations of the 4th Geneva Convention in Occupied Territories."[63]

The twenty-fifth General Council in Saskatoon in August 1972 departed from previous efforts to show an even-handed policy concerning the Middle East. It urged the federal government "to work towards and to vigorously support the implementation" of UN Resolution 242, demanding the withdrawal of Israel from the occupied territories. Since new problems had arisen recently, such as Israel's disregard of human rights in the occupied territories and the $100 million Canadian loan to Israel, the General Council decided to request an appointment with Prime Minister Pierre Trudeau "to discuss these and a number of other urgent Middle East concerns." This mission was so important to the United Church that if the Canadian Council of Churches and the Canadian Conference of Catholic Bishops were not interested in participating, the church would move unilaterally.[64] The resolutions concerning the cancellation of the loan to Israel and the delegation to the prime minister, both of which came originally from Forrest, were approved overwhelmingly. He was convinced that the

General Council supported not only his latest initiatives but also his handling of the whole situation.[65]

To implement the General Council's resolution concerning a delegation to the prime minister, Forrest prepared what he considered a "very polite and conciliatory" brief on the "Arab-Israeli Problem and the Plight of the Palestinian People."[66] But the executive of the General Council was not satisfied with the proposed text and called for "a more balanced presentation." MacDonald explained the meaning of this requirement as follows: "The interpretation which I gathered of the phrase 'more balanced' was that the supportive material ... is a unilateral denunciation of Israel without any affirmation or even indication of the fact that the Arab states have so far refused to acknowledge the existence of Israel." Wishing to obtain wide church support for its policy, the executive anticipated further revisions and editorial emendations if the Canadian Council of Churches joined in the presentation of the brief.[67]

"The history of this proposal for an interview with the prime minister reads like the Churchillian account of the paralytic centipedes,"commented MacDonald.[68] The corrected draft went to the Canadian Council of Churches for approval. During the deliberations on the subject, an informal meeting took place between the officers of the ccc and leaders of the Canadian Jewish Congress, aimed at the renewal of dialogue between the two groups. During previous years, dialogue had suffered because of the controversy over the *Observer*'s attitude to Israel. Out of courtesy, T.E. Floyd Honey, general secretary of the ccc, told the Jewish delegation about the brief and the interview with Trudeau, and he showed the brief to the cjc representatives and asked for their comments.[69]

Gunther Plaut responded on behalf of of the congress. He felt that the purpose of the delegation to the prime minister should be understood as the ccc's request to change the course of government policy. "It has been my hope that the resolution (which I consider ill-advised) would not be acted upon,[70] but apparently the current undertaking of the ccc would deny this hope." After enumerating his opposition to various aspects of the brief, Plaut stated that "it is likely to put our mutual relationships back to where we were a year ago ... the beginnings of the dialogue ... will once again be cut short." He concluded his comments appealing to the ccc "*to press for an acceptance of the idea that peace can be achieved only by negotiation*," rather than in the manner currently proposed, and he expressed his hope that the council "would reconsider both the content as well as the timing of this enterprise."[71] Responding to Plaut's comments, the ccc decided that the questions he raised were serious enough to suggest that the document "should be carefully reviewed before any further action is taken." Accordingly, a special committee was appointed to rewrite the document and to add points not covered, along with comments from various churches. Just when the revised brief was about to be presented to the CCC executive committee on 10 October 1973, however, the Yom Kippur War broke out in the Middle East, making further revisions necessary. Though the CCC agreed to a delegation to the prime minister, it demanded that the Middle East be among the subjects to be discussed, not the only one.[72]

Members of the CCIA were upset when they learned that the brief had been shown to the Canadian Jewish Congress and that the CCC had decided to rewrite the document using Rabbi Plaut's suggestions. Forrest, in an article on the *Observer*, blamed the CCC for its delay, charging it with foot-dragging. Honey responded angrily, calling Forrest's article "over-simplified to the point of distortion" and "a serious misrepresentation of the facts."[73] The CCC's delay and its intention to redraft the document led the United Church to act alone, circumventing the council. On 4 December 1973 the executive of the General Council, following the CCIA's recommendation, decided on the following resolution: "That in the light of delay and confusion in the submission of our brief on the Middle East to the prime minister via the Canadian Council of Churches, and of the extreme urgency of this situation at this time, a fresh brief be drawn to be prepared by the subcommittee and forwarded to the prime minister through the executive or sub-executive of the General Council."[74]

While the campaign over the brief was going on, the CCIA distributed a pamphlet entitled *One in Three Million*, which discussed in a vehement and bitter manner the miserable life of a Palestinian refugee. Several people strongly protested the fact that the CCIA, an official body of the United Church, was engaged in the pamphlet's distribution, which "contains obvious distortions of history, thinly disguised innuendoes and blatant contradictions." One writer demanded an apology from MacDonald and an explanation to everyone on the CCIA's mailing list, because "you have shamed Christianity."[75] MacDonald answered that the pamphlet was an informal piece of literature and "not intended as a definite historical document," though he himself did not disagree with the contents of the pamphlet. However, he admitted that he should have included a covering letter indicating that the pamphlet had been sent out after submission to the Middle East subcommittee. McLeod, the United Church moderator, requested that the subcommittee pursue a more balanced approach: "I hope that occasionally material reflecting the other side is also sent."[76] But there is no evidence that the CCIA followed his recommendation to circulate pro-Israel literature. On the other hand, the Middle East subcommittee did discuss the request of Gabriel Habib, director of the Near East Ecumenical Bureau for Information and Interpretation (NEEBII) in Beirut. Habib had inquired whether the office of the CCIA "could help in serving as a distribution center for NEEBII's future material."[77]

Looking back on the deliberations about the brief and the interview with the prime minister, one can see how deep was the impact of Forrest's original proposition and how eager the leaders of the United Church were to carry it out. The church, with its biased policy, was more radical regarding the Arab-Israeli conflict than the other Protestant churches in Canada. Even the Arab states did not request the Canadian government to cancel the loan to Israel. As already mentioned, in the 1970s the Canadian Council of Churches was reluctant to accept the unrevised version of the brief that had been prepared by the CCIA. According to David Taras, when the United Church learned that other churches hesitated to put up a fight against the loan, "the UC curtailed its own lobbying," and the loan was given to Israel "without the noisy protests and widespread opposition."[78] Probably the efforts of McLeod and Morrison, the leaders of the United Church, to pacify the Jewish community in Canada added to the quiet termination of the anti-loan campaign.

THE YOM KIPPUR WAR, 1973–1974

What is more, however, astonishing is the committee's total disregard of current events in the Middle East. The surprise Arab attack on Israel on the holiest day of the Jews, the Day of Atonement, when every Jew was praying in the synagogue, did not leave any impression on members of the CCIA, who were in charge of the United Church's foreign policy. In the thick file that makes up the CCIA correspondence on the Middle East, there is no reference to the war. The only thing that seems to have mattered was the composition of the brief which aimed to condemn Israel; the CCC's suggestion that some revision should be made "in the light of the outbreak of hostilities" was unacceptable to the leaders of the United Church.[79]

Although the committee was silent during the Yom Kippur War, the leaders of the Anglican and United churches hastened to issue a declaration. On 9 October 1973, the third day of the war, the primate of the Anglican Church of Canada and the moderator of the United Church published the following statement: "We affirm, however, our belief that Israel has the right to live in peace … We declare also our concern that the right of Palestinians and all people in the Middle East to live in peace. We call upon our Arab and Jewish brothers to condemn the inhumanity of war, and to urge upon their leaders an early peace conference, which would satisfy the reasonable claims of the Palestinians and guarantee Israel her safety."[80]

In contrast to official hesitations and "balanced" positions, a group of fourteen Catholic and United Church theologians and academians on 19 October, in the *Globe and Mail*, published a "Statement of Christian Concern about the Middle East." It rejected the anti-Zionist myth that Zionist imperialism was a Nazi-type racism which dispossessed the poor Arab population. "Zionism is not a dirty word," the statement said; its roots were in Jewish tradition and modern Jewish experience. Modern Zionism was born as an answer to Christian antisemitism. It represented an early liberation movement, a response to disillusionment with Europeans' antisemitism, which refused to accept Jews in their midst. Israel "is a resurrection symbol following the near extinction of the Jewish people" in the Holocaust. Therefore "Christians must affirm Israel as the visible and tangible manifestation of both Jewish survival and Jewish security." Israel could be criticized like any other nation, but it would be wrong to object to Israel because of its Jewish foundation. The statement recognized the plight of Arab refugees, but it rejected the moral force of the churches as an objective body to mediate between the two sides. Signatories of the document concluded that since the Arabs were threatening to drive the Jews into the sea, "Christians must … stand with Israel … without equivocation."[81] Jews in Canada were jubilant; they reprinted the article and distributed it widely. Such warm recognition from prominent Christian figures was more than they had dared to expect, particularly in light of the bitter controversy around Forrest. Emil Fackenheim, the renowned Jewish philosopher, complimented Alan T. Davies, who was the author of the "statement," saying that it was "by far the best and most profound that I have ever seen on this subject from any Christian source … It has been heart-warming and encouraging to countless people beside myself."[82]

Five days after the publication of this statement, a pro-Arab response appeared as a letter to the editor in the *Globe and Mail*, written by Lorne M. Kenny and signed by thirteen other professors in the Department of Islamic and Near Eastern Studies at the University of Toronto. The statement was termed "a surprising apology for Zionism." It was "rife with prejudice, often subtle, but nonetheless virulent anti-Semitic prejudice against the Arabs (for they too are Semites)." Kenny complained that since the Balfour Declaration, Arab rights had constantly been denied; "Should Christendom not feel some guilt for this denial?" The letter objected to the accusation that the Arabs were perpetuating a second Auschwitz, since they were not guilty of the first one.

"It is mere obfuscation to claim that Christian opinion is seeking solace in the guilt of the Jews with regard to the Palestinian refugees in order to absolve itself from its own guilt with regard to the Jews." No criticism of the indifference of Arab countries to their refugee kindred could cleanse Israel's guilt for its denial of the refugees' rights, stated the letter.[83]

The war of letters in the pages of the *Globe and Mail* led Clarke MacDonald to join in, in order to clarify the official policy of the United Church. The church emphasized its deep sensitivity to the tragedy of Jews and Arabs alike, praying for "peace and justice." MacDonald blamed the pro-Israeli letter, which "has served to polarize local feeling ... We feel that their statement is not adequate." He also blamed Israel for having different laws for Jews and non-Jews. Here he was referring to the Law of Return, the realization of two thousand years of longing for the ingathering of exiles, which recognized the right of every Jew in the world to immigrate to Israel without a visa and to automatically become a citizen. Here MacDonald showed a total misunderstanding of what the new State of Israel meant to the Jews.[84]

Expressing compassion on behalf of the unfortunate in his 1974 New Year message, N. Bruce McLeod expressed his concern about the predicament of the Israeli POWs in Syria. He complained that the Syrian authorities were preventing the International Red Cross from verifying the conditions of the Israeli soldiers, "and the world should cry out for these unarmed, defenceless hopefully still alive people."[85] In another pro-Jewish move, the CCIA in April 1974 adopted a resolution on behalf of Russian Jewry. Since the Jews in the Soviet Union had suffered harassment, unemployment, and social ostracism, the committee "expressed its solidarity" with the Canadian Jewish Congress in their common concern for the emigration of Soviet Jews. It also expressed its concern to the minister for external affairs and encouraged the presbyteries to echo this concern.[86]

The CCIA's effort to show that its criticism of certain policies of Israel did not mean that the United Church was pursuing an anti-Israeli campaign led it to seek out Israeli elements on the left that also criticized Israel's occupation and supported the establishment of a Palestinian state. Abie Nathan, who relentlessly promoted peace with the Palestinians, had bought a "Peace Ship," which broadcasted from the Mediterranean, off the shores of Israel. In 1973 the United Church contributed the sum of $6,000 to his peace initiative.[87] When an Israeli produced a movie critical of Israeli politics and of the Palestinians called *To Live in Freedom*, MacDonald contributed $500 from the CCIA budget to the production in 1973 and organized a sympathetic audience.[88] Another Israeli leftist who was outspoken in his views against the violation of Palestinians' human rights and against the Israeli occupation was Dr Israel Shahak. He condemned the entire idea of Zionism and the very concept of a Jewish state, and accused Israel of going through a process of "Nazification," creating for his readers and listeners the image of Israel cast in the Nazi mould. Sharak's extreme anti-Israeli statements were welcomed by the PLO and widely circulated in pro-Arab circles. He was also a popular lecturer abroad. "I have a tremendous regard for Professor Shahak, both for his integrity and for his courage," maintained Clarke MacDonald, who had met him several times. But MacDonald understood that this group constituted only a marginal and uninfluential element among Israelis. Therefore he looked for other avenues. "I deeply wish that there was some way in which we could communicate to our Jewish brothers and sisters that our defence of the rights of Palestinian Arabs is not a negation of our affirmation of their right to exist as a nation and as a people."[89]

At this time, Forrest and MacDonald thought that they had found the right answer to the Zionists in the person of Reuben Slonim. The conservative rabbi of Congregation Beth Habonim in Toronto, Slonim was also a talented and respected journalist and an expert on Israel. In 1963 he had published a series of articles critical of Israel in the Toronto *Telegram*. It was an "electric shock" for the Canadian Jewish community, which was "totally unready to hear so unabashed a critique from one of its own leaders," recalled Rabbi Gunther Plaut, and the community shunned him. Plaut, a spokesman for Toronto Jewry, recently admitted that "we over-reacted, and I include myself in this judgment."[90] The publication of Slonim's book *Both Sides Now*, in which he called for a more conciliatory approach to the Arabs, enraged his fellow Jews, who excluded him professionally as well as socially. Thus Slonim perfectly fitted the aims of Forrest and the CCIA – a well-known Canadian Jewish Zionist who criticized Israel's policy towards the Palestinians. Therefore in 1975 he was invited to the Middle East subcommittee, where he made a strong plea for understanding. Deanna Skeoch, the chair, commended him for his "courageous contribution in helping to create a better understanding between the Jewish community and the United Church."[91] When, after Sadat's visit to Jerusalem, Slonim called for justice and peace for the Palestinians and their inclusion in the Geneva peace conference, Forrest enthusiastically embraced him, editorializing: "So long as there are Jews ... with the compassion, insight and courage of Reuben Slonim, there can be hope."[92]

In 1974 Forrest organized a seminar on the Middle East in Ottawa for church leaders, which the CCIA approved and took under its auspices. The seminar's purpose was "to gather information from the various points of view and to discuss this from a Christian perspective." Slonim was the representative of the Zionist position. Among the other invited lecturers were Lorne M. Kenny, chair of the Department of Islamic Studies at the University of Toronto, Frank H. Epp, author of the pro-Arab *Whose Land Is Palestine*, A.C. Forrest, and Yosef Yaakov of the Israeli embassy. Since Yaakov refused to participate and Slonim was hardly a representative of the Zionist cause, the floor was left mainly to the pro-Arab speakers. As a matter of fact, this was Forrest's usual strategy: organizing a seminar with ten participants, thus giving the false impression of an even-handed approach and an opportunity to hear different points of view; yet only the Arab side was presented.[93]

Forrest's strong influence on the CCIA was apparent throughout these years. The committee accepted his initiatives, suggestions, and recommendations, whether they were a protest against the Canadian loan to Israel, the preparation of a brief and a request for an interview with the prime minister, suggesting periodicals for subscription, recommending an anti-Israeli movie, or organizing a pro-Arab study seminar under the auspices of the CCIA. Nevertheless, MacDonald and the committee's executive did not rubber-stamp Forrest's suggestions. Sometimes they refused to adopt his extreme language; when he composed an editorial in 1976 in the name of the CCIA, for example, the executive "felt the wording of this one left something to be desired. Some generalizations are questionable." And MacDonald refused to sign it.[94]

One of the most effective means for Forrest to educate the Canadian clergy about the plight of Arab refugees was what he called "the Middle East Study Seminar." Through the *Observer*, he organized three tours – in 1972, 1973, and 1974 – consisting mainly of United Church ministers, who visited Lebanon, Jordan, Syria, Egypt, and Israel, as well as the headquarters of the World Council of Churches in Geneva and the Middle East Council of Churches in Cyprus. The groups met with government officials and church leaders, visited refugee camps, discussed the situation with volunteer agencies working with refugees, and in Israel had long lectures from Israel Shahak.

Forrest made a special effort to persuade Clarke MacDonald to join these trips, finding a grant to cover his expenses. Accordingly, MacDonald participated in two study tours, in February 1973 and February 1974. "The best thing we've done in this whole area in the last while is to have three *Observer* seminars go to the Middle East to both sides. They all came back converted," disclosed Forrest to a close friend.[95] Indeed, the reports confirmed his observation. MacDonald, in his "Report to the CCIA re. Study Seminar in the Middle East," tried to convey his deep impressions of the refugee camps, Arab frustrations, technological advances in Israel, and the prospects for peace. He decided to speak frankly about the CCIA point of view, which was critical of Israel's policy, and he demanded that other United Church bodies follow this pattern, calling it "a gut reaction." He had apparently adopted Forrest's method of publishing his views without caring about the reaction of Jews in Toronto.[96]

Another report, entitled "An Expression of Concern," by twenty-five church members who had participated in the *Observer* seminar in February 1974, was also composed by MacDonald. The document expressed "deep concern" for the people, mainly for the inhuman conditions of the Arab refugees; desire that the United Church and the government of Canada should press for the implementation of UN Resolution 242; and concern for the establishment of human rights in the occupied territories. Other points mentioned were that Jerusalem should be internationalized; that the Jewish National Fund should be used in a non-discriminatory fashion; that the CCIA should "expand its present statement on the Middle East"; and that assistance to the refugees should be increased. The document concluded that "we should commit ourselves ... to do all we can, while maintaining our integrity, to be a reconciling influence" in Canada and abroad.[97] These concerns appeared more like a fairly radical draft of resolutions with new elements. On the other hand, no concern was expressed for the outcome of the Yom Kippur War on Israel. The influence, if not the fingerprint, of Forrest was clear.

Even before the Yom Kippur War, the "Key 73" program had caused some discord between the United Church and the Jews. Earlier in 1973, 130 Christian denominations in North America had launched an evangelistic program designed to "call our continent to Christ." Jewish organizations and rabbis were deeply disturbed over this missionary campaign. The Toronto Board of Rabbis, among others, expressed its concern and protested against the obvious anti-Jewish evangelistic activity of the Key 73 program.[98] Although in the United Church, missionary elements were in the minority, nevertheless, theologically the church did not want to give up the traditional Christian mission; the church's resource book, for example, instructed its members on how "to share Messiah with the Jewish people."[99] The *Observer* declared that "the United Church is part of Key 73 now" and appealed to the community to join the campaign. Later, the executive of the General Council issued a compromise statement: "The Executive, after considering claims that Jews did find Key 73 offensive, decided to continue to support the continent wide evangelical program. The Executive, however, rejected any tendency within the program to single out any group as a particular target."[100]

While the executive was prepared to support missionary intent of the campaign, Bruce McLeod, who made great efforts to restore relations with the Jewish community in Canada, declared that "there is no hidden agenda or effort to convert the Jews." Clarke MacDonald, who was probably the author of the executive decision, privately confided that he personally had "no truck or trade with this sort of thing." To reassure the Jews, who were suspicious that this was merely the latest episode in a centuries-old experience with Christian evangelism, the *Observer* printed an article entitled "Let's Forget about Converting the Jews."[101]

At the twenty-sixth General Council in 1974 new issues concerning the Middle East arose. Palestinian terrorism was condemned: "Fanatics who arise in desperation resort to appalling acts of violence, both against Israelis and against friends of Israel, but more sober Arabs know that such violence is non-productive and cannot be a solution to the basic problem." An effort was made to point out that there were two just points of view in the conflict, without taking sides. The new elements in the resolutions were the General Council's "conviction" that the Palestinians should be represented at the peace conference in Geneva and its call to support the work of the Middle East Council of Churches for the Palestinians. In an expression of the church's search for balance and justice, it appealed to Soviet Russia to allow the emigration of the Russian Jews and their resettlement everywhere, including in Israel. This resolution was adopted in spite of strong Arab opposition to a mass immigration, which would strengthen Israel.[102]

On 15 May 1974 Arab terrorists seized and murdered children in the village of Maa'lot in the northern part of Israel. The response of the United Church came from the moderator, who was careful to take an even-handed position. He issued a public statement condemning in harsh words the cowardly murder of defenceless children: "No injustice justifies such an act. No justice can be based upon it." When Israel retaliated by bombing the Lebanese refugee camps from where the terrorists came, more innocent people died. McLeod criticized this act of violence as well: "I appeal to all concerned to end the slaughter, which can only end in genocide, and return to the peace table."[103] When the United Nations adopted a resolution that equated Zionism to racism, however, several United Church courts and presbyteries protested, expressing "dismay and concern at the iniquitous resolution."[104]

THE LATER YEARS, 1974–1984

Between 1974 and 1977 the CCIA was remarkably silent concerning the Middle East, perhaps because no internationally significant events occurred in the region. Possibly Forrest's restrained position also contributed to this silence.[105] While the coverage of the Israeli-Palestinian conflict decreased, Forrest did not change his basic pro-Arab position, as the twenty-seventh General Council in Calgary in August 1977 attested. It adopted "some of the most sweeping resolutions" concerning the Palestinians, he reported. The *Record of Proceedings* read as follows: "To urge the reconvening of the Middle East Peace Conference in Geneva and to insist that the Palestinian people be represented at such a Conference. We further recommend that the Palestinian people be represented by the Palestinian Liberation Organization."[106]

The insistence on inviting the Palestinians as partners of the Geneva peace conference had already appeared in the General Council's proceedings of 1974. However, recognition of the PLO as the representative of the Palestinian people was a new development in United Church Middle East policy. "The United Church is, I understand, the first Western church to recognize the PLO," boasted Forrest. Interestingly, the resolution was approved without debate. Even Clarke MacDonald was surprised that the PLO section went through without objection.[107] The United Church was again, thanks to Forrest, the forerunner in the pro-Arab approach. Forrest himself had campaigned since 1975 for the recognition of the PLO, but only in 1977 did he suggest the idea to the General Council.[108] An examination of the CCIA's draft resolution, which was prepared in April 1977, proves that the clause about the PLO was not part of the original text, but was added later.[109] Ben Kayfetz, of the Canadian Jewish Congress, speculated that the clause was inserted "to 'compensate' … Forrest … for his election defeat" as moderator of the General Council. However, N. Bruce McLeod later insisted that "there was no ground whatsoever for this speculation."[110]

The PLO clause aroused a wave of protests from various circles. Leaders of Jewish organizations reminded the newly elected moderator, George Tuttle, that the PLO had recently adopted a charter proclaiming its aim to be the destruction of Israel: "In view of this intransigent policy we wonder at General Council's readiness to impose upon a state the requirement that it sit in council to discuss its future with a group committed to its destruction."[111] Tuttle replied that "in no way can we agree with any declared intention of the PLO that the State of Israel be annihilated"; however, the question of cooperation with the PLO was "one of practical politics." He compared it to the church's relationship with certain communist countries, in spite of those countries' commitment to cooperating with groups that would undermine democracy. Practical solutions to the Middle East problems would not come by disregarding the Palestinians' claims or by open confrontation with groups that could make more trouble.[112] Herbert S. Levy, executive vice-president of B'nai Brith, and Louis Ronson, also of B'nai Brith, invited Clarke MacDonald and Deanna Skeoch to discuss the church resolution. MacDonald found the dialogue "beneficial and we assure you of our concern to reach conclusions in this matter that are both honest and fair." He would make an effort to keep the relationship with the Jewish groups on a "very irenic level." [113]

The General Council's PLO resolution was criticized not only by Jews but by Christians as well. The Reverend Peter Gilbert, director of the Christian-Jewish Dialogue in Toronto, declared that he opposed the resolution "categorically." He argued that since the PLO had declared its purpose to be to eliminate Israel, it "does not have the right to be heard." He questioned the democratic process by which it had been elected to represent the cause of the Palestinians, and he went on to say, "It greatly distresses me that the United Church seems constantly to favor the Arab cause, and seldom, if ever, to balance their point of view by recognizing that Israel also has a just cause and a need and right to expect our support in its struggle for survival. The resolution passed by General Council can do nothing more than intensify the present hostility in the Middle East, and I would in the strongest terms register my dissent to such a statement."[114]

Barry K. Morris, of St Matthews-Maryland Community Ministry in Winnipeg, also strongly opposed the PLO section in the United Church resolution, asking the church "to reconsider sole support of the PLO." He recommended looking for Palestinian representatives other than the PLO, and he wondered whether support for the PLO was not part of the church's aim "to be conciliar and reconciling," in order to balance the support that Israel was receiving.[115] David Demson protested that "the United Church wishes Israel to be made to sit with those who will its death."[116] Answering these criticisms, MacDonald stated that in his oral report to the General Council he had reaffirmed the United Church's traditional position that "Israel must have the right to nationhood within definable and defensible borders." To appease the critics, he stressed that the PLO clause was "simply in the form of suggestion," and that it was "open to modification."[117]

Eighteen months after the approval of the PLO clause by the General Council, MacDonald had "some serious misgivings." Fraternization by Arafat with Ayatollah Khomeini of Iran and the "credit" that the PLO was taking for terrorist acts such as the murder of children in Maa'lot "continue to haunt my mind" in connection with recognition of the organization, he said. Nevertheless, he did not advocate withdrawing the resolution, particularly after Forrest's death in 1978. If that were done, he commented, "some people would conclude that now that Al [Forrest] is not with us, we were beginning to back-track on the kind of support we had given the Palestinians and consequently Dr. Forrest in that matter." However, MacDonald proposed to Deanna Skeoch "to have the matter raised and dealt with in an open and frank manner" by various United Church courts.[118]

While the CCIA supported the Palestinian cause and recognized the PLO as a political organization, it opposed the PLO's terrorism and violence. Accordingly, MacDonald issued a statement of consolation to Israel after a PLO suicide attack on 11 March 1978, in which innocent Jews were killed. "We have been shocked and dismayed at the brutal killings," the statement said; through the consul general of Israel, it expressed "our deepest sympathy" to the families of the victims. However, to balance his statement, which was prepared "in careful consultation" with his superiors on the committee, MacDonald also expressed his understanding of the violence perpetrated by the Palestinians: "We are aware of the frustrations which build up to such a point of violence in the face of unresolved injustice and unfulfilled dreams."[119]

On 8 June 1978 a statement appeared in the *Toronto Star*, signed by a hundred ministers and headed "A Call to the World Council of Churches and All People of Goodwill for a Negotiated Settlement in the Middle East." Forrest played a leading role in the genesis, drafting, and publication of this statement, as MacDonald privately disclosed.[120] Among the signatories were Robert B. McClure; Donald G. Ray, secretary of the General Council of the United Church; Clarke MacDonald; A.C. Forrest; H.R. Hunt, a former Anglican assistant bishop of Toronto; Eoin Mackay, associate secretary of the CCC; and Frank H. Epp, head of Conrad Grebel College in Waterloo. Not everyone had been prepared to sign the statement; among those who refused was N. Bruce McLeod.[121] It deplored the injustices inflicted upon Palestinian and Lebanese refugees, but the signatories also expressed their concern "for the tragic minorities of the Jewish people" in their Arab homelands, the first time this concern had been expressed in public by the churches. However, their plight was juxtaposed with that of the Palestinians, who were living under Israeli military role. Every refugee, Jewish or Arab, should be entitled to repatriation or compensation. As Christians, the signatories remembered "with sorrow and shame" that it was because of Western antisemitism that Jews were forced to look for a national home. They accepted the argument of the Arabs that Israel derived its legitimacy only from antisemitism and Christian guilt. They did not feel that Israel's existence had historical legitimacy; nor did it have the generally accepted prerequisites for nationhood. The statement followed the Arab argument that Israel was an artificial entity in the area.

It accepted the position of the World Council of Churches that, "in supporting the establishment of the State of Israel without protecting the rights of the Palestinians, injustice has been done to the Palestinians." Therefore no peace could be achieved "without a determined effort to establish justice." The statement urged the WCC "to reaffirm its findings" and renew its efforts for a just settlement.[122]

An editorial in the *Toronto Star* called the document "a divisive statement that can serve no useful end." It was "one-sided," giving a "distorted view," and "can only contribute to misunderstanding and friction between Christians and Jews." The statement would not help efforts for reconciliation.[123] Clarke MacDonald responded in a letter to the editor, arguing that the statement was "balanced."He criticized the editorial for ignoring parts of the statement and said that it had been given a "misleading interpretation."[124]

The *Canadian Jewish Outlook*, a magazine that was critical of Israel's policies, published the statement with some reservations. The document would have had more credence "had it condemned in stronger terms the use of terrorism … and had it demanded that the PLO withdraw its covenant which calls for the liquidation of the State of Israel." The journal also condemned the one-sided impression given by the statement, which implied that the policies of Israel were the only obstacles to peace.[125]

The statement received substantial publicity and elicited other angry comments and editorials. Nick Simmonds, director of communications for the Canada-Israel Committee, outlined his concerns about the "context and substance" of the document. Since Forrest, with his consistently negative attitude to Israel, had had a leading role in its publication, Simmonds questioned its objectivity and credibility. After a detailed criticism of the one-sided document, which disregarded important historical facts, he wondered whether "it is an accurate reflection of the views of all the signatories."[126] MacDonald reacted sharply to Simmonds's criticism. He opposed the argument that "as long as we are associated with Dr. Forrest nothing we say is to be taken seriously … This is an unacceptable pre-supposition and renders further dialogue extremely difficult." He emphasized the fact that the United Church was not a monolithic body, and therefore no single person could represent it. Officially, it spoke through its courts. The document signed by a hundred ministers was an "adequate reflection of the position of the United Church." MacDonald found some of Simmonds's comments "distasteful" and "totally unjustified."[127] Forrest was encouraged by reactions to the statement, the majority of which were positive, "although naturally we find the personal attacks and criticisms from elements of the Zionist community discouraging and distasteful."[128]

On 27 December 1978 A.C. Forrest died of a heart attack. The sudden death of the sixty-two-year-old energetic editor of the *United Church Observer* was a shock for his friends and admirers. The Middle East subcommittee of the CCIA particularly felt his passing, because it relied heavily on his expertise and wide connections. "The death of Al Forrest is a very great loss to our Middle East Working Group, for he was a primary source of inspiration and information. This loss implies the need for a broader base for gathering information, setting policy, and making it known," commented Deanna Skeoch.[129] Her appreciation of Forrest's contribution was particularly meaningful, since she stated it as a matter of fact and not as part of a eulogy. Clarke Mac-Donald, too, emphasized the great loss of Forrest for the CCIA: "I do not need to tell you … how greatly we miss Al's presence on the Committee, especially his leadership in regard to the Middle East situation," wrote MacDonald to Donald Ray.[130]

Indeed, his role in the formulation of the CCIA's Middle East policy was invaluable, as Forrest himself had said in 1975: "As a matter of fact, I have written many of the United Church statements myself."[131] He was right when he pointed out that the Middle East subcommittee of the CCIA was more active and productive than similar bodies in the CCC, the WCC, or the Anglican Church of Canada. "We have a pretty vigorous and reasonably well-informed Committee on the Middle East," he wrote in July 1978 to Leopoldo J. Niilus, chair of the Commission of the Church and International Affairs of the WCC, proudly reminding Niilus of the inclusion of the PLO clause in the General Council's resolution.[132] To be sure, the CCIA and other United Church bodies did not rubber-stamp Forrest's propositions. However, his knowledge, information, persistence, conviction, persuasive power, and charm enabled him to propel his plans through the various United Church bodies. Obviously, not everyone liked him or agreed with his point of view. But his ideas concerning the Middle East must have reflected the mood of many church members, as the resolutions of various General Councils attest.

An immediate result of Forrest's death was a decision to try to develop regular contact with key Middle East experts in the World Council of Churches, the Canadian Council of Churches, and the Middle East Council of Churches. "It would be very valuable to cooperate in information sharing," suggested Skeoch.[133] In February 1979, Professor Lorne M. Kenny was appointed a full member of the CCIA Middle East subcommittee, to fill Forrest's vacant chair. The new member's position on the Middle East situation was a perfect match for Forrest's and for that of the majority of the committee. A missionary for eighteen years in Egypt and currently chair of the Department of Islamic

Studies at the University of Toronto, Kenny held a pro-Arab point of view, as his letter criticizing the pro-Israeli statement in the *Globe and Mail* after the Yom Kippur War had attested. Indeed, one of the members of the CCIA remarked that "Prof. Kenny is definitely pro-Arab."[134] Reacting to MacDonald's "serious misgivings" about recognition of the PLO by the General Council, Kenny wrote, "I do not see any good reason to change our stand." Although he did not like violence and terrorism, either Israeli or Palestinian, he understood "the conviction of the Palestinians that they have no alternative." Arafat and the PLO represented the great majority of Palestinians, and "*there is no one else to represent them.*" Although the CCIA and the General Council had, time and again, supported Israel's right to exist within secure borders and had called on the Arab countries to recognize it, Kenny maintained that Arab refusal to recognize Israel had some logic, "because of their terrorism and the terrorist history of their prime minister." He denied that Israel deserved the status of nationhood or that it had any moral legitimacy.[135]

While Kenny perfectly fitted the general attitude of the committee, the opinions of Helmut L. Wipprecht, another committee member, were controversial. As a strong supporter of Israel, he was an outsider on the Middle East subcommittee, and he regarded himself as being "a lone voice" in the United Church. In April 1979 he accused the committee of being "shamelessly anti-Israeli" and criticized his colleagues for having biased pro-Arab positions:

I am disturbed at the lack of action on the part of our committee. We have nothing to say in the light of the recent momentous development [the Camp David Accord] … Now that Begin has complied, why is it that we don't sharply criticize and condemn the rest of the Arab world for opposing the Camp David accords? Why do we not condemn them for their continuing terror? … We are always ready and quick to condemn alleged Israeli acts of terror … We will NOT condemn the Arabs, since they are our bosom friends and can do no wrong … Al [Forrest] never criticized Arab terrorists, even though I urged him to do so. He would not condemn his darling friends. Are we really going to continue his biased policies? Our committee is always so tough on Israel and so cozily in bed with the likes of Arafat and company. It's sickening.[136]

Wipprecht also criticized the Middle East subcommittee for always relying on Arab sources of information: "It's no big deal to go to the Israeli consulate and get their side of the story. But we don't do it … We should at least have the decency to LISTEN to BOTH sides." The Israeli consul told Wipprecht that he used to ignore protests from the United Church "because they are openly anti-Israeli, REFUSING TO GET THE

FACTS."[137] Frustrated that the members of the CCIA disregarded his opinion, Wipprecht wrote to the Israeli ambassador in Canada. As a supporter of the Zionist cause, he "deplored the apparent situation which prevails in the United Church, a situation that is patently pro-Arab, and pro-Palestinian and pro-PLO." He wanted to inform the Israeli authorities that "there are some of us who are still pro-Israeli."[138]

Wipprecht's letter to the Israeli ambassador enraged the CCIA leaders. Skeoch felt that he was "out of line in his judgment of tone and form," while MacDonald was "appalled" by Wipprecht's appeal to the Israelis. He cited occasions when the United Church had condemned violence on both sides, and he mentioned CCIA's stand on behalf of the right of Jews to emigrate from Russia. MacDonald accused Wipprecht of being silent during the committee's deliberations. Why did he not write a minority report and submit it to the executive of the CCIA? Kenny, for his part, maintained that the committee "sincerely tried, even bent over backwards to accommodate your views." He argued that some members of the committee made a serious effort to understand the Israeli point of view.[139]

The Middle East Working Group, as the subcommittee was now called, developed a routine of protesting to the Israeli government about its actions in the occupied territories. Among them was the demand in 1979 to reopen Bir Zeit University in the West Bank, "for the interest of academic freedom." The Israeli ambassador, Mordechai Shalev, replied that the Middle East Working Group "was either not in possession of the facts, or chose to ignore them," because Bir Zeit had been reopened three weeks earlier.[140]

With the death of Forrest and the resignation of Skeoch as chair of the Middle East Working Group, Kenny was selected as convener of the group. He had a role in preparing the report to the twenty-eighth General Council (1980) which approved almost verbatim the CCIA's recommendations restating the right of Israel to exist and the right of the Palestinians to self-determination. However, while Israel was characterized as "a home for Jewish culture and tradition" – the term "Jewish people" was purposely omitted – the Palestinians had the right to "self determination" and "nationhood." The report mentioned the peace treaty between Egypt and Israel and the Islamic revolution in Iran as the two major events that had affected the area since the last General Council. However, the peace with Egypt did not solve the Palestinian question. Israel was accused of "discrimination, expulsion, collective punishment, torture and the expropriation of Arab lands" in the occupied territories. On the other hand, the report stated that "the use by the PLO of terrorist attacks on Jewish settlements is an obvious infringement of the right of the Israelis to live in peace and security." The resolutions called for a negotiated settlement and expressed concern about Israel's policies in the occupied territories, such as "collective punishment, deportation and the expansion of settlements ... [which] should impede progress towards lasting peace."[141]

When the operation Peace for Galilee was launched in June 1982, in which Israel occupied southern Lebanon in retaliation for constant Palestinian terrorist raids, the United Church issued "A Statement re the Middle East Situation." The document, signed by Donald Ray and Clarke MacDonald, declared the support of the church for "Israel's legitimate desire for security, and the rights of the Palestinians to a homeland." This was another step towards accepting the Arab position. Earlier resolutions had supported their "legitimate right to self-determination." Now the church recognized Palestinian claims for a "homeland." The statement pressed for the establishment of dialogue; it deplored violence on both sides and demanded immediate cessation of hostilities and the withdrawal of Israeli troops. Although it supported the Canadian policy of admitting that Israel had suffered Arab provocations, this fact did not justify military operations, and the statement urged the government "to use its moral and legislative leverage to press for a cease fire and to urge a negotiated settlement."[142] This statement was one of the last actions to be initiated by the CCIA.

The status of the Committee on the Church and International Affairs had been examined several times during its lifetime. In 1975, when the World Outreach and Mission in Canada divisions absorbed the Board of Evangelism and Social Service, the church appointed an ad hoc committee to recommend new terms of reference for the CCIA. Although the reappraisal did not change the committee's activity, it was a clear sign that not everyone was satisfied with its work.[143] Several reasons led to the eventual demise of the CCIA: the death of A.C. Forrest, the efforts of church leaders to mend fences with the Jewish community in Canada, and particularly the gradual domination of the Middle East Working Group of the Canadian Council of Churches. Since representatives of the United Church regularly participated in meetings of the MEWG, which had became a strong, active, and well-informed body, the church now preferred to operate ecumenically. Therefore the executive of the General Council decided in 1984 to disband the CCIA.

It was as a result of efforts by several strong-minded individuals, such as E.M. Howse, A.C. Forrest, and Clarke MacDonald, who had deep sympathy for the plight of the Palestinians, that the CCIA had become a dominant and influential policy-making body. Relying on appropriate decisions by the World Council of Churches, the Canadian Council of

Churches, and various UN resolutions, the committee had maintained a pro-Arab policy, which was endorsed by prestigious international institutions. Because of the disbandment of the CCIA, the General Council in 1984 had no original statement on the Middle East, but instead adopted a resolution which had been approved by the WCC in May 1981 – that "our work on the Middle East be guided by three basic principles enunciated in the most recent WCC statement on the Middle East" – reported the *Record of Proceedings*. These elements were the withdrawal of Israel from the occupied territories; the right of all nations, including Israel and the Arab states, to live in peace and to have secure boundaries; and the right of the Palestinians "to self-determination, including the right of establishing a sovereign Palestinian state."[144] Thus the process of gradual recognition of Palestinian claims was complete. It had grown from support for the cause of miserable refugees, through recognition of their right to self-determination, to endorsement of their right to a homeland and now to a sovereign state.

By the 1990s the United Church was preoccupied with important internal matters. Interest in the Middle East waned, and the topic was not mentioned in the 1992 General Council.[145] In 1995 George Morrison maintained that "the Church as a whole pursued an even-handed policy in the Middle East; the evidence of this chapter might suggest otherwise.[146]

The United Church and the Canadian Jewish Community

7 The *United Church Observer*
and the State of Israel,
1945–1967

The attitude of the United Church to the State of Israel inevitably involved it with the Jewish community in Canada. In the 1960s and 1970s, Canadian Jews constituted a mixture of old-timers and newcomers, of whom many were Holocaust survivors. For them, Israel was the emotional centre of Jewish existence. Canadian Jewry was affectionately committed to Israel, more than its American or European counterparts. With the exception of the Orthodox minority, many had abandoned Judaism as a religious discipline, and their identification with Israel was a substitute for their loss of faith. "The State of Israel is something tangible and visible and near religious aspiration to provide a substitute for traditional piety," wrote Reuben Slonim. Canadian Jewry, as a relatively weak and unconfident minority in Canada, stressed unity. It launched a desperate battle against assimilation, which endangered its very survival as a distinct ethnic group. Jewish education, the Hebrew language, and the Jewish way of life were in danger. Israel seemed to represent protection against assimilation. Therefore Jews closed ranks and refused to accept any deviation. Dissenters were ostracized, as happened with Slonim, who had criticized Israel's policy.[1]

Jews' readiness to defend Israel from any attackers involved them in debate with critics from United Church circles and publications. Canadian Jews volunteered to fight for Israel: "It was a true reflection of a deep and unremitting love. But love is, as the proverb says, blind … In the early and middle sixties Canadian Jews were emotionally unprepared to let anyone cast shadows of doubt across the glow of Zion restored," recalled W. Gunther Plaut, the outstanding leader of the Toronto Jewish community, who was deeply involved in upholding the Jewish cause.[2] The defensive character of Canadian Jewry, which was fighting against both antisemitism and assimilation, reinforced the dispute with the United Church, as Slonim observed: "Jews see the quarrel with the United Church not only as an unwelcome intrusion but as an addition to their already complicated identity burden. The old fear of antisemitism and the new problem of assimilation combine to make them sensitive and impatient."[3] Gunther Plaut admitted recently that the Toronto Jewish community was "over-sensitive" to any criticism. He termed it an "exercise in the psychology of the exile"; since Jews had for centuries been a defenceless, persecuted minority, they easily became excited and worried.[4]

Indeed, "sensitivity" is the key word in the quarrel; while the Jews were over-sensitive, United Church members were insensitive. The latter were unable to understand Jewish refusal to accept criticism of Israel, like any other nation. "No one spoke critically, and certainly given Toronto Jews' memory of Christians, criticism voiced by Christians was always labeled anti-Semitic. I think Christians were often insensitive to this dark memory, and were naively surprised when comments similar to those they commonly directed at other nations were categorized by this pejorative term, which catapulted discussion beyond the terms of common argument into another realm," argued N. Bruce McLeod, who was the United Church moderator during the most heated controversy (1972–74).[5] Alan T. Davies, of Victoria College at the University of Toronto, who was personally involved in the Forrest debate, recently emphasized the deep misunderstanding that intensified the controversy between the two communities as follows: "The sensitiveness was so different and each assumed the other tended to reject. Many Christians (not only Forrest) simply did not understand why Jews were so touchy when Israel was criticized and they put it down to unreason; Jews could not understand why Christians could not see what was perfectly obvious to them. Hence each grew frustrated and increasingly angry. That is partly why so many UC people rallied behind Forrest, including decent and high-minded men, such as Clarke MacDonald ... Of course there were hidden ideologies, ... but it was not just a clash of ideologies. There was a deeper level of personal misunderstanding. To put the matter in Hegelian terms, each consciousness was alienated from the other."[6]

A major factor that determined the relationship between the United Church and the Canadian Jewish community was the *United Church Observer*. Unlike the church bulletins, the *Observer* was not the mouthpiece of the church, and its editor maintained a great degree of autonomy. Freedom of the press was a sacred principle for the liberal-minded church leaders. Nevertheless, the magazine's pages reflected the mood that was prevalent among church members. Therefore a close examination of the *Observer* and its editor is crucial for understanding our subject.

During the decade of 1945–55, which was so important for the establishment of the State of Israel, the Palestinian problem received only marginal coverage in the pages of the *Observer*. Although articles and editorials that dealt with the Zionist movement and Israel were rare, their approach was unsympathetic. We have noted the articles by A.E. Prince, for example, who criticized the Zionists' narrow nationalism and called upon the Jews to relinquish their demand for a separate state in the cause of global peace.[7] A.J. Wilson, the magazine's editor-in-chief, was in total agreement with Prince's analysis. Sympathy for the Jews, the victims of Nazi persecution, had been lost because of rioting and murder by the Jewish underground in Palestine. "This is one of the most serious spiritual losses in the post-war years. It seems as though this could have been avoided had there been some elasticity shown by the Jews in their demands," maintained the editorial of March 1947.[8]

In the December issue that year, the editorial pleaded to Zionists, for the sake of humanity, to abandon their plans for independence. A month before the Declaration of Independence, Wilson reiterated his strong opposition to the establishment of a sovereign Jewish state, on the grounds that it would be "contrary to historic processes" and would endanger the peace of the world.[9] This unfriendly attitude on the part of the *Observer* was reflected in a review of the memoirs of John Glubb, the British commander of the Arab Legion. The reviewer harshly attacked the "ruthless expansionist elements" of Zionism, in the context of "the troubled background of Palestine today."[10] Thus opposition to the Zionist concept and the anti-Israeli line of the *Observer* did not begin with A.C. Forrest; he inherited it from Wilson and readily carried it on.[11] With Forrest's appointment as the editor of the *Observer* in July 1955, however, the Middle East gradually gained more attention, and after August 1967 it became, as Arnold Ages described it, an "obsession."[12]

Alfred Clinton Forrest had been born in May 1916 in Mariposa Township, near Lindsay, and he grew up in Maple, Ontario. In 1937 he graduated from Victoria College at the University of Toronto and from Emmanuel College in theology; he was ordained three years later. Forrest served as a United Church minister in various congregations, and between 1944 and 1946 he was a chaplain in the Royal Canadian Air Force. Since his college years, he had wanted to become a journalist and had contributed to college papers. During his ministries he tried to fulfill this dream, sending articles to various magazines, but without much success, as the heavy files of rejections attest. However, gradually his pieces were published, and towards the end of 1940s Forrest became a regular contributor to *Saturday Night*. In the 1950s he had a syndicated column in various newspapers, such as the *Ottawa Journal* and the *Hamilton Spectator*. During his twenty-three years as editor of the *United Church Observer*, he simultaneously published several books, including the controversial *The Unholy Land* (1971), concerning the plight of the Palestinian refugees. He also actively participated in various United Church bodies, including the executive of the General Council and the executive of the Committee on Church and International Affairs, and for many years he was a commissioner to the General Council. In 1977 he ran for the position of moderator of the United Church, but lost on the last ballot. Forrest travelled widely in North America and abroad, and was a much-sought-after lecturer and television personality. Although he was most widely known for his controversial stand on the Arab-Israeli conflict, he continued to write and lecture on other issues, including youth, morality, education, sports, alcoholism, racism, and politics.[13]

A.C. Forrest was a talented journalist and a gifted editor. Under his editorship, the circulation of the *Observer* leaped from 150,000 to 312,000, making it one of the largest church publications in Canada. Even his opponents appreciated Forrest's editorial skill, which turned the magazine into an attractive, interesting, and well written journal. Unlike other church magazines, the *Observer*, with its smaller size, coloured illustrations, and smart layout, was a popular journal. In a way, Forrest never left his pastorate. As the editor of a church publication, he wanted to be the pastor of the whole church. He tried to make the magazine a voice for the voiceless; the *Observer* therefore carried articles dealing with such subjects as urban decay, the poverty syndrome, the clergy's salaries, the housing crisis, the prison system, and loneliness. Forrest did not hesitate to engage in controversial issues such as birth control, hippies, lesbians, the church and gay rights, and women ministers. Indeed, the journal addressed such a variety of topics that people wondered whether it really was a church magazine.[14]

Arnold Ages, a writer and editor who examined issues covered in the *United Church Observer*, reached the conclusion that "the problem of Israel and the Arabs has never been a preoccupation with the magazine and has never been more than a peripheral concern; that is up until August 1967."[15] But Reuben Slonim opposed this summation, calling it "not accurate." He enumerated thirty-six issues, articles, editorials, and letters that dealt with the Middle East before 1967. In his effort to disprove Ages' argument, Slonim added thirteen issues related to Jews and Judaism that the magazine had published.[16] He was right so far as the *Observer's* preoccupation with the Arab-Israeli conflict was concerned, as this chapter will attest. Discussion of other subjects that dealt with the Jews, such as the two-hundredth anniversary of the settlement of Jews in Canada or Soviet Jewry, is part of the United Church's relations with the Jewish community in Canada, but not of the Middle East issue.

Forrest's interest in the Middle East found its expression shortly after he became the editor of the *Observer*. The editorial of December 1955 read as follows:

Strong and influential pressure is being brought to bear on the Canadian Government to send arms to Israel. But we can't believe that those who advocate this want to see Canadian men follow Canadian guns to help Israel fight Egypt to retain territory she took from Egypt, with arms purchased in Czechoslovakia with American dollars in 1948. This is a great complex problem ... All we have space to say is there are two sides to it. But Canadians are hearing mostly one side. And we are in danger of becoming victims of a smooth propaganda campaign ... We even forget that there are three times as many Christians in Egypt as there are Jews in Israel. We fail to understand that recent treatment of the Arabs has created more misunderstanding than anything the West has done since the days of the Crusades ... To raise even a quiet voice to say, let us look at the other side of this hot situation, which may lead to war, is run the danger of being called anti-Semitic ... Jews and Zionists should not be confused ... Before this gets to another Korea – Israel should have something to say about its boundary troubles.[17]

One can trace in his first public statement Forrest's basic arguments concerning the Israeli-Arab crisis. From the very beginning he justified his intensive treatment of the Arab cause by citing the one-sided media coverage of the subject. Western society was the victim of an aggressive Zionist propaganda, while the Arab side was misrepresented. In order that his readers should get a balanced picture, Forrest undertook the mission of publishing the cause of "the other side." Incidentally, precisely at this time the Committee on the Church and International Affairs adopted a resolution proposed by E.M. Howse to make an effort at a better understanding of the positions of the Arabs. Furthermore, the seventeenth General Council in 1956 approved a recommendation to place more emphasis on the Arab cause, because the Israeli side was much better presented.[18] Forrest's position, then, was not unique; he was only following Howse's reasoning. Nor was his opposition to Canadian sales of arms to Israel. The United Church had officially protested to the government of Canada about the shipping of twenty-four jet fighters to Israel.[19] Another argument that he would repeat time and again was that "Jews and Zionists should not be confused." He blamed Canadian Jewry for the fact that anyone who criticized Israel's policy was called an antisemitic.[20] Despite these critical comments, the first editorial was quite moderate. Forrest did not blame Israel for expansionism or the injustice caused to the Arabs by the establishment of the State of Israel; there was no mention of the Arab refugee problem and no demand for their repatriation.

To carry out the afore-mentioned CCIA resolution to emphasize the Arab cause, the committee recommended that the *Observer* carry an article by Claris Silcox. It is not clear from the CCIA minutes who had suggested Silcox, whose pro-Arab and anti-Zionist views were known – Forrest (who had participated in the CCIA meeting), Howse, or someone else.[21] In his editorial "Observations," introducing Silcox's essay, Forrest described Israel as "a defiant little Jewish state, with a world Zionist organization exerting pressure on its behalf throughout the world." He complained that the world had disregarded the fate of the homeless Palestinian Arab refugees. And he re-emphasized the difference between Jews and Zionists; many Canadians confused "Ben Gurion with their Jewish neighbors across the street," he said. To clarify a positive attitude towards the Jewish people, "who have so richly endowed our own heritage," Silcox had been asked to write about the Middle East situation.[22] In his article, Silcox maintained that the Zionist demand for statehood had no historical or moral justification. The establishment of Israel would spread antisemitism and endanger the peace of the world.[23]

The Jewish community was disturbed by Silcox's harsh anti-Israeli attack and asked Forrest for a rebuttal. To Forrest's credit, one should point out that on several occasions he opened the pages of the magazine to a rejoinder. In this instance he asked Abraham L. Feinberg, the rabbi of Holy Blossom Temple and a leader of Toronto Jewry, to respond. In spite of the fact that "we don't look at the Near East situation from the same point of view," Forrest wanted to show to his readers how "a very distinguished leader of the Jewish community feels about the matter." Feinberg explained the importance of Israel's existence for Jews and even for Christians. After their long period of suffering and persecution, the "recreation of a sovereign secure homeland in Palestine for the Jews … has been since the dispersion an inextricable part of a sacred Messianic hope at the core of Judaism." Nasser's threat to push the Jews into the sea was considered "Hitler-like dreams." Feinberg was sorry for the plight of the Palestinian refugees, but he stressed the concern and the burden of help to hundreds of thousands of Jewish refugees who were under the responsibility of the Jews, and he suggested a dialogue between Jews and Christians and later with Muslims.[24]

Even when there were no urgent political issues concerning the Middle East, the *Observer* continued its involvement with a series of five articles by E.L. Homewood, the managing editor of the magazine. Over several months in 1958–59 he reported on the Christian holy sites, the developing cities in Israel, the absorption of one million immigrants, and the refugee camps in Jordan.[25] Since the reports, particularly about the New Israel, were fair and even sympathetic to Israel, Homewood was criticized by a reader that he had been "brainwashed" by Israeli propaganda. For balance, he suggested inviting Dr Ernest Howse "to give the Arab side." Another reader, who had participated in the tour with Homewood, came out in defence of the author: "Such objective reports are bound to be unacceptable to some readers … But it is my belief that Mr. Homewood did not intend to take either side … Rightly or wrongly, Israel is there and is performing wonders with her resources."[26] When Rabbi Stuart E. Rosenberg of Beth Tzedec Synagogue in Toronto returned in July 1941 from a visit to the Soviet Union, the *Observer* provided space for a long article on the situation of Russian Jewry. Forrest thus granted him a forum for a call to allow Soviet Jews to immigrate to Israel, despite Arab opposition to this move.[27]

According to Slonim, the controversy between the United Church and the Canadian Jewish community began, not after 1967 with Forrest and his magazine, but three years earlier over a theological subject that had nothing to do with the Middle East. The debate started in the spring of 1964 when Marcus Long, a Jewish professor at the University of Toronto, in a lecture at Beth Tzedec Synagogue labelled a book by the former moderator J.S. Thomson, *God and His Purpose*, antisemitic. Emil Fackenheim also considered the book slanderous. Thomson's book in many ways followed *The Word and the Way*, by Donald N. Mathers, which was published by the United Church in 1962. *The Word and the Way* was a part of the "New Curriculum," which was, according to John Webster Grant, the historian of the United Church, "in many respects a classic example of Protestant modernization."[28] It was a fundamental document that represented the mainstream of United Church belief; therefore one may learn from it about the attitude of the church to Jews and Judaism. Regarding Jewish involvement in the death of Jesus, the book stated: "That was theworst thing that ever happened … Was it God that did that? Or was it the Devil? Of course it was the Devil and all his hosts: the jealousy of the Pharisees, the scheming of the Sadducees, the treachery of Judas, the hysteria of the Jewish crowd; and behind all the demonic powers of darkness."[29]

Forrest was furious about the accusation that Thomson's book included antisemitic passages. As a moderator of the United Church, Thomson had led a denomination that continually taught against "race discrimination, religious arrogance, prejudice and intolerance."In an editorial titled "WASPS" Forrest reprinted the passage that was considered offensive to the Jews. "What Jesus taught and did provoke the hostility of the Pharisee and scribe. They hated him with such fury and rage that their eyes were blinded. So when God came to them in the person of his son, they killed him." Obviously Thomson referred to the Pharisees of the first century and not to the Jews of the twentieth, so Forrest wondered whether that was antisemitism? "Pharisaism has become a dictionary word, connoting hypocrisy. It is used innocently," he maintained. If the Jews felt that there were antisemitic passages in Thomson's book, "we are expecting that this should be pointed out to us clearly and in a brotherly way by spokesmen for the Jewish community," not in a public lecture at Beth Tzedec. Forrest continued with harsh words about Jewish criticism of Christian teaching: "But they can't expect us to soft-pedal history or manage the record, or edit the New Testament to protect the sensibilities of descendants of sinners of two thousand years ago, whether they be Jew, Greek, Hebrew, Roman, Jute, Angle, Saxon, Pict or Scot. History should never be distorted for anyone or anything. We say things knowing that many United Church people are tired of being tight-lipped, white, Anglo-Saxon Protestant majorities, afraid to say what they think for fear they will offend a minority"[30]

To Forrest as a member of the United Church clergy it was clear that the New Testament was an objective history and not a statement of faith or polemical literature of the early church. The association of a liberal, non-partisan, objective stance with a normative Christian one, while others' perspectives were biased because of personal involvement, would become an ongoing theme of Forrest's arguments. The confusing of an abstract idea of objective fact with his own opinion, begun in his evaluation of New Testament texts, would continue in his pieces on Zionism and Israel, in which he would consistently argue that he was being unfairly accused of antisemitism when all he was doing was reporting the facts on the tragic situation of the Palestinian refugees who had suffered because of the actions of Zionists.

Forrest asked Rabbi Stuart Rosenberg, who had been the host in his synagogue to the criticism of Thomson's book, to respond to the charge of antisemitism and to his editorial. As a leader of the Jewish community in Toronto who wanted to keep good relations with the United Church, Rosenberg tried to keep a low profile on the debate. He therefore described Thomson's book as "most engaging," and he agreed with Forrest that Thomson "may not be labeled 'antisemitic.'"

However, he criticized Thomson's scholarship: "I am afraid I could not trust him to produce an authentic, accurate description of Judaism ... I don't say that Dr. Thomson slanders Judaism. I think rather that he has not tried hard enough to understand it, and as a result there is the inevitable tendency to be too glib and to distort essential meanings. This is a very great pity." Rosenberg was sorry that Thomson had disregarded the teachings of distinguished Christian theologians, such as George F. Moore, James Parkes, Paul Tillich, and Reinhold Niebuhr. With regard to Forrest's editorial, he maintained that it would had been better had it not been written.[31]

Slonim argued that "the seeds of a later quarrel were planted in this controversy of 1964." Forrest's subsequent criticism of Zionism and the Jewish state were considered by the Jews as a continuation of his partisan position in supporting Thomson's book, with his insensitiveness to the history of the Jewish people. "To overlook this connection is to miss an essential point in the UC-Jewish quarrel," maintained Slonim.[32]

In spite of his insistence that the quarrel had begun before 1967, however, it seems that Forrest's attitude to the Middle East crisis had meaningfully changed after the Six Day War. While after 1967 he concentrated only on the plight of the Palestinian refugees, before that time he had been able to see and write – even with some enthusiasm – about Israel's progress. During a visit to Israel in 1957 he appreciated the country's good public relations, the enthusiasm of the youth, and the religious aspects of life. Reporting on another tour in the summer of 1964 he declared, "I can't think one can ever understand his Jewish neighbor until he has been to Israel ... I can understand why most Jews thrill at the story of Israel. Here a scattered people finally found a home. They have restored a dead language in less than two decades. They are restoring a desert land very quickly." To be sure, Forrest stressed the importance of seeing both sides, and he also visited refugee camps. But he admitted that Arab UNRWA teachers were nurturing hatred not only to Israel but to the Jews as well.[33] All this radically changed after the Six Day War of 1967.

8 The Confrontation with A.C. Forrest, 1967–1971

Both before and during the Six Day War the general press in Canada reported widely on events, while the *United Church Observer* remained silent. Then in August 1967, two months after the war ended, its editorial was entitled "Christians Must Be Free to Criticize Jews." Apparently disregarding the events of May–June that year, when Egyptian president Abdel Nasser had closed the Strait of Tiran and expelled the UN peace force from Sinai, the editorial said: "While Arab threats to destroy Israel must be condemned, … it must be remembered that the provocations and threats were not all from one side." Forrest berated those Christians who hesitated to criticize Israel for fear of being charged with antisemitism, and he concluded his editorial by saying: "We must insist on the right and duty of Christians to see at least two sides of this many-sided problem. And we should be able to express objective judgments without being charged with equivocation or being compared to the ecclesiastical hand-washers of wartime Germany."[1]

The September issue also dealt with the Middle East. In the "Editor's Observations" Forrest repeated his theory of unbalanced reporting. Since the Zionists had dominated the Western media, this bias justified his focusing on the Arab side. However, he still made some efforts to maintain a balanced position. In the editorial he enumerated the ways that the churches could contribute to the effort to help the refugees. He also appealed to the Arab countries to "recognize Israel and stop threatening to drive her into the sea." Although Arabs were not expected to love Israel, nevertheless, "Israel exists, and there is no sense pretending she doesn't." He called upon Israel to let the refugees who had fled during the recent war return to their homes. In a rare display of political reality, he admitted that he was not expecting Israel to return the Golan Heights to Syria because of constant Syrian threats. Furthermore, "as long as the Arabs refuse to recognize Israel's existence, the Israelis have a logical excuse to hold what they have."[2]

Shortly after the war, Forrest visited Israel. He received a warm introductory letter from the Israeli ambassador in Ottawa and was kindly treated by Israeli officials. He toured refugee camps in Gaza and the West Bank and was shocked by the miserable and desperate conditions of the refugees. Forrest was convinced that they would receive better treatment from the Israelis than they had received before under Arab rule.[3] However, he soon became critical of the Israeli approach to the refugee issue. As a liberal, Forrest showed genuine humanitarian interest in the situation of the Palestinian refugees. When he realized that their problem was being almost totally ignored or misrepresented, he decided to launch an interpretation campaign for them, utilizing the *Observer* as a powerful tool. He soon became the centre of a heated quarrel. Jews were unable to name the moderator of the United Church or any other official, but they knew the editor of the *Observer,* who achieved notoriety through his constant attacks on Israeli policy. Significantly the Ontario Jewish Archives in Toronto has files on the United Church only from the years of the debate with Forrest, 1967–78.

The 1 October 1967 issue of the *Observer* was entirely devoted to the Palestinian refugee cause. This was an exception to the magazine's editorial policy, since for twenty-five years there had been no special issue dealing with the Jewish refugee victims of Nazism or with the Jewish refugees who were forced to flee from Arab countries. As a matter of fact, no special issue had ever been devoted to any foreign country.[4]

From the fall of 1967 on, the *Observer* was preoccupied with the Middle East question. Almost every issue carried articles and editorials on the subject. The editor also utilized other departments, such as the "Question Box," "Up Front," and the book review section, to advance the pro-Arab line. Arnold Ages, in his survey of the *Observer's* coverage of the Arab-Israeli conflict, found that the articles were almost without exception unsympathetic to Israel and the Zionist movement. He concluded, "Mr. A.C. Forrest ... has re-directed the thrust of his comments from a potpourri of musings on everyday problems to an obsessive concern with the situation prevailing in Arab refugee camps."[5]

Even Reuben Slonim, who was a friend of Forrest and of the United Church, and who criticized parts of Ages' observations, was forced to admit that Ages was right in his conclusion that the *Observer* had lost its sense of proportion on the Arab-Israeli conflict. "If a reader since 1967 were to obtain his information on the Middle East from the *Observer* as his only source, the picture would be distorted beyond recognition." Forrest's fault, according to Slonim, was not his sympathy with the Arabs, but the fact that "the editor interposes himself between his readers and the situation to be covered." An editor had a responsibility to distinguish between opinion and fact; during the years after 1967 that distinction almost did not exist. The impression given by many articles was "of a monolithic promotion, trumpeting the editor's obsession."[6] Between March 1967 and July 1969, twenty-four issues dealt with the Mideast conflict. Instead of reporting, Forrest was promoting his own ideas.

His habit of quoting anonymous sources also enraged his readers. Most of the reports from the camps describing the sufferings of refugees were attributed to an anonymous Arab man or woman. Forrest's failure to quote sources was regarded by Ages as "malicious," suggesting that the editor was quoting himself. Slonim also agreed that the frequent use of anonymous sources was a violation of journalistic principles. To avoid criticism Forrest should have identified his sources.[7]

Slonim also took issue with Forrest's argument that he needed to emphasize the Arab cause in order to balance the allegedly pro-Israeli coverage by the Western media. Balanced journalism meant the publication of both sides in the same paper side by side, said Slonim; one-sided coverage in one paper because another reports the other side is bad journalism. Forrest made several efforts to balance the pro-Arab arguments, such as publishing the reactions of the Israeli ambassador and W. Gunther Plaut to the special issue of October 1967.[8] But in terms of the total picture, "it is clear that expressions of pro-Israel sentiments in the *Observer* are mere tokenism designed to permit an harassed editor to claim fairness in presenting opposing viewpoints,"maintained Ages. "The claim is as tendentious as it is false, given the disproportionate space allotted the Arab position."[9] Even Slonim stated that "the error in Forrest journalism is that it wants balance, yet insists on proving a point."[10]

Gershon Avner, the Israeli ambassador to Canada, wrote a long rebuttal to the special October issue, requesting that it be published in the *Observer.* He attacked Forrest personally, accusing him of being an opponent of Israel "since before its establishment" and of using vicious and devious methods to bait Israel. He wondered whether readers of the *United Church Observer* were ready to become "an adjunct of the Arab League propaganda office in Ottawa." Avner recalled the fact that the Arabs had refused to accept the UN partition plan, and that since its establishment, Israel had always proposed peace agreements, which the Arabs had adamantly rejected. He quoted Arab threats to destroy Israel and accused Arab leaders of using the refugees as vehicles for their ambitions. As for the UN resolution on the repatriation of the refugees, he reminded his readers that it specified that its terms would be part of a final settlement. He also blamed Egypt for beginning the war of 1967. Generally, Avner criticized Forrest for omitting parts of resolutions when he quoted or referred to them. He concluded his letter by warning that "the dissemination of vicious one-sided propaganda can only serve to increase passion."[11]

Avner made a grave mistake by attacking Forrest personally, instead of dealing with the issues raised by the magazine, and he was wrong in stating that Forrest was anti-Israel even before 1948. Forrest rightly rejected this accusation, since he had not taken any position on Israel before the mid 1950s. "You have been badly misinformed," he wrote to Avner. "If I wanted to engage in controversy, win battles or score points, I could be very tempted to publish part of your letter." Because of a lack of space and since he wanted to publish other responses, Forrest included only a shortened version of Avner's letter in the magazine.[12]

Unlike Avner, Plaut gave a moderate point-to-point rebuttal of Forrest's arguments. This different response was partly a result of Rabbi Plaut's personality. He could be frank at times, but he was always gentlemanly. In addition, he respected Forrest and even cooperated with him in 1967 in the editing of *Ferment*, a thoughtful magazine intended to promote dialogue in a cross-section of organized religious life in Canada. Plaut was chair of its editorial advisory board and Forrest its publisher. This venture, which encouraged cooperation between Jewish and United Church leaders, was discontinued because of a lack of financial support and also because of the tension between the groups following the *Observer*'s publications.[13] In his letter to the *Observer*, Plaut criticized the "highly selective mass of materials" presented by Forrest. For instance, Forrest never mentioned that in 1967 Israel had not forced the Arabs to flee, and he did not allude to their unrelenting refusal to attend peace negotiations. He also did not report on Jewish refugees fleeing from Arab countries. Finally, the fact that Jordan had also acquired territories was not reported in the *Observer*, and certainly it was never blamed for this aggression. Only Israel, of all the nations, was expected to forfeit its national interests in deference to world opinion. Plaut concluded his article by referring to Jewish concern that, "regardless of what Israel will do, a significant portion of the Christian establishment will be highly critical of her actions."[14] Forrest welcomed Plaut's letter: "He is my closest friend among the rabbis. And his criticism is objective and impersonal. And I am grateful to have it," he told a colleague.[15] With this contribution, Plaut moved into the forefront of the quarrel, representing the Jewish side.

In the December 1967 issue of the *Observer*, Wilson Woodside, a contributor to the magazine, wrote a pro-Israeli article in which he confronted Forrest's thesis concerning Israel. In "Reluctant Conquerors" he argued that since the Arabs refused to admit defeat in their various wars with Israel, it needed to make stable and peaceful arrangements. Therefore the Israelis should "continue doing exactly what they have been doing, refusing to hand back the Arab territories," until the Arabs declared the end of their war with Israel and made satisfactory arrangements.[16]

Canadian Jews, ever sensitive to criticism of Israel, began to address angry responses to Forrest's articles. He was accused of falsification and for hatred of Jews. "The existence of the Jews is anathema to you," wrote one angry Jew. He asked Forrest why he had not protested when the Nazis had murdered the Jews or when Nasser threatened to annihilate Israel.[17] Alan Rose of the Canadian Jewish Congress, in an editorial in the *Canadian Zionist Special Report*, accused Forrest of anti-semitism. He was regarded by many Canadian Jews as "an enemy of the Jewish people," along with former Nazi Adolf von Thadden in Germany and the Soviet propagandists.[18]

Some members of the United Church were also not happy with Forrest's pro-Arab campaign. Dolores Nicholls of Norwood, Ontario, the wife of a United Church minister and a strong supporter of Israel, flooded the editor with critical letters for a dozen years. She was not disturbed by what he said in favour of the Arabs, but with what he refrained from saying in defence of Israel. She sent one of her five-page letters to various newspapers because "I want them to know ... that there are some Christians who support them [Israelis]." The national public relations committee of the Canadian Jewish Congress gladly published her letter.[19]

With these accusations and counter-accusations, the debate had begun. It was not only an angry Jewish response to Forrest and his *Observer* but also a quarrel between the Jewish community and the United Church. "Few issues provided me with more cause for both agony and resolve than did the community's quarrel with the United Church of Canada," recalled Gunther Plaut. He and Forrest symbolized the two sides of the controversy.[20] Jordan Pearlson, another leading rabbi in Toronto, was alarmed in November 1967 by the consequences of the *Observer* articles. "Much harm is being done to the friendly relationships that have been built up between the Jewish and Christian communities in Metropolitan Toronto," he observed, and he wondered how this friendship could be maintained. He complained about the biased anti-Israeli sources that had fed Forrest with false information and also that nobody in the United Church had challenged Forrest's accusations. H.E. Young, of the missionary department, suggested that the church should open a direct line of communication with the Jews "that should be frank but straightforward and open."[21]

Forrest received support from various circles. "It is refreshing to recognize a public magazine ... expressing opinions that are not dominated by Zionist propaganda," wrote R.W. Stephenson, a reader from Ottawa. He accused Israel of "practicing racial policies" and of forcing the Arabs to leave their homes.[22] I.V. MacDonald of the Department of Trade and Commerce complimented Forrest on his *Observer* pieces, "which displayed an objectivity and perspective" that were missing in the Canadian press generally.[23] Bradley Watkins of the National Council of Churches in New York commended Forrest for his "excellent piece of work, appealing equally to the reader's mind and heart and sense of justice." He was so impressed that he ordered twenty-five copies of the October special issue.[24] Probably more important and encouraging for Forrest was the support of Ernest Long, who sent an unofficial, handwritten friendly letter promising, "Anything I can do to come to your defence will be done."[25]

Arabs were also enthusiastic about the special issue of the *Observer*, ordering dozens of reprints. Forrest soon became their champion in North America. *Al Goumhouriya*, an important Egyptian newspaper, reported that he was "the only person in the world praised by the Arab League for special services to their struggle against Israel."[26] Forrest sent his articles and the October issue to Amman, Cairo, Beirut, and Jerusalem and established close contact with the Near East Christian Council. He soon became the recipient for anti-Zionist and anti-Israeli books and articles.[27] People and organizations found it necessary to share information with him concerning the Arab-Israeli scene, particularly when the approach was pro-Arab. When a group of Episcopalian Church members went to Israel on an Israeli-sponsored trip, the organizer apologized to Forrest: "We thought we would do this so that nobody could accuse us of being biased in favor of the Arabs – which we obviously are!"[28]

Forrest complained that he had "personally been subjected to a campaign of abuse such as I have never experienced from any other sources." He had been attacked by editorials, letters to the editor, and articles. He was called an "enemy of Israel" by the Jewish press; he received swastikas by mail, threatening nighttime telephone calls, and burned crosses on his lawn. "It does not bother me much," he wrote to a friend; but publicly he played the role of a martyr for the cause of the refugees. "If the price of speaking up for the refugees is to be vilified by Jews and Christians, then I for one pay that price," he said in a public address.[29] He compiled a list of criticism against him and published it under the title "What Happened When I Criticized Israel." His main complaint, which he had repeated since his first article on Israel in 1956, was that Zionists tended to interpret any criticism of Israel's policies as antisemitism. "I believe we should treat Jews exactly like Anglicans, Presbyterians, Englishmen and everybody else," he argued. He was particularly hurt by the impolite and name-calling attacks on him, which frequently misquoted him.[30]

Forrest's argument that anti-Zionism was not antisemitism and that anyone was entitled to criticize Israel's policy without being accused of antisemitism was a controversial one. As we have pointed out in the previous chapter, Christians were unable to understand the special meaning of Israel for the Jews. Within the United Church the great majority agreed with Forrest's reasoning. E.M. Howse blamed the Zionists for using the charge of antisemitism as a weapon against anyone who dared to criticize Israel; equating anti-Zionism with antisemitism was merely a tactic on their part. "The denunciation is prepared in advance. As soon as anyone questions the validity or the accuracy of a partisan line, he is automatically tarred with the anti-semitic brush."[31] Howse wrote in support of the editor of the *Observer*: "It is ironical that Forrest might have criticized any other country on earth, including his own, without arousing the torrent of abuse with which he was deluged as soon as he tried to tell the facts as he had seen them in Palestine … He could have criticized Great Britain, and not been slandered as anti-British. He could have criticized the United States, and not been suspected of nurturing an uncontrollable hatred of Yankees. But one thing he could not do. He could not criticize Israel. After that the deluge."[32]

Clarke MacDonald was convinced that to criticize Israel was not antisemitism, because one could be anti-Israeli and pro-Jewish.[33] Angus J. MacQueen maintained that anti-Zionism was not a cover for antisemitism. He sympathized with Forrest, who could not understand why the Jews reacted more heatedly than the Scots or the English when their country was criticized.[34] N. Bruce McLeod also shared the opinion that vigorous criticism of Israel was not antisemitism, "as long as the criticism [was] grounded in recognition of the country's right to exist within secure borders."[35] The issue was so important that the General Council found it necessary to justify the *Observer*'s criticism of Israel after the Six Day War. The twenty-third General Council in 1968 deplored the accusation that criticism of Israel's policies was necessarily antisemitic.[36]

Some people, including Forrest, occasionally referred to the Jews or to Israel as "arrogant Zionists." Canadian Zionists resented this label, as Gunther Plaut clearly observed in a signed editorial on 12 May 1972 in the *Canadian Jewish News*: "All too frequently anti-Zionism (as distinguished from ordinary criticism of Israel's policies) has become the cover for antisemitism, and the *Observer*'s tendency to depict Zionism as a historical evil has strengthened the heritage of latent and overt antisemitism in many readers. Surely, given the bitter facts of history, any material, which evokes such sentiments, ought to be firmly out of bounds in a Christian publication."[37]

Not only Jews but some Christians, among them devoted United Church ministers, saw in anti-Zionism "a convenient vehicle to develop an antisemitic theme," as Roland de Corneille, an Anglican priest, later stated.[38] Gregory Baum elaborated on the strong anti-Jewish bias built into Christian teaching through the centuries: "The story of Christian anti-Jewish preaching is a complex fabric woven of political, religious and pathological elements." After the Holocaust the churches were trying to purify themselves by removing "certain ideological deformations" from their gospel. However, an anti-Jewish approach had so deeply penetrated the Christian mind that it would take time and effort to root it out. An anti-Israeli attitude also unconsciously marked Christian anti-Jewish ideology. Forrest and his followers, who insisted that they were "only" anti-Zionists and not anti-Jewish, were refusing to look at inherited theological biases and were operating under what Baum termed "false consciousness" – "False consciousness disguises the actual power relations; it obscures the past." Forrest claimed to be objective and to consider only the facts. But objectivity here was "a device" for disregarding the whole historical truth. By arguing that modern Israel should be evaluated by the same universal standards as any other modern state, he "refuses to wrestle with the inherited ideology of the Christian Church. The stance of objectivity allows him to look away from the actual historical link between his group and the various peoples and religions he mentioned. To classify Israel … simply as one among several societies is to deny the entire ideological past."[39]

When Kenneth Bagnell, a United Church minister and a former managing editor of the *Observer*, delivered a lecture on antisemitism, someone from the audience called out that he had failed to mention Zionism, and "Zionists are ruling the world." The man stated that he was not against Jews but against Zionism. Bagnell concluded that "the worst obscenity of history now dresses in the vocabulary of respectability."[40] In an article in the *Toronto Star* in 1972, David Demson challenged Forrest's position on the grounds that, as a clergyman and the editor of a church magazine, he should take into consideration the history of Christendom, which was not anti-British or anti-American, but was anti-Jewish. Demson warned Christian editors and writers to be "careful, then, to avoid any continuance of an anti-Jewish attitude."[41]

Alan T. Davies belonged, along with Demson, to a minority of young intellectuals in the church who supported Israel and who criticized the pro-Arab stance of the official church bodies. In a thoughtful essay in the *Christian Century* in 1970, titled "Anti-Zionism, Anti-Semitism and the Christian Mind," Davies investigated the relationship between the two "isms." He dismissed the argument, frequently used by Forrest, that since there were anti-Zionist Jews, opposition to Zionism could not be antisemitic. "Anti-Zionism sooner or later reveals a distressing tendency to shade into anti-Semitism," maintained Davies. The fact that some Jews were critical of Zionism gave no legitimacy for Christians to oppose it. Davies depicted metaphorically the feelings of the Jews regarding the Jewish state, particularly after Auschwitz, as follows: "Israel stands in juxtaposition to Auschwitz as, to imply a Christian analogy, the Resurrection stands in juxtaposition to the Crucifixion." Jews considered the Zionist ideal as the affirmation of Jewish existence, interwoven with strong attachment to Jewish history and Palestine. "Given this reality, it is exceedingly difficult on the emotional level for the victims of the Holocaust to distinguish anti-Zionism from the anti-Semitism, however clear the distinction may seem to Gentiles." Davies emphasized the difficulty for Christians in comprehending Jewish sensitivity after Auschwitz. In addition to a failure of communication between Christians and Jews, he regarded recent changes in Christian theology as a factor in this misunderstanding. Since after Auschwitz it was politically incorrect to be an antisemite, many preferred to use the cover of anti-Zionism. "Anti-Semitic convictions can be transposed without any difficulty into the new language of anti-Zionism," stated Davies.[42]

In order to counter the critics of his anti-Israeli approach, Forrest made great efforts to find anti-Zionist Jews, who would prove that there were Jews who were not Zionists. He used to quote anonymous "great rabbis," "prominent American Jews," and "many Canadian Jewish friends" who opposed Zionism. On the other hand, privately he admitted that "it is my opinion that almost all Jews and Rabbis here are Zionists."[43] He turned to the American Council for Judaism (ACJ), a small and not very successful anti-Zionist body in the United States, composed of old-fashioned assimilationists. Although the ACJ had no influence in Canada, he asked it to recommend an anti-Zionist to write an article for the *Observer*. Eventually, after several refusals, William Gottlieb accepted Forrest's invitation. Forrest was interested in a "straightforward analysis of Zionism, showing how it differs from Judaism, and pointing out that when people criticize Israel for treatment of refugees or expansionist policies, they are not anti-Semitic." He added that, "if you can take a crack at the Zionists in the piece, so much the better."[44]

Gottlieb, a feature sports writer for the *Brooklyn Eagle* and *Sports Illustrated* and the public relations director of the American Council for Judaism, gave Forrest tips on how to handle Zionist arguments, writing: "I have some ideas about strategy and tactics which you might pursue effectively."[45]

Gottlieb delivered what Forrest had asked for; in an article that appeared in the *Observer* in 1968 under the title "An Anti-Zion Jew Tells: The Other Side of the Zionist Story," he summarized the program of the ACJ. According to this group, Judaism is "a high moral faith [which] transcends tribal and national limitations ... My organization does not consider the modern state of Israel as the homeland of 'the Jewish people.' " To prove that not all Jews held a Zionist point of view, Gottlieb quoted several eminent anti-Zionist Jews. He attacked Zionist propaganda because it was "imaginative, flexible ... half truths, quarter truths and falsehoods," and he concluded by appealing to his readers "to stand up to Zionist intimidation."[46]

The Catholic historian Edward H. Flannery was opposed to Forrest's practice of contradicting Zionists with anti-Zionists. He stated in 1970 that "the overwhelming majority" of Jews were either Zionists or pro-Zionists. He therefore regarded it as "particularly indelicate of Christians to seek out Jewish anti-Zionists in order to bolster criticisms of Israel or expose Arab interests."[47]

Forrest, nevertheless, continued his search for anti-Zionists, maintaining that there were many Jews in Canada who supported his position, but were afraid to speak out against the pro-Zionist establishment. Through publication of their point of view, he intended "to change the climate." When an anti-Zionist book, *The Decadence of Judaism in Our Time* by Moshe Menuhin, appeared in 1973, Forrest quickly recommended it; "Another prominent Jew ... has written a revealing book," he told the readers of the *Observer.*[48] Similarly, when an American Jew, Elmer Berger, reporting from Beirut, harshly criticized Israel's aggression and its treatment of Arab refugees, Forrest called him a "distinguished Jewish Rabbi" and a "modern Jewish prophet."[49]

Another American anti-Zionist Jew whose help Forrest enlisted was Norton Mezvinsky, a former executive director of the American Council for Judaism and an associate professor of history at Central Connecticut State College. For a seminar that Forrest organized on the Arab-Israeli conflict in 1970, he looked for an anti-Zionist rabbi, but was unable to find one in Canada. He therefore turned to Mezvinsky to represent this position.[50] Mezvinsky wrote a series of articles called "Israelis versus Israel: The Character of the State of Israel," which Forrest recommended be distributed by the Arab Information Office in Ottawa.[51] But he exaggerated the importance of Jews who criticized

Israel's policy, both in Israel and abroad. When he cited them, it was almost always anonymously. "Those Jews have enormous stature and seem to be increasing in number who are calling for a de-Zionist state," he wrote to William O. Fennell, principal of Emmanuel College in Toronto.[52]

In a further attempt to interpret the Middle East situation to the North American public from a point of view that he felt the media had disregarded, Forrest decided to go for a sabbatical year to Beirut. Several papers, such as the *Inter-Church Features, Presbyterian Life*, the *United Church Herald*, and the *Reformed Church in America*, commissioned him to write on the refugee problem and the Christian solution to it. In an introductory sheet, which clearly indicated the way that Forrest wanted to be recognized, he wrote: "He [i.e., Forrest] has published a number of articles all of which are critical of Israel and the injustice heaped by it upon the Arab countries and the people of Palestine." He hoped that his reports would ensure that "the grave injustices and wrongs to the Arabs and the Palestinian people may be righted."[53] This was how Forrest stated his political position to his Arab hosts in Beirut. His reports from that city, which would be syndicated in ten magazines in the United States, were considered by a friend as "an excellent opportunity for the Church and the Arab world."[54] During his sabbatical in 1968–69, Forrest travelled extensively in the Middle East, widening and deepening his connections with local organizations and individuals. Obviously, the information he gathered was from Arab sources, yet he always insisted that they were "solid facts." Thus what had begun as a report on the miserable conditions of refugee camps became a lifelong mission. Since he was reporting from the scene, supposedly observing the facts first-hand, his influence and reputation grew, particularly among those who were already inclined in his direction, and his sabbatical in Beirut added weight to his pro-Arab activity.

One report in particular from Israel in December 1968 deepened the criticism and the animosity towards Forrest. After a heartbreaking description of a poor, miserable Palestinian refugee family with seven children in occupied Bethlehem, he depicted an encounter with an American in the King David Hotel in Jerusalem: "We had dinner and ate. I suppose about half a kilo of steak between us. And he told me that this is a great country, and that he was in the hotel business and intended to interest some people back in L.A. in building a string of hotels along the Israeli coast so he can get those 'fat friends of ours who go down to Florida and sit on their fannies for six months every year to come here and spend some money and build up the country.' "[55]

This piece aroused angry reactions. The comparison of a poor refugee family in occupied Bethlehem with an American eating a lot of steak in one of the most exclusive hotels in Israel was seen as a condemnation of Israelis generally. Furthermore, the description of "fat friends who go down to Florida and sit on their fannies," although the article did not specify Jews, had antisemitic implications. Even Rabbi Plaut, who had avoided joining the chorus of attacks on Forrest, decided to criticize him. "I must now, sadly, agree that Dr. Forrest, roving reporter for the *UC Observer* and other Protestant papers, has joined the company of those who by their emotionalism make themselves inaccessible to rational argument."[56] Not only Jews but also Christian theologians and priests, such as David Demson and Roland de Corneille, were convinced that Forrest's piece on the fat man from Los Angeles was pure and simple antisemitism. They argued that everyone who was familiar with antisemitism understood that depicting a Jew as fat and wealthy and fond of Mammon was an anti-Jewish stereotype.[57] Forrest termed the Jewish criticism of him an "organized slander," but he added that "the worst of it has come from inside my own church."[58]

Was A.C. Forrest an antisemite? Most Canadian Jews at that time and even thirty years later were convinced that he was. Ben Kayfetz of the Canadian Jewish Congress recently tempered his judgment by saying, "Forrest was not an obvious bigot." He did not understand Jews; therefore it was difficult to categorize him as a clear-cut antisemite. However, in the final analysis, Kayfetz stated that, like many others in the United Church, Forrest was antisemitic.[59] On the other hand, most of Forrest's colleagues in the church, including E.M. Howse, N. Bruce McLeod, A.B.B. Moore, George Morrison, and Angus MacQueen, vehemently opposed this accusation. Forrest had grown up in a small town with few, if any, Jews and he therefore did not meet antisemitism until his college years in Toronto.[60] However, despite his many Jewish friends, his knowledge of Judaism was derived mainly from the New Testament, a not very objective source for this subject. He admitted that he was unable to understand certain aspects of Jewish behaviour: "I can't claim to understand it. I have little sensitivity to it."[61]

Indeed, Forrest's most important deficiency was probably his insensitivity to the Jews, as McLeod has pointed out. Plaut reconsidered his earlier accusations, and in later years he expressed the opinion that Forrest was not antisemitic. However, Forrest would not accept advice on certain subjects. He was stubborn and bitter, and had a "martyr complex." He "exposed some embarrassing layers of deep-seated gentile attitudes towards Jews," observed Plaut.[62] Reuben Slonim, who discussed with him his relationship with the Jews, stated that Forrest was confused about Jews and did not understand them. "Forrest is groping for some kind of definition of his relationship to Jews. Like others in the United Church ... he is in the dark about them;

therefore, he stumbles." But Slonim was convinced that Forrest was not an antisemite.[63] Alan Davies, who strongly opposed Forrest's political position and quarrelled with him publicly, stated that, although Forrest had not been influenced by antisemitic feelings, "It is possible for an individual to express views tainted with antisemitism without realizing the fact, and it is also possible for a well-meaning person to indirectly promote the ends of antisemitism without knowing that this is the net result of his labours ... The general effect of the editorial crusade in the *Observer* against Israel, I greatly fear, has been the stirring up of anti-Semitic feelings in Canada."[64]

Davies refrained from accusing Forrest of open antisemitism. He criticized him for ideological attacks on Judaism and ignorance of Jewish history, but later he retreated from this accusation. Forrest was "stubborn, bitter, obtuse and defiant ... Gradually he became so deeply involved that he lost his balance, he fought back defiantly," said Davies in 1995.[65] According to Lou Ronson of B'nai Brith, Forrest's daughter admitted that her father turned antisemitic during his long fight against Israel. Ronson himself stated that, though Forrest twisted everything to criticize Israel and his articles definitely distorted the picture, yet from his own personal experience, Forrest was not an antisemite.[66]

It seems that Forrest's almost one-man crusade in Canada for the cause of the Palestinians led to his defiant behaviour. He used harsh, critical language against Israel and made frequent negative references to "Zionists."During his all-out battle with his adversaries, he lost his temper and made mistakes, such as printing outright antisemitic material in the *Observer,* including John Nicholls Booth's article "How Zionists Manipulate Your News" and G.J. Salter's advertisement "He as God Sitteth in the Temple of God,"[67] which will be discussed in the following chapter. His eagerness to "take a crack at the Zionists," to use his own words,[68] led him to irresponsible editorship and to the use of inappropriate language. He was insensitive to the way that they would be interpreted by the Jews. Whether was Forrest an antisemite or not, many of his contemporaries thought so. He published antisemitic material in the *Observer* and was not careful or sensitive to the way in which he expressed his criticism on Israel's policies, which increased the outcry and the opposition to him, even in his own church.

The Jewish community in Canada, in any case, was agitated by the *Observer*'s constant criticism of Israel and Zionism, and did regard them as antisemitic. Jews were particularly disturbed that neither the United Church courts nor any church leader confronted Forrest and his accusations. Thus the rupture was not only between the Jews and Forrest but also between the Jewish community and the United

Church. The magazine tried to pacify the Jews without giving up its position. An editorial written in 1969 by Patricia Clarke, the acting editor in the absence of Forrest, who was on sabbatical in Beirut, read as follows: "The United Church does not wish to break fellowship with Jews. But it cannot purchase this fellowship at the expense of others. We ask Jews not to break fellowship with us. But we ask that they do their part in keeping dialogue possibly refraining from automatically branding as anti-Semitic every dissent and every dissenter."[69]

ROBERT MCCLURE AND THE JEWISH COMMUNITY

Several United Church leaders were aware of the tension between the communities and tried to find ways to ease it. "We hope to get together a small key group to begin to study the procedures of how we may best create a new understanding here in Canada," reported Long in 1968.[70] But the tension between the Jewish and the United Church communities increased with the election of Robert B. McClure as moderator in September that year. The Jewish leadership had decided to avoid public confrontation with the church as far as possible; public debate was discouraged, and responses were limited to the minimum necessary.[71] In spite of this policy of keeping a low profile, the Toronto Zionist Council invited McClure to deliver a public address at the Toronto Zionist Centre.

Robert Baird McClure, the son of Canadian missionaries, had grown up in China. After graduating from medical school at the University of Toronto, he dedicated his life to a missionary career as a doctor. He served in China for twenty-five years and then moved to the Gaza Strip for four years to work with sick Arab refugees. His election as the first lay moderator of the United Church was an unusual choice because he had controversial views and spoke openly and frankly. He was hailed as a great humanitarian, but politically he was very naive. In spite of the fact that he regarded himself "as free from racial prejudice as any WASP can be," he was unable to abandon certain Christian stereotypes of the Jews. Furthermore, his four years with Arab refugees had obviously influenced his views concerning the political situation in the Middle East.[72] Munroe Scott, his biographer, wrote: "As moderator, McClure ran headlong into Zionism … A subtler moderator might have circumvented it. For McClure it was unavoidable."[73] McClure strongly supported Forrest and refused to bend to pressure to remove him from the editorship of the *Observer*.

In January 1969 the Toronto Zionist Council requested that the moderator make an official statement about the United Church's attitude to the Jews, to Israel, and to the *Observer.* To avoid any slip-ups in such a delicate situation, McClure had prepared his speech and released a copy to the press. There was great tension in the well-packed hall of the Zionist Centre on 15 January 1969. A six-man bodyguard escorted McClure, and his hosts, too, had made great efforts to prevent violence or emotional outbursts. The moderator began his speech by proving from his own biography that he was unbiased and that he held "very positive views on racial inter-relations." Then he pointed out that to a Gentile the Canadian Jew "wears three different hats"; he was a neighbour, a member of a related religion, and someone involved with the State of Israel. McClure praised the great achievements of the first two "hats" and then reached the core of his address, the attitude to Israel. He stated that everyone in Canada supported the existence of Israel and agreed that it should have free shipping rights, both in the Suez Canal and through the Strait of Tiran. He maintained that most Canadians felt that the Six Day War was "justified." McClure then went on to say, "In the long run the Canadian Gentile, I think, is more concerned to see peace in the Middle East than he is to see Israel expand her territorial boundaries. On the other hand the nationalistic enthusiasms of the Canadian Jew seems excessive to the Canadian Gentile. For one thing he feels that if the Canadian Jew does feel so tied up with the expansion of the State of Israel why do not more Canadian Jews go out and cast their lot with their brothers there. We think that we detect a slight 'guilt complex' in the Canadian Jew caused by his living a rather comfortable and affluent existence … in Canada."[74]

McClure argued that the Canadian Gentile was seeking peace and recognized the plight of the Palestinian refugees. On the other hand, in the "excessive interest of the Canadian Jew in Israel a certain element of paranoia exists." During the question period that followed his speech, McClure stated that the *Observer* by and large reflected the position of the United Church, and he gave his total support to Forrest, whose reports he considered fair and well balanced. "Forrest is reporting what a Canadian Gentile would see, and if you don't like it, that's too bad."[75]

Robert McClure's unfavourable remarks about Canadian Jews – he called their approach to Israel "paranoid" – did not contribute to greater understanding between Jews and Gentiles. A year later, in 1970, in Montreal he said that "the Jew in North America wants action in the Middle East so he can collect money for Israel Bond drives." Gunther Plaut responded by observing that, "to put it inelegantly, he serves us a piece of baloney shot through with ptomaine poisoning."[76]

The dialogue between the Jewish community and the United Church was further complicated by remarks that McClure made at a demonstration in support of Soviet Jewry. At a large rally in Nathan Phillips Square in Toronto on 30 December 1970, a cold day, seven thousand people assembled to protest against repression of the Jews in the Soviet Union. Other civic and church leaders, including the heads of several Christian denominations, spoke about the deeper meaning of trials then going on in Leningrad and protested against the religious and national suppression of Soviet Jewry. McClure, however, spoke about the serious crime that the hijackers being tried in Leningrad had committed, although he believed that they did not deserve the capital punishment they received. He went on to speak about the Palestinian problem in the Middle East. McClure's comments provoked angry reactions. Several Russian immigrants made abusive hate calls to his home. More civilized but just as anguished were the feelings of the Jewish leaders. Sydney M. Harris, chair of the Canadian Jewish Congress, first apologized for the private nuisance and abusive calls that McClure had been subjected to, saying that he, Harris, abhorred them. But he was sorry that McClure had reduced the question to whether one was for or against hijacking or for or against capital punishment, "a gross oversimplification." McClure did not appreciate what other church leaders had understood as the real meaning of the rally.[77]

A stronger response came from Rabbi Joseph Kelman, president of the Toronto Rabbinical Fellowship. McClure's "well meaning but inconsiderate remarks ... showed both a lack of sensitivity to those present as well as ignorance of the conditions in Russia." He also blamed the moderator for what he had said to the *Toronto Star* concerning criticism of his remarks at the rally. McClure had commented to the *Star*, "It was a Zionist rally ... If I'd known you had to be a Zionist, I wouldn't have come." Kelman, who was also present on the stage, denied any connection with Zionism or Israel. McClure's remarks about the hijackers were legally "erroneous and ... and insensitive ... The freedom and well being of Russian citizens ... is more sacred and precious than concern about alleged Zionist meeting. A church leader must be relevant to facts and feelings, both of which were not evident on 30th December," wrote Kelman.[78] McClure answered Kelman with sorrow that "my words fail to express the sympathy I feel towards my Jewish brothers." His presence on the cold day of the rally, along with Ernest Long, demonstrated the concern of the United Church about the subject. "We are sorry if our words were unwelcome. I assure you our spirit was indicated by our presence." McClure went on to say that, "for any offence I caused any of the audience, I apologize." He expressed his sincere regret that during his term as moderator, "my efforts to bridge the gap between Jews and Gentiles have not been more successful." Kelman was "pleasantly surprised" at McClure's apology.[79]

Sol I. Littman, executive director of the Canada-Israel Committee, complained to N. Bruce McLeod and Don Stirling, who had participated with McClure in a trip to the Middle East, about the moderator's speech at the rally. In a letter marked "confidential, not for reproduction or publication," Littman wrote that McClure's statement "will make it extremely difficult to convince my colleagues that the United Church is sponsoring such a dialogue with an open heart and an even hand." He maintained that the moderator's statements, which displayed "a surprising lack of understanding," "have been virtually disastrous and have impeded communication" between the two communities. Littman went on to say that McClure had missed an opportunity to disprove the accusation that criticism of Israel was antisemitism. He could have shown that his pro-Arab position, as well as that of the *Observer,* was not based on hostility to the Jews, as concern for Russian Jewry would have demonstrated. But his remarks "were not appropriate, showing no sympathy, concern, or even understanding." The presence of Long on the platform with McClure reinforced the impression that the comments represented, not the position of one man, but the consensus of the United Church leadership.[80]

Long, for his part, also contributed to the deterioration in relations between the Canadian Jewish community and the United Church. He issued a circular to the religious and lay leaders of the church, recommending a television program that dealt with the plight of the Palestinian refugees "from the point of view of the Arab refugees." The fact that the secretary of the General Council, the highest ranking officer in the United Church apart from the moderator, publicly recommended a television program that was admittedly prepared from the Arab point of view widened the gulf between the two communities.[81] And the situation worsened in 1969 when Long sent a letter to Ibrahim Shukrallah of the Arab Information Office in Ottawa in which he declared that the United Church supported the Palestinian refugee cause. After the publication of this letter in the *Arab-Canada Report,* Jewish leaders felt that a meeting with the leadership of the United Church was urgently needed.[82]

Given the constant attacks by Forrest and the *Observer* on Zionists and Israel, dialogue between the Jewish community and the United Church became impossible at this time. "It is extremely difficult, if not impossible, to ease the tensions created and kept going by the words and actions" of the two communities, admitted Donald G. Ray, deputy secretary of the General Council, in a letter in March 1971. He added, "We don't know how to handle the guilt that we may feel for the actions that have been done."[83]

Forrest continued to provoke controversy. In March 1970, after an address at McMaster University in Hamilton before an Arab audience, he was asked about the disproportionate amount of space devoted to the Arab refugee issue. Forrest answered that, in a cooperative effort with other churches, the United Church had undertaken to concentrate on the Middle East, leaving other subjects to other church publications. As for the charges of antisemitism, he stated that they were a "new form of McCarthyism" that attempted to discredit and destroy anti-Zionists.[84] In December 1969 in Don Mills, Ontario, speaking before the Canadian Arab Friendship Society of Toronto, Forrest expressed his sympathy with the PLO "commandos," comparing them "to the freedom fighters of France." He retreated from his earlier demand that the Arabs should recognize Israel: "I no longer think I have the right to say any nation must recognize another state diplomatically," he declared.[85]

Jewish leaders wanted to know whether Forrest was a spokesman for the church or whether church officials disagreed with his views. "Where does your Church stand?" asked Stuart E. Rosenberg of Long. "In the name of 'humanitarianism,' the *United Church Observer* runs the most politically slanted, anti-Israeli articles, to be found anywhere in Christendom. And in the name of editorial freedom, the United Church allows the editor of its journal to disrupt and possibly destroy our interfaith dialogue … I would hope, Ernest, that you would initiate a basic review of these vital matters. It is important to spell out a statement of Church policy in the Middle East, clearly and unequivocally. We are confused. Does Mr. Forrest speak for the Church? If not, what is the Church saying for *itself*?"[86] Long answered by referring to recent decisions of the World Council of Churches that basically supported Forrest's position, and he added: "I think a more objective understanding of it is in order" – "objective," unlike the emotional pro-Israeli point of view of the Jews.[87] Defending Forrest's position, Patricia Clarke pointed out that he was saying essentially what had been said by the United Church, the WCC, the CCC, the Red Cross, and the UN.[88]

Forrest also turned to Long, asking for his public support, particularly against Anglican priest Roland de Corneille, who was pro-Israeli. Long complied with Forrest's appeal, resigning from a Christian-Jewish dialogue that was chaired by de Corneille. In his letter of resignation, he wrote to de Corneille that the latter's strong condemnation of Forrest, "intentionally or unintentionally, was a direct incitement to anger and hatred." He went on to say, "I do not always agree with Dr. Forrest, but I have complete confidence in his sincerity and in his knowledge of the total situation in the Middle East. I am sure that in the long run he will contribute far more to the creation of justice and peace in that part of the world than your methods ever will."[89]

While Jewish leaders initially believed that the official position of the United Church was meaningfully different from that of Forrest, they gradually began to feel that they were mistaken. Although several church leaders disagreed with Forrest's methods and language, they essentially supported his point of view, as the position of Long, the single most powerful man in the church hierarchy, who served as secretary of the General Council for sixteen years (1954–71), clearly indicated. When Donald V. Stirling responded to an article by Gunther Plaut and signed with his official title as chair of the Committee on the Church and International Affairs of the Toronto Conference of the United Church, Plaut wondered whether the position formerly held by Forrest alone "is now the official viewpoint of the denomination." The silence on the part of representatives of the church suggested that this conclusion was correct. Plaut warned that "it is not too late for the leadership of the Church to call a halt to this dangerous drift. If it does not, it will help to create an image which the Church will find very hard to eradicate in the years to come."[90]

In March 1970 Forrest, in the "Editor's Observations" of the *Observer*, published a list of recommended books on the Middle East, which was patently one-sided. All the books by Jewish authors were highly critical of Israel. The authors included Elmer Berger, Moshe Menuhin, Maxime Rodinson, I.F. Stone, and Uri Avneri. But the books by Arabs were also very critical of Israel and Zionism. No Arab book ever dared to criticize the Arabs. Forrest warned his readers against using pro-Israel books because they were "undisguised Zionist propaganda." Reacting to this list, Plaut commented that "there is a deep sadness in me about a church whose official organ consistently exposes its innocent readers to so distorted a world view." He lamented that Forrest was departing from the fairness expected of an editor when he recommended such a one-sided list. [91]

By 1971 the low-profile policy previously maintained by the Jewish leaders had disappeared. When they realized that their avoidance of public confrontation was useless and that quiet dialogue was bearing no fruit, they went on the offensive. Gunther Plaut now responded to every article and every insult. He decided "to deal harshly" with Forrest, but he was unhappy that the debate between the two groups had become personalized, focusing on Forrest and himself. W. Clarke Mac-Donald called it the "Plaut-Forrest syndrome," since they symbolized the two sides of the quarrel. It represented "a failure of acceptance."[92]

In August 1970, "under a certain amount of pressure," as Forrest admitted, he had decided to give space to the other side.[93] "Some of our critics have complained that the *Observer* has been one-sided in its presentation of the Middle East problem, suggesting that the Israeli and Zionist viewpoints have not been given space," he wrote in his introduction to the August 1970 issue, which carried two articles by Israelis and one pro-Israeli article. Under pressure,[94] Forrest had asked Aba Gefen, the Israeli consul general in Toronto, and Alan T. Davies to express their points of view. In addition, as usual, he enlisted an Israeli who was critical of Israel – Simcha Flapan, the editor of the *New Outlook*, a left-wing Israeli magazine.[95]

The consul general's article was entitled "A Vision of Peace Guides Israel." After rejecting reports of the mistreatment of Arabs in the occupied territories, Gefen concluded his "vision" by appealing to the Arabs to "accept Israel's extended hand for 'a peace between equals.'"[96] Davies, in his "Why Critics of Israel Must Be Careful," examined the origins of political Zionism, which was "a Jewish response to Western anti-Semitism." He emphasized the influence of the Holocaust on the establishment of Israel: "Auschwitz is the great watershed in modern Jewish history, but few Christians understand its terrible meaning for Jews … For the post-Auschwitz Jew, the Holocaust and the State of Israel are linked together in a fashion that, for the Christians, suggests the historical and religious interwining of the death and resurrection of Jesus himself … If Christians really wish to criticize Israeli policies, they must be careful how they sound. An anti-Zionism that sounds too much like anti-Semitism thoroughly deserves the repudiation." To be sure, Davies did not object to fair and judicious criticism that took into consideration the moral dilemmas of the region.[97] Not surprisingly, the Jews were grateful for such support from a professor of religion who happened to be a United Church minister, and Plaut and Littman commended Davies for his article.[98]

Not everyone was satisfied with Davies' analysis, however. The Reverend David R. Wood of Brantford, Ontario, was disturbed because Davies' plea for Christians not to criticize Israel injudiciously "tastes of Neville Chamberlain's Christian unhealthy care to treat Hitler's complaints 'fairly.'" He maintained that "it was a Christian duty" to condemn strongly Israel's violation of international law and its aggression.[99]

About this time, Max Shechter, chair of B'nai Brith Canada, commended Forrest for his effort to "balance biased statements with objective presentations." Nevertheless, he criticized him for an earlier article, which was full of "deductions, omissions and inaccuracies." He complained about the constant attacks by the *Observer*, which "add fuel to the fire … [and] create a polarization amongst good friends in our home community." Forrest replied that he was ready to risk a certain amount of polarization for the higher purpose of peace in the Middle

East, which could only be reached if "reasonable Jews" put pressure on the Israeli government to adopt a more flexible policy.[100]

Forrest then turned to a Rabbi Dr I.M. Rabinowitch, asking him to write an article or a letter opposing the statements made by Gefen and Davies. He requested Rabinowitch to make "a reference to the fact that you are Jewish and a faithful Jew and an Orthodox Jew, but what you think of Zionism, would make quite a point."[101] When the rabbi refused to criticize Israel publicly, particularly in a church magazine, Forrest managed to find another anti-Zionist Orthodox Jew.[102] In 1972, when he organized a Middle East seminar, he was "anxious that some of the top-notch people in the States who are fighting quite a fight against the repercussions in the occupied area etc. be at such a symposium. I think their input would be very valuable to all of us and might attract some attention from the press."[103]

Forrest's constant and harsh criticism of Israel made him a controversial public figure. People reacted to him with great passion, either strongly supporting him or vehemently attacking him. "To protect my blood pressure I shall have to drop the coming issues of the *Observer* in the wastepaper basket unread," wrote one reader.[104] Forrest received many letters admiring his daring in coming out openly against Israel. They supported his argument that Zionists dominated the media: "Thousands of Christians watch aghast as only one ethnic group gets publicity and feel it amounts almost to a wonder that your letter was published. We pray that you will be able to tell the truth as our letters do not see the light on the pages of the local newspapers," complained Ella Sienkiericz.[105] Among Forrest's critics were important United Church ministers. "I am startled sometimes by the numbers of people in that category (well-read, intelligent ministers of the church), who don't [support me]. I have been surprised by some of the top N.D.P. [New Democratic Party] people, such as Stanley Knowles, who are pro-Israeli and almost uncritically so," he wrote.[106]

Indeed, only a small group of sensitive intellectuals in the United Church dared to confront Forrest publicly concerning the Palestinian issue, principally Alan T. Davies, David Demson, and R.M. Freeman of Queen's University. They were "an isolated minority, subject to considerable criticism." Forrest, as the editor of the church magazine, had "the advantage of an unique public platform which his critics [were] denied," claimed Davies.[107] This small group of intellectuals was important to the Jews. They felt that a voice of criticism would be effective only if it came from within the United Church. "Something from within the Church ought to be done to disassociate it from becoming identified" with antisemitism, warned Plaut.[108]

Another stage in the growing animosity between Forrest and the Jewish community in Canada was the publication of *The Unholy Land* in 1971. After returning from his sabbatical in Beirut, Forrest wrote this book, which summarized his position on the Palestinian-Israeli crisis. In it he called Israel "a racist and aggressive state" that brutally oppressed innocent Arabs. The dream of the Zionists of establishing a new moral society had become a nightmare, according to Forrest. He pointed to Israel's increasingly friendly relations with apartheid South Africa and compared the two reactionary regimes. However, the Israelis "made the South African whites look like babes in the wood when it comes to practicing apartheid and keeping another race in its place and misleading the world about it." Forrest felt that there were strong similarities between the Israelis and the Nazis. "I do not like to refer in any way to Israel's treatment of the Arabs as Nazi but the parallels are so numerous and so similar that Arabs speak of Nazi tactics and practices."[109] There was nothing new in this book that Forrest had not said or written earlier. However, by concentrating his criticism in one volumn, he made the comments more persuasive. Members of the Jewish community, however, refrained from public debate or reaction to his accusations.[110]

Apparently, *The Unholy Land* was not a great success in Canada, and it sold poorly. Coles bookstores ordered seventy-four copies for display, but after a month the company returned them to the publisher since only eleven had been sold. Forrest accused the chain, whose executive director, Jack Cole, was a Jew, of bowing to outside pressure in its decision to stop selling the book. Cole strongly denied this charge and said that the only reason for the withdrawal of the book was that "it was not selling well."[111] The campaign that Forrest launched against the Coles bookstores helped slightly to increase sales of his book.[112] Not surprisingly, Arab reaction to *The Unholy Land* was positive. F. Bahman, director of the Near East Ecumenical Bureau for Information and Interpretation in Beirut, suggested that it be translated into Arabic. It soon appeared in that language and was distributed in the Middle East.[113]

To ease the tension, Jewish leaders turned to Long, asking that discussion with the United Church be resumed. Long reacted cautiously, saying that he was anxious to continue the dialogue, but that he should consult his colleagues,[114] but it seems that a serious and meaningful dialogue was almost impossible in the current atmosphere. Following the election of A.B.B. Moore, a former president of Victoria College in the University of Toronto, as moderator in 1971, Davies and Freeman applied to him to intervene on behalf of better Jewish-Christian relationships. They stated that, freedom of expression aside,

Forrest had "violated the canons of both good journalism and Christian responsibility." They complained about his "profound insensitivity" to the plight of the Jews. "Wise ecumenical statesmanship will be able to heal the present wounds," concluded Davies and Freeman. Moore answered that he intended "to initiate some discussions about the way in which our relationships with the Jewish community may be improved." Although he did not "entirely agree with the *Observer*'s position," he promised to ameliorate his working relations with Forrest.[115] Speculating on whether Moore would be "good to the Jews," Demson remarked that, though he would be an improvement over McClure, he "is not a 'good friend' in the sense of someone who can be relied on to fight for our cause."[116]

THE CHURCH'S POSITION
IN THE CONFLICT

The question in many minds was: What was the official policy of the United Church? Was it represented by the anti-Israel statements of Forrest, by the reporting in the *Observer*, by Robert McClure's controversial speech at the Zionist Centre, or by the report made by three leading church members on their return from a trip to the Middle East? No official declaration was published to confirm or reject any of these points of view. Therefore Sol I. Littman of the Canada-Israel Committee wrote an article in the *Toronto Star* appealing to the United Church to clarify its position. "In the light of many pronouncements by prominent leaders, the United Church owes a clear and unequivocal statement of its own position to the public," he said. "Such a declaration will be helpful to all parties."[117]

Responding to Littman's article, Ernest Long and A.B.B. Moore hastened to clarify the official policy of the United Church. In an other article in the *Star* they expressed the church's concern over its relationship with the Jewish community. They regarded the recent situation as a "misunderstanding of the nature of the United Church." Although the General Council was entitled to speak officially for the church, the United Church "is not an authoritarian body, which demands a uniform acceptance of official position. Members, officials and even organizations within the church have full freedom to express their opinions or convictions, and often these are not in harmony with official statements." The authors cited the official policy of the church regarding the Middle East which had been issued at the twenty-fourth General Council in 1971.[118]

Forrest was jubilant: "I have always maintained that my position is consistent with the position of the United Church, with that of the wcc and with the facts as they are."[119] Yet this was not quite true. While his basic criticism of Israel was accepted, many United Church leaders disagreed – as we will see later – with his methods of using the media, with his harsh language, and with his employment of the *Observer* for constant anti-Zionist attacks. Forrest's new target for criticizing Zionists and Israel was Jewish emigration from the Soviet Union. Unlike the leaders of other Christian denominations in Canada, who demanded unconditional emigration, Forrest tied the problem of Russian Jewry to Israel's treatment of the Palestinian refugees. According to the editorial in the August 1971 issue of the *Observer*, both the Soviet Union and Israel had violated the basic human right of free travel to and from their countries. Forrest maintained that mass emigration to Israel would be a threat to the Arabs, and he therefore opposed it. "This is one more chapter in the ugly and successful plot to drive out the Palestinian Christian and Muslim people, and give their lands and homes to Jewish people," read the editorial.[120]

Forrest did not want to be a lone warrior for the cause of the Palestinians, however. On the model of the pro-Arab organization in the United States called Americans for Middle East Understanding, in November 1971 he organized a group called Canadians for Middle East Understanding (CAMEU), which later changed its name to the Canadian Committee for Palestine. He turned to the Catholics, the Orthodox, the Unitarians, the Mennonites, and other Protestant denominations to join his group, which would tell Canadians the story of the Palestinians. Forrest hoped that the group might change the atmosphere in Canada in order to encourage anti-Zionist Jews to speak out freely on behalf of Palestinian refugees. Among CAMEU's objectives were the promotion "of understanding of the Arab-Israeli problem and to work for peace, justice, and compassion in the Middle East." The group affirmed the right of Israel to exist, along with the right of Palestinians to justice, according to UN Resolution 242. To avoid worldwide confrontation, Canada should play a part in the achievement of a peaceful settlement. Among the first members were the following: N. Bruce McLeod and John Morgan (minister of the First Unitarian Congregation, Toronto), co-chairs; Deanna Skeoch, secretary general; and Mary Bardvill, Jack Cowan, Frank Epp, A.C. Forrest, Bishop H.R. Hunt, Dr Ahmed Kadry, P. Leblanc, J. Murphy, Dr Wilfred C. Smith, and D. Tushingham.[121]

The same month, Forrest took another step that alienated the Jewish community. Reacting to criticism that the churches had not done anything during the Holocaust, he editorialized: "We hear this slander repeatedly, especially from Christian Zionists who emphasize that the Church did so badly by the Jewish people in times of the past it must now throw all its support behind Israel … Just for the record it should be remembered that in order to stop Hitler, a good many hundreds of thousands of Western soldiers, sailors and airmen died."[122]

The editorial caused a storm of angry protests, some of them in the *Globe and Mail,* such as those from Davies and Demson. Professor H. Weinberg blamed Forrest for repeating the "blatantly anti-semitic canard, that the Allies fought the war in defence of Jewish interests. This is not only a perversion of the truth, but a grave insult to the Jewish people."[123] To be sure, the editorial did not specify that the Allies had entered the war in order to save Jews. However, since Forrest's argument was not precise, "it is not surprising that the quotations from the editorial were also careless," observed Slonim. So Forrest could easily have defended himself, saying that the critics had misquoted him. But as Gunther Plaut argued later in a calmer atmosphere, "The implication was clear: the war against Hitler had been fought in order to save the Jews. All the dead of the war could be laid at the Jewish doorstep. The West owned nothing to us."[124] Even Slonim admitted that although the editorial was not antisemitic, "it did, however, display a lack of sensitivity to a tragic era."[125] Several months later Forrest admitted that the German church had failed during the war: "I know that there was a massive failure of Christians there." This statement appeared to contradict his earlier editorial.[126]

Criticism of Forrest was not limited to the Jews or to known supporters of Israel; even leading United Church members disagreed with the editor. In a private letter in March 1972, Angus J. MacQueen expressed his truthful opinion of Forrest's handling of the magazine: "Al Forrest and I have disagreed on a number of things, one being his November editorial. There are times when I question his judgment, his objectivity, his sensitivity to the feelings of the Jewish community, and his naivete in not realizing that certain articles and emotive words are bound to create a storm among the Jewish people, and foment anti-Jewish prejudice among our own people."[127]

While MacQueen confided his disagreement with Forrest privately, Donald R. Keating, a United Church minister and a community worker in Toronto, did so publicly. In "An Open Letter" to the United Church moderator, the Anglican primate, and the Halton Presbytery, he protested against Forrest's writings: "What does it say of the United Church when a man can write such editorials and still be employed by the *Observer.*" He wondered why "nobody [was] doing anything about him" and called for action – "Not radical action … Just plain basic fundamental Christian action." "Is he not lighting the candles that stoke the fires that turned to smoke and ashes the bodies of six million Jews in the Holocaust? ... I can no longer stay even on the outside of the same house. I'm resigning today."[128]

E.M. Howse came to Forrest's defence. In an article in the *Toronto Star*, he responded. Forrest's critics, many of them Christians, had not taken the trouble to confront his facts; rather, they "quickly introduce Hitler ... But ... Hitler's cruelties cannot be made an excuse for obscuring the cruelties and injustices that have happened in the world since," wrote Howse, hinting at injustices against the Palestinians by the establishment of the State of Israel. He praised Forrest's reputation as a "responsible and competent journalist" and maintained that in a free society, issues should be openly discussed and differing views equally heard. "But those critics who, without taking the trouble to inform themselves, have done nothing more than denounce the editor's temerity in daring to criticize Israel as frankly have said nothing," concluded Howse.[129]

His article in the *Star* received many responses. There were supporters such as Charles E. Hendry, who expressed his admiration of Howse's courage in coming to Forrest's defence.[130] However, most of the reactions were negative. The *Canadian Jewish News* criticized Howse's past record of anti-Israeli positions. The article in the *Star* was "a one-sided disk [*sic*] of little merit and reflects no credit" on a former moderator. "Name calling is no substitute for reasoned debate," maintained the *CJN*.[131] Other criticism came from respected Christians. David Demson disagreed with Howse's perspective and tone, and opposed his argument that criticism of Israel should be the same as criticism of any other nation. He also took issue with Howse's tone, in which he referred to Forrest's critics in degrading terms.[132] G. Douglas Young, president of the American Institute of Holy Land Studies in Jerusalem, attacked Howse's article from a different angle. As a churchman and educator who was living in the Holy Land and knew the situation first-hand, he argued that "Forrest's facts are wrong." The editor's "sin" was not in criticizing Israel but "in playing on the human misery of some in an attempt to force world public opinion to a political solution that has never worked elsewhere and which cannot and will not work here." According to Young, Forrest confused the issues and Howse "made a serious mistake in trying to 'cover' for him."[133]

Keating's resignation created headlines, and church leaders were embarrassed. It contributed to the polarization between the Jewish and United Church communities, because Keating had protested not only against Forrest and his magazine but also against the silence of the church leaders, who refused to censure the editor. "I find myself aghast at the United Church's inability to feel for Jews," he complained.[134] The impression made by Keating's resignation did not last long, however, because for several years after, he did not function as a minister and he had had no influence within the church before his resignation.[135]

By March 1972, when the *Observer* published John Nicholls Booth's article "How Zionists Manipulated Your News," relations between the Jewish community and the United Church were at the boiling point. An effort was made at reconciliation; after some deliberation, the board of governors of St Andrew's College, a United Church institution in Saskatoon, offered an honorary doctorate in philosophy to Professor Emil Fackenheim of the University of Toronto, an internationally renowned Jewish philosopher who had dealt extensively with the meaning of the Holocaust in both Jewish and Christian theology. The statement issued by St Andrew's College read: "In honouring Prof. Fackenheim, St. Andrew's College is acknowledging the contribution to theological and philosophical scholarship of one of the most perceptive thinkers of our time. During the past decade … there have countless students … for whom the Jewish 'philosopher of the Holocaust' has had a profound and prophetic influence … We Christians live with the mark of Cain on us as we contemplate our guilt through indifference, acquiescence, and theological irresponsibility in that anti-Semitism which manifested itself so incredibly in the murder of six millions. And we confess how quickly we have forgotten Auschwitz."[136]

The statement also pointed out that, in a time of polarization, Fackenheim had maintained a "steady commitment to a Christian-Jewish dialogue." It is true that he had remained committed to dialogue, but he was also a staunch defender of the Jewish community in Toronto. As such, he was directly involved in debates with Forrest and was known as a critic of the United Church for its reluctance to silence the editor. Therefore the choice of Fackenheim by a United Church college was a clear political message that Forrest did not represent the whole church. Not everyone in the church was happy with the St Andrew's decision. Robert McClure, for example, said that "Fackenheim is positively paranoid" on the question of the United Church's responsibility for the *Observer*.[137] In Jewish circles there was some discussion of the propriety of his accepting the degree. Saul Hayes, executive vice-president of the Canadian Jewish Congress, was suspicious of the church's attitude to the Jews. "We were further troubled because we do not think that the United Church is being very truthful … I don't think they are all in a very good faith … I never believed in these brotherhood meetings."[138]

Fackenheim consulted Gunther Plaut on whether to accept the degree. "I strongly urged him to go to Saskatoon, accept and make the kind of strong statement of which he was eminently capable," Plaut recalled.[139] On his advice, Fackenheim received the honorary degree and utilized the public relations opportunity, delivering a strong attack on the United Church and the *Observer.* He discussed the deep-seated anti-Jewishness of Christian theology and pointed out that the church still continued it in practice, under the guise of anti-Zionism. "The *Observer* has shown an ever-increasing anti-Jewish bias, and the United Church officials, while seeking refuge behind the editor's freedom of speech have either themselves kept silent, or else used their own freedom of speech only to defend the policies of the editor, or even to attack, often vociferously, those who opposed these policies ... No official I know of has made use of this freedom of speech to oppose the anti-Jewish policies of the *Observer.*"[140]

There were mixed reactions both to the United Church's award of an honorary doctorate to Fackenheim and to his address. Davies was enthusiastic, commending St Andrew's College for its "significant decision." "Such a gesture on the part of a United Church institution, at a time when relations between the United Church and the Canadian Jewish community are seriously disturbed, reflects the basic logic of Christian identification with the oldest victims of Gentile misunderstanding and prejudice ... It serves also to refute ... the increasingly distorted interpretations of Judaism which appear in the *United Church Observer,* which tragically have tended to colour the image of the entire United Church community."[141]

Ben Smillie, a professor at St Andrew's College, suggested to Forrest that he publish Fackenheim's address in the *Observer* without editorial comment. Since there were conciliatory elements in the speech, its publication would prove that Forrest was willing to open the magazine to the Jewish side. "It would give you a more wider and more sympathetic hearing for your legitimate concerns for the Arab people." Forrest, however, declined to print the address on technical grounds. But it seems that the real reason for his refusal was the long personal animosity between himself and Fackenheim.[142]

Not everyone in the United Church was as happy as Davies. W.W. Sedwick maintained that he agreed with Fackenheim concerning the growing antisemitism in the United Church. However, he maintained that Fackenheim himself was the reason for this phenomenon.[143] Earl S. Leutenschlager, of Emmanuel College at the University of Toronto, had a similar complaint. When Fackenheim "threw at us ... all the old Jewish accusations against the Christians, I then and there stopped giving support to the Jews. They don't welcome supporters evidently."[144]

The gesture of offering an honorary doctorate to Emil Fackenheim did not improve relations between the Jewish community and the

United Church. Growing criticism of Forrest's handling of the *Observer*, not only from Jewish circles but also from his own church leaders, pushed the editor to make grave mistakes. The publication of John Nicholls Booth's article "How Zionists Manipulate Your News," as mentioned above, was- a case in point.[145] This article and its implications for the quarrel with the United Church after March 1972 is the subject of the next chapter.

9 The Booth Article and the B'nai Brith Libel Suit, 1972–1973

The debate between A.C. Forrest and the United Church, on the one hand, and the Jewish community, on the other, reached its climax in 1972–73. While Jewish leaders criticized his arguments through editorials, articles, and letters to the Toronto newspapers, several angry individuals wrote him uncomplimentary letters. Forrest felt personally beleaguered. He was particularly disappointed that members of his own church were among his critics. But the more he was criticized, the more adamant he became. He was determined to fight back and not to change his course. His eagerness to publish anti-Zionist material drove him to cross the line between anti-Zionism and antisemitism. The publication of J.N. Booth's article "How Zionists Manipulate Your News" was, according to Angus J. MacQueen, "a serious mistake, but it was obviously a reaction by an editor who has got his back up and is determined not to be intimidated or pushed around."[1] Robert F. Nielsen, editor-in-chief of the *Toronto Star*, stated, "Forrest, a stubborn man, has allowed himself to be pushed by criticism from the Jewish community into a posture that is biased against Israel." But he also wrote that he was convinced Forrest was not an antisemite.[2]

In September 1971 Forrest had invited Booth to contribute an article to the *Observer* that would deal with the problem "of pressures to keep quiet about Israel." He was familiar with Booth's sermons and articles, and had considered quoting them in his *Unholy Land*; he suggested to Booth that he write an introduction "and then do the rest with a bit of scissors and paste, but I want my readers to hear from some informed person about the powerful Zionist influence in this country and the repressive techniques they use."[3] The Reverend John Nicholls Booth was the Canadian-born pastor of a Unitarian-Universalist congregation in Gainesville, Florida. He was known for his antisemitic sermons and articles, which were printed in the right-wing *American Mercury* and the *Cross and the Flag*. Gerald L.K. Smith edited the latter; it was a publication known for its anti-Black and antisemitic polemics.[4] Thus when Forrest initiated the publication of Booth's article, he knew what it would include, both in substance and in style.

"How Zionists Manipulate Your News" opened with the accusation that, during its few years of existence, Israel "has left a trail of global tensions, the longest and blackest record of international censures against any nation … Unable to challenge the truth about their territorial greed, maltreatment of refugees and defiance of UN resolutions, they have tried instead to silence their critics, keep them off platforms and out of newspapers, and discredit those who manage to be heard with the red herring cry of anti-Semitism." The article then elaborated on Zionists' efforts to suppress anti-Israel reports through character assassination of distinguished people such as Arnold Toynbee, Bertrand Russell, William E. Hocking, Millar Burrows, Bayard Dodge, Dorothy Thompson, and Vincent Sheean. Booth argued that the Zionists used economic pressure on editors and publishers to coerce them to give the major part of their space to pro-Israel reports.

The author focused his attack on the Anti-Defamation League of B'nai Brith, saying that it "exercised 'surveillance' of Israel's critics" and that its files contained "dossiers on thousands of North Americans." He accused B'nai Brith of engaging in political activities in spite of its tax-exempt status as a charitable organization. Booth recounted the efforts of B'nai Brith to silence him, "maligning me with innuendoes and calling for a countrywide surveillance of my movements." Church organizations were intimidated into not mentioning Israel from the pulpit. "Israeli intelligence, through B'nai Brith's ADL [and other] Zionist organizations … penetrate every part of our nation." He quoted Jean-Paul Sartre, the French philosopher, mistakenly referring to him as Jewish. According to Booth, Sartre regarded "some threat of anti-Semitism as essential to hold Jews together. If there is no actual anti-Semitism then it must be created." Booth called upon the press to counterbalance Zionist sources of information in order that "no group can throttle our right to hear and express all responsible points of view."[5]

The Booth article raised "temperatures in both communities to fever pitch," recalled Reuben Slonim.[6] Even Forrest admitted that "this is the first time since 1968 I have taken a solid swing at that type of Zionist activity."[7] The Jews unanimously accused him of antisemitism. For them, the Booth article clearly demonstrated that anti-Zionism and antisemitism belonged to the same family of ideas. Ben Kayfetz, in a private letter to Norman Edell of the Jewish Welfare Federation, expressed a temperate point of view: "Forrest ... has been our major pain in the neck hereabouts these last few years, far more disturbing in a real sense than the neo-Nazis ... Our complaint against Forrest is not so much that he is anti-Israel, whether we like it or not, it is his privilege, but in his anti-Israel stance he reveals a supreme indifference to the facts of modern Jewish history and the needs and aspirations of the Jewish people. His Christian conscience applies to one side only ... He is found to be making common cause with people whose materials appear in periodicals such as those of Gerald L.K. Smith and other 'classical' antisemites."[8] Kayfetz, as well as Rabbi Gunther Plaut, maintained that Forrest's collaboration with antisemites whose material had appeared in well-known antisemitic publications made his anti-Zionist approach an antisemitic one, despite his protests that he was only anti-Zionist. Plaut argued that "the *Observer*'s tendency to depict Zionism as an historical evil has strengthened the heritage of latent and overt antisemitism in many readers."[9]

Another accusation made against Booth was that his article had already appeared, almost verbatim, in both the *American Mercury* and the *Cross and the Flag*. He responded that both publications had used his sermons without his permission. Whether or not this was true, the fact that racist and right-wing papers were interested in printing his sermons meant that his ideas conformed to their anti-Jewish points of view.[10]

The Jewish leaders preferred to let Christians protest against the Booth article; as Ben Kayfetz wrote: "We have been following, or trying to follow, a policy of non-confrontation as far as the Jewish community is concerned. We do however, aim and aid Christian opponents who want to and are capable of confronting him."[11] The editorial in the *Canadian Jewish News* maintained that the Jewish community should not deal with Forrest, but rather, his own church should: "He has been and continues to be a problem to the United Church of Canada, the body which has entrusted him with their official publication."[12]

One of the leading critics of Forrest and the *Observer* regarding the publication of Booth's article was Gregory Baum. He was shocked that the *Observer* had distorted Sartre's writing to suggest the "scandalous idea" that Jews must invent antisemitism as a myth necessary for their survival. Baum criticized Forrest for printing a "plainly anti-semitic article." He further denounced the *Observer* for failing to fulfill the vital task of eliminating the centuries-old Christian bias against Jews, particularly in the face of the Holocaust. Baum's attack was painful to Forrest, because in the past they had been friends. "I rated him very high.

He started to cut me up, or let others cut me up, and imply I was an anti-Semite, without checking with me," complained Forrest.[13]

Baum was not alone in his criticism. United Church ministers denounced the publication of Booth's article from their pulpits and in letters to the press.[14] One piece of criticism that did not receive publicity came from F.G. Brisbin of the United Church division of communication. He wrote a paragraph-by-paragraph commentary, because "such an article cannot be treated lightly in the present circumstances." Brisbin criticized the opening sentence concerning Israel's "longest and blackest record of international censures," regarding it as "more inflammatory than helpful ... It is a distortion of the nature of this century's history." He blamed the author for giving "facts" without bringing any evidence to support them, such as "1,200,000 Zionist mailings ... monthly," or the "fact" that the ADL files contained dossiers on thousands of North Americans. As for Booth's accusation that B'nai Brith had organized a boycott against Japan for refusing to trade with Israel, Brisbin reminded Forrest that the United Church had "taken similar action against South Africa, and [was] engaged in many kinds of political pressure activities, but still [claimed] to be a religious organization." He commented that "it might have been better had you deleted the unsupported charges rather than lay yourself open to the counter-charge of smearing the opposition." Summing up his comments, Brisbin argued, "I believe this article rendered more of a disservice than service to your particular cause."[15]

As a matter of fact, the publication of Booth's article was a disservice not only to Forrest's cause but to the United Church as a whole. It put the leaders of the church in an embarrassing situation; they opposed the article but refrained from criticizing Forrest publicly. Angus Mac-Queen regarded the Booth article as "a serious mistake," but he declined to enter "publicly into the fray at this time."[16] A.B.B. Moore also "often disagreed with Forrest's position and in particular thought he had gone too far in publishing the antisemitic article in the *Observer*." However, he maintained that Forrest was not antisemitic, since he did not reject Jews "because of race, religion, culture and history."[17] George Morrison opined that Forrest "did not reflect the general approach of the rank and file membership of the United Church, and particularly in his 'later excesses' re: John Booth's article."[18]

Booth complained in April 1972 to Forrest about the lack of reaction to his piece in the *Observer*. Forrest, who had been flooded with angry responses, answered, "I rather wish that were true."[19] Charles W. Brodie of Richmond, British Columbia, deplored "the use of this material in the issue of any church magazine; it can only cause rancor, hatred, discord, suspicion etc." S. McMillan of Winnipeg disapproved of the *Observer*'s policy "on what the thinking United Church member should be exposed to in their magazine." She wondered why the editor considered Booth's article wise or fair, and warned, "You are destroying your credibility." John Patton of Ottawa, who regarded himself as "critical of Israeli policy," claimed that Christians failed to distinguish between fear of antisemitism and promotion of Israeli aggrandizement, and he called "for a moratorium "on criticism of Israel. J.W. Doherty, also of Ottawa, argued that, since the *Observer* was not a magazine of international affairs, the editor "does a disservice to the United Church by using its official paper as a means of presenting his own viewpoint on the Arab-Israeli situation." To Forrest's credit, he published all these letters of criticism in the *Observer.*[20]

The Reverend John Short criticized him in the *Globe and Mail,* saying that material like Booth's article caused harm to Jewish-Christian relations. Forrest answered in a personal letter that Short's involvement in the public debate concerning the Middle East is "harmful … [and] playing directly into the wrong hands."[21] A. Roy Eckardt, an American pro-Israel Christian theologian, described Forrest as "Canada's most notorious and perhaps most denominationally protected Christian anti-Semite."[22]

Forrest had his supporters as well. Lorne M. Kenny, who had expressed pro-Arab opinions as a member of the Committee on the Church and International Affairs, defended him publicly. In a letter to the editor of the *Toronto Star* he indicated the importance of editorial freedom as "one of the essentials of a free and open society." Forrest, who had showed "the highest regard for Judaism and the Jewish heritage," could not be regarded as anti-Jewish. Kenny strongly denied that political criticism of Israel was tantamount to antisemitism. On the contrary, the right to criticize Israel in the interest "of preserving truth and justice" should be cherished and supported. "It is high time that the Canadian and American publics … stopped letting the Zionist leaders dictate our thinking regarding the State of Israel," Kenny concluded.[23]

The constant criticism of the *Observer* fell on the fertile soil of insensitivity to the Jews, as the Reverend Maurice Whidden, minister of Donminster United Church in Don Mills, Ontario, attested: "What impresses me is the insensitive way so many of our United Church Christians relate to the Jews, and this includes a surprising number of clergymen. We become very defensive or digress to the area of grievances, which justify a negative attitude toward Jews."[24]

In such an atmosphere it is not surprising that certain people wrongly interpreted Forrest's campaign for the Palestinians and his criticism of Israel's policies. M.P.B. Wrixon of Victoria, British Columbia, who was of southern Irish origin, wrote a letter of support to Forrest that clearly demonstrated his antisemitic feelings, despite his denial of them: "I am not anti-semitic as I have many very good Jewish friends. However, I am very much opposed to the power of the Jewish people in the world of 1972. Of course this power is based on money and the power of the Jewish vote in the U.S. without which no president can hope to be elected. That is all wrong … Of course, the power of the Jewish communities in Montreal, Toronto, Winnipeg and Vancouver is enormous … I just wanted you to know that you are not alone in your fight."[25]

B'NAI BRITH CONFRONTS FORREST

While the Canadian Jewish Congress had decided to avoid confrontation with Forrest, leaving it to Christians,[26] B'nai Brith took a more aggressive approach. Its Anti-Defamation League had a standing policy of publicly confronting attackers of Jews. After five years of frustration, local chapters of B'nai Brith exerted pressure on their own leaders to criticize Forrest and his anti-Israel campaign. Accordingly, at the beginning of 1972, before Booth's article was published, a piece by Alfred Green appeared in the *Digest*, the publication of the Toronto lodge of B'nai Brith, entitled "The President's Message." In the opening paragraph Green reflected the feelings of his co-religionists, writing: "We, the Jews, have controlled our emotions for centuries. A hush hush policy was adopted which stifled our inner feelings, forcing us to carry the yoke of brutal persecutions and inhuman attacks upon our dignity. Over the years we slowly – but slowly – emerged from the ghettos and animal-like existence, and were given recognition … We paid a terrible price to arouse ourselves from our stupor which engulfed us for centuries … From biblical times, there has always appeared a Pharaoh, or in plain language, an anti-Semite, who attempts for ulterior motives and by nefarious means, to besmirch and throttle the Jews. Such a character is Dr. A.C. Forrest, the Editor of the *United Church Observer* … Dr. Forrest is constantly taking advantage of his position as Editor to attack Jews and Israel. The Church, by its silence, condoned these attacks."[27]

Green expressed what the leaders of B'nai Brith felt but were afraid to say openly.[28] Forrest was shocked by Green's accusation that he was an antisemite. "That was the nastiest piece of obvious libel I had seen … This violated the limits," he later told Reuben Slonim. Forrest discussed the matter with friends, lawyers, and fellow editors, and they recommended initiating a libel suit. "You've got to stop this thing; it is getting out of hand," they said to him.[29] Accordingly, Forrest launched a libel suit against Alfred Green and the *Digest*. "There was a great excitement around. I was told from the start that I would probably make my point and let it go." He hesitated over whether to accept this advice, because he did not like to start a suit that he could not finish. "I don't like to bluff," he wrote to a friend, but eventually he decided to do just that.[30]

Although Forrest initiated a libel suit, the leaders of the United Church were not interested in litigating, particularly against a Jewish organization. A meeting was therefore held on 10 February 1972 with the leaders of the United Church and B'nai Brith, along with their lawyers. Those present agreed "to cool" the matter and keep it "within bounds." They decided to make an effort"to eliminate the possibility of a small fire turning into a conflagration."[31]

On 15 March the sub-executive of the United Church discussed Forrest's plan to initiate proceedings against Albert Green and B'nai Brith. It welcomed the decision of the meeting with B'nai Brith "to minimize if possible the seriousness of the incident," and it appointed a small committee to confer with the editorial advisory committee of the *Observer* "concerning the terms of reference of the Committee and the procedures followed by it, in the light of this particular crisis." The moderator appointed Long, Morrison, H.R. Parker, and B. Robert Bater to this committee. The sub-executive also appointed another committee to examine the financial implications and the responsibility of the church in the coming libel suit.[32]

The sub-executive took the libel issue very seriously, calling the situation "a crisis." The appointment of the committee to discuss matters with the editorial advisory committee was a sign of dissatisfaction with Forrest's handling of the *Observer.* It called upon the advisory committee to strengthen its supervision of the magazine's policy. The new committee was appointed in order "to enquire into the whole matter and see what can be done to effect a satisfactory resolution of the problem that has bothered so many people on both sides of the controversy," reported F.G. Brisbin.[33]

Then in the March issue of the *Observer,* the Booth article appeared, drastically matters. Instead of a cooling-off period, the atmosphere now reached the boiling point. Leaders of the United Church criticized Forrest not only for the content of Booth's article, as Brisbin's comments indicate, but also for the bad timing of its publication. "Certainly when you were considering issuing a Writ for libel, the article on Zionism should not have appeared in the last issue of the *Observer,*" argued F.R. Murgatroyd, chair of the division of communication and Forrest's superior.[34] Following the publication of the Booth article, the situation deteriorated further. B'nai Brith issued a notice of libel against Forrest, the *Observer,* and the United Church. It was the first time that an important agency of the Jewish community and the

United Church of Canada were suing each other, and both sides lined up for the battle.[35] Heavy pressure was exerted on the officials of the church to silence or dismiss Forrest. This demand came not only from Jewish leaders, including Emil Fackenheim, but also from within the church itself. Forrest claimed that there was an organized pressure group in the advisory committee that was influenced by the so-called academics (Davies, Demson, and Freeman).[36] Howse agreed that "a good many" voices were demanding Forrest's removal. According to Howse, one could provide "an impressive list" of Forrest's opponents even inside the United Church.[37]

The meeting of the special committee with the *Observer*'s editorial advisory committee was highly critical of Forrest and his constant attacks on Israel. "Fred Murgatroyd and a few others gave me a bad time in a meeting of the advisory committee," complained Forrest.[38] Murgatroyd, who was responsible for the church magazine, led the discussion, proposing a resolution that neither Forrest nor the *Observer* mention the Middle East for one year. While, publicly, the United Church leaders' excuse for their non-intervention in Forrest's handling of the *Observer* was the sacred principle of "editorial freedom," behind closed doors they did try to silence him. Forrest bitterly complained that "nobody in that committee ... protested the chairman of the division's expression of hope that I'd have nothing to say about the Middle East for a year."[39] He had underestimated the seriousness of repercussions caused by the Booth article and the harm it had inflicted on his own church. In a letter to Ernest Long, he ridiculed the term "crisis," which the sub-executive had used, and he was "a bit taken aback by the seriousness with which Fred Murgatroyd and others seemed to take the Zionist reaction to the Booth article."[40] Brisbin explained to Forrest that"the Church has to be concerned not only about its tradition in law on a subject of this nature, but also about its relationship with the Jewish community in Canada."[41] Not everyone at the meeting of the special committee was critical of Forrest. Angus MacQueen, the chair of the advisory committee, defended the principle and tradition of editorial freedom. Forrest appreciated MacQueen's help, saying that he "came through for me beautifully."[42]

The special committee and the advisory committee reviewed the latter's terms of reference and recommended that the executive supervise the magazine more closely;[43] the executive endorsed these recommendations.[44] By May 1972 Forrest felt that heavy pressure was being exerted on him. He admitted, "I am aware that I have bowed to some of the pressures that have come from the 9th floor and the chairman of the division [of communication] and others."[45] In a letter to John Nicholls Booth, Forrest candidly depicted his difficult situation. Although his case against B'nai Brith was "solid," it could take two years to come to court, "and then could drag on and on. The Church and the publishing house [of the United Church] have no stomach for it." His lawyers advised him to publish a "weasel-like apology." "I fight against this idea because I know that any sort of apology which I don't feel is wrong, but secondly, people just read it as an apology and what they will remember is that Forrest had to apologize to the Jews. However, the Church and the Publishing House are involved and their lawyers advise that this is done."[46] Although he agreed to publish an apology, Forrest promised Booth, "I will not give up this fight but I do have to fight it carefully." He would have many chances to speak on radio and television, and "they can't stop me on this."[47]

Bowing to the pressure of his church and his lawyers, Forrest published an apology in the June issue of the *Observer.* It pointed out that the Booth article referred to B'nai Brith in the United States and not to the Canadian branch. "We are sorry if the article in question has caused offence to the B'nai Brith Foundation of Canada and extend this apology."[48] Since the "apology" did not repudiate Booth's statements and was not a real retraction, the Jewish leadership was disappointed. The apology "is not only inadequate but totally unacceptable, that in fact, its wording aggravates the offense," was the unanimous opinion of the Jewish establishment.[49] When the B'nai Brith lawyers complained about its inadequacy, a United Church lawyer made clear that "no further apology would be published in the *Observer.*"[50] Indeed, the compromise wording of the apology satisfied nobody; as Forrest reported, "there has been a bit of showdown inside the establishment here. I think there was a move on which might be interpreted as an attempt to placate some of the North Toronto rabbis, without upsetting the editor of his advisory committee. It did not work. North Toronto was not placated and the editor of his committee was not happy."[51]

The publication of the apology did not end the quarrel between the United Church and the Jewish community. Furthermore, it did not even conclude the debate inside the church. The special committee recommended close supervision of the editor and of the magazine's policy.[52] Accordingly, the United Church solicitor reported that the church "has now activated an 'Editorial Committee' for the purpose of keeping a constant check on the proposed contents of the *Observer* and to guard against such material ever appearing again."[53] However, supporters of Forrest and of the principle of editorial freedom appealed, asking that these recommendations be reconsidered. Eventually, they succeeded in cancelling the attempt to restrict Forrest's independence.[54]

The vacillation by the United Church bodies reflected the dispute that was taking place in the church between the universalists and the pragmatists. The universalists were less concerned with the traditional issues of the church than with messianic utopianism. This group supported subjects popularly called "progressive forces" and "liberation movements," and it engaged in criticizing colonialism, racism, and Israel's expansionism. Members advocated a militant, internationalist, politically aware policy for the United Church. The pragmatist group was more concerned with church matters, such as union with the Anglicans, and with social action in Canada, not abroad. This group opposed internationalist intervention because it undermined the church's strength in Canada. Forrest belonged to the universalists, while the pragmatists considered his policy harmful to the church in Canada.[55]

In the end, although no official restriction was imposed upon Forrest's editorship, he was urged to ease off on Middle East coverage. Angus MacQueen supported editorial freedom, but he asked him to take "a more moderate and responsible approach."[56] Forrest's lawyer not only requested him to refrain from publishing articles such as Booth's, but also strongly advised him "to have as little to do with Dr. Booth as possible."[57] As Forrest told John Sutton, the executive director of the pro-Arab Americans for Middle East Understanding, "Some pretty strong pressures have been placed on church officials recently and there were signs of some bending to the pressures for awhile, but I think I've got that stopped … we must be very careful not to further tensions between the 'Jewish community' and the United Church."[58]

The publication of Booth's article and the libel suits with B'nai Brith also caused controversy between Forrest and leading church members. B. Robert Bater, minister of Eglinton United Church in Toronto, a New Testament scholar, and a distinguished member of the church, regretfully pointed out that "we seem to be at such distance from one another both in thinking and feeling." Bater praised Forrest's courage for defending the underdog, particularly the Palestinian cause, and regretted the "ganging up" on him by some church officials. However, he criticized Forrest "for not being able to see that after Auschwitz confessed Christians can only take sides against Jews when it is clear that there is human tragedy which will be intensified if *they* don't act … and even then with terrible agony and heart-searching that everything could align a Christian against Jews again." He regretted that he did not find such awareness in Forrest. Bater wondered whether the editor had not increasingly developed a strong anti-Jewish – not an anti-Zionist or anti-Israeli – bent. Despite his disagreement with Forrest, however, he did not believe that the church should drop the Arab cause simply for the sake of keeping itself "in a good shape."[59]

Another friend and close collaborator who criticized Forrest's one-sided policy was Kenneth Bagnell. An ordained United Church minister, he had worked with Forrest as the magazine's managing editor but had become a columnist for the *Globe and Mail* after resigning as managing editor. He pointed out that "the *Observer* does not reflect church policy; that the issue in the Middle East defies the one sided judgment reflected in my resignation and finally that there should be room for diversity of opinion on the Middle East." However, Bagnell refused to consider Forrest anti-Jewish: "Unfair, perhaps, but not anti-Semitic"[60] was his summation.

The United Church's failure to silence or dismiss the editor of the *Observer* was a source of ongoing controversy. The Jewish community refused to accept the claim about the independence of the *Observer* and its editorial freedom, since the journal's opening pages declared in large letters, "The *Observer* is the official publication of the United Church and is produced by the Publishing House of the United Church for the membership of the United Church."[61] Despite the fact that the *Observer* had an editorial advisory committee and a board of directors and was responsible to the General Council or its executive or sub-executive, it was independent in editorial policy and administration, claimed the church. "The *Observer* is not a house organ, like say the *IBA News*. The editorial board has complete freedom as do preachers in the United Church," N. Bruce McLeod later wrote.[62] In an editorial entitled "Unofficial: Who Speaks Officially for the United Church? The General Council," Forrest clearly stated the independent role of his magazine: "The Church is flexible and the resolution is not to be taken as law but as a guide ... As far as the *Observer* is concerned we repeat what we have said in the past. We [are] sometimes called even in political documents the 'official church paper.' But it is not an official voice. We try to be loyal to the teachings of the United Church, but sometimes the best way to express our loyalty is to make loud unofficial noises, in the official church paper, about official policies we think should be officially changed."[63]

Douglas Fisher, a regular contributor to the *Observer* before he resigned and went into politics, stated that the *Observer* "has been a forum, not a 'one voice' publication ... The United Church and the *Observer* are not monolithic, not authoritarian [,] not exclusive."[64] Similarly, A.B.B. Moore commented later that the *Observer* "was not a house organ promulgating church propaganda. It was rather a newspaper with its right to publish even though it was critical of the Church that published it ... Those of us in the office of the Council respected that right although there were times when we confronted the Publishing Board and the Editor."[65]

The *Canadian Jewish News*, not independent as the *Observer* was, reflected the interests and position of the Canadian Jewish Congress and the United Jewish Welfare Fund. The editor answered to the board of directors. The *CJN* "serves the community, but not independently," maintained Reuben Slonim.[66] The Jewish community was accustomed to the paper's role as a "house organ," as indeed were the journals of other denominations. It was therefore unable to accept the idea of the *Observer*'s "editorial freedom," regarding it only as an excuse. Thus misunderstanding and suspicion deepened the rupture between the two communities. "I don't think they are all in very good faith," observed Saul Hayes, executive vice-president of the CJC.[67] Lou Ronson of B'nai Brith later suggested that economic considerations had motivated the refusal of church leaders to silence Forrest; the steady income from the *Observer* prevented officials of the church, which had a deficit, from intervening.[68] No source from the time seems to corroborate this argument, though.

In spite of the pressure, Forrest refused to give up his fight. He struggled to clear his name and rehabilitate his reputation. In a "Draft of Proposed Statement on the Middle East," which he prepared on 11 May 1972, he gave his side of the dispute with the Jewish community. He denied accusations that he was anti-Jewish under the shabby disguise of anti-Zionism, that he was unfair to his opponents, and that he was too critical of Israel. He repeated the argument that there were many Jews and even Zionists who supported his criticism of Israel's policy concerning the Palestinian issue. After criticizing Israel for its refusal to comply with UN resolutions, he pointed out that the *Observer* had a balanced policy. It published pro-Israel articles and then letters in rebuttal. After he had been personally harassed and his life threatened, he said, "I have wished I had never heard of the Middle East. Many times I have been tempted to get out of this discussion." Many editors and churchmen "backed away from this discussion and grew quiet." However, because of the churches' failure to speak up during the Nazi era, he found it crucial, on behalf of the churches, to show concern for the sufferings of people in the Middle East. Forrest concluded his long "statement" by criticizing Emil Fackenheim and by defending the principle of editorial freedom.[69] It is not clear whether this statement was ever submitted for publication.

As for Booth's article, even after the apology, Forrest strongly maintained that Booth had written only solid "facts" and that none of the fault-finders had disproved them. Although privately he admitted, "I may be insensitive to certain language Booth used," as to the facts, he was convinced that Booth had depicted the real character of Zionist influence on the media in North America.[70] Slonim, however, confronted Forrest's argument that there was nothing "incorrect or false" in Booth's article. First of all, "accuracy demands not only the facts but the right tone." But "aside from its tone, the Booth piece abounds in inaccuracies ... mistakes, misleading and misinformed statements like faded rosebuds." The most obvious mistake was the statement that Jean-Paul Sartre was a Jew. Slonim enumerated one by one Booth's "egregious mistakes," saying that Forrest, as a skilled editor, "should have checked it for accuracy and judged it for journalistic balance."[71]

During the spring and summer of 1972, the animosity between the two communities did not diminish. The beleaguered Forrest, disappointed at the criticism he was receiving both from the Jewish community and from many members of his own church, sometimes reacted forcefully. In a television interview he was very critical of the Jewish community in Toronto. "I suppose I over-reacted a little bit," he admitted later.[72]

The executive of the General Council could not stand by and remain silent about the position of the United Church in the ongoing debate between the two religious communities. In a statement on 5 May 1972 the executive said that it was "deeply concerned about the indications of a climate of alienation and mistrust between the United Church and a large part of the Jewish community ... We cannot absolve ourselves as a Church from our share in the heavy responsibility for allowing this deterioration of Jewish-Christian brotherhood to take place." But it indicated that the Church would not repudiate Forrest's editorial freedom. The executive disavowed "the allegation that the leadership of the United Church of Canada is, or has been, anti-Jewish."[73]

The Jewish leadership was disappointed at this long-awaited official response from the church after five years of silence concerning the *Observer*'s anti-Israeli policy. The seriousness with which the church addressed the question of antisemitism was welcomed. Indeed, the statement was "clearly meant to open the way to reconciliation," wrote Gunther Plaut in a signed editorial in the *Canadian Jewish News*. However, it "regrettably falls short of what we had hoped it might have said." The statement did not disavow Forrest's editorial practice, particularly Booth's article. "We are disappointed and saddened that the leaders could not find it possible to say 'no' to such dirt." Plaut wondered what the United Church would do about the *Observer*. "Will they persist in letting matters go on as before?"[74]

Although the statement by the executive went only halfway, it was a sign of truce if not of peace. Then came the twenty-fifth General Council in Saskatoon in August 1972, which was later regarded as a slap in the face of the Jewish community. The council urged the Canadian government to cancel a $100 million loan to Israel and invited other denominations to join forces in asking for an interview with the prime minister to discuss Israel's policies. These resolutions had been suggested and backed by Forrest. Indeed, he received a standing ovation from the members of the General Council, who called out that "we love you, Al." Forrest regarded this response as a message of support for his Middle East policy and for the way he had handled the *Observer*'s pro-Palestinian coverage. "I was tremendously cheered, I got a standing ovation. There was no criticism whatsoever of my handling of the Middle East situation and I felt almost unanimous support of my work," he wrote.[75] To J.N. Booth, Forrest indicated that the General Council's action "has been very disconcerting to the Zionist community in Canada who have worked very hard to discredit me and get the church to disavow me."[76]

Forrest was right: the Jewish leaders were disappointed. They had always hoped that he did not represent the United Church at large. Now they learned the hard way, as Gunther Plaut observed, that "despite all disavowals, it was apparent that Forrest did at that point represent the Church."[77] Jews regarded the council's enactment of the resolutions as a definite "yes" to what the *Observer* had written about the Zionists and Israel since 1967. Plaut recommended that the Jewish community concentrate on "more fruitful avenues" and cease wasting time and effort on a sterile dialogue with the United Church.[78]

Yet it is possible that the Jewish community misunderstood the mood of the council. It may not have signalled an agreement with Forrest's views and a backing of his policies but, rather, a warm embrace for a persecuted brother. N. Bruce McLeod stated that outsiders failed to comprehend the "family nature" of the United Church, where, despite disagreements, church members supported Forrest as one of the family who had been under "personal pressures of incredible magnitude" to resign. The delegates to the council were anxious to assure him personally of their love and respect. Those who called for his dismissal "could not have found a more effective way of rallying the whole United Church of Canada behind this able man," said McLeod.[79]

THE BEGINNING OF A NEW ERA

It seems that the General Council of Saskatoon was a turning point in the quarrel between the United Church and the Jewish community. On the one hand, it represented the peak of anti- Israel resolutions and of warm personal support for Forrest. On the other, the election of Bruce McLeod as moderator and George M. Morrison as secretary of the General Council introduced a friendlier atmosphere towards the Jews. McLeod had been a member of a United Church delegation to the Middle East in 1970, and he returned a convert to the Palestinian cause. As such, he became chair of Forrest's pro-Arab Canadians for Middle East Understanding. Therefore Forrest and John Sutton, the chair of the parallel Americans for Middle East Understanding, were pleased at McLeod's election as moderator.[80] At the General Council, McLeod warmly supported Forrest: "We have the best editor of a church paper in Canada and I will back him up any chance I get," he said.[81] McLeod invited David Demson, a critic of Forrest, to lunch and asked him to refrain from attacking the editor.[82] For this action, many Jews regarded him with deep suspicion.

However, after his election McLeod declared that one of his first tasks would be to try to bridge the rift between the two communities. "The building of bridges between the Christians and Jewish communities was one of the priorities that was on my heart," he said a year later.[83] To combat deep-seated Christian antisemitism, he delivered lectures and published articles in which he pointed out that the New Testament encouraged antisemitism and that the Gospels were unfair to the Jews.[84] This ambivalent position on McLeod's part, supporting Forrest, on the one hand, and expressing sympathy to the Jews, on the other, led Jews to question his credibility.[85] But the serious conciliatory efforts he made gradually changed Jewish attitudes towards him. He stressed the importance of "being sensitive" and "listening to the feelings" of the other.[86] In August 1972 McLeod lunched with Plaut at Holy Blossom Temple, and both felt that it was "a great encounter." They therefore agreed to exchange pulpits in future.[87]

After sixteen years of Ernest E. Long's service as the strongman of the United Church, the election of George Morrison as secretary of the General Council also brought a change in the church's attitude to the Jews. "A warm, gentle, outgoing person whose experience and compassion made it impossible for him to endorse the policy on which the Church and the *Observer* had embarked," Plaut recalled of his friendship with Morrison.[88] The appreciation was mutual, as Morrison later recollected: "I know and respect Gunther Plaut deeply, and turned to him early in my term as secretary of the General Council for help and advice and count him a close friend and confidant."[89]

The first sign of McLeod's conciliatory approach came when eleven Israeli athletes were murdered at the Olympic Games in Munich in September 1972. The terrorist attack shocked not only the Canadian Jewish community but Christians as well. The moderator strongly denounced the murder, saying that "it is vital in the interests of the oneness of the human family, for non-Jewish Christians to be quick with unambiguous condemnation of the shameful and inexcusable violence." He hastened to offer the church's hand to its Jewish kin in condemning the strategy of terror.[90] While Forrest also joined McLeod to "condemn utterly such vicious acts," he could not withstand the temptation to criticize Israel, writing, "But we deplore, too, the violence under which the Palestinian refugees are forced to live." He was particularly critical of the Israeli reprisals, which produced "several hundred" Arab victims.[91]

Encouraged by the moderator's approach, Plaut invited him to speak at his temple before some of the Jewish leaders. With McLeod's talk, a new hope for a successful dialogue arose. McLeod returned the invitation, asking Plaut to deliver a sermon at Bloor Street United Church. On a bright Sunday morning in November 1972, the rabbi arrived to a crowded church, accompanied by several carloads of bodyguards. Plaut was "frank without being harsh." He used the opportunity to speak candidly to a Christian audience about Jewish feelings on the debate with the United Church. He argued that the church's refusal to censure Forrest and the *Observer* reflected traditional Christian anti-Jewish teaching. The resolutions of the Saskatoon council, including the appeal to other Christian denominations to ask the Canadian government to cancel the loan to Israel, according to Plaut, constituted "a Christian-Jewish confrontation." He blamed the United Church for setting "the Christian citizens of Canada against its Jewish components." The rabbi wondered about the silence of the churches in 1967. He reviewed Forrest's harsh criticism of the Zionists, arguing that anti-Zionism was a cover for antisemitism. Because of world silence during the Holocaust, "Jews will not listen to any kind of Christian moralizing." Christians had lost their credibility; they could not instruct Jews on how to be moral or how to act in a glorious fashion. The support of the United Church for the Arab cause might solve their own moral dilemma, but that support "clearly help[s] to engender anti-semitism at home." After the sermon, the congregation rose with prolonged applause, quite unusual in the Bloor Street church.[92] McLeod complimented Plaut for his "special combination of graciousness and frankness."The audience had applauded him, not because it agreed with his arguments, but for being there "and sharing himself as a man honestly and forthrightly with us."[93]

Although Gunther Plaut felt after his speech that "we had turned the corner," actually there were no formal relations with the United Church at that point because of the latter's refusal to disavow the Booth article. In a letter to Alan Rose marked "confidential and not for publication in any form," Plaut reviewed the situation at the beginning of November 1972. Despite the Saskatoon ovation, "Forrest is gravely embattled." The United Church leaders could not disavow the article because Forrest had threatened to resign. They considered doing so, nonetheless, because some felt that he was bluffing, and they did try to put so much pressure on him that he would mute his discussion of Middle East. Plaut suggested two preconditions before Jews could enter into any dialogue with the United Church: that it disavow the Booth article and its contents, and that it not implement the resolution of the Saskatoon General Council concerning the $100 million loan. He strongly suggested avoiding any media debate. [94]

According to Plaut's assessment, "Morrison represents a new chapter in the leadership of the Church ... he is serious about his objectives and finds himself at total variance with Forrest."[95] Plaut was right regarding Morrison's seriousness. In January 1973 the secretary of the General Council decided to convene the leaders of the church for a one-day retreat. He turned to Plaut to present the Jewish case. The rabbi recommended Rose, the associate executive director of the Canadian Jewish Congress. "Plaut was a tower of strength in opening up probing leads in the Jewish community, as well as warm trust between us. I sought his guidance in securing a Jewish presence with our Inter-Faith and Inter-Church Committee," recalled Morrison.[96]

"Anxious to comprehend the attitude of the Jewish community to the United Church," the members of the Inter-Church and Inter-Faith Committee listened with great interest to Rose's presentation. For many hours, he spoke with frankness and great passion, emphasizing the importance of the Holocaust and Zionism for an understanding of the feelings of the Canadian Jewish community, whose members were first- or second-generation survivors of persecution. He dealt with Jewish suspicion of Christians in the light of centuries of Christian abuse. He stressed the biblical yearning for Zion and pointed out that, contrary to Forrest's argument, "virtually all Canadian Jews, except for an insignificant fringe group, are committed to the survival and well-being of Israel." Rose went on to discuss with complete frankness the issue of Jewish resentment of Christian accusations. He quoted James Parkes, who had emphasized the need to understand the catastrophic experience of the Jews before launching any criticism of Israel.

As for relations with the United Church, Rose pointed out that since 1967 the *Observer* had "constantly followed a blatantly hostile policy to Israel ... there was neither objectivity nor balance." He discussed Booth's article, which he regarded as "an obscenity," and he criticized the General Council's decision to appeal to other Christian denominations to join it in a delegation to the Canadian government to request the cancellation of the loan to Israel. "Thus, the United Church had embarked on a policy of mobilizing the entire Christian faith against Israel." Rose blamed the one-sided attitude of the General Council, which concentrated only on Israel's sins disregarding Arab terrorism and the treatment of Jews in Syria and the Soviet Union. This focus was what had convinced Jews "that the United Church and the *Observer* are anti-Israel, prejudiced, and not above publishing obscene antisemitic diatribes." He wondered how one could reconcile this practice with the moderator's call for opening a dialogue. Rose stressed the two preconditions for reconciliation: disavowal of the Booth article and the assurance that the Saskatoon resolutions concerning the Middle East would not be implemented. His lecture left a deep impression on the audience. The chair of the committee said that members were "truly overwhelmed and deeply troubled, but much wiser." The discussion continued for more than nine hours. In his report to Jewish organizations, Rose added his observations that, despite the ovation, Forrest was in a difficult position and McLeod and Morrison seriously meant to "cool" the dispute. Rose felt that they were determined to open a conciliatory dialogue with the Jewish community, and he concluded, "I think that my appearance served a useful purpose."[97]

Alan Rose's presentation was a great success, and members of the interfaith committee continued to discuss the subjects he had raised. Morrison commended Rose for "the long term results of a relationship" he had established. The secretary of the General Council expressed his hope that the meeting would lead to "a continuing growth of openness and understanding between the Jewish community and our Church ... We must continue to seek ways and means ... to be constantly more sensitive to the reactions."[98] Morrison thanked Plaut for his recommendation of Rose and was enthusiastic about Rose's lecture. "His person and presentation were of integrity. He shared with us freely and openly and I think he elicited from our members a responding openness and frankness, which I think, bodes very well for improved and deepening relationships between our two communities."[99]

McLeod's talk at Holy Blossom Temple and Plaut's address at Bloor Street United Church were the first steps towards reconciliation. Then came Rose's moving presentation, which helped to warm the chilly atmosphere. McLeod and Morrison were determined to end the debate with the Jewish community, which meant dealing with the two preconditions set by the Jewish leaders. Silencing Forrest was difficult because of the principle of editorial freedom and because of Forrest's threat to resign (although he denied that he intended to do so). And the Jewish demand not to implement the resolutions of the General Council concerning the Middle East presented a dilemma. How could the moderator and the secretary disregard the decisions of the highest court of the United Church? They decided not to push the implementation of the plan concerning the loan to Israel. Since neither the Canadian Council of Churches nor the Catholic bishops were eager to participate in a delegation to the prime minister, they let the subject die. As for disavowing the Booth article, since many leaders of the church regarded the piece as shameful and outrageous, there was a need only for a carefully worded declaration.

The most pressing items in the dialogue with the Jews were now the libel suits with B'nai Brith. Both organizations were eager to end the suits, in order to avoid headlines in the media about prolonged court deliberations. Thus the stage was set for negotiations between the United Church and B'nai Brith. Secret discussions were carried on from February to April 1973 between Bruce McLeod and George Morrison, on the one hand, and Herbert Levy, Canadian executive vice-president of B'nai Brith, and Lou Ronson, district court chief judge and League for Human Rights commissioner of B'nai Brith, on the other. (The LHR had replaced the Anti-Defamation League in 1971.) B'nai Brith closely consulted with the Canadian Jewish Congress.[100] Some leaders of the Canadian Council of Churches offered Gunther Plaut their services as mediators between the two communities. In a meeting held at Holy Blossom Temple, Floyd Honey of the CCC participated, along with officials of the United Church. Forrest complained that he was not invited and was advised not to come.[101]

After months of negotiations, it was agreed that both sides would withdraw their libel suits (Forrest dropped his suit independently of this agreement), and a carefully drafted accord was signed on 4 May 1973 by McLeod and Morrison for the United Church and Sydney Maislin and Herbert Levy for B'nai Brith. "We in the United Church deeply regret and disavow the insensitivity and the inaccuracies contained in an article by John Nicolls Booth in the *United Church Observer.* We of the B'nai Brith deeply regret and repudiate invective as a form of expression and communication," read the main part of the "peace pact," as the agreement was called. The United Church recognized the interest of Canadian Jews in the survival of Israel; it also expressed regret at the "deep wedge of misunderstanding and acrimony" between the two communities and pledged to begin a dialogue of reconciliation. The church went on to declare, "As we in the Church recall the record of the centuries, we acknowledge the church's sorry role in fostering hostility between Christians and Jews." It pledged to pursue a better future of tolerance. Toasts and handshakes concluded the well-publicized ceremony at the offices of B'nai Brith in Toronto.[102]

Jewish leaders welcomed the agreement, which ended a state of uncertainty. Sol Kanee, president of the Canadian Jewish Congress, expressed "great satisfaction with the statement … This welcome development is of the utmost significance to Jewish-Christian relations in Canada."[103] Sydney Maislin, president of B'nai Brith, said that "it is a happy occasion to bury our differences." Bruce McLeod was jubilant; "I am happier than I can express to reach the point of mutual acceptance that we are going to leave our animosities behind," he exclaimed.[104] The editorial in the *Canadian Jewish News* was more reserved. Although it declared that "a new and better era has begun in the relationship of the United Church and the Jewish community," it added that "it now remains for the words of the declaration to be translated into action." Nevertheless, it concluded with an optimistic comment, calling the agreement "an historic event and a good omen for the days to come."[105]

Although all the negotiators should be credited, Lou Ronson appears to have played a major role in the rapprochement. Bruce McLeod appreciated Ronson's "fairness and ... sensitivity to problems George [Morrison] and I were coping with, [he was] instrumental in our making what progress we did." Sol Kanee also deeply appreciated the"extraordinary skill" with which Ronson conducted the negotiations.[106]

Despite the joy that greeted the signing of the "peace pact," it is interesting to see what was missing from the document. Forrest was not mentioned, and he did not take part in the negotiations. There was no suggestion that his writings would be curbed or his editorial freedom restricted. As a matter of fact, no steps were taken to prevent the repetition of a Booth incident, "though the chances of it happening again are relatively remote," said McLeod. Morrison added: "We have trust and confidence in our editorial staff to practice restraint."[107]

Forrest strongly opposed the agreement, which repudiated Booth's article. He was embarrassed by it and thought it a mistake. He had had no part in the negotiations, although he saw the various drafts and commented on them. On 19 April, two weeks before the signing of the statement, Forrest expressed his opposition to it. Since it "pulled the rug from under me," he decided not to be silent but to provide comments on the agreement. Although he did not want to fight the moderator and the secretary, he thought that "this sort of thing is naive and far too much simple a reaction to pressures from the Zionist establishment."[108] According to his aforesaid intention, on the day the pact was signed, he prepared a "statement for the press." Since the *Toronto Star* refused to publish it, Forrest printed it in the *Observer*. The way that the magazine reported on the agreement with B'nai Brith is worth noting. The journal reported that four individuals, not the representatives of two organizations, had signed a personal agreement. The executive of the United Church had held a meeting the same week, yet it was not consulted and not asked to approve the statement. After publishing only part of the short agreement, Forrest added his comments, as if they were a response to questions from reporters. He said that he was glad to learn that B'nai Brith had repudiated invective. As to "inaccuracies" in Booth's article, "if anyone points out inaccuracies ... we will be pleased to make corrections." In regard to "insensitivity" to the

Jews, "it is very difficult to express our sensitivity over the continued sufferings of the Palestine refugees."[109]

Forrest also drafted a long and candid letter to McLeod and Morrison. He maintained that the pact was harmful to the Palestinian cause. It was a mistake to sign an agreement with B'nai Brith, since this group did not represent the Jewish community. He strongly opposed the reference to "inaccuracies" in Booth's article and considered the pact "very unfair" to Booth. He questioned the wisdom of issuing such a statement without mentioning the Palestinian refugee problem; the Arabs and anti-Zionists would conclude that "the United Church had capitulated to pressure from influential persons," at the expense of weak groups that had no influence in Canada. The incorrect impression that he had been involved in the peace pact "seriously undermined" his credibility. Forrest termed the recent crisis "the most depressing incident I have experienced during my years in this office, depressing to me because ... I was deceived." He concluded his letter with an invitation to clarify the misunderstandings; indeed, instead of mailing the letter, he discussed its contents personally with McLeod and Morrison.[110] It seems that Forrest accepted the advice of his lawyer to refrain from taking a harsh position, but a year later he changed his mind and had a "guilty conscience about not slapping back hard" at the moderator and the secretary.[111]

The pact with B'nai Brith also met opposition in certain United Church circles. Frank Brisbin of the division of communication, who had criticized Forrest for the publication of the Booth article, objected to the wording of the agreement, since it failed to mention the constant virulent attacks on Forrest by Jewish groups, which, in his opinion, amounted to "organized character assassination." The pact could be interpreted as the repudiation not only of the Booth article but also of the editor. As well, Brisbin questioned whether the moderator and the secretary could speak as individuals without carrying the weight of their offices.[112] Clarke MacDonald also criticized the personal nature of the agreement, which disregarded the executive of the General Council, in session at the time of the agreement's release. He further complained about the omission of any discussion of the Palestinian problem and of the deep concern on the part of the United Church for human rights in the Middle East.[113]

While these criticisms of the pact were private, the attack by Hugh McCullum was public. McCullum, the editor of the Anglican *Canadian Churchman* and a friend of Forrest, criticized the United Church leaders in a signed editorial in the *Churchman*. He accused McLeod and Morrison of giving in to Jewish pressure. For the price of reconciliation, they had allowed the Jews to interpret the agreement as if the

United Church had repudiated Forrest and his fight for the Palestinian refugees. But "Al Forrest is not going to stop his campaign, nor is he going to quit his job."McCullum maintained that giving up freedom of the press was too high a price for reconciliation with the Jews. "When church leaders, no matter how well motivated, diminish that freedom we believe they diminish the freedom of Christian people to know what is being done, said and thought."[114]

As Forrest predicted, Arabs regarded the agreement as capitulation by the United Church to the Jews. "United Church Surrenders to Zionism," read the headline in the *Toronto Star,* printing the response of Faoluzu Gassan, president of the Arab Palestine Association. The Palestinian community in Toronto was "shocked and dismayed" by the agreement. Gassan accused the church of surrendering its moral stand for justice and peace in the face of Zionist pressure and of following a regressive path, preferring a policy of "retreat to that of truth, cowardice to that of courage, moral turpitude to that of integrity."[115] John Booth also protested to McLeod about the repudiation of his article. He complained that the accusation of "inaccuracies" and "insensitivity" discredited his scholarship. "I am appalled by your breach of decency and fair play," he wrote to McLeod. Booth, who was "thunderstruck" by the peace pact, appealed to Forrest to issue a disavowal of the agreement, but Forrest refused to do so.[116]

Although he was hurt by the agreement, Forrest wanted to show that he would not capitulate. He made it clear that he had no intention either of backing off from publicizing the plight of the Palestinian refugees or of allowing the *Observer* to be silenced. "Anyone who thinks that the United Church is going to muzzle their editor does not know the United Church, and if anyone thinks that I will ban comment on the Palestinian problem he does not know me."[117] To Booth he promised "to hit hard again on the Palestinian thing, probably with materials from Israel Shahak." Evaluating the reaction from the street, he concluded that "we did not lose anything on this."[118]

Despite these strong declarations, the pressure eventually bore results. Forrest agreed, though reluctantly, to reduce coverage of the Israeli-Palestinian crisis, although not to change its content. In a lecture to the Christian Congregation of Mississauga, Ontario, he took "an extremely low-key, soft-sell approach ... For someone with Forrest's record and background it was surprisingly mild and innocuous almost ... a 'Zionist speech,'" reported Ben Kayfetz.[119] The number of items in the *Observer* dealing with the Middle East decreased, while the articles on Canadian politics increased. Forrest was more cautious in his criticism, although he did not change his basic position. "After our agreement with B'nai Brith officials, there was a softening of Al

Forrest's rigid stances toward Israel," recalled George Morrison. In April 1973, when Booth offered to publish another article in the *Observer*, Forrest diplomatically refused it.[120]

The Jewish community tried to learn from the bitter quarrel with the United Church by imposing some discipline over public speeches and writings. Neither the church nor the name of Forrest was mentioned. This strategy helped to create a better atmosphere for interfaith dialogue. As well, the Canadian Jewish Congress entered into a dialogue with the Canadian Council of Churches.[121] Another outcome of the heated debate over the Booth article and the libel suits was increased supervision of the *Observer*. Although editorial freedom was still honoured, the newly founded board of directors of the magazine, chaired by Angus MacQueen, kept a watchful eye over its editorial policy.[122]

Thus the most trying period in relations between the United Church and the Canadian Jewish community reached a stage of armistice, though not of peace. There would be occasional flare-ups from Forrest and the *Observer*, but what was probably the worst phase was over. In May 1973 the *Canadian Jewish News* predicted "a new and better era" in relations between the Jewish and United Church communities; the next chapter will examine whether this forecast came true.[123]

10 The Truce, 1973–1993

After the agreement with B'nai Brith in May 1973, a truce was reached between the United Church and the Canadian Jewish community. Each side made great efforts to cool the atmosphere and initiate dialogue. However, the church made no official commitment to curb the editorial freedom of the *Observer.* Forrest, a proud fighter, was deeply hurt by criticism from colleagues in his own church, and he was determined to show that he would not yield to the "Zionists," Jewish or Christian. Therefore he continued, though less frequently, to publish material on the Arab-Israeli crisis, with his usual anti-Israeli tone. The Jewish community regularly refuted his criticism, and the moderately tranquil atmosphere was repeatedly disrupted. Thus while, after May 1973, the quarrel between the United Church and the Jewish community had apparently ended, the debate between the Jewish community and Forrest continued, though at a slower pace and with fewer irruptions.

In the May issue of the *Observer* a letter appeared from a reader who was concerned with the "Zionization of Jerusalem," which he felt threatened the presence of Christians in the Holy Land. He suggested to the editor that this matter of special concern to Christians be brought to the attention of the Canadian public.[1] In this issue, Forrest did not confine himself to printing others' articles or letters to the editor. He also contributed a piece of his own, in which he reported on a nineteen-day tour that he had just taken to the Middle East. He depicted the miserable living conditions of the Arabs, which existed even while the West had been sending Phantom jets to their enemies.

"When you travel you learn something about the deprivation and injustice that have brought terrorism into being," wrote Forrest in justification of Palestinian terrorist acts against civilians.[2]

There was nothing new in this article, except the fact that it appeared only a week after the signing of the peace pact between the United Church and B'nai Brith. The *Canadian Jewish News* commended that "trouble has again developed," and it interviewed the signatories of the pact as to whether the *Observer*'s article represented a breach of the agreement. George Morrison maintained that "we didn't say we would no longer be critical of one another's communities. In no way are we going to stifle justifiable criticism." Bruce McLeod also argued that just because of the agreement, "we are not going to start a completely passive approach to one another." Differences would continue, but they should be solved by mutual understanding. Even Herbert Levy of B'nai Brith held the opinion that the article did not violate the agreement. Other B'nai Brith leaders were less sure,[3] and Jewish leaders were worried about the spread of Forrest's influence. Alan Rose complained to Morrison about the fact that Forrest's writings had been quoted in neo-Nazi papers, including the notorious *Deutsche National Zeitung* and the fascist *Western Guard*.[4]

A full-page advertisement that appeared in the March 1974 issue of the *Observer* again put Forrest and his magazine in the middle of a storm of angry protests. The ad, by G.J. Salter of Haliburn, Ontario, was entitled "He as God Sitteth in the Temple of God." It contained pseudo-biblical revelation and apocalyptic prophecy with a heavy and coarse admixture of crudely expressed hate propaganda directed against the Jews, Israel, the Catholic Church, and the organized Protestant churches. In fact, it covered a fairly wide spectrum of hatred. The ad referred to the old antisemitic theory of a global Jewish conspiracy that ruled the world through money and power. The Jew "has now given her power unto the beast (Europe ruled by Judah) by joining the European Common Market."[5] The ad represented the fundamentalist antisemitic beliefs of the British Israelite Federation. These ideas infuriated not only Jews and Catholics but also members of the United Church, because they contradicted the principles of liberalism, modernism, and the social gospel. In fact, it was surprising that Forrest, with his generally liberal views, would allow the ad into his magazine.

The same advertisement had appeared at the time of the Yom Kippur War in a number of Canadian dailies – in London, Ontario, in Vancouver, and in other places. Most papers later apologized, orally or in print, explaining that their editors had not noticed the inflammatory language. In an inter-office letter, Ben Kayfetz commented that "it's incredible that it was accepted in the United Church *Observer* – as it's not only vulgarly anti-Semitic but anti-Catholic (and anti-Protestant) in the crudest possible manner and tone."[6]

Forrest received a huge number of letters. "How could such a scandalous thing appear in our magazine? What standards are used to judge what is fit to print?" asked Ian M. Hablane, a reader of the *Observer*. "It's all there, classic rabid anti-Semitism … Mr. Morrison, please … enough! What must we do to stop this?" asked Dolores Nicholls.[7] The *Globe and Mail's* editorial reprimanded the *Observer*: "The *United Church Observer* recently published an ad … which any publisher with a proper sense of taste would have rejected immediately. Unfortunately, the *Observer* has not had such a sense of taste for a long time."[8]

Out of the many letters that it received, the *Observer* in its May issue carried seven which strongly criticized the policy of the magazine. Two of these were from principals of United Church theological colleges. William O. Fennell, of Emmanuel College in Toronto, wrote that in the past he had tried to defend the magazine. "No defence of this advertisement is possible. It is theologically irresponsible. It is anti-Semitic. It is anti-ecumenical." C.H. Parker, acting principal of Queen's Theological College in Kingston, Ontario, wrote in the same vein. As a firm supporter of the *Observer*, he was dismayed to find an ad that was "an invitation to join in the worst kind of anti-Semitism."[9]

Given with such a unanimous outcry, Jewish organizations avoided public criticism, leaving that to others; but privately they protested to United Church leaders. J.C. Horwitz, chair of the National Joint Community Relations Committee of the Canadian Jewish Congress, wrote to N. Bruce McLeod, and Alan Rose appealed to George Morrison. McLeod replied to Horwitz that he was "personally embarrassed and distressed" by the ad. He conveyed Forrest's explanations of how and why it happened, and quoted the apology that the editor would include in the upcoming issue of the magazine. "Through you may I apologize to members of the Jewish community for this unfortunate and unintentional offense," concluded the moderator.[10]

Morrison, in his reply to Rose, quoted a resolution of the Montreal Presbytery, which stated that such an ad in the *Observer* "cannot but raise questions as to the objectivity vis-a-vis the Jewish faith," and that even from a Christian point of view, "such a distortion of scripture should not appear in an organ purporting to be the official organ of the UCC." Therefore the presbytery went "on record as taking strong exception to the printing of such an ad in the pages of the *United Church Observer*." Morrison added that "this reflects the feeling of our Church, generally." Indeed, fifteen presbyteries adopted this kind of resolution.[11] Because of these almost unanimous critical reactions, the Salter ad appears not to have caused a rupture between the two communities.

However, relations between the Jewish community and Forrest worsened. Reaction to the ad was so extensive that he became convinced that it was the outcome of a "well-organized campaign." In the May issue of the *Observer*, he apologized, admitting that he was "taken off guard" by the strong reaction to the ad. He had not considered the British Israelites to be antisemitic, and he did not take them seriously. Since the ad had already been printed in several Canadian papers, Forrest had considered it "a harmless expression … with which we didn't agree." The magazine frequently published opinions with which it disagreed; however, "we confess we didn't read it carefully, or we would have rejected it on the grounds of taste." He stated that he had checked with Salter, who denied being antisemitic. Forrest also apologized to readers who found Salter's biblical interpretations racist or anti-Catholic. But he dismissed the fears of those who considered the ad anti-ecumenical or not in conformity with United Church theology; he felt that such heresies were not damaging to the church.[12] The advertising manager, J.D. Wells, wrote in a private communication that the magazine opposed censorship: "There is less danger to the church members from freedom than from censorship."[13]

While Jewish leaders were prepared to understand the editor's oversight in not reading the advertisement carefully, Forrest's written apology infuriated them. J.C. Horwitz, in the name of the Canadian Jewish Congress, described the apology as "inadequate and most unsatisfactory." Forrest said that he should have rejected the ad "on the grounds of taste," but how could he refer to the strong antisemitic views of the advertisement as a matter of "taste"? "The editor treated this rather casually. We are sorry," commented Horwitz. Furthermore, Forrest had written to the author of a bigoted, antisemitic item to ask him if he were an antisemite and had glibly accepted his denial. "Such trusting naivete on the part of a man who parades as a sophisticated, prodding, hard-nosed journalist is nothing less than laughable, if not malicious," wrote Horwitz. Forrest's argument that, since several daily newspapers had printed the ad, it could not be harmful was unacceptable to Horwitz. A religious paper should have different criteria and policies than the dailies.[14]

McLeod agreed with Horwitz's criticism: the ad was "indefensible." He wished that the editorial had ended after its first paragraph, and he told Horwitz that he had said so to Forrest. "All of us regret immeasurably the appearance of the advertisement." He concluded with the hope that such a "regrettable mistake" would not do any harm to current positive interfaith relations.[15]

Did Forrest learn from this blunder? Was his apology serious? The magazine's subsequent issue gave at least a partial answer to these questions. In June 1974 the *Observer* featured an interview with Don Andrews, the leader of the neo-Nazi Western Guard Party. It was written by Nils Johanson, who added an analysis of the racist and antisemitic character of the Western Guard. In their introductory comments, the editors expressed their unanimous opposition to Andrews's opinions. However, they wrote, the interview had been published because church members deserved to be acquainted with the ideas of other groups and to know how they justified their deeds in the name of God and Christianity.[16]

Roland de Corneille, who was a critic of Forrest and of the *Observer*, praised the magazine's criticism of racism and antisemitism in its introduction to the Andrews interview. "This, in my opinion, is the first evidence of a very clear and practical stand by the *Observer* against at least some form of anti-Semitism. There is nothing ambiguous about this article." De Corneille wrote confidentially to Jewish leaders that he believed that the strong protest by Horwitz to McLeod, as well as the criticism from inside the church by prominent leaders and presbyteries, was what had motivated the apology in the May issue of the *Observer*. He felt that the printing of the Andrews interview, too, was a response to widespread displeasure with the Salter ad, and that the June article should be regarded as "a real genuine form of apology for the Salter advertisement which is more meaningful than had there been an unambiguous and well-worded apology in the May issue." De Corneille saw the Andrews article as "a new plateau of communication and understanding" in the efforts of the Jewish and Christian communities towards rapprochement since the Booth article. Although there was no change in the *Observer*'s attitude to Israel, he stated that "communication is improving."[17]

Was de Corneille's optimism justified, or was it premature? In Forrest's attitude towards Israel there was no improvement. In a speech in Ottawa he declared, "Zionists repeat, repeat and repeat lies."[18] In the June 1974 issue of the *Observer*, a reader wrote to the "Question Box," suggesting that other readers remember that God had promised Israel the land of Canaan. Therefore, she suggested, when discussing the Arab-Israeli conflict, people should keep in mind that "by divine law that land belongs to Israel." Responding to the question, the editor selected an answer given by Christian theologians and scholars, which rejected the idea of a chosen people. God was no respector of persons, and he had made all nations dwell together.[19]

Towards the end of 1974 the recognition of the Palestine Liberation Organization became a widespread subject of debate. The UN General

Assembly passed a resolution that recognized the PLO as a legitimate claimant to the territory of Israel. A group of theologians and scholars of religious studies reacted with a letter which they published on 9 December 1974. They declared that the UN resolution was "illegal, null and void and a threat to peace." The letter was composed by Alan Davies and signed by twelve scholars. Among the signatories were Terry Anderson, Gregory Baum, David Demson, and William Fennell. They affirmed their solidarity with the people of Israel, repented of past Christian indifference to the suffering of the Jews, including during the Holocaust, and rejected missionary attempts to convert Jews. They wrote that "the maintenance in the land of Israel of the Jewish people and their faith is an integral part of their witness to the one God, and therefore also a proper matter of Christian concern," and they called upon Canadian churches "to uphold the security and integrity of the state of Israel" and to continue to reject PLO claims to Israel's territory.

The signatories to the letter also recognized "the justice of the claim of the Palestinian Arabs to their own form of statehood," and they urged Israel to negotiate with the Arabs concerning the implementation of UN Resolution 242. Accordingly, they supported Canadian recognition of an "eventual Palestinian state," which would be the outcome of the implementation of that resolution. The signatories declared that "Christians have no specific interest in the form which the future of Jerusalem should take," as long as freedom of access for pilgrims and worshippers was secured. Finally, they called upon members of the Canadian churches to work towards the implementation of these principles.[20]

In a speech at the University of Windsor in March 1975, Forrest reacted. In response to the call by the theologians "to uphold the security and integrity of Israel," he asked, "How can I uphold a racist state? Israel doesn't need to have integrity upheld; it needs an injection of integrity." Despite his strong words, the constant opposition of the pro-Israeli ministers and scholars troubled him. "I felt a sense of frustration that I had been betrayed in part by my church, by the media and by my government," he confessed to a sympathetic audience, which had been organized by the Canadian Arab Federation of the University of Windsor.[21]

In the spring and summer of 1975 Forrest seems to have reached a breaking point. During the controversy over the Booth article and the B'nai Brith libel suit, he had been in a fighting mood, but by 1975 he felt tired and betrayed by his friends and his church. He reached the stage where he did not want to be identified solely as a Middle East expert. When Israel Shahak sent him some anti-Israeli material to publish, he refused. He wrote candidly to John Booth: "My problem here is not to become a bore or a one-issue person and I have repeatedly identified with this issue and nearly every time I am asked to do anything on TV it's on the Middle East. So, I've done more calculating in my timing and the use of my pages on the issue."[22] Forrest also planned to write a book on the Middle East, which would be different from his *Unholy Land*. It would not be controversial, but would depict the modern Arab world in a positive manner.[23]

Yet Forrest did not give up the fight for the Arab cause. Instead, he concentrated on certain issues, such as recognition of the PLO. From August 1975 on, the *Observer* repeatedly called for its recognition as the legitimate representative of the Palestinians in the Geneva peace conference. Following the resolutions of the World Council of Churches in June 1975 and the Antiochian Orthodox Church in the United States, Forrest demanded that the PLO be invited to the peace conference, since the Palestinians "have no other organization." He blamed an "imbalanced press, uninformed politicians, naive clergy," and irresponsible acts by a minority of Palestinians for distorting the image of the PLO into a "wild-eyed terrorist" organization.[24]

When, in the summer of 1975, Prime Minister Trudeau refused to allow PLO representatives to participate in a conference of a UN agency in Canada, Forrest editorialized: "Let's welcome the PLO." He refuted the "distorted" view that the organization was a terrorist group, but he admitted that "some Palestinians are terrorists. Some of the organizations under the PLO umbrella have committed terrorist acts and others applauded terrorist acts ... We reject violence and condemn it." However, the PLO represented the great majority of the Palestinians, and therefore the dismissal of their representatives by Canada "would look ridiculous in the eyes of the world."[25]

Many remained unconvinced by Forrest's argument that the PLO was not a terrorist group. The October issue of the *Observer* carried three letters criticizing the editorial that had welcomed the organization. "Surely their record of cold-blooded murders, hijacking and assassinations speaks for itself," wrote L. Karagianis. L.W. Lindsay complained of the "double standard" of the United Church in regard to killing: "it is permissible to kill innocent people, but not murderers," such as the PLO. Robert Campbell hoped that "this band of murderers is not the representative of the Palestinian people." He declared his opposition to terrorism, whether carried out by a small group or a large one.[26]

Forrest continued to demonstrate his anti-Israeli bias. In January 1976, while visiting Israel, he became sick. True to his political views, he preferred to be treated in the St Joseph Hospital in Old Jerusalem, rather than in the more modern Hadassah.[27] When *Time* magazine revealed that Israel had nearly used atomic bombs during the Yom Kippur War, he rushed to editorialize: "Why Doesn't Somebody Scream?" He urged church leaders, who he felt should be responsible for creating public opinion, "not [to] ignore the *Time* revelation and what it means" because the Middle East "is moving inexorably towards Armageddon."[28]

Forrest's eagerness to publish anti-Israeli material sometimes flew in face of journalistic principles. In October 1976 he published an editorial relying on Israel Shahak, the extreme critic of Israel. Shahak had submitted an article from the Israeli newspaper *Maa'riv*, reporting that an immigrant to Israel from Yugoslavia had not been allowed to join an Israeli soccer team because he could not prove that his mother was Jewish. Forrest regarded this incident as racism, commenting that "in South Africa you call it apartheid."[29] Upon investigation, however, it came out that the Yugoslav soccer player had neither an immigration certificate nor a visa, and it was on these grounds that the Ministry of Interior had not allowed him to join the team. When Forrest was confronted with these facts, he admitted that he had not seen the Israeli newspaper; nor would he have been able to understand it, since it was in Hebrew. He had simply not bothered to get any confirmation of the story. Thus he had compromised editorial ethics in order to publish an anti-Israeli item. David Demson was furious; he wrote to Angus MacQueen "to ascertain why the editor thought he could employ direct quotation in his editorial from an article he had himself never read or verified."[30]

This was not the only time that Forrest was criticized for editorial abuse. In November 1977, *Massada*, the Zionist student publication in Toronto, reprinted an article by R. Emmett Tyrrell Jr from *Harpers* magazine entitled "Chimera in the Middle East." The piece discussed the history of the Jewish-Arab confrontation, using harsh and insulting words about Arabs and Muslims.[31] Forrest attacked the diatribe, quoting the derogatory phrases. He emphasized the fact that a Zionist publication, whose editorial adviser was Emil Fackenheim, had disseminated it. "The circulation of these vicious lies is a disgrace to a civilized community concerned with dispelling racism and religious bigotry … How ironic it is then, to find Zionists circulating this."[32]

Jewish leaders were upset by the *Observer* article. Lou Ronson complained that the article was "artfully pieced together to create the impression that a Jewish publication is engaging in the practice of disseminating hate propaganda." Nowhere in Forrest's editorial did he mention that a non-Jewish author in a non-Jewish magazine, *Harpers*, had written the original article. Rabbi Jordan Pearlson was even more critical. He complained to Clarke MacDonald, "Al's distortive use of quotations out of context ... is a classic case of editorial abuse." He called Forrest's habit of turning everything against the Zionists "a pathological element." MacDonald responded in a noncommittal manner.[33]

The publication in 1977 of Reuben Slonim's *Family Quarrel: The United Church and the Jews* was a sign that a crucial phase in the debate between the United Church and the Jewish community was over and time was ripe for reconciliation. Slonim attempted to discuss the quarrel between the two communities in an unbiased manner, aiming at reconciliation between the United Church and the Canadian Jewish community. Furthermore, he wished to improve relations between Christians and Jews generally. He analyzed various aspects of the bitterness, beginning with the centuries of Christian anti-Jewish persecution, which had caused deep Jewish suspicion, and continuing up to the conflicts about the Palestinian refugees, mainly since the war of 1967. Slonim not only treated the immediate causes of the conflict between the two communities, but also provided insight into the history of the Jewish people and into their psyche. Trying to be non-partisan, he criticized both sides, which awakened resentment in both. The Jews did not like his labelling of them as weak, insecure, and over-sensitive. The United Church leaders were uneasy with his description of their insensitivity to Jewish devotion to the State of Israel, particularly after Auschwitz. Answering the question "Will the United Church and the Jewish community ever find an accommodation?" he concluded that "feeling and emotion, combined with a lack of awareness of the facts, keep the United Church and the Jews apart. Reason says we must get together."[34]

Slonim's unusual book – a rabbi preaching morality to Christians – received thoughtful responses from some Christians. Angus J. MacQueen wrote a book review in which he called the book "impartial, with careful documentation and temperate language ... It is a good book, well written and objective." He could not agree with Slonim that whenever the church expressed its concern for the Palestinians, it should at the same time assert its support for Israel's survival. Also, he felt that Slonim was ambivalent about the editorial freedom of the *Observer*: "I wish he were as committed to freedom of speech and the press as he is to amicability and peace within the 'family,'" said MacQueen. But he hoped that in the long run the book would create better understanding between Jews and Christians.[35]

Hugh McCullum, reviewing Slonim's book in the *Observer*, was more critical. He complimented Slonim for his "fascinating, thorough, courageous, if sometimes insensitive," fair, and well-written book. He did not like Slonim's tone, however, which he said "verges on patronizing, as the non-Jewish reader is lectured on his inability really to understand." Slonim had criticized the *Observer* for being insensitive and for failing to understand, but McCullum charged that Slonim "show[ed] a similar lack on occasion." His major criticism, like MacQueen's, was of Slonim's failure to take the idea of freedom of the press seriously. "Freedom of press is not a highlight of this book," commented McCullum.[36]

In a review for the *Globe and Mail*, Kenneth Bagnell also praised Slonim's fair and balanced treatment of the subject in general and of Forrest in particular. He criticized Slonim for not interviewing two major Jewish participants in the debate, Gunther Plaut and Stuart Rosenberg. Because of this oversight, the book failed to depict the deep emotions that had swept the Toronto synagogues during the controversy. Bagnell wondered whether Slonim's attempt to bring about reconciliation between the two communities was too ambitious. According to Bagnell, "there is a chasm so wide that the deepest compassion may never bridge it."[37] Ken Adachi, the *Toronto Star* book editor, also found fault with the book's "air of a finger-waving school-masterly lecture to two groups of wayward children." The book was "pertinent and thoughtful," but its weakest feature was Slonim's aim of reconciliation. "His hopes for a gentle amelioration and his trust in the future in open-hearted dialogue bypass the lacerating memories," maintained Adachi.[38]

One may deduce from these reviews that in 1977 reconciliation was more wishful thinking than fact. Indeed, in 1977–78 Forrest energetically resumed his activities on behalf of the Palestinians, successfully dragging the United Church along with him.[39] To the very end, he maintained his pro-Palestinian stance. His reaction to the Camp David Accord in November 1978, a breakthrough on the road to peace between Egypt and Israel, was characteristic. While the world press printed the now famous photograph of the smiling Anwar Sadat, Menachem Begin, and Jimmy Carter shaking hands, the *Observer* published a picture of two hungry-looking Palestinian children. While the world press praised Begin's courage and statesmanship in signing a peace agreement with Egypt, Forrest called the Israeli prime minister "a tough, one-time terrorist."[40]

In August 1977 he succeeded in having a resolution passed by the General Council stating that the PLO should represent the Palestinians at the Geneva peace conference.[41] However, the assembly refused to back his candidacy for moderator. In later years, Angus MacQueen reflected that Forrest lost because the commissioners thought "that his election to the highest office in the United Church would be an act of hostility, or defiance, towards the Jewish community." Alan Davies added that "not everyone liked Forrest personally or trusted him as a spokesman for the Church." According to MacQueen, Forrest took his defeat very hard: "He felt that his own Church had rejected and disowned him."[42] MacQueen wondered whether Forrest's failure to be elected contributed to his death in December 1978.[43] Sixteen months had passed since the election, so perhaps there was no direct link. Nevertheless, Forrest was deeply disappointed at the rejection by his friends and by members of his own church, and complained about it repeatedly.

Ever since the negotiations with B'nai Brith in 1973, Forrest had been regarded by certain leaders and members of the United Church as a burden, rather than an asset, and as an obstacle to the improvement of relations with the Jewish community. However, his funeral service at St Andrew's Church on Bloor Street in Toronto was a demonstration of love and affection for his personal charm and integrity and a testimony to his courage. The church was packed with editors, friends, and admirers. The *United Church Yearbook* described Forrest as the "most widely known and influential churchman."[44] N. Bruce McLeod later recalled that "he was greatly loved and respected, though not always agreed with." Because of his knowledge and conviction, continued McLeod, Forrest "greatly influenced the United Church position on the Middle East."[45] While he gained wide media coverage, other opinions in the United Church had failed to receive headlines. Forrest had proved how a single person with knowledge and determination could bypass the main courts and make his own opinion represent the policies of the entire church.

Many Jews believed that Forrest was the sole reason for the quarrel with the United Church. Had he been more moderate in his anti-Israel criticism, the debate might have been avoided. "That is a misleading assumption," claimed Slonim. "Forrest did help to precipitate the quarrel and gave it shape … But the quarrel was not only of Forrest's making; the seeds of dissension between the two communities existed from the founding of the United Church in 1925." While Jewish groups maintained open and cordial communication with Catholics, Anglicans, and the Canadian Council of Churches, "the gap to be spanned with the United Church itself remains as wide as ever," Slonim wrote in 1976.[46] Gunther Plaut also maintained that, years after Forrest's death, Jewish relations with the United Church remained unresolved. Warm contact with the church leadership was missing, though "friendliness and civility" prevailed. Plaut was particularly sorry that the controversy with Forrest was transferred to personal enmity, which he was never able to repair, and he wondered whether a less vigorous Jewish response would have changed the tone of the debate.

"Perhaps it was good that it had aired, for with it were aired many feelings that ran below the surface; it was a time for catharsis for all of us."[47]

After the death of A.C. Forrest, a definite effort was made by both the United Church and the Jewish community to improve relations. One of the expressions of this endeavour was interfaith dialogue. On the initiative of the World Council of Churches, the Inter-Church and Inter-Faith Committee of the United Church met in 1982 at Holy Blossom Temple to discuss guidelines for a Christian-Jewish theological dialogue. "This ought to be the beginning of a most intense and rewarding theological reflection of United Church people on our historical and contemporary relationships with the Jewish community," reported the *United Church Yearbook*. John H. Berthrong, secretary of the Inter-Faith Dialogue Committee, felt that "we are entering a new and hopeful era of Christian-Jewish dialogue."[48] As a symbolic gesture of friendliness, the moderator invited the officers of the Canadian Jewish Congress to the induction ceremony for the United Church General Council in 1984. This was the first time that representatives of the Jewish faith had been invited to participate and speak at such a ceremony.[49]

These efforts notwithstanding, the pro-Arab policy of former decades prevailed, although Israel's right to exist was always mentioned. When Israel invaded Lebanon in June 1982, the United Church issued a statement that supported the "rights of the Palestinians to a homeland," a step just short of recognition of a Palestinian independent state.[50] In January 1983 Berthrong reported, "All of us in the United Church felt that we must find a more effective way to deal" with questions of Middle East policy.[51] However, the disbanding of the Committee on the Church and International Affairs in 1984 and the meaningful involvement of the Canadian Council of Churches in Middle East affairs led the United Church to adopt the CCC's statements and resolutions and not to initiate independent policy.

The *United Church Observer* went through a metamorphosis after Forrest's death. Under the editorship of Hugh McCullum (1979–92), a friend of his, the Middle East almost totally disappeared from the pages of the magazine. In June 1982, Jerusalem was treated in a balanced way.[52] Ten years later, in August 1992, the General Council requested that "the content of the magazine be a balance of the pastoral and the prophetic."[53] To carry out this new policy, a new editor, Muriel Duncan, was chosen; she introduced more direct religious content into the *Observer*. Even subjects such as events in the Philippines,

Russia, and South Africa were linked to faith and religion.In October 1993, when Israeli prime minister Yitzhak Rabin shook hands with Yasser Arafat in the presence of President Bill Clinton, the *Observer* printed a photograph of the event, a graphic contrast with its failure to include a similar image in 1978.[54] The pictures of refugee children and elders disappeared from the pages of the *Observer*, another drastic change from Forrest's editorship. The magazine's retreat from the Palestinian question did not harm its journalistic distinction; it may even have added to it. In 1992, in a competition sponsored by the Canadian Church Presses and the Association of Church Presses, the *Observer* won twelve awards for general excellence and was named "the best magazine in the general interest."[55]

In December 1987, with the beginning of the Intifada, Christian attitudes to Israel underwent a meaningful change. Gregory Baum, who had supported Israel and criticized Howse, Forrest, and their followers for their attacks on its policy, changed his mind. He spoke of the Christian dilemma of being involved in dialogue with Jews and strongly opposing antisemitism, on the one hand, and supporting the struggle for the self-determination of oppressed people, including the Palestinians, on the other. But many church members, fearing accusations of antisemitism, refused to publicly criticize Israel's human rights violations in the occupied territories. At this time, however, Jews, both in Israel and in North America also began to criticize the Israeli government for its suppression of the civilian uprising. Thus Christians were able to resolve their dilemma: "Christians are now free to speak out because Jews publicly criticize the State of Israel," declared Baum.[56]

The Intifada and Baum's new position coincided with growing criticism of Israel's civil rights policy by various circles in the United Church, as well as in the Anglican Church and the ccc. In July 1988 N. Bruce McLeod called upon Israel to engage in self-examination. Aware that since he was a Christian, his criticism of Israel might be misunderstood, he concluded, "While some criticism of Israel emerges from darker motives, mine is a cry of pain for what Israel was meant to be."[57]

This new critical attitude to Israel in the 1990s was apparent at the Toronto Regional Conference of the United Church, one of the church's largest church conferences. At its annual meeting on 30 May 1993, the conference adopted a resolution critical of Israel's "gross violations of basic human rights" in the West Bank and Gaza. If Israel disregarded the Geneva Convention with regard to human rights, the Canadian government should turn to the un to send "protecting power" to defend the Palestinian people in the occupied territories.

The conference stated that there was wide international consensus that Israel's practices constituted a "major block to peace." The motion was adopted in spite of warnings from several delegates that it might upset ongoing Christian-Jewish dialogue.[58]

The Toronto Regional Conference's resolution was "disappointing but not surprising" to the members of the Canada-Israel Committee. It was "consistent with the one-sided, unbalanced and excessively judgmental statements made in recent years by the United Church," read a CIC inter-office memo.[59] The Canadian Jewish Congress also protested, saying that the "grossly unbalanced resolution contains a shameful denunciation of Israel." The congress, "shocked and saddened" by the anti-Israel resolution, pointed out that the Toronto Conference should also denounce Arab terrorism.[60] Even fifteen years after Forrest's death, the United Church maintained the unbalanced approach to the Arab-Israeli conflict that it had begun to show in the mid-1950s; nothing fundamental had changed.

While still critical of Israel, the United Church progressed in its attitude to Jews and Judaism, however. In 1997 a report entitled *Bearing Faithful Witness: United Church–Jewish Relations Today* was sent by the General Council to the churches for comments. It aimed to mend fences with Jews. The document proposed "guidelines for the relationship with Jews and Judaism and for the related interpretation of Scripture within the United Church." After examining various anti-Jewish passages in the New Testament, the study concluded that they were "argumentative and often present a skewed picture of Judaism." It therefore recommended that congregations "adjust the picture of Judaism that they present with information from the Hebrew Scriptures" and from other contemporary sources: "It clears away potential use of disrespect." In the guidelines for the use of the Scriptures the study indicated emphatically, "We must always be ready to revise our understanding of the Palestinian context ... in which Jews lived."[61]

The study also recommended that the church stop trying to convert Jews to Christianity, stop interpreting the Scriptures in a way that would lead to anti-Jewish feelings, and depart from the belief that Christianity had replaced Judaism. "Christianity does not supersede Judaism," declared Bill Phipps, the moderator of the United Church. He pointed out that the document did not compromise the Christian faith, but rather, it abandoned the effort to criticize other faiths and cast aspersions on other traditions. He said that the most important aspect of the document was making congregations aware of the fact that anti-Jewish teachings could be found in most worship services.[62]

The Canadian Jewish community hailed the report as a major breakthrough in relations between the two communities. "I think it deserves the highest accolades," observed Rabbi Reuven Bulka, chair of the Religious and Interreligious Affairs Committee of the Canadian Jewish Congress.[63] It was a genuine effort to reach out to the Jews; this new trend of mutual understanding was promising.

Although these last chapters have focused on the position of the United Church towards Israel and the Jewish community in Canada, these subjects were marginal to the main concerns of the church in the 1990s. In that decade the United Church faced serious internal problems. The internal divisions between evangelicals (conservatives) and social activists (liberals) were deeper than ever before. Mistrust existed between the church administration and rank-and-file members. The church now had to determine what its attitude should be to Native Canadians, whether the Bible should be "the" fundamental authority for church life, and what approach to take regarding gays, lesbians, and same-sex covenants. There was no consensus on these issues or on many others. In 1990 John Webster Grant, the distinguished historian of the United Church, summarized the situation as follows: "After 65 years of union the United Church seems less *united* than ever before. Our current disagreements have brought to light such a diversity of conviction and such an intensity of emotion that pain, alienation, and a measure of schism have been the only possible results."[64]

In October 1992 the *Observer* editorial was entitled "Seeking an Honorable Peace." It referred, however, not to the conflict in the Middle East, but to that between the liberal and conservative elements in the church. After four years of bitter controversy, a compromise was finally reached between the two sides at the thirty-fourth General Council.[65] In 1993 the council approved the ordination of a gay church member. Opponents wondered, "Is ordination still necessary?" A "same-sex covenant," which would allow gay or lesbian couples "to solemnize relationships in church ceremonies," was also discussed.[66]

These controversial debates led to a sharp decline in church membership, church school enrolment, and church income. Members voted "with their feet and with their wallets" on church policies. Many United Church members moved to the Christian Congregational Church or the Reformed Church, swelling their ranks with dozens of new congregants. In 1991 the *United Church Yearbook* admitted that the *Observer* had experienced a drastic decline in circulation: "The magazine suffered some of the General Council fallout as individual members protested decisions by canceling subscriptions or leaving the denomination." The circulation of the magazine declined from 312,000 in the 1970s to 200,000 by the end of 1991.[67] Grant summed up the situation by saying, "There is no doubt that the United Church is in trouble."[68] Thus, to put our study in perspective, the church's attitude towards the Middle East, particularly in the last decade, has not been high on its agenda and should be understood in that light.

Other Canadian
Protestant Churches,
the Holocaust, and the
State of Israel

After our examination of the attitude of the United Church of Canada to the Holocaust and to the Middle East, it is interesting to investigate the position of its fellow Protestant church, the Anglican Church of Canada, regarding these subjects. How did the Anglican Church respond to the rise of Nazism, the persecution of Jews in Germany, and the refugee problem? What role did it take in efforts to change the restrictionist policy of the Canadian government? What has been the approach of the Anglican Church in the last decades towards teaching and remembering the Holocaust? And how did church members overcome the antisemitism and missionary zeal of some of their predecessors?

The attitude of the Anglican Church to the State of Israel must be seen as part of its approach to the Jews as a whole. Unlike the United Church and the Canadian Council of Churches, it largely disregarded the Middle East until the late 1980s, despite the fact that there were Anglican churches and institutions in Jerusalem. How can we explain the decades of indifference? How, why, and when did the Anglican Church change drastically from disregard to involvement, and from a balanced position to a pro-Arab approach? The aim of this chapter is to deal with these questions.

ANGLICANS AND THE HOLOCAUST

The Anglican Church of Canada is an autonomous religious denomination, part of the worldwide Anglican Communion. The Church of England operated officially in Canada from the eighteenth century on.

Originally known as the Church of England in Canada (CEC), it became the Anglican Church of Canada in 1955, though the term "Anglican" applies to its adherents even before the church was officially called by that name. The census of 1961 recorded 2,409,068 members of the Anglican Church and 3,600 individual churches, served by 2,400 clergy. Its thirty dioceses were located in four provinces, each headed by an archbishop.[1] Since then, there has been a serious decline in church membership, variously attributed to growing secularism in society at large and to divisive issues within the church, such as movements for the liberalization of church attitudes towards women priests and towards homosexuals.[2]

In the first half of the twentieth century the church maintained a traditionally conservative Christian attitude towards Jews and Judaism. In 1936 the Reverend C.B. Mortlock called Judaism "a monstrous creation of human ingenuity" and referred to the Jews as "God killers."[3] The traditional Christian point of view found its expression in a sermon by the Reverend F.D.V. Narborough entitled "The Danger of Pharisaism," which was published in the official organ of the Church of England in Canada, the *Canadian Churchman*. It was even reprinted in that journal in February 1943, despite widespread knowledge of what was happening to the Jews in Nazi death camps at that time.[4]

One of the characteristics of the church in this era was its missionary zeal towards the Jewish community. The annual report of the Missionary Society to the General Synod in 1946 began, "In obedience to our Lord's command and in response to our Church's zeal we heed the words, 'Go yea there to the lost sheep of the House of Israel.' With these marching orders we present the following report."[5] Two active missionary institutions operated during and after the war, one in Toronto and the other in Montreal, the cities where most Canadian Jews lived.[6] The rise of antisemitism and the problems of Jewish refugees around the world were viewed as an opportunity to work for Jewish conversion. The primate of the Church of England in Canada, the head of the church, stated in his Good Friday pastoral letter in 1938: "The presence in the world today of all that is meant by the term 'anti-Semitism' and its consequences, gives to the Jews a new claim upon our sympathies ... We have witnessed with horror and regret the sufferings and injustices, which have been done to them. This distress also lends urgency to the need of evangelism among them."[7]

At the same time as some CEC members denounced antisemitism, others expressed more overt anti-Jewish feelings in articles and in sermons, even during the Nazi era. Some claimed that the Jews deserved their punishment, saying, for example, "We all condemn the folly and violence of the attacks upon the Jews in Germany ... But to both Jews and Socialists some words of warning are necessary. Many Jews were responsible for the violence of the Russian Communists ... It is they who first of all made the appeal to violence ... Therefore, it is equally legitimate for a Nazi [to use violence]."[8]

Several Anglican priests supported Hitler, and others wrote that the Jews deserved their persecution because they had failed to adopt redemption. However, these anti-Jewish voices were a minority in the church. On an official level, the Anglican courts increasingly denounced the Nazi regime and its brutality. In September 1934 both houses of the General Synod, the highest bodies of the Church of England in Canada, condemned the persecution of the Jews in Germany. During the Olympic Games in Germany in 1936, as well as after Kristallnacht in 1938, the editors of the *Churchman* sympathized with the Jews and warned of growing antisemitism in Canada.[9]

The Council for Social Service (css), a national body of the Anglican churches in Canada, whose aims were education and social welfare, was vocally sympathetic to the Jewish cause. Led by Canon W.W. Judd, its general secretary, a devoted, liberal-minded Anglican priest, the council was the mouthpiece of the cec on the issues of antisemitism and refugees throughout the Nazi years. In 1937, when the Canadian Council of the World Alliance for International Friendship passed a resolution that condemned antisemitism, the executive committee of the css followed suit. It stated in November 1937 that it viewed "with great sorrow" the spread of antisemitic propaganda in Canada by various agencies, and it called upon church leaders "to ignore such propaganda and as far as it bears the imprimatur of 'Christian' organizations, to repudiate it as utterly un-Christian and foreign to the mind of Christ." Adopting this recommendation, the annual meeting of the css strongly criticized antisemitic propaganda in Canada.[10]

While opposed to antisemitism, the Church of England in Canada still balked at the idea of actually inviting Jews to settle in Canada. As Alan Davies and Marilyn Nefsky point out, it was a challenge for the church, given its strong attachment to the Anglo-Saxon people, to sympathize with the admission of non-British refugees. "With its Anglo-Saxon roots and its fervent imperial loyalties, the suggestion that Canada should suddenly open its doors to masses of non Anglo-Saxon, non-British, non-Christian and frequently destitute strangers – constituted a moral test of no small proportion."[11] Indeed, the executive committee of the css felt that "an undue proportion of Southern Europeans [were] coming to Canada." Therefore in May 1937 it decided that "this executive go on record as being in favour of a large proportion of British immigration."[12] Even during the war, while condemning Nazi racism, the *Bulletin* of the council published an article that "definitely expressed the interest of our Church people in keeping Canada British by the desire for more British immigration and for the maintenance of British ideals in the future political and cultural life of our country."[13]

Despite its desire for more British immigration, the CSS felt that "it was a Christian duty that Canada assist [refugees] in some small way." Therefore the executive committee, "having due regard to the sufferings of these unhappy people, ask the Government to allow selected political refugees from Austria and Germany to enter Canada."[14] Anticipating Canada's role at the Evian Conference, which was to discuss the refugee problem, the council in 1938 appealed to the Canadian government to "continue to explore the possibilities for the immigration of selected groups of Jewish people ... as far as possible and desirable, and thus assume a share of the responsibility of finding a home for these unfortunate victims of political persecution."[15] It was aware of strong opposition in Canada to the admission of refugees in general and of Jewish refugees in particular, and it confined its request to the admission of "a selected group of a reasonable number of desirable Jewish people." With the establishment of the Canadian National Committee on Refugees and Victims of Political Persecution in December 1938, the CSS unreservedly supported the new organization, and Judd served as CSS's representative to the committee.[16]

In 1940 the General Synod ordered a special report on the problem of immigration. This report, prepared by Judd, was adopted by the synod, but it did not make much of impact, partly because public attention was focused on the war. The CSS's annual reports time and again called upon the government to liberalize its immigration policy and upon the general public to support such a move, but the church body was crying in the wilderness.[17]

Thus Anglican attitudes about antisemitism and the refugee issue during the Holocaust were not clear-cut. Traces of antisemitism were evident in certain Anglican circles, particularly among missionary groups. Like other Protestant churches in Canada, Anglicans were relatively silent, as Brian Prideaux, the ecumenical officer of the Anglican Church during the 1980s, has admitted.[18] However, several Anglican leaders, including Judd and especially the Council for Social Service, were not silent at all, though they were ineffective. Davies and Nefsky conclude, "Church journalists, ordinary priests and laymen, diocesan and national synods as well as some bishops and archbishops made their voice heard ... If a religious community is identified with its leaders and officers, the Anglicans were far from silent: indeed they were surprisingly vocal ... The Church of England in Canada cannot be compared unfavorably to the United Church of Canada with respect to the Jewish refugee crisis; neither church did as much as it could and should have done, but neither church was as inert as it might have been. Morally speaking, both were more creditable than the elected government and parliament of their country."[19]

Davies and Nefsky perhaps ignore the silence of the General Synod. Furthermore, their comparison of the moral responsibility of the churches with that of elected politicians is questionable. However, the Church of England in Canada, along with the United Church, was more outspoken in favour of Jewish refugees and against antisemitism than other Protestant and Catholic denominations in Canada, as Irving Abella and Harold Troper have pointed out.[20]

After World War II the CEC took little interest in the Jewish people or in the Middle East conflict. In the late 1950s the Anglicans entered into dialogue with several Christian denominations, such as the Roman Catholics and the United Church. Jews, however, were not included.

Beginning in the 1960s, Roland de Corneille, an Anglican priest in the diocese of Toronto who was later elected as a Liberal member of the House of Commons, initiated a dialogue as a vehicle to bring together the Anglican and Jewish communities in Canada. As secretary of the missionary Nathanael Institute in Toronto, he lamented the ineffectiveness of traditional missionary methods. He therefore proposed the dialogue approach in 1961 as a more effective and modern method of evangelizing: "on the whole, the missionary method of the past is not acceptable. Any realistic missionary method that intends to represent a serious approach by the Church as a whole cannot be satisfied that it is sincere until it faces up to the new world that has dawned … That means that before we can approach people with the Gospel, we shall have to first remove, with their help the barriers that are an offence … Out of this kind of situation, the missionary tactics of the Dialogue Approach has been born."[21]

When he first suggested a dialogue, Jews were skeptical. The Orthodox circles opposed any kind of dialogue, and even liberal leaders, such as Rabbi Jordan Pearlson, hesitated, because Jewish experience with Christians throughout the centuries had taught them to be suspicious. When the church spoke about Christian love, Jews became nervous, commented Pearlson. As a matter of fact, de Corneille's original "dialogue approach" justified Jewish suspiciousness.

Despite this initial response, de Corneille's plan for reconciliation between the two communities gradually took shape. As a step towards a better understanding of Jews and Judaism, forty parishes in the Toronto area attended classes on Judaism, visited synagogues, and participated in the celebration of a Jewish Passover seder. In March 1967 the *Churchman* published a symposium entitled "Learning to Discover the

Man Next Door: Preparation for a Dialogue." Articles by Christian and Jewish authors discussed various aspects of interfaith dialogue.[22]

Lou Ronson of B'nai Brith Canada later praised de Corneille's role in reconciliation between Anglicans and Jews, saying that among Anglicans the priest stood out for his understanding of Jews and Judaism. Furthermore, as a strong supporter of the Sate of Israel, he counterbalanced the pro-Arab elements among Anglicans. The Israeli government appreciated de Corneille's sympathetic attitude and invited him to visit the country as its official guest. He was so highly regarded by Jewish groups that they appointed him the first non-Jewish director of the Human Rights department of B'nai Brith Canada.[23]

The history of the Third Collect of the Good Friday service provides an interesting barometer of Jewish-Anglican relations in the second half of the twentieth century. In August 1965 the House of Bishops of the Anglican Church demonstrated its desire to improve relations with the Jews by deciding to eliminate this collect, a prayer for the conversion of the Jews, from the prayer book, and the house requested that bishops "authorize their clergy to omit the Collect on future Good Fridays." Such good intentions must not have been easy to carry out, however, because twelve years later, in February 1977, the House of Bishops needed to reaffirm its earlier decision, and two years later, in 1979, the primate, Archbishop E.W. Scott, found it necessary in his pastoral letter to remind Anglican archbishops and bishops of the decision. "I believe that we must take deliberate steps to clarify our interpretation of Scripture, whether in liturgy or in preaching, which might be interpreted as causing offense to the Jewish people," he wrote[24] The General Synod finally approved the deletion of the collect only in 1992.[25]

In 1973 Anglicans had participated in the Key '73 campaign, arousing Jewish concern and protest. Archbishop Scott responded by stating on 4 May that the church "disavows any approach which is geared to proselytizing Jews." He admitted that "through misdirected zeal or insensitivity" of some people, Jews might be offended. "We have learned from the bitter lessons of history that such efforts inevitably result in creating misleading comparisons, which falsely portray the faith of non-Christians. This has always has resulted in misrepresentation, hostility and alienation … We should reassure our Jewish neighbors that we respect their spiritual patrimony and the vitality and relevance of Judaism today. Above all, we should guard scrupulously against advertisements, arguments, actions and avowals, which single out or compare another religious community and its faith negatively to our own." Archbishop Scott indicated that the Anglican Church had re-examined its relations to the Jews and that consequently it was seeking a positive dialogue with them.[26]

But there were other voices in the Anglican Church. In 1972 Beth Sar Shalom, the congregational arm of the American Board of Missions to the Jews, published an advertisement in the *Toronto Star* that showed a group of smiling men. The words under the picture read: "So many Jews are wearing 'that smile' nowadays ... The love of Jesus has come into their lives." The ad led to a controversy on the pages of the *Churchman.*[27]

The Anglican approach to the Jews in the 1960s and 1970s was not coordinated nationally. As J.B. Boyles, the ecumenical officer, stated in 1981, "concern for Jewish-Christian relations at the national level of our church has not been expressed in a highly organized way." But in June 1981, within the framework of the Inter-Church Inter-Faith Relations Committee, the primate established a subcommittee on Anglican-Jewish relations, chaired by the Reverend Canon E.D. Fleming. The new subcommittee was authorized to deal with potentially sensitive areas.[28] Moe Seidman, chair of the Canadian Jewish Congress, reported that year that the Anglican Church considered the new subcommittee "a high priority."[29] Another sign of Anglican goodwill to the Jews was the invitation extended in 1986 to representatives of the Canadian Jewish Congress to participate in the General Synod. This was the first time that Jews had been invited to the highest court of the Anglican Church.[30]

The issue of antisemitism was prominent in the media in 1985 because of the Ernst Zundel trial and because of attacks on Temple Sholum in Vancouver. Archbishop Scott took pains to reiterate the position taken by the General Synod, which strongly denounced antisemitism in Canada. "Antisemitism, or any other kind of prejudice based on race or religion, has no place in our society," wrote the primate in a letter to Alan Rose. He spoke of the friendly relations between the two communities, which went "a long way to breaking down misunderstanding and stereotypes. It would be a tragedy if the acts of a few bigots were to overshadow this important development." Scott assured the Jews "of the concern and support of their Anglican friends."[31]

The dramatic change in Anglican attitudes towards the Jews can be seen in its views on the Holocaust by this time. In 1983 the General Synod "deplore[d] recent expressions of antisemitism in Canada and called upon all the people of our Church to reject the same." It urged Anglicans "to renounce racism and to work towards the eradication of all expressions of it." The synod assured the Jewish people that it would "persist in fighting antisemitism wherever it exists,"[32] and it confronted the denial theory, acknowledging "the reality that the Nazi regime executed millions of Jewish people ... on account of race."

Furthermore, it requested that "reference to the acts of genocide" be included in courses on World War II in all school systems in Canada.[33]

Following the synod's recommendation, the Sub-Committee on Anglican-Jewish Relations prepared a kit for the purpose of reviewing and revising the teaching of the Holocaust, which aimed "to counter-act false teaching regarding the Holocaust." After several drafts, the study, which had been approved by Alan Rose of the CJC, was completed in October 1989. Entitled *From Darkness to Dawn: Rethinking Christian Attitudes toward Jews and Judaism,* it was distributed throughout the Anglican churches and became the starting point for teaching the Holocaust in Anglican parishes and schools.[34]

The Anglican Church had changed meaningfully since World War II; by the 1980s it was less aristocratic, less British, and more concerned about maintaining good relations with other communities, including the Jews. Ironically, denunciations of antisemitism and of Holocaust denial were more vocal and frequent during the 1980s than they had been during the Nazi era.

ANGLICANS AND THE STATE OF ISRAEL

Following this review of the Anglican Church of Canada's attitude to the Jews and to the plight of Jewish refugees, it is worthwhile to discuss its position on the establishment and the reality of the Jewish state. In spite of the fact that there were vested Anglican interests in Jerusalem, it is surprising how little attention was given to the Arab-Israeli conflict before the late 1980s. The issue received very little coverage in the *Churchman,* for example. But in view of the fact that, unlike the more liberal United Church, which was deeply involved in world affairs, the conservative Anglican Church dealt mainly with church and Canadian internal affairs; this neglect is understandable. While the *United Church Observer* was a colourful and wide-ranging journal, the *Canadian Churchman* was primarily a church bulletin, preoccupied with religious matters. Among the issues that dominated its pages was the church's attitude to Native Canadians, Catholics, and homosexuals; its stand on abortion, AIDS, and the ordination of women were also discussed. As well, internal church matters, such as union with the United Church, inter-church and interfaith relations, and religious television domi-nated the pages of the *Churchman.* Often, when the journal discussed non-religious subjects, such as nuclear testing, the famine in Biafra, or issues related to Pakistan, Bangladesh, Uganda, South Africa, and Zim-babwe, readers did not like it. A reader in 1974 complained, "We are tired of being told about drought and famine … We are tired and we just want to be like everyone else." The *Churchman* apologetically stated that such an opinion "does not sound much like going into all the world to all people with the message of love and hope and trust and faith."[35]

In 1963, in a statement against nuclear testing, the General Synod had found it necessary to justify its interest in foreign matters, declaring, "Christians must always be vigilant of their responsibilities in the matter of their stewardship of time, talents and possessions."[36] The history of the Committee on International Affairs clearly reflects the low priority that Anglicans gave to international relations. The first time that the term "international affairs" appears is in the 1945 annual report of the Council for Social Service. The reference concerned the establishment of the United Nations.[37] But after World War II there was a growing sense that churches should be more involved in international affairs. "It is incumbent upon Christian people ... to seek the solution of inter-racial and international problems in the light of the moral law. It is sound, too, that organized departmental bodies of the Churches and inter-church bodies should seek to influence rulers and international statesmen to act in conformity with that moral law," stated the annual report of the csc in 1947. The Anglicans, however, lacked a body on international relations and were represented by several organizations.[38] A decade later, in 1957, the establishment of a standing committee on international affairs, with diocesan subcommittees, was discussed, and in 1959 an independent committee was finally organized devoted to "study on a long-range-basis of the ethics and moral principles in international relationships."[39]

The new committee was flooded with suggestions for study. Among the topics proposed were disarmament and arms control, nuclear testing, international trade, external aid, the UN, world population, immigration, Africa, Cuba, Latin America, Vietnam, Rhodesia, the new left, and pollution. The Middle East was not mentioned as an area of interest.[40] Because of a lack of funding, expertise, and interest, the committee was able to undertake annually only one or two studies of specific areas. During its short life the very existence of the committee was repeatedly questioned, and it was transferred from one sponsor to another – from the Council for Social Service to the Program Committee. Each time its terms of reference were examined.[41] After a decade, in October 1969, the International Affairs Unit, as it was now called, was disbanded. However, the area of world affairs was not totally abandoned. One staff member became responsible for this subject and was requested to prepare "recommended actions for task forces on international affairs from time to time, as needed."[42]

The establishment of a Jewish state in 1948 and the fight by Jews for independence had not been acknowledged by Anglican leaders in

Canada. No official statement was issued either by the House of Bishops or by the primate. The *Churchman* devoted one editorial to the subject, in July 1948. Christians "were anxious that the Jews shall have fair treatment from all the nations of the world and be allowed to develop according to their own ideals," it stated. The editorial defended British policy on Palestine, declaring that "no country in the world has done more for the Jewish race than the British Empire." The Church of England had been working in Palestine for many years. Therefore it could not "easily look on it without interest." The Christian Arabs, who were faced "with severe tests …, should be constant in our minds and in our prayers," concluded the editorial.[43] The General Synod of 1949 did not discuss the Palestinian problem or the establishment of the State of Israel, and there was no discussion of the protection of the holy sites or of the internationalization of Jerusalem.[44]

This limited but balanced coverage changed in 1967 after the Six Day War. The Anglican Church, along with other Christian denominations in Canada, did not express any concern for Israel's survival, and no definite statement of support came from any official Anglican body.[45] But in August 1967, after the war ended, the General Synod adopted a resolution that supported the efforts of the Canadian government "to achieve a just peace in the Middle East." The resolution went on to urge that "international guarantees be sought to assure free access to the holy places in Jerusalem" for members of the three religions.[46] The demand for international guarantees meant that the church did not rely upon Israel's assurances that it would allow free access to the holy sites. No such guarantee had been sought when Jordan occupied East Jerusalem, despite the fact that Jews had been denied access to the Wailing Wall. The General Synod also adopted another resolution, this one regarding the refugee problem. It declared "its concern that Canada play a full and responsible role in seeking a lasting solution to the Middle East refugee problem," and it called upon the Canadian government to enlarge its financial support for the United Nations Relief and Works Agency, to admit refugees into Canada, and to initiate diplomatic steps to find a permanent solution for the refugees. The synod declared its willingness "to cooperate to the full in implementing these measures."[47] These resolutions, modest as they were, constituted the beginning of the Anglican Church's support for the Palestinian cause in the Middle East conflict.

Although the church was an autonomous organization, it preferred to act ecumenically. This was the case particularly with the Middle East situation, to which the church gave little attention.[48] Furthermore, as mentioned above, its International Affairs Unit had no experts on the subject and no staff to carry out intensive research. Unlike the United

Church, the Anglican Church was "slow in … getting out statements that might be considered the voice of the church," Anne M. Davison of the IAU later wrote.[49] Therefore when, in 1969, the IAU formulated a resolution on the Arab-Israeli conflict, it preferred to rely upon resolutions that had already been adopted by worldwide church bodies, such as the World Council of Churches and the Lambeth Conference, a consultative gathering of Anglican bishops from around the world held every ten years. The Lambeth Conference of 1968 viewed "with concern the continuing tensions in the Middle East; the tragic plight of hundreds of thousands of Arab refugees who have lost homes and means of livelihood."[50] The aim of this statement was to shape "public opinion, having some understanding of the complex and tragic state of things, and some insight into the part played by religious factors."[51]

In February 1969 a statement had been released to the press signed by, among others, the Anglican primate, urging the Canadian government to permit the immigration to Canada of Jewish refugees from Iraq, Syria, and Egypt and also of Arab refugees from the Middle East. When the General Synod passed its resolutions in August that year, it also supported the "welcoming of Palestinian refugees into Canada," but it omitted the part of the statement that referred to Jewish refugees from Arab countries.[52]

Judging by the deliberations of the IAU and the resolution of the General Synod of 1969, we can conclude that the Anglican Church was reluctant to adopt the pro-Arab resolutions of the WCC, preferring a more moderate, balanced policy. This position was made clear by a statement issued in June 1971, which expressed deep concern for people who had been deprived of the basic requirements for adequate living. The statement went on to say that "we understand that words from Canada are unlikely to resolve differences between Israel and the Arab world. We recognize that in a situation at once so delicate and so dangerous, silence may be our wisest policy."[53] The statement avoided criticism of Israel and did not even mention the Palestinian refugees. Thus there was a real difference between the Anglican Church's attitude, which in regards to the Middle East crisis was that "silence may be our wisest policy," and the outspoken position of the United Church of Canada.

The *Canadian Churchman* exercised editorial independence and took a different path from the General Synod. Although the journal served as the official bulletin of the Anglican Church and was supervised by a synod-elected Board of Trustees, it was "encouraged to speak its own mind in editorials and present its news and features responsibly." A 1979 editorial, for instance, emphasized its independent role, stating that the magazine provided "for the expression of disparate and conflicting views, including those, which dissent from existing editorial policies and those, which dissent from the church's official position."[54] But as a church journal, the *Churchman,* we have seen, was mainly devoted to religious matters, inside and outside the Anglican Church. It published reports on tours to the Holy Land, excavations there, and visits to religious sites, such as Bethlehem, Jerusalem, and Nazareth. Some of the articles were neutral, and some depicted Israel in a positive way.[55]

After the Suez crisis of 1956, the *Churchman* had expressed its concern about the increase in Cold War tension. The journal blamed the Soviets for their role in the Suez campaign. The very existence of Israel, established with the help of the United States, caused "turmoil" in the region. In order to keep the Soviet Union away from Middle East oil and to diminish Arab suspicion, the journal called upon the United States to favour the Arabs. The editorial stated, "It is obvious that to be effective in the Middle East, America must be prepared to act in her own interest and that of the Western world as well as in the interest of the Arab states themselves before Russia becomes entrenched ... Russian control of Middle East oil could win the Battle for Europe without a shot being fired."[56]

After 1967, the *Churchman* did not adopt as moderate a stance as the General Synod; rather, A.C. Forrest influenced its position. In an editorial that summarized the activities of the Anglican Church during that year, the *Churchman* echoed Forrest's style: "We responded with great fervor to appeals for help from Israel in her time of need against the Arab hordes. Little Israel fighting and winning against overwhelming odds caught our imagination. But we sort of forgot thousands of starving hopeless refugees kept from their homeland by little Israel. And when some of our Christian leaders deigned to chasten victorious Israel, we left them to the wolves rather than rock the boat."[57]

In December 1968 the *Churchman* even printed an article by Forrest, "A Christmas Story," which had also appeared in the *Observer.* The antisemitic overtones of this article led to a debate on the pages of the *Churchman.*[58] Bishop L.S. Garnsworthy and Roland de Corneille termed it "hate literature." They wrote that it contained "images, caricatures and stereotypes which are entirely too similar to those found in anti-Jewish hate-literature and this is in extremely bad taste," and they criticized the *Churchman* for its departure from "balanced and reliable journalism."[59] Another reader complained that the editor had published the article, despite Forrest's "well-known bias." He called for a "balanced" account of the Arab-Israeli situation. The editor responded, "Dr. Forrest, we know, is not anti-Semitic, nor is the *Canadian Churchman.* Dissent with the State of

Israel does not constitute antisemitism." This controversy continued to simmer on the pages of the *Churchman* for months.[60]

In April the following year the *Churchman* published a report by the National Council of Churches that was critical of Israel. Rabbi Gunther Plaut protested in a letter to the editor that the report had been reprinted without an editorial comment. He contended that the report was a political, rather than a religious, message.[61] Plaut's remarks drew angry responses. G.K. Watts of Lethbridge, Alberta, wrote: "I think it is a tragedy that so many Arabs are displaced by the Israelis who have been most brutal in their punishments … Rabbi Plaut has written a lot, but said little."[62] The Reverend F.L. Elias of Charlottetown, Prince Edward Island, was even more blunt in his criticism. He complained that the editor gave a good deal of space to Plaut, but did not publish other points of view. He also attacked the Zionists' claim to a God-given right to Palestine. "If this 'monopoly on God attitude' persists, Zionism will some day claim the whole world." Elias wondered whether Israel would be the second nation in the world to use the atomic bomb, and he asked: "Is it possible that Christians are still victims of Zionist propaganda?"[63]

Neither an editorial nor a report appeared in the *Churchman* on the Yom Kippur War of October 1973. However, in the November issue an article by Forrest was published, which criticized Israel's refusal to comply with UN resolutions. Forrest chastised the churches for their neglect of the Middle East, and he particularly accused the Canadian Council of Churches of "foot-dragging."[64]

In his introductory remarks to that issue, Hugh McCullum maintained that the primate was compelled to issue a "guarded" statement about the Yom Kippur War because he "must weigh public opinion," which was pro-Israel. However, as a church magazine, "we feel that Christians have a particular need to see the war and the crisis in perspective." McCullum stated that Forrest had presented in his article "an accurate and fair account of the situation." The editor argued that the churches should state their concerns about the Middle East "clearly and unequivocally, not in a foot-dragging manner."[65]

While the official courts of the Anglican Church considered silence on the Middle East conflict to be their "wisest policy," members of the church thought otherwise, as the pages of the *Canadian Churchman* attested. The majority of the letters in the "Letterbasket" during the 1970s were critical of Israel. Readers complained of "unbalanced reports" by the Western press, which, they said, censored anti-Israel news. They rejected the Zionist claim of a legitimate right to Palestine, since for nineteen hundred years Arabs had lived there; therefore the Palestinians were entitled to claim it as their land.[66]

Arab oil, particularly the oil embargo in 1974, was mentioned as a reason for support of the Arab cause. "We can no longer ignore the Arabs, not when some of them become as rich as Croesus at the expense ... of a great part of the world," maintained Maurice Western.[67] E.W. Abraham of Victoria, British Columbia, argued that "the Bible does not sanction Israel's territorial claim."[68]

Balanced viewpoints about the Middle East crisis appeared in the *Churchman*. Jerry Hames, the future editor of the *Churchman*, returned in April 1970 from a visit to Israel with mixed feelings: "Israel is breathtaking in its beauty ... But its beauty is marred by ugliness of hate, distrust and stubborn rigidity on the part of Jew and Arab." P.F. Gilbert of Willowdale, Ontario, called upon the readers of the *Churchman* to "dispense with partisanship."[69] But there were also pro-Israel articles. Francie Miller reported with excitement about the "haunting beauty" of Israel. Few visitors left the country disappointed, "because Israel offers all the excitement, meaning and diversity anyone could ever wish for."[70] After the journal in May 1977 published an article by Ann Benedek that described Israel in a positive manner, readers protested about the one-sidedness of the magazine. Margaret J. Howell of Vancouver agreed with Benedek that Israel "performed remarkable works," though these were financed by European and American money. However, she criticized the author's disregard of the Arab cause.[71] Another reader, Michael E. Marmura, a Palestinian Anglican and professor of Near Eastern and Islamic studies at the University of Toronto, commended Howell "for her courageous letter." He recalled the earlier terrorist role palyed the newly elected Israeli prime minister, Menachem Begin, whose underground Irgun was responsible for the Dir Yassin massacre in 1948. Marmura blamed the Anglican Church for being "very timid in facing up to the moral issues of the Palestine question and the devastating injustice incurred by the indigenous Arab population."[72]

The *Churchman* disregarded the dramatic visit by Egyptian president Anwar Sadat to Jerusalem in 1977 and the peace negotiations between Egypt and Israel in the following months. In March 1979 the journal published an item about Begin and Sadat signing the peace treaty in Washington. Although it entitled the piece "History in the Making," it devoted to this important event only three lines and a picture of the two smiling leaders.[73] In November 1981, after the assassination of President Sadat, the first discussion of the peace between Egypt and Israel appeared in the journal. "Anwar Sadat will be remembered as a man who dared the improbable in his quest for peace and stability for his country. His death is a tragic loss for all who worked for the same goals for the Middle East," read the editorial.[74]

Following the Israeli invasion of Lebanon in 1982 and the beginning of fighting in Beirut, an editorial in the *Churchman* called for the establishment of a sovereign Palestinian state and the recognition of the PLO. "Self-determination for Palestinians, including provision for a homeland, is a worthy and just goal that is long overdue. It is ironic that the Jewish people, who fought for the right to establish such a homeland after the terrible persecution of the Holocaust, deny the same right to Palestinians."[75] An anti-Israeli article that pointed to similarities between Israel and racist South Africa followed this editorial. "The growing bond of the axis is irrefutable," it said. The author praised the PLO and criticized Israel for its refusal to recognize "the most credible and internationally recognized organization."[76]

To his credit, the editor frequently allowed rebuttal of the criticism of Israel. Reader Dean Jon Donald of Nelson, British Columbia, wrote that the equation of South Africa and Israel was "if not anti-Semitic, at least a biased opinion based on selected facts." Although he admitted that the two countries had blundered, for which they should be criticized, he felt that "selecting two 'bastard' nations and labeling them 'Zionist conspirators,' while not once mentioning Arab or Black African terrorism, is discriminatory."[77]

During the civil war in Lebanon in 1982, when Christian Falangists massacred Palestinian Muslims in the Lebanese refugee camps of Sabra and Shatila, the Canadian churches were silent. The *Churchman* opposed this silence, stating that "such inhumane butchery against helpless women and children ... is an indelible stain against the Christian church and against all for which it stands." A number of Anglican Church leaders in the Middle East declared that the Christian Falangists who carried out the massacre did not deserve to be called Christians.[78]

Thus to summarize the *Canadian Churchman*'s coverage of the Middle East conflict in these years, unlike the *United Church Observer*, the editor showed no obsessive concern with the plight of the Arab refugees. Although the journal published editorials and articles supporting the Palestinian cause more clearly and more frequently than any statements made by the General Synod, it also printed rebuttals in favour of Israel. Similarly, the Anglican Church, when compared with the United Church or the Canadian Council of Churches, was much more restrained in its rare resolutions on the Middle East. Internal matters and foreign concerns of those countries where it had missionary activities were more important for the church than the Israeli-Palestinian crisis.

But in the second half of the 1980s this approach changed drastically. Several factors played a role in the evolution of the Anglican

Church's attitude towards the Middle East and Israel. The growing influence of the Middle East Council of Churches, which was mostly Arab, led to increased interest by the Canadian churches in the Israeli-Palestinian conflict, and the pro-Arab position of the Canadian Council of Churches in the second half of the 1980s naturally influenced its member denominations. In 1988 the CCC prepared a "Position Paper on the Middle East," which was sent for comments and review to its member groups, including to the Anglican Church of Canada.[79]

The position paper was referred to the subcommittee on Anglican Jewish relations. It discussed the contents and considered the paper "unbalanced." Members felt that "it could negatively affect Christian-Jewish relations." Accordingly, the House of Bishops decided that the paper should be amended. It asked the primate to set up a Middle East task force "to prepare a response from the Anglican Church to the CCC's Statement."[80]

The Anglican Middle East Committee (AMEC), as the new task force was later called, was established on 17 February 1989, with Professor Peter Slater as convener. John Rye, Shafik A. Farah, and Robert Assaly were the other members. The first meetings were devoted to the Anglican response to the CCC statement. After deliberations, the committee recommended that the original draft be amended. It also decided to enlarge its membership. Among the new members were the primate, Archbishop Michael Peers, the ecumenical officer, Brian Prideaux, Edith Land, and Professor Michael E. Marmura. The committee recommended support for the overall document, but added a statement on the Intifada, "noting the Israeli government's violations of human rights and international conventions during the intifada, and deploring the diplomatic delays to the peace process as opportunism, thus forever scarring the next generation."[81]

Brian Prideaux, later rector of the Anglican church of St John the Baptist in Toronto, who had worked for Anglican reconciliation with the Jews, including preparation of the study *From Darkness to Dawn*, about the Holocaust, tried to moderate the extreme anti-Israeli expressions in the AMEC response. He was surprised to learn that in the paragraph about the Intifada the words "as opportunism, thus forever scarring the next generation" had not been crossed out, contrary to what had been agreed upon by the committee. Therefore he asked to be disassociated from these words.[82]

The AMEC's next assignment was the preparation of a resolution on the Middle East for the General Synod. For this purpose, the Anglican Church of Canada turned to its own Anglican links to the Middle East. These were the Lambeth Conference and the Anglican Consultative Council. The latter body served as a liaison between the various Anglican national churches. (This approach was different from that of the United Church, which, because it was a national and not a worldwide denomination, tended to turn to inter-church bodies such the WCC, the CCC, and the MECC for information on the Middle East.)[83] In June 1989 the General Synod adopted the text of the Lambeth Conference resolution of 1988 but omitted several parts of the statement prepared by the Anglican Consultative Council, because they were considered too extreme. The resolution on the Israeli-Palestinian conflict read as follows:

1. Adopt the 1988 Lambeth Conference resolution LC 88/24 which:

a. Affirms the importance of the Church in the exercise of its prophetic role by standing on the side of the oppressed in their struggle for justice, and by promoting justice, peace and reconciliation for all people of the region.

b. Affirms the existence of the State of Israel and its right to recognized and secure borders, as well as the civic and human rights of all those who live within its borders.

c. Affirms the right of the Palestinians to self-determination, including choice of their own representatives and the establishment of their own state.

d. Supports the convening of an international conference over Palestine/Israel under the auspices of the UN and based on all the UN resolutions in relation to this conflict, to which all parties of the conflict be invited.

e. Commits itself to continued prayer for Israelis and Palestinians … for the achievement of justice, peace and reconciliation for all.

2. Continues to work with our Anglican, ecumenical and other partners to achieve these ends.[84]

The synod omitted from the text of the Consultative Council the paragraph that rejected "the interpretation of the Holy Scripture, which affirms the special place of the Present State of Israel in the light of biblical prophecy." It also rejected the words "calls attention to the injustice done to the Palestinians in consequence of the creation of the State of Israel." Finally, the Anglican synod did not mention the PLO as the representative of the Palestinians at the peace conference.[85] The importance of the synod's 1989 resolution was that it "provided the basic guide for the future work of the Committee," as the *Journal* of the General Synod stated.[86]

Gradually, the AMEC's position became less balanced, until it eventually supported the Palestinian cause openly. Several factors played a role in this development, such as the Intifada, the Anglican Communion's critical approach to Israel, and closer relations with the MECC and the Middle East Working Group of the CCC. Another reason for the committee's pro-Arab position was the contribution of several pro-Arab members, among them Shafik Farah, Robert Assaly, Michael E. Marmura, and Beth Davies.

The Reverend Canon Shafik A. Farah was a Palestinian, born near Nazareth, who had studied in Lebanon. In 1953, after graduation, he was not allowed to return to Israel, and he immigrated to Canada. "The bitter experience of not being able to go home stayed with me," recalled Farah in 1990. He dedicated his life to helping the Palestinian people "to arrive at peace with justice."[87] Farah used every opportunity to promote the Arab cause. From 1985 on, he was a member of the MEWG as the representative of the Anglican Church. In January 1988 he met with Archbishop Peers and requested that the church take "a pronounced role in addressing itself to the Palestinian-Israeli situation." In light of various resolutions, including those of the CCC and the Anglican Consultative Council, he requested that the church "make its plea for a just peace, the preservation of the human rights of the Palestinian people and their right to freedom, self-determination and statehood." Farah offered to make himself "available to you for interpreting the Palestinian-Israeli situation to any group or committee or on the pages of the *Churchman* or in conference."[88]

On 9 February 1988, in response to Farah's plea, Peers read his telegram to the House of Bishops which said: "I pray you take a stand and speak out for peace with justice … for how long should we wait?" Accordingly, the House of Bishops adopted a resolution in which it "deeply regret[ed] the acts of violence" in the West Bank and the Gaza Strip and endorsed the Consultative Council's resolution concerning an international peace conference, "in which all parties affected would be present."[89] While the bishops denounced Israeli violence in the occupied territories, Peers, in his pastoral letter, "understood" – though he did not justify – Palestinian violence. "The use of violence becomes a 'Third World' reality not because they enjoy it, but because it is the only language which will make it through our media and into our consciousness."[90]

Even after the 1988 resolution of the House of Bishops, Farah continued his pressure on the primate. In January 1990 he and several Anglican Palestinians requested of Archbishop Peers "that our Church and its leaders take a more public stand on the Palestinian Israeli conflict … We are disappointed by the silence of our church. The Church must speak out now and loudly lest future generations accuse it of having remained silent in the face of great evil and great suffering."[91] Farah complained to Peers that the media had disregarded church resolutions concerning the Middle East, such as that of the Anglican Consultative Council, and he urged the primate to publicize these resolutions, particularly among church members.[92] Thus as an active member of AMEC, Farah was able to promote the cause of the Palestinians in the Anglican Church from the late 1980s on.

Another active member of the committee was Robert Assaly, a student of Lebanese descent at Trinity College in the University of Toronto. Particularly after Israel's invasion of Lebanon, he became very critical of Israel. Beth Davies, a student of religion at the University of Toronto, was also highly critical of the Israeli occupation. After one visit to Lebanon she considered herself an expert on the Middle East, and as such, she joined the AMEC as a full member.[93] Although Farah later insisted that "we talked objectively" on the committee,[94] it seems that the biased opinion of several members had some influence on the AMEC's attitude to the Middle East crisis. On the other hand, Brian Prideaux tried to moderate the resolutions.

The subject of public relations was discussed at AMEC meetings. Members of the committee complained repeatedly about the failure of the church to publicize the Middle East problem. But the AMEC seemed unable to implement its suggestions for educating the Canadian people.[95] At Farah's suggestion in April 1990, it recommended that Bishop Samir Kafity of Jerusalem be invited to speak to the General Synod. "We are trying to raise the profile of the church in the Middle East," read the minutes of the committee.[96]

The Anglican Middle East Committee had a short life. After two or three years of activity it disbanded for several reasons. For one thing, the accomplishments of the committee were too small to justify its continuation. Also, several members of the AMEC, such as Farah, Assaly, Prideaux, and John Rye were also members of the active and influential Middle East Working Group of the Canadian Council of Churches, and thus they were able to operate through the CCC. Prideaux later maintained that there was a desire "to work ecumenically ... rather than have a separate Anglican group."[97]

Another factor that contributed to the change in the Anglican attitude towards the Middle East was the outlook of Archbishop Michael G. Peers, the primate of the church. While his predecessor, Archbishop E.W. Scott, had been interested in Africa, where Anglican missionaries had operated, Peers became involved in Middle East matters. He participated in the Lambeth Conference in the summer of 1988, at which the Intifada was widely discussed, and he praised the role played at the conference by Bishop Kafity and Canon Naim Ateek of the diocese of Jerusalem in "helping people grow from conventional North American and Western European views about the Palestinian issue."[98]

In January 1990 Peers was a member of a delegation of Canadian church leaders that visited Ethiopia and Israel. The Canadian Jewish Congress had been consulted prior to the visit. Alan Rose was enthusiastic, regarding this consultation as "something of a breakthrough," because on earlier occasions such visits had been made in cooperation with the MECC, without consulting any Jews.[99] Douglas duCharme was also in touch with Peers. He wished to influence the primate to increase "Anglican interest, support and commitment to work in the Middle East."[100] The delegation visited Gaza, the West Bank, and Jerusalem. It then went to the MECC assembly in Nicosia. Peers returned to Canada wholly sympathetic to the Palestinian cause.[101]

The primate related his impressions of the tour in his pastoral letter to the Anglican clergy called the "Ember Letter" of Lent 1990. The visit to the refugee camps in Gaza and the West Bank was "a distressing experience." Since 1967, the people had been living under military occupation without any protection of their human rights. Peers wrote that only a minority of the Palestinian people had committed terrorist acts: "Those who live in the occupied territories do so, for the most part, in misery and oppression. They suffer daily assaults upon their dignity and freedom, and I believe we must not allow our sense of guilt toward Jews to silence us in the face of the reality of the Palestinians." The primate maintained that Jews had suffered from antisemitism, not from Arabs, but from Europeans, and the Arabs were not responsible for the Holocaust. For the balance, he reviewed the "unfortunate and at times tragic" history of Christian-Jewish relations. He admitted that "echoes of anti-Jewish attitudes are discernible in the Scriptures," and that these had formed Christian anti-Jewish attitudes. The primate therefore called for "acts of repentance about the history of Christian anti-Semitism. I don't think we may deny it, avoid it, or justify it."[102]

The Ember Letter provoked angry responses from Jewish leaders, as well as from Anglicans involved in dialogue with Jews. The Canadian Jewish Congress issued a statement in which it referred to the primate's letter as an attack upon the Jewish people. The CJC regarded the letter as a retreat from what had been accomplished in the Christian-Jewish dialogue. But members of the AMEC argued that "since the *Intifada* nothing is the same. We cannot ignore this reality in our dialogue." They felt that the reaction of the CJC was "milder than what they warned they would say."[103]

Archbishop Peers was "disappointed" at the Jewish criticism and maintained that his letter had been "misunderstood." He stated that he had not tried to deal with the Palestinian-Israeli conflict or with the history of Israel. "We value the relationships we have built between the Anglican and Jewish communities over the years," he said. The significant changes that had been made in Anglican teaching and liturgy attested to this statement. The primate called for a "continued dialogue and openness" over controversial subjects.[104]

Although Peers tried to reassure the Jews, he did not give up his point of view. On 20 April 1990, in an address entitled "Israel and the Occupied Territories: The Role of the Churches in Promoting a Just Peace," given in a synagogue before a mixed Jewish and Christian audience, he continued to criticize Israel. Reporting on his visit to Israel, he emphasized that he came as a witness, rather than as an expert. In the first section of the address he talked about why it was legitimate for the churches to be involved in the Israeli-Palestinian conflict, which was beyond their own jurisdiction. The area was important to them because it was the birthplace of Christianity and millions of Christians were living there. The churches, according to the Gospels, had a moral obligation to help those who suffer. Church partnership had become a dominant theme in the theology of mission, and the steady decline of the Christian population in the occupied territories was a source of concern.

The explosive anger demonstrated by the Palestinians had been caused by Israeli military rule, policies of containment and restriction, diminished access to health care, bureaucratic delays, closure of schools, and the imposition of curfews, Peers said. The anger had resulted in violence: "Herein lie the seeds of the Intifada. The hopelessness and despair of Palestinians finally erupted in 1987 and provoked a major uprising of popular sentiment against the Israeli occupation, and a major political crisis within the Israeli government." The primate blamed not only Israel for the eruption of the uprising but also the international community for failing to deal with the Palestinian problem and for tending to identify the Arabs as terrorists. The refusal of Western countries to distinguish between the Palestinian issue and the larger problem of the Israel-Arab conflict was also a cause of the international lack of interest in the Palestinian problem.

Peers went on to praise the unity of the Middle Eastern churches. He was so enthusiastic about the Middle East Council of Churches that he made the following questionable statement: "Politically, the Council has tried to avoid a posture of uncritical endorsement of partisan positions taken by the various interest groups in the regional power struggle." According to the primate, the moderate position of the MECC provoked hostility in both Jewish and Arab extremists. "There is a cost involved for moderation," he maintained.

Peers argued that the methods used by the Palestinians were "entirely peaceful and non-violent." The Israeli authorities, however, aimed at suppressing not only the uprising but also Palestinian development. The prospect of settlement by Russian immigrants on Arab land was also a cause for concern on the part of Palestinians. Accommodating this new wave of immigration would encourage Israel to implement an expansionist policy, they feared.

Archbishop Peers outlined the role that the Canadian churches should play in the achievement of peace and justice in the Middle East. He suggested that church members be encouraged to study the CCC's "Middle East Statement"; that they undertake educational programs concerning the various aspects of the Palestinian-Israeli conflict; that they support Canadian independent foreign policy, including its even-handed approach; that they increase the Canadian churches' contribution to development projects in occupied territories; that they encourage alternative tourism; that they express solidarity with the Palestinians by joining the MECC's program of prayer on Palm Sunday; and finally, that theological colleges be encouraged to include in their courses "perspectives of Palestinian Christians" and the history of Christian-Jewish relations.[105]

The primate's address was a turning point in the attitude of the Anglican Church towards the Palestinian-Israeli conflict. The position taken in his 20 April speech was not new; it was similar to the policy of the World Council of Churches and the Canadian Council of Churches. However, this was the first time that the Anglican primate had expressed a clear pro-Arab approach in a public address. It was not a passive position, in response to other statements, but an active policy, proposing the actual steps to be taken. The address was carefully prepared and distributed in advance. It therefore represented a well-thought-out policy, rather than an impulsive statement. Jews were shocked at the address. Les Scheininger, president of the Canadian Jewish Congress, challenged the primate's integrity and criticized Peers for having "fully thrown in [his] lot with the Palestinians and, indeed, become their advocate."[106] On the other side, Bishop Samir Kafity of Jerusalem commended the primate for his "courageous" address. "We need such genuine and important support," he wrote to Peers.[107]

On 25 June 1990 Archbishop Peers lectured at a UN North American regional seminar on the question of Palestine, in a continuation of his public statements on the Middle East. It was the first time that an Anglican primate had participated in a seminar on such a topic; in 1987 the Anglicans had refused to take part in a similar symposium. "It is not likely that the Anglican Church of Canada would send its own representative to the UN-sponsored symposium on Palestine," Brian Prideaux had written in his letter declining the invitation.[108]

The primate's lecture on the subject of the Intifada was mainly based on his address of 20 April. As a North American Christian, Peers pointed out that American involvement in the Middle East conflict had "not always been helpful or well intentioned," because the decisions were "often made for reasons which have more to do with the perceived interests of the United States of America than those of the

Middle East itself." Relying on statements by the heads of the Christian communities in Jerusalem, he repeated his criticism of the deprivation of the fundamental rights of people in the occupied territories. "The international community can no longer wait for events to get worse. Now is the time to convene an international conference through the offices of the UN to begin the implementation of the human rights of the Palestinian people." Peers called for the active support of the great powers in peace negotiations that would include the PLO. He recognized the sensitivity of the Jews, who had suffered from Christian persecution and who had a "desire for homeland," but he repeated the argument that Christians' sense of guilt towards the Jews should not prevent their support of the Palestinians. Therefore he recommended intensive peaceful negotiations.[109]

Archbishop Peers's public criticism of Israel's policy and his support for the Palestinian claim to an independent state ended the period of Anglican efforts to maintain a balanced policy. Another factor that played a role in the change in the Anglican Church's policy to the Palestinian-Israeli conflict was the Arabization of the Middle Eastern churches. Growing Arab nationalism and the rise of Palestinian self-determination led to the domination of the churches by Arab priests. This was the case not only with the Middle East Council of Churches, as we have seen in chapter 1, but also with the Anglican Church in Jerusalem. Instead of Western archbishops, such as George Appleton of England, in the 1970s, Arab bishops took the lead in the Anglican diocese of Jerusalem. Appleton had prepared the way for autonomy in the Anglican church in the Middle East. In 1976 the direct jurisdiction of Canterbury came to an end, and a new autonomous province of the Anglican Communion came into being. Bishop Frank Ibrahim Haddad was appointed the first Arab bishop of the Episcopal diocese of Jerusalem. Haddad had been born in Palestine during the British mandate, and after 1948 he had been the minister of a large Episcopal refugee community in Amman.

The new diocese of Jerusalem had fifteen local Arab clergy and eleven Arab expatriates from Israel.[110] Bishop Graham of London, chair of the Council of Jerusalem, complained in 1982 to Archbishop E.W. Scott: "I am concerned about the function of the Cathedral and its Close as a focal point of the Anglican Communion, as it is taking on increasingly an Arab character … This policy of the present bishop does not make things easy for the Dean."[111] Bishop Elias Khouri, a Palestinian Anglican, was a member of the PLO executive committee, and in 1986 he was photographed with Yasser Arafat, the PLO leader.[112] This trend led naturally to the nomination of Samir Kafity in 1984 as the Anglican bishop of Jerusalem. Kafity, a Palestinian, promulgated the Palestinian cause aggressively in England, the United States, and Canada. He appealed to the Anglican leaders in those countries to be involved in the Palestinian cause, to denounce the Israeli occupation, and to protest violations of Arab human rights.[113]

Bishop Kafity's criticism of Israel coincided with the new pro-Palestinian approach taken by the Anglican Church of Canada. In October 1990 an Anglican staff retreat responded to his appeals. Archbishop Peers reported that at the retreat it had been decided that the churches should "give prominence to the Anglican Diocese of Jerusalem … both in terms of inter-Anglican cooperation and in broader ecumenical terms."[114] Accordingly, the Anglican Church protested several times about Israeli violations of Anglican interests in the Middle East. In 1987 Peers had already protested a travel ban imposed on Canon Riah Abu Al-Assal, rector of Christ Evangelical Church in Nazareth. Al-Assal was accused by Israeli authorities of smuggling money to the PLO. Because of his position in the church, he was not arrested, but he was prohibited from travelling. Joe Clark, the Canadian secretary of state for external affairs, informed Peers that the primate's protest "was an important element of our representation" to the Israeli government.[115] Responding to a request by Samir Kafity, Peers in August 1989 appealed to Clark "to make our Government's strong disapproval" of an Israeli attack upon the Arab Ahli Hospital in Gaza, an institution that Anglicans had been helping, know to the Israeli government.[116] In March 1994, after the massacre at the Tomb of the Patriarchs in Hebron, the primate issued a statement expressing his "sorrow and outrage at the ruthless slaughter of so many worshippers" in Hebron. He called upon the government of Canada "to raise its voice in urging the Government of Israel to take those steps which only it can take to end the unconscionable situation in the occupied Palestinian territories." He also appealed to the world to respond "not only with sympathy and outrage, but with determination and resolution."[117]

The concern of the Anglican Church of Canada for the Anglican diocese of Jerusalem was also expressed financially. After the 1967 war, in response to a call by the World Council of Churches, Anglicans in Canada contributed $25,000 for Arab refugees.[118] In 1987, out of a total expenditure of $4,341,738,71 for the Primate's Fund Projects, the Palestine Refugee Development Program received $25,000, exactly the same amount as two decades earlier.[119] In 1990 the Anglican Church granted $23,423 to various institutions of the church in Jerusalem and $25,000 to churches suffering in Lebanon.[120]

Despite these warm and close relations between the Anglican Church of Canada and Bishop Kafity of Jerusalem, the Gulf War of 1990–91 became a disputed issue between them.[121] The Canadian churches denounced the occupation of Kuwait by Iraqi forces and the use of military force against Saddam Hussein by countries in the coalition. On 10 January 1991 Canadian church leaders, including Archbishop Peers, issued a statement that called for "a just and peaceful resolution to the Gulf Crisis by means other than war."[122] A week later the primate issued a separate statement in which he rejected the notion that war in the gulf was justified. "It is beyond dispute that Saddam Hussein's invasion of Kuwait … is unacceptable and contemptible. Nevertheless, the decision of the Canadian government to commit our forces to war … is deeply problematic." He called for the settlement of disputes "through diplomatic, economic and political means without recourse to the brutalities of war."[123]

While Samir Kafity had asked for church intervention in the Palestinian-Israeli conflict, he opposed the intervention by the Canadian churches in the Gulf War. He demanded that the churches take sides with the Palestinians, but he asked them to stay out of the gulf conflict, because it was "an inter-Arab crisis." Although no territorial occupation by force was acceptable, "one must see the crisis in its totality. It must be seen as a regional domestic problem, an Arab problem," he maintained. Kafity objected to the fact that the churches took sides in the Gulf War. "The church redeems situations, does not judge nor should it condemn," he declared.[124]

The address given by Bishop Kafity on 21 June 1992 to the General Synod of the Anglican Church of Canada, an extraordinary honour, and the resolutions adopted were the climax of Anglican intervention in the Palestinian-Israeli conflict. The bishop delivered a moving lecture on behalf of the Palestinian cause at the synod's special session on the Middle East. He recounted the decades of Palestinian suffering under Israeli occupation, reminding the audience of his twenty-three years of experience in the area. Christian Arabs had fled from occupied territories, and he warned of a decrease in the Christian population in Jerusalem. Kafity appealed for an "evenhanded" attitude. He understood the sense of remorse felt by Western Christians because they had persecuted the Jews, but why could they not be friends to two peoples? "We don't ask the West to abandon their friends the Jews, but we want their friendship too." Kafity appealed to the churches to be more involved in the Middle East crisis. "Christians have been spectators for 44 years. It is high time that the Christian church rose up from a position of passive support … How long will the world be silent?" He insisted that the Palestinians wished "for peace with justice, integrity and honor as equals." Kafity concluded his address by calling upon the Anglican synod to consider seriously "evenhandedness, objectivity [and] opting for peace."[125]

Following Bishop Kafity's presentation, the General Synod adopted a set of resolutions concerning the Middle East situation and the church's position regarding the Jews. It agreed to support the MECC and the diocese of Jerusalem; to deepen education in order to create awareness of the Middle East crisis and the "exodus of Christians from Jerusalem"; and "to affirm the right of the Palestinians to self-determination, including their right to choose their representatives in the peace talks and their right to the establishment of their own state alongside the State of Israel." The synod also resolved to concentrate on the solution of the Palestinian refugee problem; "to urge the UN to offer protection" to the people in the occupied territories; and finally, to encourage alternative tourism for Anglicans. In an effort to balance this strongly pro-Arab set of resolutions, the synod declared that criticism of Israel's policies was "a separate matter in no way implying prejudice against Jewish people." It reaffirmed earlier resolutions denouncing antisemitism and "repudiating the continuing dissemination of Neo-Nazi propaganda in Canada and the revisionist theories concerning the Holocaust." Church leaders were urged "to take positive action" to reject antisemitic expressions and neo-Nazi sympathizers, and clergy were asked to avoid anti-Jewish interpretations of the Scriptures and "blaming the Jews for Jesus' death."[126]

In response, Alan Rose challenged Kafity's figures concerning a decrease in the Christian population in Jerusalem, and he complained about the lack of balance in the synod's resolutions. Since the resolutions originated in part with the MECC, which had "a long and undistinguished record with regard to Israel," Rose was not surprised.[127] One can see that the Anglican Church of Canada had travelled a long way in regard to its attitude to the Jewish state. Nevertheless, as far as Anglican-Jewish relations were concerned, the dialogue between the two communities continued in a friendly atmosphere.[128]

Towards the end of the 1980s a radical change had taken place in the attitude of the Anglican Church towards Israel, from apathy to involvement, from neutrality to a pro-Arab position. A combination of internal and external factors produced this change, among them the Israeli invasion of Lebanon, the Intifada, and the Arabization of the Middle East Protestant churches, including the Anglican church in Jerusalem. Other factors were the growing influence of the Middle East Council of Churches, the deep involvement of the Canadian Council of Churches in Middle East affairs, and the personal interest of the primate, Archbishop Michael G. Peers, in the Palestinian-Israeli conflict.

12 The Presbyterian Church in Canada

In the twentieth century the Presbyterians and the Baptists in Canada were small denominations compared to the United and the Anglican churches. While those churches had global interests, the smaller groups were mainly preoccupied with internal church matters and did not concern themselves with the Israeli-Palestinian conflict.[1]

The Presbyterian Church in Canada had both Scottish and American roots. In the eighteenth and nineteenth centuries it had suffered from sectionalism and division. However, in 1875 all branches of Canadian Presbyterism united, adopting the name of the Presbyterian Church in Canada. The union was followed by five decades of growth, so that in 1925 it was the largest Protestant denomination in the country. But at this time a bitter controversy arose over a proposed merger with the Methodist and the Congregationalist churches. Between 1903 and 1925 the Presbyterians had been deeply divided over whether to join the proposed United Church. In the west and in new congregations the great majority supported the union. By establishing one church, the unionists wanted to avoid factionalism. Furthermore, in small communities people did not have the financial ability to maintain several churches with small congregations.

The Presbyterians who opposed the merger were a less homogeneous group than the unionists. Many of them were recent Scots or Irish immigrants who still considered themselves to be living in exile in Canada. For them, the idea of a national Canadian church was not appealing. Some disliked the evangelism, social action, and liberalism of the Methodists. Many feared unknown elements that might join the union. In 1910 those opposing the merger formed an organization to campaign more effectively. Called the Presbyterian Association for the Federation of the Churches of the Protestant Denominations, it gradually gained momentum. In 1925, in the crucial election, approximately one-third opposed the union, refusing to join the United Church. Most of the leaders, elders, and ministers and almost all overseas missionaries joined the United Church. The liberals and the theologians also preferred the new organization.[2]

The schism within the Presbyterian Church left deep scars on its members. "It is difficult to think of any event in Canadian church history that left such a residue of bitterness, breaking up not only congregations but personal friendships and family loyalties," wrote John Webster Grant.[3]

Those who remained outside the United Church were faced with many challenges in their efforts to preserve the Presbyterian Church as an independent body. The seven hundred congregations who did not join the union had to erect new buildings and acquire the necessary supplies, which led them into heavy debt. It was even more difficult to find new leaders, new ministers, and new missionaries to operate abroad. The independent identity of the Presbyterian Church in Canada was considered a crucial matter. Subsequently, the church participated fully in ecumenical activities, joining the Canadian Council of Churches and the World Council of Churches. The turning point came after World War II when debts were paid and the suburbs began to grow. Urbanization helped Presbyterians to establish new congregations in the suburbs, and the church's recovery was under way. "The question before the PCC in 1925 was ... whether it would survive as an effective entity, and it has triumphantly survived," observed Grant.[4]

More difficult to recover was the church's denominational identity. Since most of the Presbyterians had joined the United Church, those who remained outside wondered who the "real" Presbyterians were and what Presbyterianism meant. Articles in the *Presbyterian Record*, the official organ of the church, frequently discussed the subject of self-definition. This concern led also to a re-examination of the theological foundations of the church. But the Presbyterian Church in Canada not only survived the great schism; it grew. While in 1925 approximately 127,000–130,000 members had opposed the union, in 1994 the General Assembly reported 152,684 members and 62,969 adherents (who were allowed to participate in church life but were not official members).[5]

THE PRESBYTERIAN CHURCH AND THE HOLOCAUST

In light of the painful schism, the Presbyterians were preoccupied in the 1930s and 1940s with the need to rebuild their church and organize its boards. They had to develop lay leadership, recruit ministers, gain recognition, pay debts, and establish their theological identity. Their sense of weakness caused the Presbyterians to focus upon their own problems. This preoccupation could partly explain Presbyterians' disregard of the Holocaust, the persecution of the Jews, and later the Middle East conflict.[6]

What was the dominant character of the church in these years? The rejection of union was fundamentally conservative. Furthermore, in searching for new ministers, the churches tended to recruit graduates of conservative seminaries. The theological re-examination also arrived at conservative conclusions. Comparing the Presbyterian to the United Church, Grant concluded that, despite their similarities, the Presbyterians were concentrated "at the conservative end of the register."[7]

Another aspect of the Presbyterian Church was its worldwide missionary activities. Missionaries were active in India, Korea, Manchuria, Japan, Italy, and several African countries. Among the missionary enterprises was one to the Jews. The leading personalities in the Presbyterian Church who were involved in converting Jews were the Reverend Morris Zeidman, a born Jew and director of the Scott Institute's "Mission to the Jews" in Toronto, and the Reverend W.M. Rochester, editor of the *Presbyterian Record*. In 1936 the presbytery of Chatham pointed out the existence among Jews of "an increasing appreciation of Jesus and his message in modern Judaism." It therefore proposed to the General Assembly that it "invite leaders of Judaism to meet leaders of the PCC ... with a view of developing a deeper spirit of friendship between Judaism and Christianity." The overture was rejected, perhaps for procedural reasons, and no action was taken.[8]

Morris Zeidman was very active in missionary enterprises. He boasted that his Scott Institute in Toronto was "one of the most effective on the North America continent." In 1938, in view of the Nazi persecution in Germany, the rise of antisemitism in Europe and Canada, and the refugee problem, he wrote, "the Presbyterian Church has now the great opportunity of acting the good Samaritan, the friend-in-need, to the Jews. Being tossed to and fro, being hated and calumniated, the Church should stretch out the hand of friendship."[9] Zeidman reported great success; twelve Hebrew Christians had been preaching the Gospel among Jews in North America.[10]

As a matter of fact, Zeidman's optimism was baseless. In 1941 he resigned as superintendent of the Presbyterian Mission to the Jews, and the report of the following year, written by someone else, presented a different picture: "When we look at the field, we say truthfully that merely the fringes of the work have been touched ... It seems impossible to Christianize the Jews ... Even the poorest Jews look upon the Gentiles as Gayim [*sic*] – Heathen – and worshippers of a dead carpenter. They despise our Savior, sneer at His miraculous birth and deny His resurrection." Although the task was "tremendously difficult," the missionaries did not give up their effort, because every soul was important, and as they visualized each success, "our hearts bound for joy."[11]

Another potential opportunity for the evangelization of Jews arrived with the establishment of the State of Israel. Missionary groups took advantage of the fact that mass immigration to Israel had brought serious economic hardship. Calvin H. Chambers, a former convener of the Presbyterian Committee on the Christian Approach to the Jew, visited Israel in 1961 and analyzed the possibilities for conversion. He observed that the average Jew resented missionary work. Particularly after Auschwitz, "it is unlikely that the Jew will give up his religion." Nevertheless, Chambers insisted that "the church cannot side step her responsibilities to the Jewish people in Israel."[12]

The missionary zeal of the Presbyterians did not abate with the time. When Ray Drenvan, a minister who was serving in Mauritius, declared in 1988 that he had not come to that country to convert people to Christianity, much debate followed. An editorial in the *Presbyterian Record* confronted Drenvan's opinion. "ultimately I think it has to be said that we are indeed to convert others." The editor went on to say that "the traditional missionary task is with us. Perhaps it is to be done in new ways, with a new sensitivity and with a greater openness to others. But it is to be done, and with decisiveness and vision."[13] While the primate of the Anglican Church of Canada had declared in May 1973 that his church disavowed "any approach which is geared to proselytizing Jews,"[14] the Presbyterian Church in 1988 still rejected any notion of changing its evangelistic mission.

The attitude of the church to the Jews and the Holocaust followed this conservative approach, including, for many members, the traditional derogatory Christian remarks about the Jewish people. A characteristic example was Lord Tweedsmuir, the governor general of Canada. In January 1938, addressing the General Council Alliance of Reformed Churches, he lamented the decrease in morality in Canadian society. Speaking "as a Presbyterian to fellow Presbyterians," he cited the example of Pharisaism, "which might be defined as loyalty to conventions which have lost any binding spiritual force." This leading

Presbyterian figure stated that obedience to Jewish religion "is no basis for value." As a religious Presbyterian, he believed in the immorality of Judaism.[15] Possibly he did not intend to treat Jews in a derogatory fashion; rather, like most Christians of his day, he simply did not connect the New Testament Pharisees in any way with modern Judaism. Davies and Nefsky have called Lord Tweedsmuir's comment "inappropriate" and "unthinking." However, they point out that he was not an antisemite and that he sympathized with the plight of Jews, even supporting their entrance into Canada.[16]

Another distinguished Presbyterian was W.L. Mackenzie King, the Canadian prime minister. Unlike the governor general, he had an anti-Jewish bias, as antisemitic remarks in his personal diary attest. As a religious Presbyterian, King regarded the Jews as aggressive, ruling the world by their money. He met Hitler and was impressed by the German leader's personality. King strongly opposed the relaxation of Canadian immigration regulations. While his anti-immigration policy mainly derived from political and economic considerations, his anti-Jewish bias and the influence of his meeting with Hitler probably played a part in his position as well.[17]

Some Presbyterian ministers during this period stated that the Nazi persecution of the Jews was a divine punishment for the Jews' refusal to accept redemption. John Inkster, the Scottish-born minister of Knox Presbyterian Church in Toronto, the largest Presbyterian congregation in the country, complained in November 1938 after Kristallnacht that Jews were turning to the world for help, "instead of confessing their sins and asking God for forgiveness for themselves, especially the sin of unbelief and denial of Christ." God had used the Nazis as his stick to punish the Jews. There were other ministers who, like Inkster, "understood" the Nazi persecution of Jews, even if they did not condone it.[18]

Was the Presbyterian Church antisemitic at this time? Davies and Nefsky argue that "there is no evidence to suggest that antisemitism was more widespread in their ranks than in the rest of Canadian society, in spite of the antiquated anti-Jewish theological ideas cultivated by some of their more conservative preachers." The General Assembly was more direct, in 1989 adopting a resolution that declared: "We repent of the sin of antisemitism."[19] Probably this anti-Jewish sentiment, along with other factors, contributed to the disregard by the church of the problem of Jewish suffering under Nazi rule.

To be sure, most Presbyterians did not sympathize with Hitler and the Nazis. As British descendants, they supported Britain and its democracic tradition. Their attention was focused upon the Protestant church's struggle in Germany, which diverted their consideration away from the Jewish predicament. Christian suffering in Germany had more appeal than the image of a suffering Jew, possibly another reason for Presbyterian disregard of the Jewish plight in Germany.[20]

A notable exception to the Presbyterian silence concerning the Jewish persecution and admission of Jewish refugees into Canada was a leading Presbyterian laywoman, Senator Cairine Wilson. In 1939 she established the Canadian National Committee on Refugees and Victims of Political Persecution (CNCR). As president of this committee, she tried to educate the Canadian people to recognize the plight of Jewish refugees.[21] Another exception was Morris Zeidman, who had been born to a Jewish family in Poland that was murdered in Treblinka. He was the only one who reported in the *Presbyterian Record* about Nazi atrocities and massacres in Eastern Europe.[22]

In 1943, when the mass murder of the Jews was well known and difficult to disregard, the General Assembly discussed and approved an overture presented by the Saskatoon presbytery, entitled "On Behalf of the Jewish Race," which read as follows:

Whereas, never before, perhaps in the history of Christianity have the ancient race of Israel been tortured and persecuted as at the present time ...

We, as a Church, are sympathetic to the Jewish Race in their trials and persecution in every part of Europe, and urge it to do all in its power to mitigate the suffering of God's ancient Race, to open the doors of our Dominion to a fair share of the refugees as opportunity presents itself, and to provide as far as possible for the immediate necessities of such refugees as may come to us from time to time during the war ... And we would still further petition the Venerable, the General Assembly, to urge the people of our Church to denounce anti-semitism wherever found.[23]

The following year the moderator of the General Assembly joined with the heads of the Anglican, United, and Roman Catholic churches in issuing a statement that supported the appeal by the CNCR to the Canadian government to admit Jewish refugees. The Board of Evangelism and Church Life and Work of the Presbyterian Church discussed this statement and, "after considerable discussion of a knotty point," agreed to approve it, reported the *Presbyterian Record*.[24]

Was, then, the Presbyterian Church in Canada silent? A historical review prepared by a committee appointed by the General Assembly, whose report was printed in the *Acts and Proceedings of the General Assembly* of 1990, concluded: "It is significant to point out that no other mention of the persecution of the Jews in Europe, with the above two exceptions, is recorded in the records of the church's highest court or in its official periodical in this pre-1945 period. While the Presbyterian Church in Canada did not remain entirely silent on the subject of the

'Holocaust' and the 'final solution,' it is concluded that individual voices who stood up and were counted did not receive the widespread and visible support of the official church bodies, and there is little indication that the Church attempted, or was prepared, to take action in this regard."[25]

Davies and Nefsky also argue that the Presbyterian Church "was not silent with respect to the Jews, but it was less vocal and less involved than the larger United and Anglican Churches."[26] Nearer to the facts was the resolution approved by the General Assembly in 1989, which said: "We deplore the total inaction and nearly total silence of our Church during the Second World War when the scattered descendants of those who gave to us our faith were being crucified at the hands of those who called themselves Christians."[27]

THE PRESBYTERIAN CHURCH
AND THE STATE OF ISRAEL

What was the attitude of the Presbyterian Church to the establishment of the Jewish state and the Middle East crisis? To understand the church's approach to the Palestinian-Israeli conflict, we must first consider its general policy on international affairs. As we have pointed out, the Presbyterian Church had struggled for survival during the decades following the schism of 1925, focusing on internal matters, and naturally, it was unable to give much attention to world affairs. However, its department of Overseas Missions was concerned with those countries where its missionaries operated. Missionary groups were particularly sensitive to the importance of international affairs, which "dominated many aspects of our national life." Furthermore, Christians had a responsibility "for witness and prophetic utterance in world issues." Since the Presbyterian Church had "no appropriate instrument" to investigate these subjects, the General Board of Missions recommended to the General Assembly in 1959 that a special committee be responsible for this field.[28]

The eighty-fifth General Assembly that year endorsed this recommendation and authorized the moderator to name a committee to study the subject.[29] Although the Committee on International Affairs (CIA) was officially approved by the General Assembly in 1961, four years later its activity was confined to sending participants to the CCC's equivalent committee and to an inter-church seminar in Ottawa. "I hope we may be able to move forward in developing a program for the Committee ... even though its main function so far has simply been to line up a delegation for the annual Inter-Church seminar,"reported E.H. Johnson, the CIA secretary.[30] One reason for the committee's inability to conduct independent research into international affairs was a lack of money; its annual budget ranged from $300 to $400.[31] Pressures from the presbyteries finally activated the CIA, however. In 1966, responding to an appeal by the synod of Toronto, the committee prepared a statement on Vietnam.[32] That year "a reappraisal of the Committee function and responsibility was made and plans laid," according to the report of the CIA to the General Assembly.[33]

While in its first decade the CIA prepared a statement only on Vietnam, gradually it extended its interest to other countries, such as South Africa, China, Nigeria, Ireland, and Pakistan. The committee was particularly interested in political liberation movements. In June 1972 the secretary of the committee wrote: "We cannot dismiss the concern in these statements for the victims of actual political oppression." As a sign of solidarity with national liberation movements, the committee recommended that the Presbyterian Church reduce its support to Portugal, which was suppressing national liberation movements in its African colony.[34]

The Middle East was not mentioned as an area of interest for the committee. Furthermore, it lacked experts in this field and had to rely upon other groups. "In areas where we have little or no background, e.g. the Middle East, we would support and assist other denominations in the Canadian Council of Churches," reported the CIA to the ninety-eighth General Assembly in 1972. As an outcome of this cooperation with the CCC, the committee distributed the council's pamphlet *Search for Understanding in the Middle East.*[35]

If the Committee on International Affairs showed a lack of interest in the Middle East, so did the General Assembly and the *Presbyterian Record*. The General Assembly did not issue any statement regarding the Palestinian-Israeli conflict until 1967. The *Record* did not report on the UN resolution on the partition of Palestine in November 1947, nor did it cover the fighting and the establishment of the Jewish state in May 1948. Later the Arab refugee problem gained some attention. During the first decade of the Israel's existence, several articles depicted the situation of the Arab refugees. They were "discouraged, bored, unemployed, insecure, unhappy, sometimes hungry and dirty … As such they have a claim on the sympathy and respect of Christian men and women," wrote Mildred McAfee in February 1953. The author solicited help for the refugees, without criticizing Israel and without offering any solutions. She recommended leaving the political situation to the politicians.[36] The journal also published several reports on visits to the Holy Land, depicting Christmas in Bethlehem, Easter in Jerusalem, and excavations in the Holy City. These articles either disregarded the establishment of a new state in the Holy Land or mentioned it without comment and without animosity to either side.[37] Some stories depicted Israel in a positive way. In 1964 a writer commented, "Modern Israel ... is a land of progress, but care has been taken to keep intact the historical and holy sites."[38]

Only a few articles focused upon the problematic situation in the region. Alexander Ferguson, a reporter and a minister working for the National Council of Churches in the U.S.A., analyzed the conflict and discussed the positions of the Israelis and the Arabs. Trying to be fair to both sides, he declared that "it is ever difficult to determine which side is at fault when war comes." To solve the "grave and deep-seated" issues, he proposed that Arab leaders be ready "to settle for something other than repatriation," that they allow open trade routes for Israel, and that they "receive Israel into their family of nations." Israel should retreat to the UN partition line and limit the number of immigrants it admitted. To Christians, he advised that they be aware of the problems, support the Christian churches in the region, and contribute financially to the refugees.[39] Apparently, such appeals for financial help did not generate much response. In 1955 the Presbyterian Church contributed $18,990 to the CCC to be distributed among churches in Belgium, Austria, Italy, and Indonesia. It also gave $1,000 for flood relief in Pakistan and for the churches of Istanbul. However, the church made no financial contribution to Arab refugees.[40]

Like other denominations, the Presbyterian Church was affected by the Six Day War of 1967. In June that year the General Assembly adopted a resolution, probably its first in regard to the Palestinian-Israeli conflict, which noted "with deep concern the tragic events in the Middle East with their sad aftermath of homeless refugees, aggravated hostility and tension ... and the increased threat of world war." The assembly expressed its sympathy with the victims of the war, Israelis as well as Arabs, and pledged its help to provide relief and rehabilitation. It appealed to church members to support those who were suffering and to pray for a "just and lasting solution." It encouraged the Canadian government to press the United Nations to establish a peacekeeping force that would restore confidence in the area, and to take steps towards solving the problems of the region, particularly the refugee issue. The assembly also expressed its support for the general secretary of the UN for his efforts to reach a solution to the Middle East conflict.[41] Unlike the Heraklion resolution of the WCC from August 1967,[42] the Presbyterian statement refrained from taking sides. It avoided criticism of Israel, although it did not mention Israel's right to exist in secure boundaries.

In October 1967 the *Presbyterian Record* published a rare editorial on the Middle East conflict. It reprinted the Heraklion resolution and added some suggestions for action that individuals and congregations could take: they could support refugees either through the Presbyterian inter-church aid committee or by appealing to the Canadian government to contribute to UNRWA. The editorial also called upon the major powers to find "some permanent placement for the dispossessed" and to be aware of the problems of the region.[43]

Presbyterians in the 1960s and 1970s continue to take only a minor interest in the Middle East, and the *Presbyterian Record* had little coverage of the area. In these decades it published several articles by Forrest, but unlike his articles in the *United Church Observer*, these were relatively moderate.[44] To balance Forrest's pieces, the editors printed pro-Israeli articles, such as those of G. Douglas Young.

The president of the American Institute of Holy Land Studies in Jerusalem, Young was the son of a Presbyterian missionary to Korea and Japan; he was a Christian Zionist and a staunch friend of Israel. In 1969 he denounced certain reports of church delegations to Israel, which he called "misinformation." As one who had lived in Jerusalem for ten years and knew the facts first-hand, he criticized those "inspectors" who came for a few days and returned with reports based on "partial and sometimes even faulty sources." He maintained that accusations against Israel for its occupation and its approach to the refugees were "motivated by political considerations rather than considerations of truth." Young argued that "we feel at peace and at ease in our united city as Christians." Israel had repaired the holy sites and churches that had been damaged in the war of 1948. "The problem is not one of refugees, of occupations, of borders. It is a problem of either peace or genocide for the Jews ... It becomes, not a cause for uneasiness or uncertainty to Christians abroad but rather a very deep moral issue as to whether they will lend encouragement to Arab nations, whose plans include more war and possible genocide, or whether they will use their influence for the negotiation for peace now," argued Young.[45]

Another pro-Israel piece appeared in the *Presbyterian Record* in 1976. The story of Nes Ammim exemplified the possibility of understanding and cooperation between the two religious communities. It was a small Christian settlement in Israel that supported itself by growing roses. "This remarkable farm stands as a silent witness to Christian understanding and support of Israel," wrote DeCourcy H. Rayner.[46]

James E. Solheim, the editor of *Event*, the American Lutheran magazine, had published an article in the *Presbyterian Record* from a Christian point of view in 1971. He examined the role of religion in the life of Israel. Since Israel was a "politically secular state," the author questioned its relation to the people of the Bible. Despite its cultural and sociological continuity with the biblical Israel, he stated that "as a Christian I find it very difficult to accept a theological continuity." He expressed the traditional Christian concept that "it is the church, the people of the new covenant in Jesus Christ, who are the true Israel … It is we who are in continuity with the biblical Israel … The God I meet in the Old Testament will not dance a Zionist jig for a political-secular state." Solheim also criticized the role of the Middle Eastern churches in the peace process. Because of the fact that Christians in the Middle East were a small minority, they tended "to compensate for their minority status by being vocally nationalistic, to the point of embarrassment. Arab Christians … were as rigid in their condemnation of the Israelis as any Arab." Solheim was disappointed to learn that the church did not play a role of reconciliation in the region.[47]

The officers of the Presbyterian Church or its assembly occasionally issued statements on the Middle East or joined ones that were initiated by other denominations. In February 1969, after the hanging of Jews in Baghdad, the Presbyterian moderator joined a group of leading Canadian church leaders who sent a telegram to Ottawa asking the Canadian government to assist those people who were living in danger and distress. "Bearing in mind the recent tragic hangings in Iraq, we urgently call upon our government to arrange for permission for all Jews living in Iraq, Egypt and Syria who wish to emigrate to Canada to be free to do so, and to assist them to get to Canada as quickly as possible." The telegram also recommended that the government extend an invitation to Palestinian refugees to immigrate to Canada.[48]

In 1972, after a terrorist attack in the Israeli airport at Tel Aviv in which fifteen Christian pilgrims and nine Israeli civilians were massacred, the General Assembly instructed the CIA to demand that the Middle East countries "secure free and safe passage for pilgrims of all faiths." The assembly hoped that cooperation among the states of the region would bring reconciliation. There were no words of condolence for the families of the victims of the massacre and no condemnation of the terrorist attack.[49] T. Meron, the Israeli ambassador in Ottawa, responded. He wrote that Israel had taken "various steps to prevent the recurrence of such senseless acts of violence." He reminded the Presbyterians that certain Arab countries were sheltering and supporting terrorist organizations, and he called upon nations to take "immediate steps to put an end to air piracy and air terror."[50]

The Yom Kippur War of October 1973 was totally disregarded by the CIA, the General Assembly, and the *Presbyterian Record*.[51] However, two years later, in 1975, the committee decided to learn more about the complicated subject of the Middle East. Desiring to hear both sides, it invited representatives to a symposium entitled "Towards a

Just Solution for Israel and the Palestinians." Rabbi Erwin Schild of Adath Israel Congregation, chair of the Canada-Israel Committee's central region, represented the Zionist point of view. James Peter, a professor at Ryerson Polytechnic and former president of the Canada-Arab Federation, presented the Arab position. A member of the Canadian Council of Churches discussed the approach of a Canadian Christian to the problem. This was a fair and balanced effort to learn about the problem from different angles.[52]

As we have seen, in the period 1945–82 the Presbyterian Church in Canada was not really interested in the Middle East conflict. Until 1967, the area was almost totally disregarded, and even after that date, statements and editorials were rare and vague, though balanced. This apathetic attitude changed after 1982: instead of neutrality, the Presbyterian Church became involved; instead of a balanced approach, it adopted a pro-Arab policy. What were the causes of this drastic change? The increasing involvement of the CCC in the Middle East conflict during the 1980s and its close cooperation with the Middle East Council of Churches led its member denominations, including the Presbyterian Church, to support the Palestinian cause. Glen Davies, a Presbyterian minister, represented the church in the Middle East Working Group. Douglas duCharme, whose function as the CCC's liaison to the MECC was partially financed by the Presbyterian Church, contributed to the shift of the church towards support of the Palestinians.[53]

The first sign of a growing interest in the Middle East conflict on the part of the church appeared in a list of topics prepared in 1982–83 by the Committee on International Affairs. The Middle East was ranked at the top of subjects that were classified as of "major interest."[54] Indeed, 1983 was the year that ended the long silence of the Presbyterian Church with regard to the Middle East. The CIA published a resolution in which it stated that it had been "much saddened and deeply troubled by … the invasion of Lebanon and the massacre of Sabra and Shatila, which brought death and destruction to so many." The committee called upon church members "to embrace and assert the cause of peace." In 1983 also, the General Assembly called upon the Canadian government to press for the "withdrawal of all outside military forces from Lebanon," though without mentioning Israel and Syria.[55]

Although in 1984 there were other bloody disputes in the Middle East, such as those between Iran and Iraq and in Lebanon, the General Assembly considered the Palestinian-Israeli conflict as "the key Middle East crisis." It therefore renewed its call for the Canadian government to "press for the solution," which should be based "on the right of Israel to have secure and recognized boundaries, and the right of the

Palestinians to have a homeland of their own in a clearly defined territory."[56] The Reverend Dr Raymond Hodgson, secretary of the Committee on International Affairs of the Presbyterian Church, later reflected that Presbyterians were not tough enough with regard to ensuring Israel's territorial security. Although every statement did mention the right of Israel to exist in secure boundaries, he believed that the church's full support of the Palestinians, and later of the PLO, sometimes contradicted Israel's security.[57]

From the mid-1980s on, the Presbyterian Church in Canada had "closer relationships with church partners in the Middle East."[58] In 1987 the *Acts and Proceedings of the One Hundred and Thirteenth General Assembly* published an excerpt from a report by Ghassan Rubeiz of the WCC, who discussed the migration of Christians from Israel and particularly from the occupied territories.[59] The General Assembly adopted a resolution that commended the Board of World Missions for its support of the Middle East Council of Churches and warned Presbyterians visiting Israel to "be aware of the political significance of the arrangements they make." It recommended that they visit Christian institutions while in Israel.[60]

A sign of growing Presbyterian support of the MECC was the selection of Gabriel Habib as the recipient of the E.H. Johnson Annual Award for 1988. Habib received this prestigious award because "of his contribution in that area of Christian Witness." In his address, delivered in June 1988 to the General Assembly, he criticized Western missionaries, "who instead of respecting Muslims and their faith, arrogantly proclaim that they are coming merely to save the Muslim from Islam."[61] Besides listening to Habib's address, the General Assembly dealt with the CIA report on the Middle East, which described the crisis in the area as potentially the "next world war." Accordingly, the assembly adopted a resolution that called upon the Canadian government to demand an international peace conference.[62]

The following year, 1989, the General Assembly took a step closer to an unbalanced approach to the Israeli-Palestinian conflict.[63] It reaffirmed the need "to recognize the concerns of both parties" when the human and political rights of one side could not be fulfilled at the expense of the other, and it specified UN Resolutions 242 and 338 as the bases for a peace settlement, "with consideration for the changes that have occurred in the situation since 1967," particularly since the Intifada. It also called for the convening of a UN-sponsored peace conference, at which the PLO would represent the Palestinians. The acknowledgment of the PLO as the legitimate representative of the Palestinians was a new phase in the church's recognition of Arab rights. The General Assembly turned to its congregations and presbyteries "to build greater awareness" of the conflict and to facilitate a dialogue between Jews and Arabs in Canada. An additional recommendation urged the Canadian government "to exert pressure on the Government of Israel to bring an immediate end to human rights abuses by Israeli forces in the occupied territories and to bring to justice those guilty of such abuses." This last clause was rejected, however, because it was considered "counterproductive."[64] The report, which had been prepared by Douglas duCharme, clearly reflected the ideas of the MEWG of the CCC. Thus duCharme was instrumental in the development of a closer relationship between the Presbyterians and the MECC.

Some members of the General Assembly were alarmed by the church's growing criticism of Israel and increasing support for the Palestinian cause. The 150th assembly therefore adopted a resolution in 1989 which stated: "Before addressing any issue affecting the State of Israel or our Jewish kinfolk in the faith, the PCC within the holy Catholic Church proclaims that although we come before the State of Israel with contrite hearts, we come not with clean hands. We publicly disown and repent of the long and ancient record of wrongdoing committed by the Christian church in most of its history ... We repent the sin of antisemitism ... We also are alarmed at injustice being done to our Palestinian brothers and sisters. But because we repent past misdeeds, we urge that all future pronouncements of our Church affecting the Israeli-Arab relations will be prefaced with this preamble."

Several members of the assembly disagreed with the last sentence. It was therefore decided that the words "But because ... with this preamble" should be deleted. In line with the statement of repentance, the assemby moved to ask the Committee on History to prepare a historical review of Christian-Jewish relations through the ages and to report on the subject to the next General Assembly.[65] Accordingly, at the 16oth assembly in 1990, this committee provided a historical account of Christian anti-Jewish relations. It stated, "We must acknowledge our own weakness ... We must recognize that we have our own cultural biases and that may affect our behaviour."[66]

Nevertheless, the Presbyterian Church continued its warm relations with the MECC and deepened its involvement in Middle East affairs. In 1990 the moderator, Dr Harrold Morris, joined other Canadian church leaders in a trip to Israel. After visiting the West Bank and Gaza, he said about the Intifada: "They are attempting to increase the self-worth and pride of Palestinians who have been treated as second and third class citizens, and not even as citizens." The delegation participated in the MECC convention in Cyprus and returned to Canada converted to the Palestinian cause.[67] The CCC's "Position Paper on the Middle East" was presented and endorsed by the General Assembly of the Presbyterian Church that year. It was printed in its entirety in the *Acts and Proceedings*, the official record of the assembly, which recommended that it be distributed together with a study guide.[68]

The CIA report of 1991 discussed the massive emigration of Russian Jews to Israel in 1990–91. It stated that this influx had brought "sweeping changes" to the region and "introduced a new and volatile element" into the conflict. The new immigrants were taking jobs and housing from the Arabs, expanding new settlements, increasing the demand for water, and supporting the incumbent right-wing Israeli government.[69] The General Assembly that year deplored the "recent alarming increase in anti-semitic and anti-Arab acts and remarks in Canadian society." It rightly pointed out that "the term 'anti-semitic' … is understood to mean 'anti-Jewish.'"[70] This clarification undermined Arab response to the accusation that Arabs were antisemitic. Bishop Samir Kafity argued that Arabs were also Semites, saying, "I can't be anti-Semitic, because I would be anti myself."[71]

The continuing influence of Douglas duCharme on the Presbyterian approach to the Palestinian-Israeli conflict was clear in the report of 1992. To explain the background of Middle East events of the previous year, the *Acts and Proceedings* reprinted his article "The Middle East: Where Peace Is Broken and Where There Are Signs of Hope."[72] The recommendations adopted by the assembly were also characteristic of duCharme's concerns: "That steps be taken to strengthen the partnership between the Presbyterian Church in Canada and the Middle East Council of Churches; that congregations be encouraged to make use of Middle East mission study materials prepared for 1992–1993 as a means of deepening an understanding of the Middle East and its people."[73]

On 13 September 1993, in Washington, DC, Israel and the PLO signed a declaration of principles. This agreement was hailed by the General Assembly's report that year as "a new beginning and a positive step towards peace … a sign of hope and a turning point in the history of the Middle East." The report introduced a new element, the centrality of Jerusalem, and it rejected "all attempts for exclusive control over the city by any religious or political entity." The city's destiny should be decided by a "genuine partnership" between the three religions.[74]

In conclusion, we can say that early in this period the Presbyterian Church in Canada was mainly preoccupied with internal matters. Its principal interests abroad were in countries with missionary activities. The Middle East conflict therefore attracted only minor attention. From the mid-1980s on, this approach changed as a result of several factors, including growing criticism of Israel's policies because of its invasion of Lebanon, the Intifada, the increasing influence of the

Middle East Council of Churches on Canadian churches, and the influence of Douglas duCharme. But did the Presbyterian Church have a balanced Middle East policy? One might agree with Dr Raymond Hodgson, the former secretary of the church's Committee on International Affairs, who in 1995 commented that "if I were a historian, I would say that the Presbyterians' position was biased in favour of the Arabs."[75]

13   The Baptists in Canada

The earliest Baptists were a product of the sixteenth-century Protestant Reformation. They opposed the baptism of infants and instead required adult believers to be baptized upon profession of faith. They believed in the liberty of the soul and in personal freedom to interpret the Scriptures. Each congregation constituted a fellowship of believers who had experienced a spiritual conversion. Local churches were independent in religious, as well as in administrative, matters. This congregationalist character, where individual churches are self-governing and have theological independence, contributed to divisiveness and schisms which prevented the establishment of one national church. Accordingly, Canadian Baptists are divided into five major and several minor bodies. In 1981 all the Canadian Baptist groups totalled 696,850 persons, including children and adherents.[1] While the first Canadian Baptists were the descendants of seventeenth-century British immigrants to the American colonies, there were fellowships made up of other ethnic groups, such as German and Swedish Baptists. Strong religious conservatism and opposition to modernism and liberalism have characterized Baptists in Canada.[2]

THE BAPTISTS AND THE HOLOCAUST

The attitude of the Baptists to Jews and Judaism "reflected the general misconceptions and endemic ignorance of Jewish history and religion that pervaded the Christian world in pre-Holocaust times, as well as certain anti-Judaic sectarian strains," write Alan Davies and Marilyn

Nefsky.[3] Of the various Baptist publications, I will focus upon the *Canadian Baptist*, the official bulletin of the Baptist Convention of Ontario and Quebec and the Baptist Union of Western Canada, because the great majority of Canadian Jews lived in these parts of the country. Hence the Baptists in these areas had the most frequent contact with Jews. Since the *Canadian Baptist* was a church journal, Bible lessons and religious articles appeared frequently. In the lessons Jews were sometimes depicted in a traditional derogatory manner. The Pharisees were regarded as "self-righteous, haughty and hypocritical people"; they "exalted tradition above the Word of God itself," and by "sheer hypocrisy," they used tricks to escape responsibility for taking care of their parents. The "true religion" obviously contradicted the teachings of the Pharisees. Even after World War II, this Christian anti-Jewish teaching continued.[4]

The Baptists' attitude to Nazi totalitarianism and to the persecution of Christians and Jews varied. Baptists of German origin, particularly in western Canada, enthusiastically supported Hitler. Later, when the persecution of the German churches became known, they were reluctantly silent. In September 1934 the *Canadian Baptist* reported on the gathering of the Baptist World Alliance in Berlin. Nazi racist measures were "condemned as unchristian. Anti-Semitism was particularly specified." However, the journal stated that the movements in Germany against the Jews "were not religious or racial, but political and economic." During the 1920s, 200,000 Jews had migrated to Germany from the East: "Most of these were Communist agitators against the government." The magazine elaborated on the great influence of the Jews, who had "monopolized a majority of the government, educational and economic positions." While Jews constituted 1 per cent of the population of Berlin, they occupied 75–100 per cent of the positions of influence, "using these positions for self-aggrandizement to the injury of the German people." At the Institute of Science, for example, all the workers were Jews. "No Aryan or Christian was permitted in it." Obviously, Germans resented this state of affairs. "Naturally excesses occurred and irresponsible persons committed some atrocious deeds. But at the worst it was not one-tenth as bad as we had been made to believe." The Nazis were "the agent of adjustment of positions proportionate to population," reported the *Canadian Baptist* from Berlin, echoing official German propaganda.[5]

In September 1938 the Toronto-based *Canadian Baptist* printed an article by Hans Luckey, a tutor in the German Baptist College in Hamburg, who strongly defended Nazi Germany. Referring to the question of whether Hitler was a Christian, he maintained, "It is conceivable that Hitler is a Christian who does not think denominationally, but I should like to present him as a religious romantic who looks too far to be an atheist." Luckey justified the events in Germany: "the street battles, the moral purification of the community, the destruction of noxious literature, social peace, the increase of matrimonial morality – all these things give greater possibilities for the proclamation of the Gospels than any before." He insisted that there was "religious freedom" in Germany. The editor of the *Canadian Baptist* introduced the article by saying that it was"very interesting reading as it gives a German viewpoint."[6]

Watson Kirkconnell delivered the presidential address to the Baptist Union of Western Canada in Winnipeg in 1939. He spoke of his appreciation for the"ruthless but effective way" in which the dictators of Europe solved their countries' economic and social problems. Hitler had succeeded in reorganizing German industry and had given pride and new meaning to the lives of his embittered, humiliated people. "Any analysis of the totalitarian states that omits these positive achievements will merely delude us," said Kirkconnell. However, such achievements had a high price, namely, the "ruthless extermination of liberty, an appalling persecution of individuals and minority groups … Concentration camps like those at Dachau and Sachsenhausen are sinister symbols of that rule." Kirkconnell mentioned fascist movements in Canada that were imitating the Nazi dictator. To avoid a revolution and to preserve liberty and democracy at home, he advocated setting "our house in order, economically, politically and socially," Something that could be accomplished by "applying Christian zeal and Christian intelligence."[7] Although he spoke about the persecution of "minority groups" and about concentration camps, Kirkconnell avoided mentioning the Jews by name.

A different approach, although a rare one in the *Canadian Baptist*, openly criticized Germany for its persecution of the Jews. In 1933–34, during the first year of Hitler's accession to power, several articles in the journal had protested Nazi anti-Jewish policy. "If a fraction of the atrocities against Jews with which Germany is charged to-day be true, Hun is the only word that can be used to describe the Hitlerite Teutons," read an article on the front page in April 1933. Ancient barbarism was less horrible than German cruelties against Jews. "The entire world is horrified by the tales of barbarism" coming from a country that was the birthplace of Protestantism. The journal argued that Berlin would be "an impossible meeting place" for the coming Baptist World Alliance (which eventually did meet there in September 1934). From the cruelty with which the Germans treated the Jews, it seemed that German Christians must have forgotten that "the Christ whom German Protestants and Catholics alike worship was a Jew," concluded the article.[8] In the same month, the journal quoted the British *Baptist Times*, which also criticized the ill-treatment of the Jews and called upon the Christian church to "unite in protest against these outrages." The British Baptists declared that the "Jews have our sympathy."[9]

Along the same lines, an article appeared in the *Canadian Baptist* in March 1934, criticizing Christian attitudes to the Jews. Since the author was a Gentile and not a Jew, he wrote that he was exempt from the "insults and penalties that a Christian world is heaping to-day on the heads of the nation from which came my Christ." He discussed the Nazis' racial policy, the persecution of Jews, and the confiscation of their money and their forced flight from Germany. He praised the Jewish emphasis on education and ambition to succeed. "If I were a Jew to-day," the author wrote, "I might wonder how one who professed to love Jesus, the Hebrew, could treat my race so despicably."[10]

After Kristallnacht, sympathy for the Jewish victims increased. Several Baptist leaders participated in anti-Nazi rallies in various Canadian cities. The *Canadian Baptist* carried a number of items discussing the Jewish problem, and a few resolutions were adopted in favour of the admission of Jewish refugees to Canada. "With the great wave of sympathy with the Jews that many lands are now showing, as a result of Berlin's and Rome's barbarous attack upon the race, there ought to be a great dearth of 'Gentiles Only' signs at the lakes and rivers next summer," wrote the editor. In November 1938 the Moose Jaw Ministerial Association, a Baptist group, adopted a resolution that, "whereas there has broken out a fresh and bitter persecution of Jews in Germany, ... Be it resolved that we express our deep and prayerful sympathy for these suffering people."[11] An editorial in 1935 had discussed Canada's economic need for immigrants and concluded that it would be "a tragedy of supreme magnitude" to admit many newcomers: "No one loves an immigrant any more." But the editorial disregarded the problem of refugees and the country's moral responsibility for them.[12]

While the editor of the *Canadian Baptist* refused to press for the admission of Jewish refugees to Canada, the Baptist Convention of Ontario and Quebec felt otherwise. In June 1939 the convention, aware of the great need for a haven for Jewish and European Christian refugees, resolved to "urge upon the proper governmental authorities the desirability of admitting to Canada a carefully selected individuals or groups of refugees, as being desirable not only from humane and ethical standpoints, but also because such immigration should prove a valuable addition to our national economy, by introducing skilled workers and new arts, crafts and industries."[13]

In November 1938 the Moose Jaw Baptist Church had also adopted a resolution that called upon Canada to take part in the solution of the refugee problem by receiving "a generous quota of these unfortunate Jewish refugees." It maintained that "we shall rather make a place for these persecuted people than waste our energies in condemnation of the persecutors," and it suggested to the government that it take advantage of "an unparalleled opportunity" to show its international spirit. This was one of the few resolutions adopted by official Baptist bodies in favour of Jewish refugees.[14]

In addition to the few voices of support for the cause of the Jews, there were many expressions of criticism of the totalitarian regime of the Nazis. In May 1939, when war was imminent and the "dictators of Europe [were] drunk with the wine of God's wrath, ... mad with a desire to over-run and steal territory that does not belong to them," Baptists turned to pray to Almighty God.[15]

As part of the British Empire, Canada joined the war against the Axis Powers. Condemnation of Nazi Germany therefore had a political and not only an ideological motivation. For the Baptists, the entrance of Canada into the war was also a religious issue. Did the war have moral justification? Was there more at stake than simply self-interest? In the spring of 1939 W.R. Matthews, dean of St Paul's Cathedral in London, had issued a pamphlet entitled *The Moral Issues of the War*, in which he justified war against Nazi Germany as a fight to save Christendom: "Few can doubt but that a victory for Nazi Germany would be a defeat for Christian civilization and for the humane values."[16] The pamphlet was quoted in the *Canadian Baptist*. According to T.N.T. Tattersall of Toronto, God would approve the war against the Nazi evil. Although "force must be met with force," he also called for repentance.[17] The editor clarified the aims of the war for the readers of the journal by quoting the bishop of Gloucester, who said, "We are fighting to free Europe and the whole civilized world from a greater tyranny than it has ever known before."[18]

Preoccupied with the war, most Baptists entirely disregarded the persecution of the Jews and the problem of Jewish refugees.[19] Even after the war, when the horrors of the mass murders were known, the fate of the Jewish victims was not a subject of interest. On the other hand, the attitude of the European churches to Nazi Germany and the rehabilitation of the German churches were widely discussed. Bishop Bell of Chichester was quoted as saying that the Christian churches in Europe had been "among the most determined adversaries of Nazism," though he admitted that church opposition was not "on the same scale in every country."[20] Apparently, the German Baptists did not belong to the category that Bell had spoken of, since the editor of the *Canadian Baptist* observed in June 1945 that "there must be an awakening of the Baptist and Methodist leaders in Germany who would appear not to have taken any stand as did the Evangelical Reformed under the inspiring leadership of Martin Niemoller," since he had opposed the suppression of the freedom to preach in Germany.[21]

THE BAPTISTS AND THE STATE OF ISRAEL

What was the Baptist attitude to the establishment of the Jewish state and to the Israeli-Palestinian conflict? The founding of Israel in 1948 was mentioned in the *Canadian Baptist* as an event of great magnitude, along with the signing of the North Atlantic Security Pact and the entry of Newfoundland into the Canadian Confederation. Palestine's unsolved problems were regarded as the outcome of intensification in the deadlock between East and West. The emergence a new Jewish state had deep religious meaning for Baptists. Their major focus was on Israel's holy places, on Jerusalem, and on evangelistic prospects in the country. Not surprisingly, Baptist interest in the region was religious rather than political. Thus little was written about the Israeli-Arab crisis.[22]

The first editorial acknowledging the formation of the State of Israel appeared in January 1949. It contained a mixture of admiration for the survival of a nation and hope for its eventual conversion to Christianity: "It is difficult to realize that this idealistic spiritual term [the Commonwealth of Israel] has now assumed tangible reality in the formation of a new nation for the Jews. It is difficult, too, to be fully aware of both the political and spiritual setting up of this tiny commonwealth on the battle-scarred soil of Palestine." The editorial admired the success of the Jews in maintaining their religious and cultural identity throughout two thousand years of exile. Their survival was an incomparable event in the history of humankind. The Israeli Declaration of Independence "vindicated and illuminated" the predictions of the great Jewish prophets. The editorial then went on to say: "We who are Christian cannot help but feel that the future of this tiny Hebrew nation will be marked by recurring storms and frustrations, as of old, until Israel become the New Israel – not only the 'Israel of God' but of His Son, Jesus Christ our Lord."[23] Another editorial, in April the same year, emphasized Israel's democratic character, which represented "a seedling of democracy in the Near East." This fact was considered important in light of communist expansion into Asia and Africa. The editorial predicted that "a new Israel will wield an influence far beyond its physical strength upon the events of the entire world order."[24]

The conflict between the Israelis and the Arabs was described in a less complimentary manner in the *Canadian Baptist*. In 1950 Duke McCall, who had toured the Middle East on behalf of the Southern

Baptist Missions, termed Israel "a modern immoral miracle." "For the people who have built a nation in just two years, I have profound admiration. For the future of the nation I have great hope. For the way the nation began there must be some atonement." McCall referred to the Dier Es-Siem (*sic*) massacre, where soldiers of the Etzel, an underground anti-British group, had killed many Arab civilians. The author compared this incident with the Nazi premeditated mass murders at Lidice and Dachau, adding, "Hitler never sank lower." Trying to show the "two sides of the problem," he expressed sympathy for the Jews, who had finally won a national home and yet had "won all my sense of justice for adequate recompense for the displaced Arabs."[25]

The Middle East as a political problem was mentioned only rarely in public debates and in official publications, however. Baptist conventions and the pages of the *Canadian Baptist* were devoted mainly to internal problems. Some of the important issues were observance of the Lord's Day, temperance, how to deal with obscene publications, lotteries, religious broadcasting, Christian schools for girls, abused women, abused children, abortion, surrogate mothers, and single ministries.[26] The problem of cooperation with other Baptist groups, as well as with other denominations, was often discussed. According to William H. Jones, editor and manager of the *Canadian Baptist* in the 1980s, Baptists had the "fault of not getting along with one another."[27] The question of affiliation with the World Council of Churches and the Canadian Council of Churches was also part of the public debate. Baptists had a real difficulty with the councils of churches, because there was no single Baptist Church in Canada. They carefully avoided the term "church," identifying themselves as fellowships, conventions, unions, or associations. After many debates, the Baptists decided not to join the World Council of Churches, and after participating in the ccc since the 1940s, they finally left in 1980.[28]

From 1967 on, there was a growing demand for Baptists "to assume a more active role" in foreign affairs. That year the eighth assembly of the Baptist Federation of Canada stated that there were national subjects on which Baptists should voice their opinion; therefore it authorized its national council "to make public statements on … demanding issues." In 1968 the Baptist Convention of Ontario and Quebec encouraged its members "to concern themselves with the problems and issues of international affairs and Canada's role therein."[29] Following the pattern of the Washington-based Baptist Joint Committee on Public Affairs, the Canadian Baptists in 1978 founded a Baptist Joint Committee. They not only voiced protests against the abuse of civil rights in Latin America, but also initiated or helped to finance projects, particularly in countries where they had missionary activities.[30]

The religious duty to "save" non-Christians by conversion was a frequent topic in the *Canadian Baptist*. Discussions were carried on about the "purpose of evangelism," with advice on how to adapt new tactics to changing situations. William R. Wood, pastor of Highland Baptist Church in Kitchener, Ontario, gave precise instructions on how to reach the hearts of non-Christians. "Feel around the rim of a friend's life until you find the crack. It's at that point people open most easily to God's love and grace." Canadian Baptists had active missionaries in India, Indonesia, Sri Lanka, Bolivia, Brazil, Zaire, Kenya, Angola, China, and Ghana.[31]

Baptist missionaries also operated in Israel. As always, such activities were strongly opposed by Jewish communities, and an extremist Jewish group vandalized and burned down Baptist centres in Jerusalem and Acre in 1987. William H. Jones, the editor of the *Canadian Baptist*, protested against such religious intolerance. Although he declared his sympathy for some of Israel's territorial claims and its democratic government, he felt that it should "demonstrate tolerance and religious freedom. That includes the freedom to worship and to undertake missionary work."[32] While freedom of worship was a sacred principle that Israel dutifully preserved, the right to carry on missionary activities was a controversial issue. Most Israelis strongly rejected evangelism, but they did not support violent acts such as burning down churches.

The readers of the *Canadian Baptist* were interested, not in the political crisis between Israel and the Arabs, but in the holy sites where Jesus had lived – Bethlehem, Nazareth, the Sea of Galilee, Jericho, and Jerusalem. Many articles dealt with the religious aspects of the Holy Land. In passing, they described modern life in Israel, usually in a positive manner. An editorial in 1972 described the changes that had taken place in Israel after the Six Day War. The modern highways, the well-organized tours, the good guides, and the efficient tourist services impressed the editor. Local church ministers had assured him that "their religious interests were cared for … All of their religious properties were well maintained." He advised would-be tourists to "see the Holy Land now – while it is still unspoiled by modern progress."[33] In 1968 J. Gordon Jones, in a series of articles about the "Lands of the Bible," wrote about the religious places as well as about the new political situation. He recommended that efforts be made to reach peace in the region: "It is everybody's business to help Isaac and Ishmael, Jews and Arabs, to live together side by side in friendship and peace."[34] R. Lindsay, pastor of Jerusalem Baptist Church, maintained in 1981 that "all Christians have been able to freely celebrate Christmas in Bethlehem."[35] Michael Lipe reported five years later about the peaceful life in Bethlehem: "Contrary to the popular media presentation of Israel as a land torn by terrorism, none is to be found here [in Bethlehem]."[36]

The occupation of the West Bank and Gaza in 1967 and the intensification of the refugee problem went almost unnoticed among Canadian Baptists. A rare report appeared in the *Canadian Baptist* in March 1969, which described a panel discussion led by the Women's Missionary Auxiliary on Rhodesia, Czechoslovakia, and the Middle East. Murray Luft, who had worked with Arab refugees in Lebanon, gave "a sympathetic account of the Arab predicament in the Middle East." He called for more Canadian awareness and understanding of Arab problems and Arab rights.[37] More critical of Israel was the report of R.M. Bennett, a former Baptist missionary in India and secretary of the Canadian Council of Churches. In February 1970 he wrote about his trip to Israel. Bennett depicted a totally different situation from that observed by some other pilgrims. Everywhere he went, he saw "confusion, breakdown of morale and panic." He left the country "terribly depressed" because of the injustices done to the Arabs. The refugees were bitter and frustrated, "without hope, without commitment, condemned to a life seemingly without purpose." Bennett called Israel a "military state."[38]

This harsh criticism of Israel, uncharacteristic of the *Canadian Baptist*, was reprinted from the *United Church Observer*[39] and revealed the differences between the two journals. While the editor of the *Canadian Baptist* gave a neutral title to Bennett's article, "A Journey in Israel," Forrest's title for it in the *Observer* was "Israel-Sorrow, Injustice, Distrust." When Forrest prepared a special issue of the *Observer* on Israel in October 1967, it was entirely devoted to the Palestinian problem. In the *Canadian Baptist's* special issue on Israel in November 1979, the Israeli-Palestinian conflict was not discussed at all. Rather, its articles dealt with archaeology and the holy places. The editor refused to take a stand on the conflict: "We have an opinion on these matters ... The solution to these problems must come from the goodwill of the persons involved in the issues, and can hardly be imposed from editors who write at an uninvolved distance."[40] The fact that in the 1980s the Baptists were not affiliated with the Canadian Council of Churches probably contributed to their remoteness from the Middle East conflict. As we have seen, in that decade the CCC and its member churches became highly involved in the Israeli-Palestinian crisis, supporting the Arab cause.

The beginning of the Intifada in December 1987 changed the approach of Baptists. "We see inhumanity as a method in subduing the people of Gaza," stated the editorial and commentary of March 1988. The editors had "great sympathy for Israelis trying to settle a land for themselves, victims also of prejudice and war. But we cannot abide the treatment by official Israeli leaders of the Palestinians." The stones thrown by frustrated Palestinians were understandable, though not justified. However, the editors wrote that they had made a determined effort "to avoid throwing rocks too hard at either side."[41] Less restrained and balanced was the description of Bethlehem under Israeli occupation written by Martin Bailey, former director of communications for the National Council of Churches in the U.S.A. He complained about the harsh measures that the Israeli authorities had employed to check Arab terrorism: "When the Israelis respond to their fears of some extremist attack they seem intent on demonstrating both their authority and their determination to crowd Palestinians into smaller and smaller enclaves." The author described how difficult it was to reach the holy places in Bethlehem, because of the frequent Israeli checkpoints, but he failed to mention that these security measures had been taken to protect Christian pilgrims, after several buses of Christian worshippers had been attacked there by Palestinian terrorists. The article, based upon the testimony of Robert Assaly, the CCC's liaison with the MECC, gave an imbalanced picture.[42]

In conclusion, a reserved attitude characterized the Baptists' approach to the Holocaust and the State of Israel. Although Canadian Baptists did not remain silent over the Jewish problem during the Holocaust, "no mass outcry erupted from the rank and file," observe Davies and Nefsky. A combination of factors – theological conservatism, individualism, and a lack of outstanding, courageous leadership – led to religious narrow-mindedness and a disregard of the Jewish cause during the Holocaust.[43]

This theological conservatism also caused the Baptists to regard Israel simply as the Holy Land, with its holy sites. In addition, the evangelical prospect presented by the Jews in the newly established state attracted the attention of Baptist missionary groups. Lack of a national united church and of cooperation with church councils, such as the WCC, CCC, and MECC, prevented political involvement in the Middle East conflict. With the exception of two periods – the years immediately after the establishment of Israel, 1948–50, and the years following the eruption of the Palestinian civil uprising in 1987 – the religious interests of Canadian Baptists dominated their attitude to the State of Israel. This approach was entirely different from the deeply involved political position of the United Church of Canada.

Conclusion

The silence, though not total, of the Canadian Protestant churches during the Holocaust and their critical attitude to the State of Israel stemmed mainly but not exclusively from Christian teachings about the Jews and Judaism, whether consciously or unconsciously. The very existence of Israel contradicted some fundamental tenets of Christianity. The churches therefore attempted, not always with success, the difficult task of finding a way to reconcile the permanent existence of the State of Israel with their theology. However, there were many Protestant Zionists among conservatives, fundamentalists, evangelicals, and Presbyterians. Among the Presbyterians, the influence of the Swiss-born theologian Karl Barth was especially important. He believed that the survival of the Jews was a sign of divine providence, although he did not take up the question of the Jewish state.

Criticism of Israel created a long and enduring debate. Some members argued that the State of Israel should be judged by the same universal standards as any other modern state. On the other hand, those who sympathized with Israel claimed that the anti-Zionism of these individuals was a cover for antisemitism and that there was a clear link between the two attitudes. To be sure, Israel as a state was led by human beings, who unquestionably made mistakes that could legitimately be criticized. Honest criticism of its policy was perfectly valid; but despite strong denials on the part of the critics, behind such views was a deep-seated hatred of the Jews. After the Holocaust, antisemitism was no longer politically correct, and church leaders disassociated themselves from it and were reluctant to speak negatively about Jews.

Instead, they criticized Zionism, which sounded more objective. Alan Davies has observed that A.C. Forrest, by his constant attacks on Israel, "crossed the line of legitimate criticism into illegitimate assault again and again in more outrageous ways."[1] However, there were United Church members who supported Forrest and regarded him as a martyr.

How can one differentiate between legitimate criticism and anti-Zionism as a cover for antisemitism? Zionism is sometimes used as a codeword for Judaism; Forrest, for example, referred several times to Jews as "Zionists." When someone declared that twelve million Zionists were supporting Israel, he simply substituted "Jews" for "Zionists." Another way to assess the relationship between antisemitism and anti-Zionism is to show that a double standard operated. Zionism and the State of Israel were judged according to one measure, the Arab countries according to another. Criticism of Israel's violation of the human rights of the Palestinians totally disregarded violations of Jews' human rights by Syria and other Arab countries. While liberal church leaders supported national liberation movements, including that of the Palestinians, they opposed the efforts of the Jews to establish an independent state. Criticism of Israel's military actions against Palestinians disregarded the Arab terrorism that had provoked Israel's retaliation. Under the pretext of a "balanced approach," church establishments adopted the Arab cause. Recognition of Israel's existence, included in most statements on the Middle East, was sometimes only lip service, as Presbyterian leader Raymond Hodgson later admitted.[2]

What should the church leaders have done? How could they have criticized the Jewish state without being accused of antisemitism? As has been pointed out, Israel made real mistakes, including violating human rights and using force against civilians to suppress popular uprisings. For such actions, criticism would have been legitimate. However, because of centuries-old Christian anti-Jewish teaching, church members should have examined their conscience before attacking Israel. As Gregory Baum has pointed out, "If the Christian wants to express his own critical views of Israeli policies, he can do so with honor only if he reveals that he is also wrestling with his own ideological past."[3]

The rise of Arab nationalism during these years led to the Arabization of the Middle East churches and, by extension, of the Middle East Council of Churches. The growing influence of the MECC on the World Council of Churches and the Canadian Council of Churches resulted in increasing involvement by the Canadian churches in the Middle East conflict, generally on the side of the Palestinians. Thus political and ecumenical considerations contributed to the churches' support of the Arab position. Most Protestant denominations solved their dilemma of conscience by relying heavily on support for the underdog – the Palestinian refugees.

Some voices in the churches called for a revision of traditional theology and for support of Israel, but since they were in the minority, they were unable to change the course of church policies.

The churches in this study differed in their religious and political outlook, which in turn influenced their attitude to the issues. The United Church, with its emphasis on liberalism and the social gospel, as well as its interest in international affairs, was a leader among the Canadian denominations in expressing, clearly and frequently, its biased position on the Israeli-Palestinian conflict. Other denominations that were theologically and socially more conservative, such as the Presbyterian Church and the Baptists, were more interested in internal church or national matters than in events abroad. They were unsympathetic to the Jews during the Holocaust and essentially apathetic to the Middle East crisis. While the Presbyterians and the Baptists represent this group in the study, Lutherans and Mennonites, among others, also belong to this category. They either were apathetic to the Israeli-Palestinian conflict or supported the Arab cause.

During the first decades of the State of Israel's existence, there seems to have been an intentional effort within most of the denominations to maintain a balanced position on the Middle East conflict. But Israel's invasion of Lebanon in 1982 and its military suppression of the Palestinian civil uprising in 1987 led to a radicalization in the attitude of the Canadian churches to the conflict. Probably, the strong response to these events demonstrated by leading Jews in Israel and around the world, with their first open criticism of Israel's policies, contributed to a more vocal Christian anti-Israel position. From the mid-1980s on, as a result of pressure from the MECC and the WCC, the CCC and its affiliated members deepened their involvement in the Middle East, adopting a critical approach to Israel's policies.

In the past, Christians were often insensitive to their own antisemitism, which skewed their approach to the Middle East. A great deal of theological baggage from the past still distorted their perceptions of the Jews. This bias, in addition to their failure to understand how important Israel was to the Jews, sometimes created animosity between the Christian and Jewish communities in Canada. Not many Christians today want to be anti-Jewish, but they are often confused by Jewish reactions to their attempts to make amends for the past, and they feel misunderstood. On the other hand, Jews' oversensitivity – what Gunther Plaut called their "exile psychology"[4] – in regarding almost any action taken by Gentiles as antisemitism and their failure to distinguish between legitimate criticism of Israel's policies and anti-Jewish intentions intensified the distrust and deepened the quarrel. But dialogues at denominational and inter-denominational levels have gradually succeeded in restoring better understanding between the communities.

While Canadian churches maintained their imbalanced approach to the Israeli-Palestinian conflict, the attitude of the mainstream churches to Jews and Judaism meaningfully improved. The Anglican Church abolished an anti-Jewish prayer and strongly condemned Holocaust deniers and rising antisemitism in Canada. By the end of the twentieth century, the United Church was considering adopting a statement that opposed conversion of the Jews and called upon its members not to interpret the Scriptures in a way that would lead to anti-Jewish feelings. It also departed from the church's traditional belief that the Cross had superseded the Star of David, that the church had replaced the synagogue. Can a theological development such as the abandoning of Christian supersessionism really have a political impact? Many people are doubtful. The carefully worded statements of various denominations show that they are far from resolving the practical and political questions these issues pose. However, the various statements repudiating supersessionism, condemning aggressive proselytizing, and recognizing that the State of Israel is central to Judaism move in the right direction. The churches do not pretend to have complete answers, either theologically or politically. Their statements simply express a determination to seek an understanding within a framework that acknowledges God's ongoing covenant with the Jews. Despite these reservations, this new trend of mutual understanding is promising. Rabbi Gunther Plaut's remarks a quarter-century ago are still relevant today: "In full recognition of our mutual defects and errors in the past, we can now proceed to a relationship which will have all the aspects of dignity and promise."[5]

Notes

CHAPTER ONE: INTERNATIONAL COUNCILS
OF CHURCHES

1 Conway, "The Founding of the State of Israel and the Responses of the Christian Churches," 2. I thank Professor Conway for his kindness in showing me this unpublished paper.
2 Flannery, "Anti-Zionism and the Christian Psyche," 174, 178–9, 181.
3 Millar Burrows, in *Christian Century*, 14 July 1948, 701.
4 Prince, "The Global War," *United Church Observer*, 15 December 1945, 4; see also Fishman, *American Protestantism*, 31–8.
5 Prince, "The Global War," *United Church Observer*, 1 January 1946, 28; see also ibid., 15 January 1946, 25.
6 UC, *Record of Proceedings of the Eighteenth General Council*, 1958, 149.
7 Fishman, *American Protestantism*, 11, 27, 179; Conway, "The Founding of the State of Israel," 6.
8 By 1989 more than three hundred churches were members of the WCC. See "WCC Presentation on Palestine," 24 February 1989 (CCC, MEWG, 1989, b.183); A.C. Forrest to McCullough and Diana Skeoch, 24 January 1973 (UCA, CCIA, 88,088C, b.7, f.8); Clarke MacDonald, "An Expression of Concern," n.d. (ibid., b.2, f.4); "Church Leaders Urge Israel to Quit Occupied Land," *Toronto Star*, 8 June 1978.
9 Fishman, *American Protestantism*, 11–2, 27–8, 38, 88–92; Brockway, "WCC and the Jewish People."
10 Fishman, *American Protestantism*, 155; WCC, *The First Assembly of the WCC: Official Report*, 160–4.

11 Fishman, *American Protestantism*, 158.

12 *Christianity and Crisis*, 11 June 1951, 78–9.

13 Fishman, *American Protestantism*, 133–5, 139.

14 Matthews, "Lobbyist or Prophet," 4.

15 Longley, "Can WCC Grants to Guerilla Movements Be Defended?"; "Political Involvement of World's Churches Is Criticized," *Canadian Churchman*, 105 (January 1979): 12; Smith, "The WCC and Its Critics"; the quotation is from July–August, 22.

16 "WCC Central Committee Adopts Statement on Middle East," 25 August 1967, (ACCA, GS files, CSS, GS-75-106, b.11, CIA, Minutes).

17 "Consultation on the Palestine Refugee Problem, Held at Nicosia, Cyprus, 29 September–4 October 1969" (UCA, CCIA, 88,088C, b.2, f.1); WCC, Middle East Task Force, John B. Taylor to "Dear Friends," 5 September 1975 (UCA, CCIA, 82,250C, b.7, f.9).

18 "WCC Appeals to the UN Assembly to Rescind Resolution on Zionism," 13 November 1975 (UCA, ACF, 86,104C, b.21, f.10).

19 Gilbert, "Exploring Christian-Jewish Relations."

20 Plaut, *Unfinished Business*, 281–2.

21 "Statement Issued by the Sixth Assembly of the WCC in Vancouver," 14 July–10 August 1983, 8 (CCC, CIDA, METG, Dialogue, 1983–84).

22 "Middle East Information Distorted, Angry Jewish Groups Tells WCC," *Canadian Churchman*, 106 (November 1980): 10.

23 "Statement Issued by the Sixth Assembly of the WCC in Vancouver."

24 Ghassan Rubeiz, "Lebanon/Palestine – 1988," January 1988 (CCC, CJP, MEWG, 1988).

25 WCC, "Statement on the Occupied Territories," n.d.; WCC, Central Committee, "Message to the Heads of the Christian Communities in Jerusalem," n.d. (CCC, CJP, MEWG, 1988). On another occasion the Central Committee urged the churches to press their governments for an international peace conference and to pressure Israel to halt new Jewish settlements and consider dismantling the existing ones. See "Council Seeks Middle East Peace," *Anglican Journal* 115 (October 1989): 5.

26 "WCC on Palestinian Declaration of Independence," Ecumenical Press Service, 3 January 1989.

27 "WCC Presentation on Palestine," 24 February 1989 (CCC, MEWG, 1989, b.183).

28 Rubeiz to Robert Sternberg, 19 September 1983 (CJCNA, DA 15,1, b.2, f.36).

29 MECC, "Background on Ecumenism in the Middle East,"n.d. [ca. October 1986] (CCC, 1985–86, MEWG, 1986).

30 Fishman, *American Protestantism*, 137–8.

31 CCC, "Member Churches of the Middle East Council of Churches," n.d. (CCC, MEWG, n.d.).

32 MECC, "Summary Background of a Meeting in Geneva, 14–5 November 1989" (CCC, MEWG, 1989, b.183).

33 MECC, "Message to the Churches: Consultation on Service to Palestine Refugees," Nicosia, Cyprus, 4–8 November 1979 (UCA, CCIA, 88,088c, b.3, f.3).

34 MECC, "Ecumenical Travel Office," 19 November 1985 (CCC, CIDA, MEWG, 1985); Gabriel Habib to Donald Anderson, 27 March 1986 (ibid., 1986); CCC, MEWG, "MECC Alternative Tourism," Minutes, 6 November 1987 (CCC, CWC, MEWG, 1987).

35 See Fishman, *American Protestantism*, 152–4.

36 Niilus to CCC, 8 August 1983; Mitsui to Niilus, 27 September 1983 (CCC, CWC, MECC, 1983); CCC, MEWG, Minutes, 29 February 1988 (CCC, CWC, MEWG, 1985–87).

37 MECC, "The Palestinian Conflict on the MECC Agenda," 1994, 1–2 (CCC, MECC, 1994).

38 Habib to Donald Anderson, 2 February 1988 (CCC, CJP, MEWG, 1988).

39 "Jerusalem Heads of Churches Statement," 22 January 1988 (CCC, MEWG, 1989, b.383).

40 Donald Anderson to general secretaries, CCC member churches, 26 January 1988 (CCC, CJP, MEWG, 1988); see also "Statement by the Heads of the Christian Communities in Jerusalem," 27 April 1989 (CCC, MEWG, 1989, b.383).

41 MECC, "Closing Message, MECC's Fifth Assembly," Cyprus, 22–29 January 1990 (CCC, MECC, 1990).

42 Forrest to John Sutton, 5 November 1970 (UCA, ACF, 86,104c, b.19, f.6); 23 August 1972 (ibid., b.20, f.5).

43 Diana Skeoch, "Middle East News Gathering Event," 25 January 1979, UC, CCIA, Minutes, 25 January 1979 (UCA, CCIA, 88,088c, b.3, f.2).

44 Fishman, *American Protestantism*, 12.

45 Genizi, *American Apathy*, chapters 3–4; Nawyn, *American Protestantism's Response*, 156–8.

46 Fishman, *American Protestantism*, 27–32. For a discussion of theological opposition to the Zionist idea, see above in this chapter.

47 Ibid., 32–5.

48 Ibid., 181.

49 NCC, Executive Committee, "Resolution on Crisis in the Middle East," 7 July 1967 (ACCA, GS files, CSS, GS 75–106, b.11, Minutes).

50 Editorial, *Christian Century*, 26 July 1967, 954.

51 For details of the Heraklion and Canterbury resolutions, see above in this chapter.

52 John H. Davis to A.C. Forrest, 22 May 1975 (UCA, ACF, 86,104c, b.21, f.8).

53 See, for example, Jean Caffey Lyles, "No Peace without the PLO?" *Christian Century*, November 1980, 1147–8; Richard Slusser, "Who Killed Lebanon?" ibid., 11 October 1989, 900–1.

CHAPTER TWO: THE CANADIAN COUNCIL
OF CHURCHES

1 Grant, *The Church in the Canadian Era*, 136–45.

2 Davies and Nefsky, *How Silent Were the Churches?* 1–10.

3 Ibid., 128.

4 Grant, *The Church in the Canadian Era*, 160–83.

5 Ibid., 216–23.

6 Matthews and Pratt, *Church and State*, ix.

7 Greene, *Canadian Churches and Foreign Policy*, 1–8.

8 Matthews, "The Christian Churches and Foreign Policy," 161.

9 Matthews, "Lobbyist or Prophet," 1–2.

10 Grant, *The Church in the Canadian Era*, 238–43.

11 WCC, "Canadian Committee, WCC, 1942," 6 February 1943 (UCA, GC, ser. ix, 82,001C, b.197, f.3); WCC, "Canadian Committee: Report of Activities, 1944" (ibid., b.197, f.5).

12 UC, "Committee on Overseas Relief," Minutes, 8 October 1947 (UCA, Committee on Overseas Relief, 82,00060C, b.1, f.1); *United Church Observer*, 1 November 1949, 16.

13 ACC, CSS, "Canadian Council of Churches and Refugees," Executive Committee, Minutes, 21 February, 12 September 1951 (ACCA, GS files, 75–106, b.5).

14 Baun et al., "Peace, Justice and Reconciliation in the Arab-Israeli Conflict."

15 DuCharme, "Learning to Live with the Enemies," 50–1. The CCC was ready in 1956 to sponsor Charles Malik, the Lebanese ambassador to the UN, to deliver a series of lectures presenting the Arab side in six or seven Canadian cities; see UC, CCIA, Minutes, 1 February 1956 (UCA, CCIA, 88,088C, b.1, f.1).

16 Forrest to John H. Davis, 4 December 1970; Forrest to E.S. Mackay, 6 January 1971 (UCA, ACF, 86,104C, b.19, f.6).

17 Forrest to Charles Forsyth and Floyd Honey, 15 October 1969 (UCA, CCIA, 80,250C, b.4, f.6).

18 CCC, CIA, *Search for Understanding: A Study Booklet on the Middle East*, n.d. [ca. 1970] (UCA, CCIA, 88,088C, b.6, f.5); see also CCC, "Report of Commission on World Concern," Central Committee, Minutes, November 1970; CCC, "Excerpts from Report on Middle East Study Tour, 2–23 September 1970" (UCA, ACF, 86,104C, b.19, f.6).

19 "Canadian Council of Churches Called Antisemitic," Toronto *Telegram*, 17 December 1970.

20 Nesis to Plaut, 6 December 1972 (OJA, MG8/S, b.54, f.41).

21 For a detailed discussion of the controversy between the Canadian Jewish community and the United Church and A.C. Forrest, see chapter 8.

22 Rose to W. Gunther Plaut, 4 December 1973 (OJA, MG8/S, b.54, f.41).

23 UC, *Record of Proceedings of the Twenty-Fifth General Council*, 1972, 263; Gunther Plaut to Floyd Honey, 12 July 1973; Honey to Robert Matthews,

Eoin Mackay, and Clarke MacDonald, 9 August 1973; Honey to Forrest, 1 November 1973 (UCA, CCIA, 82,250C, b.7, f.8); Forrest "The Middle East Story," *United Church Observer*, November 1973, 31.

24 Roland de Corneille, "Development of Christian Attitudes toward the Middle East" (ACCA, GS files).

25 CCC, News Release, 23 November 1973 (OJA, MG8/S, b.54, f.41).

26 CCC, News Release, Norman Berner, and Floyd Honey, 16, 17 May 1974 (UCA, CCIA, 82,250C, b.7, f.9).

27 Honey to Plaut, 15 August 1975 (CJCNA, CJC, NA, ZA, 1975).

28 "A Proposal to the Canadian Council of Churches," 22 December 1975 (UCA, ACF, 86,104C, b.5, f.14).

29 Memorandum, Tad Mitsui to CCC Executive Committee, Re: Middle East tour, 20 January 1983 (CCC, CWC, ME, 1983).

30 CCC, "Empowered to Participate," report of the Commission on World Concerns, CCC triennial assembly, Halifax, May 1985, 101 (CCC, CWC); hereinafter cited as "Empowered to Participate."

31 Tad Mitsui to CCC Executive Committee, 20 January 1983 (CCC, CWC, ME, 1983).

32 "Statement on the Invasion of Lebanon," 25 June 1982 (UCA, CCIA, 88,088C, b.6, f.5). The statement was signed by the leaders of the United, Anglican, Presbyterian, Lutheran, Greek Orthodox, Coptic Orthodox, Reformed, and Christian churches and the Society of Friends. See also "Church Leaders Condemn Israeli Invasion of Lebanon," "News from the CCC," 28 June 1982; WCC, "Church Leaders React to Israeli Lebanon Actions," Ecumenical Press Service, 1 July 1982 (CCC, MEWG, 1989, b.183).

33 Mitsui to CCC Executive Committee, 20 January 1983 (CCC, CWC, ME, 1983).

34 Tad Mitsui to Pierre E. Trudeau, 23 December 1982; Allan J. MacEachen to Donald Anderson, 10 April 1983 (CCC, CWC, ME, 1983). See also the baseless complaint about the closing of Bir Zeit University in Nablus: M. Shalev to Clarke MacDonald, 3 August 1979 (UCA, CCIA, 88,088C, b.3, f.3).

35 CCC, Minutes, CCC-CAF Dialogue, 14 April 1984; CCC, MEWG, "To members of the Christian delegation to the talks with the Arab Federation," n.d. (CCC, CIDA, METG, Dialogue, 1983–84).

36 Robert Matthews to Robert Sternberg, 23 October 1984; CCC, Meeting of church representatives in CCC-CAF Dialogue, Minutes, 12 October 1984; John Berthrong to Tad Mitsui, 8 February 1984 (CCC, CIDA, MEWG, Dialogue, 1983–84); Memo: Mitsui to Brown, 2 August 1989 (CCC, MEWG, 1989, b.383).

37 "An Account of a Dialogue," n.d. (CCC, CIDA, MEWG, Dialogue, 1983–84); duCharme, "Learning to Live with the Enemies," 52–3.

38 "Empowered to Participate," 102.

39 Mike Milne, "Canada's Overseas Role: An Ecumenical Perspective," *One World* [WCC publication], July 1986, 9.

40 "Canada's International Relations: An Alternative View," 29 November 1985, 79–82 (CCC, CIDA, MEWG, 1985).

41 Anderson to Habib, 2 December 1985 (CCC, CIDA, MEWG, 1985).

42 "Proposed Working Group on the Middle East, Terms of Reference" (CCC, CIDA, MEWG, 1985).

43 Marjorie Ross to general secretaries, member churches, re: formation of MEWG of CCC, 3 October 1985; Marjorie Ross to "Dear Friends," 1 November 1985 (CCC, CWC, METG, 1985).

44 "Members of MEWG, CCC," 16 December 1985 (CCC, CIDA, MEWG, 1985); MEWG, "Membership List," September 1990 (CCC, MEWG, 1990).

45 MEWG, Minutes, 11 February, 12 May 1986 (CCC, MEWG, 1985–86).

46 Gabriel Habib, "Staffing Proposal for a Canadian-Sponsored Position with the MECC," January 1987 (CCC, CJP, MEWG, 1988).

47 Habib to Glen Davies, 21 January 1987 (CCC, CWC, MEWG, 1987).

48 "An Account of a Dialogue," n.d. (CCC, METG, 1985–86).

49 Douglas duCharme to Leopoldo Niilus, 5 June 1986 (CCC, MEWG, 1986).

50 "Position Description – (Second Draft)," December 1987; "Proposal for Canadian-Sponsored Staff Position with Middle East Council of Churches," 29 April 1987; CIA, Minutes, 21 September 1987 (CCC, CWC, MEWG, 1987).

51 Interview with Douglas duCharme, 5 June 1995. For further information on the relationship between CCC and MECC, see duCharme, "Learning to Live with the Enemies," 47–59; "Proposal for MECC/CCC Cooperation from September 1991," March 1990 (CCC, MECC, 1990).

52 CCC, MEWG, Minutes, 7 January 1987 (CCC, MEWG, 1986).

53 Anderson to Habib, 5 December 1985 (CCC, CIDA, MEWG, 1985); "Proposal for MECC/CCC Cooperation from September 1991" (CCC, MECC, 1990).

54 CCC, MEWG, Minutes, 7 January, 9 February, 29 May, 21 September 1987; Marjorie Ross to "Dear Friend," 25 August 1987 (CCC, CIA, MEWG, 1987–88).

55 CCC–Middle East visit, 25 September–2 October 1987 (CCC, MEWG, 1987).

56 CCC, Communiqué, 2 October 1987 (CCC, CJP, MEWG, 1988); CCC, *Old Patterns, New Possibilities: Thoughts on the Middle East from Delegates of the CCC, September, 1987*, April 1988 (CCC, MEWG, 1988).

57 CCC, MEWG, Minutes, 6 November 1987 (CCC, CWC, MEWG, 1987).

58 CCC, *Old Patterns, New Possibilities*, April 1988 (CCC, MEWG, 1988).

59 Edward Scott to Joe Clark, n.d. (CCC, CWC, MEWG, 1987).

60 Douglas duCharme, "Trip Report, Palestine Human Rights Campaign, Annual Conference, Chicago, 12–20 September 1986," Minutes, 7 January 1987 (CCC, CWC, MEWG, 1987); see also the file NCC, Division of Overseas, Middle East Committee (CCC, MEWG, 1985–6).

61 CCC, MEWG, Minutes, 21 September; 7 December 1988 (CCC, MEWG, 1988, 1989); Marion Boulby, ed., "Whose Will Be Done: Report of a 1989 Study Tour Group to the Holy Land"; Robert Assaly, "Outline Proposal for 1990 Middle East Trip" (CCC, MEWG, 1989).

62 Interview with Canon Shafik Farah, 23 June 1995. See, for example, Farah's address to the triennial meeting of the CCC on 11–16 May 1991, "Where I Came From, Where I Need to Arrive and the Inevitable Way of the Cross" (CCC, MEWG, 1990). For a discussion of Farah's pro-Arab views, see chapter 11 below.

63 CCC, MEWG, Minutes, 18 May, 25 October 1988 (CCC, MEWG, 1988).

64 CCC, MEWG, Minutes, 30 October 1989, 2 November 1990; duCharme to MEWG, 14 November 1986 (CCC, CWC, MEWG, 1986).

65 See the file CCC, Palestine, 1988 (CCC, CJR, MEWG, 1988); Alison Rose to Marjorie Ross, 7 March 1989 (CCC, MEWG, 1989).

66 Edward Scott to Joe Clark, n.d. (CCC, CWC, MEWG, 1987).

67 Douglas duCharme, "Where Mission Began," 8 August 1988; CCC, MEWG, Minutes, 6 April 1988 (CCC, CJP, MEWG, 1988); duCharme's report of activities, 2 September–6 November 1989 (CCC, MEWG, 383, 1989); "Douglas duCharme, the CCC Liaison Officer to the MECC," ACC, Anglican Middle East Committee, Minutes, 23 October 1990 (ACCA, GS files, GS, 93–11, ME, 1989–1991).

68 CCC, MEWG, Minutes, 29 February 1988 (CCC, CWC, MEWG, 1985–87); duCharme to Don [Anderson], 7 March 1988 (CCC, CJP, MEWG, 1988).

69 The CCC three official policy statements were *Search for Understanding* (1970), *Peace, Justice and Reconciliation* (1979), and "A Study Guide of the Position Paper on the Middle East," draft, 6 June 1990 (ACCA, GS files, GS 93–11, MW, 1989–91). See also Douglas duCharme to Ian Kegedan, 22 March 1988 (CCC, CJP, MEWG, 1988); Harvey Shepherd, "Churches Confront Controversies – but Take Few Bold Steps," *Montreal Gazette*, 21 May 1988.

70 Michael McAteer, "Churches Speak Out on Mideast Question," *Toronto Star*, 7 October 1989.

71 "Sharing Gifts: Resolution #3: Middle East Statement," CCC Triennial Assembly, Montreal, May 1988, 13 (CCC, CJOP, MEWG, 1988).

72 Heather Johnston to Bob Matthews and Marjorie Ross, 22 May 1988 (CCC, Responses to the position paper, 1989).

73 William F. Ryan to Stuart Brown, 15 December 1988 (CCC, CJP, MEWG, 1988).

74 ACC, House of Bishops, November 1988 (ACCA, GS files, GS 93N, Middle East); METF to Archbishop Michael Peers, primate, 5 April 1989 (ACCA, GS files, GS 93–11, Middle East, 1989–91). For a detailed discussion of the Anglican response, see chapter 11 below.

75 Heather Johnston to Bob Matthews and Marjorie Ross, 22 May 1988 (CCC, Responses to the position paper, 1989).

76 "CCC Statement on the Middle East," n.d. (ACCA, GS files, GS, 93N, ME); CJDM, Minutes, 9 December 1988 (CCC, Jewish-Christian Dialogue). The Canadian Christian Jewish Consultation was established in 1977 with the purpose of serving as a liaison committee between Christian and Jewish communities in Canada. It consisted of representatives of the Canadian Jewish Congress, the Canadian Conference of Catholic Bishops, and the CCC, and it discussed "mutual concerns for promoting understanding and encouraging joint efforts wherever possible." See CCJC, "Report to the CCC Triennial Assembly, May, 1991" (CJCNA, DA5, b.31, f.7b).

77 Jeno Kohner to Stuart Brown, 14 December 1988 (CCC, CJP, MEWG, 1988); CJDM, Minutes, 9 December 1988; General meeting, "Re: Statement of ME delegation," 6 January 1989 (CCC, Jewish-Christian Dialogue). See also the responses from Marsha Levy and Howard Joseph (CJCNA, DA5, b.31, f.1; b.10, f.11); (OJA, MG 8/s).

78 R. Gordon Nodwell to Stuart E. Brown, 14 March 1989.

79 Alan Rose to Stuart Brown 8 December 1988, "Canadian Council of Churches Statement on the Middle East," n.d. (CCC, MEWG, 1989, b.283).

80 Marjorie Ross to members of the General Board, 27 September 1989 (CCC, MEWG, 1990); News release, "Churches Approve Position Paper on Middle East," 16 October 1989; CCC, "Position Paper on the Middle East: A Study Guide" (CCC, MEWG, 1989, b.183).

81 Dorris Sallah to president and general secretary of the CCC, 3 November 1989 (CCC, Responses to the position papers, 1989); see also "Council Supports Palestine," *Anglican Journal,* 115 (November 1989): 1.

82 Canadian Christian-Jewish Consultation, Minutes, 15 November 1989; Louis Guay (for Rev. Canon Jeno G. Kohner) to the general secretary of CCC, 12 February 1990 (CCC, Responses to the position paper, 1989).

83 Editorial, "Palestinian Homeland," *Western Catholic Reports,* 30 October 1989.

84 Michael McAteer, "Churches Speak Out on Mideast Question," *Toronto Star,* 7 October 1989.

85 DuCharme to Stuart Brown, 11 November 1989 (CCC, MEWG, 1989, b.383).

86 Les Scheininger to Stuart Brown, 19 October 1989 (CCC, MEWG, 1989, b.283); Alan Rose to Heather Johnston, 6 October 1989 (CJCNA, DA5, b.30, f.12).

87 Friedberg to Bishop Donald W. Sjoberg, 8 November 1989 (CCC, Responses to the position paper, 1989).

88 McAteer, "Churches Speak Out," *Toronto Star,* 7 October 1989.

89 CCC, MEWG, Minutes, 13 April 1989; see also Donald W. Sjoberg to Stuart Brown, 30 June 1989 (CCC, MEWG, Minutes, 1989, b.183).

90 CCC, MEWG, Minutes, 7 December 1988 (CCC, CWVC, MEWG, 1985–87).

91 CCC, MEWG, "Submission to the Department of External Affairs," 6 January 1989 (CCC, MEWG, 1989, b.183). A more detailed brief from the Canadian

Council of Churches to the UN Commission on Human Rights was presented to the Canadian ambassador to the UN; see CCC, "Submission on Palestinian Human Rights and Israeli Settlement Policy in the Occupied West Bank and Gaza to the Canadian Ambassador to the 40th Session United Nations Commission on Human Rights,"n.d. (CCC, CWC, MEWG, 1989).

92 Andrew N. Robinson to [Tad] Mitsui, 13 March 1989 (CCC, MEWG, 1989, b.183).

93 B'nai Brith Canada, "Discussion Paper of the Institute for International Affairs, in Response to the Brief Prepared by the MEWG CCC for the Consultations in Preparation for the 45th Session of UN Commission on Human Rights," 19 June 1989 (CCC, MEWG, 1989, b.183).

94 "Brief Prepared by the MEWG, a Specialized Body of the CCC, for the Consultations in Preparation for the 46th Session of the UN Commission on Human Rights, 22–3 January 1989," to Department of External Affairs and International Trade Canada (CCC, MEWG, 1990); "Human Rights in the Middle East: A Brief to the Department of External Affairs and International Trade Canada, Human Rights and Social Affairs Division," submitted by the MEWG, CCC, 12 December 1991 (ACCA, GS files, SA, 73N, ME).

95 Brown to Habib, 6 June 1989 (CCC, MEWG, 1989, b.283).

96 "Message of the CCC to MECC Fifth Assembly, Larnaca, Cyprus, January, 1990, Delivered by Bishop Donald Sjoberg, CCC President" (CCC, MEWG, 1989, b.183).

97 DuCharme to Stuart Brown, 19 February 1990 (CCC, MEWG, 1990). Brown invited Habib as a guest of the CCC, but without a delegation; see Brown to Habib, 15 October 1990 (ibid.).

98 Brown to duCharme, 27 July 1990 (CCC, MEWG, 1990).

99 CCC, MEWG, Minutes, 2 November 1990 (CCC, MEWG, 1990).

100 "Douglas duCharme Appointed to CCC Post," *Presbyterian Record*, March 1992, 44; CCC, "Together in the World of the Gospel: Middle East Working Group," Triennial Assembly, May 1994, 54 (CCC, MEWG, 1994).

101 Stuart Brown to Brian Mulroney, 28 November 1990 (CCC, CWC, MEWG, 1990).

102 "Joint Communiqué of the Delegation of the CCC and the MECC," 20 January 1991 (CCC, MEWG, 1990).

103 "Church Leaders Unite against War in Gulf," *Anglican Journal* 117 (January 1991): 1; "All of the mainline churches … have spoken unambiguously and with one voice … that armed buildup by Western forces … cannot be justified" (Robert Assaly to the editor, *Toronto Star*, 12 December 1990).

104 Donald W. Sjoberg to Alan Rose, 18 January 1991; Sjoberg to James Kafieh, 25 January 1991 (CCC, MEWG, 1990).

105 Rose to Dan Pekarsky and Rob Ritter, 21 January 1993 (CJCNA, DA5, b.52, f.22).

CHAPTER THREE: THE UC AND THE HOLOCAUST

1 Davies and Nefsky, *How Silent Were the Churches?* 19.

2 Grant, *The Canadian Experience of Church Union*, 5–101; Grant, "What's Past Is Prologue," 125–9.

3 Dirks, *Canada's Refugee Policy*; Neatby, *The Politics of Chaos*; Abella and Troper, *None Is Too Many*; Betcherman, *The Swastika and the Maple Leaf.*

4 Davies and Nefsky, "The United Church and the Jewish Plight," 57.

5 *United Church of Canada Year Book*, 1927, 116–17.

6 "Mr. Black's Bible Class: When Religion Becomes Selfish," *New Outlook*, 26 August 1936, 797; "When Patriotism Goes Bad," ibid., 2 March 1934, 322.

7 "The German Peril," *New Outlook*, 22 March 1933, 251.

8 *New Outlook*, 9 August 1933, 584; 8 July 1938, 658.

9 Editorial, *New Outlook*, 21 November 1934, 1029; "Our Readers' Forum: Why Dictatorship?" ibid., 8 July 1938, 658.

10 Fair Play, "Germany and the Jews," *New Outlook*, (5 February 1936, 130.

11 23 February 1939 (OJA, MG8/S B1PR 131.5, 23).

12 *Globe and Mail*, 5 December 1939.

13 Davies and Nefsky, "The United Church and the Jewish Plight," 61; see also Nefsky, "The Shadow of Evil"; Davies and Nefsky, *How Silent Were the Churches?* 30–47.

14 Davies and Nefsky, "The United Church and the Jewish Plight," 67.

15 *New Outlook*, 29 March 1933, 267.

16 Richard Roberts, "If Jesus Went to Germany," *New Outlook*, 15 November 1933, 805.

17 For a detailed discussion of Silcox's anti-Nazi and pro-refugee activities during the Nazi era, see the following chapter.

18 Editorial, "The Limit Has Been Reached!" *New Outlook*, 22 January 1936, 73.

19 "Canadian Christians and German Refugees: A Manifesto," *Social Welfare* 16 (March 1936): 25–6.

20 Editorial, "A New Phase in Germany," *New Outlook*, 25 November 1938, 1116.

21 Editorial, "Facing the Storm," *New Outlook*, 6 May 1938, 432.

22 "James Parkes' Visit to Canada," November–December 1938 (OJA, MG8/S B1PR 160.3).

23 *United Church Observer*, 15 June 1940, 1.

24 W.J. McCurdy, "Fascism a Danger," *United Church Observer*, 15 March 1944, 11; see also "Roots of Hitlerism Must Be Removed to Save Civilization," ibid., 15 February 1942, 3, 27.

25 C.A. Lawson, "Christianity's Debt to Judaism," *United Church Observer*, 1 January 1942) 11; see also Alice A. Chown, ibid.

26 Editorial, "The Atrocities," *United Church Observer*, 15 September 1944, 4.

27 "Speech of Dr. Slater of UCC to the Protest Meeting of the Canadian Jewish Congress in Toronto,"1 October 1944 (CJCNA, b.5, f.3).

28 *New Outlook*, 23 October 1935), 1025. See also Hoffmann's comment: "The present plight of the Jews … was a direct challenge to the Church and the Church must deal with it." He suggested playing "the part of neighbor to the Jews," rather than establishing a Jewish mission (*Globe and Mail*, 25 January 1939).

29 See Genizi, *American Apathy*, 106–9; also Davies and Nefsky, "The United Church and the Jewish Plight," 58–60.

30 Editorial, "The Jewish New Year, 5694," *New Outlook*, 13 September 1933, 660.

31 Davies and Nefsky, "The United Church and the Jewish Plight," 58.

32 "Canadian Christians and German Refugees: A Manifesto," *Social Welfare* 16 (March 1936): 26.

33 *New Outlook*, 20 May 1936, 469; "Appeal for the Persecuted," ibid., 12 August 1936, 747.

34 *New Outlook*, 15 July 1938, 574.

35 For the history of the CNCR, see Craft, "Canada's Righteous."

36 E. Crossly Hunter, "The Marks of Anti-Semitism," *United Church Observer*, 15 March 1941, 10; emphasis in the original. See also "Messages from the Co-Chairmen, E.C. Hunter," *Fellowship* [monthly bulletin of the Canadian Conference of Christians and Jews, Toronto], June 1940, 3.

37 A.J. MacQueen to the author, 2 May 1995. Because of a lack of definite proof, I must rely on personal recollection.

38 Editorial, "Is It Nothing to You?" *New Outlook*, 10 February 193, 120.

39 A.B.B. Moore to the author, 10 May 1995.

40 UC, BESS, Thirteenth Annual Report (1937), 37 (UCA).

41 UC, BESS, Fourteenth Annual Report (1938), 10, 30, 52 (UCA).

42 Quoted in Daves and Nefsky, *How Silent Were the Churches?* 147n33.

43 UC, *Record of Proceedings of the Eighth General Council* (Toronto, September 1938), 54–5.

44 UC, BESS, Fifteenth Annual Report (1939), 55, 101 (UCA). The sub-executive of the General Council also endorsed a resolution of the CNCR to join with other churches in drafting a united petition to submit to the Canadian government; see Davies and Nefsky, *How Silent Were the Churches?* 148n63.

45 *United Church of Canada Year Book*, 1939, 54.

46 UC, BESS, The Sixteenth Annual Report, (1940), 26, 66–8, 86–8, 92 (UCA).

47 *United Church of Canada, Year Book*, 1940, 18.

48 UC, BESS, Seventeenth Annual Report (1941), 27–8 (UCA).

49 UC, BESS, Nineteenth Annual Report (1943), 62, 132 (UCA).

50 Quoted in Davies and Nefsky, *How Silent Were the Churches?* 41, 149n76.

51 *United Church of Canada, Year Book*, 1941, 17.

52 UC, Commission on the Church, Nation and World Order, Minutes, July 1941 (UCA, 82,046C, b.1).

53 UC, Commission on the Church, Nation and World Order, Minutes, 4 March 1943 (UCA, 822,046C, b.1).

54 UC, Commission on the Church, Nation and World Order, Norman F. Black to the Commission, 24 January 1944 (UCA, 82,046C, b.1).

55 UC, Commission on the Church, Nation and World Order, "Report to the Eleventh General Council, 1944" (UCA, 82,046C, b.1, f.6.)

56 Davies and Nefsky, *How Silent Were the Churches?* 57.

57 Abella and Troper, *None Is Too Many*, 51; see also 284.

58 Morrison to the author, 24 June 1995.

59 Davies and Nefsky, *How Silent Were the Churches?* 46.

60 McLeod to the author, 29 May 1995.

CHAPTER FOUR: CLARIS E. SILCOX

1 Graham Rockingham, "Biographical Notes" (UCA, CES, 86,208).

2 Silcox to W.H.P. Faunce, 11 September 1928 (UCA, CES, 86.208, b.11, f.3).

3 Silcox, "Can the Church Survive?" undated MS. (UCA, CES).

4 Silcox, "Religious Peace in Canada?" *Canadian Association for Adult Education*, October 1941, 7.

5 Silcox, "The Crisis of the Christian Social Council of Canada: Statement to the Board of Directors by the General Secretary," 4 March 1939 (UCA, CES, b.8, f.56).

6 Van Stempvoort, "Search for Social Unit," 92; see also 87–92.

7 UCA, CES, 86,208 b.8, f.1.

8 Silcox, "The German Psychosis," *New Outlook*, 16 August 1933, 598.

9 "Canadian Christians and German Refugees: A Manifesto," *Social Welfare* 16 (March 1936): 25–6.

10 *Social Welfare* 18 (winter 1939): 61.

11 Abella and Troper, *None Is Too Many*, 44–5; Rome, *Clouds in the Thirties*, 667–71.

12 Abella and Troper, *None Is Too Many*, 46; CNCR, "Should Canada Admit Refugees? Some Considerations and Arguments Submitted for Consideration of the People of Canada," revised, July 1939 (UCA, CES, 86,28, b.12, f.28).

13 Silcox, "Should Canada Provide Sanctuary for European Refugees?" broadcast, CFRC Radio, Kingston, Ont., 1 November 1938 (UCA, CES, 86,208, b.5, f.18).

14 Silcox, "Why Anti-Semites Hate Christ," *Canadian Churchman*, 1 January 1941, 13–14.

15 Silcox, "The Challenge of Anti-Semitism to Democracy," January 1939 (UCA, CES, 86,208, b.12, f.25).

16 See a whole file of clippings of press reports in UCA, CES, 86,208, b.18, f.6.

17 Silcox, "The Historical Background of Jewish-Christian Relations," *Reconciliation* (Fellowship of Reconciliation) 1 (July 1944) 3–5. (UCA, CES, 86,208, b.13, f.17).

18 Silcox, "What Do We Owe to the Jews," *Teacher's Quarterly* (United Church Publication House) 6 (July–September 1943): 1–4.

19 Silcox, "Will the Jews Enlist?" *Saturday Night* (Toronto), 7 October 1939, 5.

20 Silcox, "Canadian Post Mortem on Refugees," 21 March 1939 (UCA, CES, 86,208, b.5, f.19).

21 *Leader Post* (Regina), 9 January 1939 (UCA, CES, 86,208, b.18, f.6).

22 Bennett to Silcox, 27 May 1939 (UCA, CES, 86,208, b.11, f.4).

23 *Evening Free Press* (London, Ont.), 22 June 1940; *Hamilton Spectator,* 30 April 1940.

24 Silcox to Henry J. Stern, 3 July 1940 (OJA, MG8/s, b.2, f.208).

25 Silcox, "Second Report of the Director, Canadian Conference of Christians and Jews, 29 December 1941" (UCA, CES, 86,208, b.7, f.13).

26 Ibid.

27 E.E. Gelber to Julius Miller, 9 February 1945; Canadian Jewish Congress to "Dear Friend," 23 October 1944; A.B. Bennett to "Dear Parent," 23 October 1944 (OJA, MG8/s, reel 1, f.30).

28 "Official Declaration by the Canadian Jewish Congress on Religious Instruction in the Public Schools,"April 1945 (OJA, MG8/s, reel 1, f.30).

29 Maurice N. Eisendrath, "Religion and the Public School," *Holy Blossom Pulpit* (Toronto) 2, no. 4 (16 November 1941); Abraham L. Feinberg, "Religious Instruction in the Public School," sermon delivered 18 February 1945 (Holy Blossom Archives, Toronto, A9); "Memorandum re- Interview with Minister of Education Dr. Duncan MacArthur Regarding Religious Instruction in Public Schools," 3 June 1943 (OJA, MG8/s, reel 1, f.30–1). The Ontario Jewish Archives contains many files on this subject.

30 Silcox to E. Crossley Hunter, 18 December 1945 (UCA, CES, 86,208, b.11, f.5).

31 Silcox, "Religious Education and the Schools," *United Church Observer,* 1 August 1952, 11; see also Silcox, *Religious Education in Canadian Schools* (n.d.) (UCA, Pam. LC, 114, s44).

32 See, for example, *Canadian Commentator,* 10 May 1961 (UCA, CES, 86,208c, b.18, f.16).

33 Silcox, "Address on Palestine and Balfour Declaration" (1948), 1 (UCA, CES, 86,208, b.6, f.68); Silcox, "The Crisis in the Middle East," 5.

34 Silcox, in *Fellowship,* January 1943.

35 Silcox, "The Crisis in the Middle East," 5.

36 Silcox, "Address on Palestine and Balfour Declaration," 2 (UCA, CES, 86,208, b.6, f.68).

37 Silcox, "Impasse in the Holy Land," 128.

38 Ibid., 132.

39 Silcox, "The Crisis in the Middle East," 5.

40 Silcox, "Address on Palestine and Balfour Decleration," 7–11 (UCA, CES, 86,208, b.6, f.68).

41 Ibid., 12.

42 Silcox, "Address on Zionism and Palestine," n.d. (UCA, CES, 86,208, b.6, f.68); Silcox, "The Palestine Question: Outline of Address," given at Rotary Club, Bramton, 19 July 1948 (ibid, f.67); Silcox, "The United Nations Should Reconsider Palestine," *Globe and Mail*, 28 February 1948.

43 Silcox, "The Crisis in the Middle East," 26.

44 Ibid.

45 Silcox to E. Crossley Hunter, 18 December 1945 (UCA, CES, 86,208, b.11, f.5).

46 Ibid.

47 Minutes, Joint Public Relations Committee, Canadian Jewish Congress, 13 March 1946 (OJA, MG8/S, b.3, PR 131.2).

48 CCCJ "Announcement of Administrative Committee's Action on Letter of Resignation from Dr. Silcox and Proposed Re-Organization," 14 February 1946 (UCA, CES, 86,208, b.11, f.6).

49 Interview with Ben G. Kayfetz, 1 March 1995.

50 Silcox, "The Crisis in the Middle East," For a discussion of this subject, see the following chapters.

51 Alice M. Wolfe to Rabinowitz, 3 February 1928; Silcox to unidentified, n.d.; "Report on the Forum Meeting at Lawrence, Mass" (UCA, CES, 86,208, b.5, f.2).

52 Silcox, "The German Psychosis," *New Outlook*, 16 August 1933, 598.

53 Silcox, "The Challenge of Anti Semitism to Democracy," January 1939 (UCA, CES, 86,208, b.12, f.25); see also Silcox, "Canadian Universities and the Jews," *Canadian Student*, 16 (January 1934): 94–9.

54 Quoted in Abella and Troper, *None Is Too Many*, 284.

55 Silcox, "Plea for Germany," *Canadian Commentator*, March 1960, 2.

56 Silcox, "The Challenge of Anti Semitism to Democracy," January 1939, 2 (UCA, CES, 86,208, b.12, f.25); Silcox to Arthur Maheaux, 8 July 1942 (ibid., b.11, f.5).

57 Silcox, "The Challenge of Anti Semitism to Democracy," January 1939, 16 (UCA, CES, 86,208, b.12, f.25).

58 Silcox, "Impasse in the Holy Land," 132.

59 Interview with Alan T. Davies, 9 February 1995.

CHAPTER FIVE: ERNEST MARSHALL HOWSE

1 Angus J. MacQueen to the author, 2 May 1995.

2 "Ernest M. Howse, 1903–93," *United Church Observer*, 1 March 1993, 15; see also "United Church Leader Provokes Controversy," *Montreal Gazette*,

24 April 1965; "United Minister Calls Dr. Howse 'Foolhardy,'" *Toronto Star,* 3 May 1965; *Edmonton Journal,* 28 April 1965.

3 Howse, "I Speak for the Jew," 11 October 1942 (UCA, EMH, 87,043C, b.6, f.11).

4 Howse, "Christian Canada and the Refugees," and "The Refugee Policy for Canada," Westminster UC, Winnipeg, April 1939 (UCA, EMH, 86,049C, b.2, f.9).

5 The quotation is from Walter Ruchmann to Howse, 3 March 1943 (UCA, EMH, 87,043C, b.6, f.16). See also Mrs Vincent Massey to Howse, 18 August 1941; Howse to Lady Tweedsmir, 26 February 1941; Constance Hayward to Howse, 19 March 1942; Alic Russel to Howse, 13 June 1944 (UCA, EMH, 87,043C, b.6, f.7, 16).

6 Letter, signed Elizabeth R, n.d. (UCA, EMH, 87,043C, b.6, f.16).

7 J.R. Mutchmor to Howse, 25 October 1948; Karl Kolodziej to Howse, 23 December 1952 (UCA, EMH, 86,149C, b.2, f.4; b.6, f.9, 10, 16); Howse, "His Name Is John," *Saturday Night* (Toronto), April 1946.

8 See the MS. of two undated articles, nos. 179–80 (UCA, EMH, 87,043C, b.3, f.7); it is not clear where they appeared.

9 "Winnipeg Forms a Round Table of Christians and Jews," *Fellowship,* November–December 1942, 7.

10 Howse, "We Can Lead the Way to Greater Religious Understanding."

11 Interview with Slonim, 3 April 1995 .

12 See an untitled and undated MS. beginning with the words "Rabbi Feinberg and I" (UCA, EMH, 87,043C, b.6, f.2).

13 "Palestine and Post-War Jewish Problems," *Fellowship,* November–December 1942, 5.

14 Ibid.

15 "Dr. Howse Invited to Christian-Muslim Conference, Bhamdoun, Lebanon, 22–27 April 1954," *Church Tower* (bulletin of Bloor Street United Church, Toronto) 2, no. 3 (April 1954).

16 Garland Evans Hopkins to James R. Mutchmor, 22 April 1957 (UCA, EMH, 82,250C, b.13, f.2; see also UCA, EMH, 88,088C, b.1, f.1); Minutes, 14 June 1955 (UCA, EMH, 86,149C, b.11); The movement terminated in 1957 because of a lack of funds and increasing hostility in the Middle East; see Howse's untitled and undated MS. beginning with the words "Rabbi Feinberg" (ibid., 87,043C, b.6, f.2.)

17 Howse's papers contain several files of books and pamphlets dealing with the Israeli-Arab crisis (UCA, EMH, 86,149C, b.12, f.8; b.13, f.2, 8.). The vast majority of them are from Arab publications or hold a pro-Arab point of view. However, there are a few Israeli publications, such as Michael Comey's *The Future of Arab Refugees.*

18 "The Situation in the Middle East Today" (UCA, CCIA, Minutes, 5 January 1956, 2–3, 88,088C, b.1, f.1).

19 Ibid., 3.

20 CCIA, Minutes, 17 May 1956, 7 April 1956 (UCA, CCIA, 88,088C, b.1, f.1).

21 UC, *Records of Proceedings of the Seventeenth General Council, September, 1956,* 141–3. For a detailed discussion of the decisions of the General Council of 1956, see the following chapter.

22 See CCIA, Minutes, 5 January, 1 February, 7 April, 30 October 1956 (UCA, CCIA, 88,088C, b.1, f.1).

23 "Crisis Answer Seen by Cleric," (UCA, EMH, 87,043C, b.3, f.6).

24 Three-page MS. article no. 184, beginning with the words "The Eichmann kidnapping ..." (UCA, EMH, 87,043C, b.3, f.7).

25 Howse, "The Rabbi Is Wrong."

26 Howse, "Who Should Control Jerusalem?" The article appeared in *Ferment,* but my quotations were taken from the second draft of Howse's MS. 23 June 1967 (UCA, EMH, 86,149C, b.12, f.7).

27 Plaut, *Unfinished Business,* 282. The reference to the economic revenue is missing in the second draft MS.

28 Howse, "Reject That Hate Law."

29 Howse, Untitled and undated twelve-page MS. beginning with the words "Rabbi Feinberg" (UCA, EMH, 87,043C, b.6, f.2).

30 For Howse's support of Forrest, see chapter 8 below.

31 Quoted in Slonim, *Family Quarrel,* 91.

CHAPTER SIX: THE CCIA

1 Prince, "The Global War," 28; see also *United Church Observer* 15 January 1946, 25; Slonim, *Family Quarrel,* 60–5.

2 Editorial, "The World Scene," *United Church Observer,* 15 December 1947, 8.

3 Ibid.

4 Editorial, "Palestine," *United Church Observer,* 1 April 1948, 4.

5 Lorna Francis, "A Challenge to Christians," *United Church Observer,* 15 March 1944, 11; see also "Palestine and Post-War Jewish Problems," *Fellowship,* November–December 1942, 5.

6 A.B.B. Moore to the author, 10 May 1995.

7 UC, Commission on the Church, Nation and World Order, "Report to the Eleventh General Council," September 1944, 11 (UCA, Commission on the Church, Nation and World Order, 82,046, b.1, f.6); emphasis in the original.

8 "Why Does a Christian Think He Has Something to Say on International Affairs?" UC, *Record of Proceedings of the Eighteenth General Council, 1960,* 394.

9 "The Committee on the Church and International Affairs," *United Church of Canada, Year Book, 1954,* 133; see also UC, *Record of Proceedings of the Fifteenth General Council, 1952,* 132.

10 UC, CCIA, Minutes, 20–21 June, 17 September, 2, 30 October 1947, 14 January, 26 February 1948 (UCA, CCIA, 88,088C, series 1, b.1, f.1).

11 UC, CCIA, Minutes, 8 April 1948 (UCA, CCIA, 88,088C, b.1, f.1).

12 Henry Langford and J.R. Mutchmor to members of the CCIA, 1 June 1948 (UCA, CCIA, 88,088C, b.1, f.1).

13 UC, *Record of Proceedings of the Thirteenth General Council, Vancouver, September 1948*, 138–40.

14 UC, CCIA, Minutes, 5 April, 1954 (UCA, CCIA, 88,088C, b.1, f.1).

15 UC, *Record of Proceedings of the Sixteenth General Council, September 1954*, 141–3, 148–9.

16 See chapter 4 above. Silcox provided an article, in which he called for a better understanding of the Islamic world and criticized Israel; see Silcox, "The Crisis in the Middle East."

17 UC, CCIA, Minutes, 5 January, 7 April 1956 (UCA, CCIA, 88,088C, b.1, f.1).

18 UC, *Record of Proceedings of the Seventeenth General Council, September, 1956*, 141.

19 Ibid., 142–3.

20 UC, CCIA, Minutes, 30 October 1956 (UCA, CCIA, 88,088C, b.1, f.1).

21 The cable is quoted ibid.

22 UC, CCIA, Minutes, 3 December 1956 (UCA, CCIA, 88,088C, b.1, f.1).

23 "Dr. Mutchmor Gives Views on World," *Ottawa Times*, 28 August 1959.

24 See, for example, "Church and International Affairs," n.d. (UCA, CCIA, 88,088C, b.1, f.1); see also the reports of the CCIA to the General Council in *United Church Yearbook* and UC, *Record of Proceedings*.

25 Taras, "A Church Divided," 86–7. See, for example, UC, CCIA, Minutes, 24 February, 29 March, 30 November 1961 (UCA, CCIA, 88.088C, b.1, f.2).

26 UC, *Record of Proceedings of the Eighteenth General Council, 1958*, 148. It is remarkable, that A.C. Forrest participated in the preparation of this report, which was favourable to Israel; see UC, CCIA, Minutes, 28 March 1958 (UCA, CCIA, 88,088C, b.1, f.1).

27 UC, *Record of Proceedings of the Eighteenth General Council, 1958*, 148.

28 Ibid., 150–2.

29 Editorial, "Christians Must Be Free to Criticize Jews," *United Church Observer*, 1 August 1967, 8.

30 Slonim, *Family Quarrel*, 4.

31 Angus J. MacQueen, "Israel and the United Church of Canada" (MS., 1991). I thank Rev. MacQueen for his kindness in showing me this manuscript.

32 UC, CCIA, "Recommendations for Peace Settlement in the Middle East," Minutes, 20 September 1967 (UCA, CCIA, 88,088C, b.1, f.4).

33 WCC, "Central Committee Adopts Statement on Middle East," 25 August 1967 (ACCA, GS files, GS-75-106, b.11, Committee on International Affairs, Minutes).

34 "Middle East Policy: Executive of the General Council Declaration," UC, *Record of Proceedings of the Twenty Third General Council, September 1968*, 442–3.

35 For a detailed discussion of the *United Church Observer's* pro-Arab policy and the debate between Forrest and the Canadian Jewish community, see the following chapter.

36 "Where Does the United Church of Canada Stand on the Arab-Israeli Conflict?" *United Church Observer,* 15 March 1968, 11.

37 Slonim, *Family Quarrel,* 38.

38 "Middle East Policy: Action of General Council," UC, *Record of Proceedings of the Twenty Third General Council, September, 1968,* 443–4.

39 Ibid., 443; see "The Middle East Policy of the United Church of Canada," UC, *News,* January 1969.

40 C.P. Wright to Mrs M. Pitman, 24 August 1968 (UCA, CCIA, 866,250C, b.3, f.12).

41 J.R Mutchmor to C.P. Wright, 29 October 1968 (UCA, CCIA, 86,250C, b.3, f.12).

42 C. Forsyth to Colwell, 12 March 1969 (UCA, CCIA, 82,250C, b.3, f.13).

43 Frank E. Epp to Charles Forsyth, 17 February 1970 (UCA, CCIA, 82,250C, b.4, f.3).

44 UC, CCIA, Minutes, 24 October 1969 (UCA, CCIA, 88,088C, b.2, f.1).

45 Forrest to Mohamed Chouiri, 13 July 1970; see also Forrest to Yoon Gu Lee, 13 July 1970 (UCA, ACF, 86,104C, b.19, f.2).

46 Bruce McLeod to the author, 29 May 1995.

47 UC, CCIA, Minutes, 30 October 1969, 16 April 1970 (UCA, CCIA, 88,088C, b.2, f.1; "Search for Understanding". See also "Excerpts from Report on Middle East Study Tour, 2–23 September 1970" (UCA, ACF, 86,104C, b.19, f.6).

48 Forsyth to W.A. Monagham, 3 June 1971; see also the letter of Maurice Whidden to the editor, n.d. (UCA, CCIA, 82,250C, b.4, f.8).

49 "Findings" (UCA, ACF, 86,104C, b.19, f.4); see also Robert B. McClure, "Forget History – Look Ahead," *United Church Observer,* November 1970, 30; Bruce N. McLeod, "Not the Facts, but the Fears," ibid.

50 "McClure Says Hatred Dwindling in Mideast," *Toronto Star,* 26 August 1970.

51 "Canadians for Middle East Understanding," November 1970 (UCA, ACF, 86,104C, b.19, f.10.); interview with Gunther Plaut, 11 May 1995.

52 CCIA, "Presentation by Rev. Donald Stirling Regarding the Middle East," UC, CCIA, Minutes, 24 September 1970 (UCA, CCIA, 88,088C, b.2, f.2); UC, "B'nai Brith and the UC Committee Urge Government/Red Cross Aid to Jordan Wounded," UC, *News* 25 September 1970 (UCA, CCIA, 82,250C, b.4, f.5).

53 W.S. McCullough, "The Situation in the Middle East," UC, *Record of Proceedings of the Twenty Fourth General Council, 1971,* 294–7. Note the one-sided bibliography recommended; ibid., 297.

54 Ibid., 327–8.

55 Forrest, "Draft Resolution on the Middle East for the General Council," 11 December 1970 (UCA, ACF, 86,104C, b.19, f.6).

56 UC, CCIA, Minutes, 25 November 1970 (UCA, CCIA, 88,088C, b.2, f.2).

57 MacDonald to Slonim, n.d. (UCA, CCIA, 82,250C, b.7, f.9); MacDonald to Donald Keating, 12 November 1973 (UCA, CCIA, 88,111C, b.1, f.3); MacDonald to Charlotte McEwen, 4 April 1974 (ibid., b.1, f.5).

58 Interview with Lou Ronson, 14 July 1995; Forrest to MacDonald, 21 February, 1 March 1972 (UCA, CCIA, 88,111C, b.1, f.1; UCA, ACF, 86,104C); see also MacDonald to Slonim, n.d. (UCA, CCIA, 82,250C, b.7, f.9).

59 McCullough to MacDonald, 1 October 1972 (UCA, CCIA, 88,111C, b.1, f.1); "Canadians for Middle East Understanding" (UCA, CCIA, 82,250C, b.7, f.8).

60 Forrest to MacDonald, 7 June 1974; MacDonald to *Palestine Digest*, 5 July 1974 (UCA, CCIA, 88,111C, b.1, f.6); MacDonald to Kathryn Huenemann, 3 April 1975 (UCA, CCIA, 88,88C, b.5, f.3).

61 MacDonald to Mitchell Sharp, 1 October 1971; the Department of External Affairs replied that Israel Bonds were not exempt from income tax; see Robert Ellison to MacDonald, 8 November 1971 (UCA, CCIA, 82,250C, b.4, f.10).

62 "For Immediate Release," Ottawa, January 1972 (UCA, CCIA, 82,250C, b.7, f.8).

63 "Canadian Loans to Israel," n.d. (UCA, CCIA, 88,111C, b.1, f.1); UC, CCIA, Minutes, 27 January 1972 (UCA, CCIA, 88,088C, b.2, f.3); Executive, CCIA, 8 February 1972 (ibid., b.2, f.4).

64 UC, *Record of Proceedings of the Twenty Fifth General Council, 1972*, 263. Forrest suggested sending a delegation to the prime minister; see UC, CCIA, Minutes, 25 January 1973 (UCA, CCIA, 88,088C, b.2, f.4). See also Taras, "A Church Divided," 96.

65 Forrest to Yehia Abubaker, 31 August 1972; Forrest to John Sutton 30 August 1972 (UCA, ACF, 86,104C, b.20, f.5). Regarding the controversy between Forrest and the Jewish community, see the following chapters.

66 Forrest to McCullough and Deanna Skeoch, 24 January 1973 (UCA, CCIA, 82,250C, b.7, f.8); Forrest to McCullough, 24 January 1973 (UCA, ACF, 86,104C, b.20, f.9).

67 Clarke MacDonald to Ronald Stirling and Deanna Skeoch, 9 February 1973 (UCA, CCIA, 82,250C, b.7, f.8).

68 MacDonald to Floyd Honey, 20 August 1973 (UCA, CCIA, 82,250C, b.7, f.8).

69 Alan Rose to Gunther Plaut, 21 August 1973 (OJA, DA5, 46/4). When Honey was criticized for showing the brief to the Jews, he apologetically stated that he had only responded to the Jewish request "to receive a copy of the brief and have the privilege of commenting on it"; see Honey to editor of *United Church Observer*, 1 November 1973 (UCA, CCIA, 82,250C, b.7, f.8).

70 George Morrison and Bruce McLeod promised Alan Rose that the Saskatoon resolutions to the government "would more or less be disregarded."

Kayfetz of the CJC was worried that the inclusion of the Saskatoon resolution, with its request to cancel the loan to Israel, "would become the main burden of the discussion in the oral presentation." See B.G. Kayfetz to J.C. Horwitz, 28 June 1973 (OJA, MG8/S, b.56, f.160a).

71 Plaut to Floyd Honey, 12 July 1973 (UCA, CCIA, 82,250C, b.7, f.8); emphasis in the original.

72 T.E. Floyd Honey to Robert Matthews, Eoin Mackay, and Clarke MacDonald, 9 August 1973; "Presentation on Brief on the Middle East to the Prime Minister," CCC, CIA, Minutes, 17 September 1973 (UCA, CCIA, 82,250C, b.7, f.8); Honey to editor of *United Church Observer*, 1 November 1973 (ibid.).

73 "If the members of the church wonder why the modern church is so ineffective in these matters, here is an account of how things work"; Forrest, "The Middle East Story," *United Church Observer*, November 1973, 31. See also Honey to editor of *United Church Observer*, 1 November 1973 (UCA, CCIA, 82,250C, b.7, f.8).

74 UC, CCIA, Minutes, 25 October 1973 (UCA, CCIA, 88,088C, b.2, f.4); George Morrison to Clarke MacDonald, 4 December 1973 (UCA, CCIA, 82,250C, b.7, f.8).

75 Daniel S. Maas to Clarke MacDonald, 20 July 1973 (UCA, CCIA, 82,250C, b.4, f.8). Mrs Von Baeyer, a member of the regional committee of the CCIA in British Columbia, protested in similar way. She wondered why the CCIA was distributing "hate literature" (ibid.).

76 MacDonald to D.S. Maas, 21 August 1973 (UCA, CCIA, 82,250C, b.4, f.8); MacDonald to McLeod, 10 September 1973 (UCA, CCIA, 88,111C, b.1, f.3); McLeod to MacDonald, 16 October 1973 (UCA, CCIA, 82,250C, b.7, f.8).

77 Habib to Clarke MacDonald, 11 March 1974; MacDonald to Habib, 26 March 1974 (UCA, CCIA, 88,088C, b.6, f.5).

78 Taras, "A Church Divided," 96. Although Taras does not cite any source to confirm his statement, the lack of evidence that the brief was actually handed out in an interview with Prime Minister Trudeau supports that view.

79 "Correspondence Middle East, 1972–3" (UCA, CCIA, 82,250C, b.7, f.8); BGK [Ben G. Kayfetz], re. CCC brief, 29 June 1973 (OJA, MG8/S, b.54, f.41).

80 Anglican News Service, "For Immediate Release," Toronto, 9 October 1973 (OJA, MG8/S, b.54, f.41).

81 "Statement of Christian Concern about the Middle East," *Globe and Mail*, 19 October 1973. Signatories of the document included Edward A. Synon, president of the Pontifical Institute of Medieval Studies; Gregory Baum of St Michael's College and John M. Kelly, president of St Michael's College, the University of Toronto; Alan T. Davies, Victoria College; William O. Fen-

nell, principal, Emmanuel College, the University of Toronto; David Demson, Emmanuel College; and B. Robert Bater, minister of Eglinton United Church, Toronto.

82 Fackenheim to Alan T. Davies, 23 October 1973 (UCA, ATD, 98,087V). See also, Slonim, *Family Quarrel*, 14.

83 "Fourteen University of Toronto Professors See Anti-Arab Bias in Pro-Israel Argument," *Globe and Mail*, 24 October 1973.

84 Clarke MacDonald, "Statement of United Church Official on Mideast," *Globe and Mail*, 30 October 1973.

85 "Humanity Diminished if No Response: Affluent Canadians Asked to Face Up to Famine in World," *Globe and Mail*, 29 December 1973. Jewish leaders appreciated McLeod's initiative in this area; see R.L. Ronson to McLeod, 3 January 1974 (Ronson's private collection); Gunther Plaut to McLeod, 31 December 1973 (OJA, DA5, b.46, f.4).

86 MacDonald to B. Kayfetz, 4 April 1974. Sydney M. Harris, president of the CJC, appreciated this resolution in this vital humanitarian cause and said that he was looking forward to further cooperation; see Harris to George Morrison, 21 March 1974 (OJA, MG8/S, b.59, f.99a–b).

87 Clarke MacDonald to George Morrison, 26 October 1973; MacDonald to Floyd Honey, 6 June 1975 (UCA, CCIA, 88,099C, b.6, f.6); The Anglican and Presbyterian churches also supported A. Nathan; see UC, CCIA, Minutes, 23 March 1972 (ibid., b.2, f.4).

88 Forrest to MacDonald, 29 November 1973; MacDonald to Robert Torrence et al., 6 December 1973; MacDonald to Des McCalmont, 31 January 1974 (UCA, CCIA, 88,111C, b.1, f.3, 6).

89 MacDonald to Charlotte McEwen, 4 April 1974 (UCA, CCIA, 88,111C, b.1, f.5). For a critical view of Shahak by the B'nai Brith's Anti-Defamation League, see "Israel Shahak and Lea Tsemel Anti-Israel Propaganda Tours," 30 September 1977 (ADL): "Although some in Israel regard Shahak as a traitor, he continues to write and to speak freely in the framework of Israeli democracy, and to travel freely to Europe and the United States." See also Lou Ronson and H. Levy to Clarke McDonald, 26 October 1977 (UCA, CCIA, 82,250C, b.7, f.10).

90 Plaut, *Unfinished Business*, 279–80.

91 UC, CCIA, Minutes, 24 April 1975 (UCA, CCIA, 88,088C, b.2, f.4); see also "Rabbi Recognizes Rights of Palestinians," *United Church Observer*, February 1973, 45. "Peace with justice can not come to the Middle East until the rights of Palestinians are recognized," wrote Slonim, in "Justice and Peace for Palestinians Too?" *Toronto Star*, 22 November 1977. MacDonald and Slonim developed a personal friendship, and Slonim invited MacDonald to deliver a sermon at his Congregation Habonim Synagogue in Toronto; See MacDonald to Slonim, 25 May 1977 (UCA, CCIA, 88,088C, b.6, f.5); Slonim to MacDonald, 30 January 1978 (UCA, CCIA, 82,250C, b.7, f.10).

92 Editorial, "Rabbi Says Include Palestinians," *United Church Observer,* January 1978, 8.

93 Forrest to Eoin S. Mackay, 7 May 1974 (UCA, ACF, 86,104C, b.21, f.3); UC, CCIA, Minutes, 2 May 1974 (UCA, CCIA, 88,088C, b.2, f.5); Clarke MacDonald to "Dear Friends," re: Middle East Seminar, Ottawa, 13–15 June 1974 (UCA, CCIA, 82,250C, b.7, f.9).

94 MacDonald to Norman Vale, 9 July 1976 (UCA, CCIA, 82,250C, b.7, f.10).

95 Forrest to John N. Booth, 8 April 1974 (UCA, ACF, 86,104C, b.8, f.74); MacDonald to Charlotte McEwen, 4 April 1974 (UCA, CCIA, 88,111C, b.1, f.5).

96 Clarke MacDonald, "Report to the CCIA re: Study Seminar in the Middle East," n.d. [ca. 9 March 1973], (UCA, CCIA, 88,088C, b.2, f.4).

97 Clarke MacDonald, "An Expression of Concern" (UCA, CCIA, 88,088C, b.6, f.5).

98 *United Church Observer,* February 1973, 42; Slonim, *Family Quarrel,* 25; MacDonald to Jordan Pearlson, 9 February 1973 (UCA, CCIA, 88,111C, b.1, f.4).

99 See Donald A. Gillies, "Let's Forget about Converting the Jews," *United Church Observer,* April 1973, 34; but also "Salvation Is of the Jews," ibid., 15 December 1947, 24; J. Berkley Reynolds, "Long Live the Old Evangelism! The United Church Has Forgotten It and Thus Forsaken Its First Responsibility," ibid., 1 May 1967, 14–5, 26.

100 Patricia Clarke, "The Rush for Evangelism: Not Just Key 73, but Door 74," *United Church Observer,* October 1972, 6–7; "Church Supports Key 73, but Not Converting Jews," ibid., April 1973.

101 "Christian-Jewish Relations in Canada: A Statement by N. Bruce McLeod, Moderator, UCC, 5 November 1973, Iona College, the University of Windsor" (copy in the possession of the author); Donald A. Gillies, "Let's Forget about Converting the Jews," *United Church Observer,* April 1973, 34–5; MacDonald to Jordan Pearlson, 9 February 1973 (UCA, CCIA, 88,111C, b.1, f.4).

102 UC, *Record of Proceedings of the Twenty Sixth General Council, 1974,* 328–9. Clarke MacDonald used to point to the fact that the United Church took a stand on behalf of the right of Jews to emigrate from Russia to their homeland as a proof of its even-handed policy; see MacDonald to H.L. Wipprecht, 24 July 1979 (UCA, CCIA, 88,088C, b.3, f.3).

103 UC, "News for Immediate Release," 24 May 1974 (OJA, MG8/S, b.59, f.99a); see also the CCC's "News Release," 17 May 1974 (UCA, CCIA, 82,250C, b.7, f.9).

104 See, for example, the Waterloo Emmanuel United Church congregation's statement in *Kitchener-Waterloo Record,* 11 December 1975.

105 McLeod to the author, 29 May 1995. For a detailed discussion of the controversy over the *Observer*'s Middle East policy, see the following chapters.

106 UC, *Record of Proceedings of the Twenty Seventh General Council, August 1977*, 617.

107 MacDonald to Deanna Skeoch, 23 February 1979 (UCA, CCIA, 88,088C, b.3, f.3).

108 Editorial, "Hope for the Middle East Settlement," *United Church Observer*, May 1975, 8; editorial, "Let's Welcome the PLO," ibid., August 1975, 9.

109 UC, *Record of Proceedings, 1977*, 617; "News," *United Church Observer*, October 1977, 20.

110 Ben Kayfetz, "Demand that the PLO Represented at Geneva Talks Draws Jewish Protest," *Canadian Jewish News*, 7 September 1977; N. Bruce McLeod to the author, 29 May 1995.

111 *Canadian Jewish News*, 7 September 1977.

112 George Turtle to Jack Jacobson, 18 November 1977 (OJA, MG8/S, JCRC, 1977).

113 MacDonald to Levy, 19 October 1977 (Lou Ronson's private collection); MacDonald to Jordan Pearlson, 14 September 1977 (UCA, 88,088C, b.6, f.5); Ronson to MacDonald, 21 December 1977 (UCA, CCIA, 82,250C, b.7, f.10).

114 Gilbert to MacDonald, 8 September 1977 (UCA, CCIA, 988,088C, b.6, f.5).

115 Barry K. Morris to CCIA, 11 January 1978 (UCA, CCIA, 82,250C, b.7, f.10).

116 David E. Demson, "Letter to the Editor," *Globe and Mail*, 8 August 1977.

117 MacDonald to Peter Gilbert, 26 September 1977 (UCA, CCIA, 88,088C, b.6, f.5); MacDonald to Barry K. Morris, 18 January 1978 (UCA, CCIA, 82,250C, b.7, f.10).

118 MacDonald to Skeoch, 23 February 1979 (UCA, CCIA, 88,088C, b.3, f.3).

119 "Statement on the Middle East Situation on Behalf of the CCIA of the United Church of Canada," 15 March 1978 (OJA, MG8/S, b.70, f.122). Note also George Morrison's sorrow and protest; Morrison to Theodore Meron, Israeli ambassador, Ottawa, n.d. (UCA, ACF, 86,104C, b.23, f.15).

120 MacDonald to H.L. Wipprecht, 24 July 1979 (UCA, CCIA, 88,088C, b.3, f.3).

121 UCA, ACF, 86,104C, b.21, f.17.

122 "Church Leaders Urge Israel to Quit Occupied Land," *Toronto Star*, 8 June 1978; "Clergy Efforts towards Mid-East Peace," *Canadian Jewish Outlook*, June 1978, 3.

123 Editorial, "Bound to Divide," *Toronto Star*, 8 June 1978.

124 "Clergymen Called for Mideast Peace," "Letters to the Editor," *Toronto Star*, 19 June 1978.

125 "The Editor's Comment," *Canadian Jewish Outlook*, June 1978, 3.

126 Simmonds to MacDonald, 6 July 1978 (UCA, CCIA, 82,250C, b.7, f.10).

127 MacDonald to Simmonds, 26 July 1978 (UCA, CCIA, 82,250C, b.7, f.10).

128 To "Signers of the Statement calling for the WCC to make a renewed effort to seek peace in the Middle East," 25 July 1978 (UCA, CCIA, 88,088C, b.6, f.5).

129 Skeoch, "Middle East News Gathering Event," 25 January 1979 (UCA, CCIA, 88,088C, b.3, f.2).

130 MacDonald to Ray, 26 February 1979 (UCA, CCIA, 88,088C, b.3, f.3).

131 Forrest to editor of *Windsor Star,* 24 April 1975 (UCA, ACF, 86,104C, b.21, f.7).

132 Forrest to Leopoldo J. Niilus, 5 July 1978 (UCA, ACF, 86,104C, b.21, f.17).

133 D. Skeoch, "Middle East News Gathering Event," 25 January 1979 (UCA, CCIA, 88,088C, b.3, f.2).

134 "Fourteen University Professors See Anti-Arab Bias in Pro-Israel Argument," *Globe and Mail,* 24 October 1973; H.L. Wipprecht to Israeli ambassador, 24 May 1979 (UCA, CCIA, 88,088C, b.3, f.3).

135 Kenny to MacDonald, 28 February 1979; see also Lorne Kenny, "The Palestinian Problem, Known as the Middle East Question," a lecture delivered in the CCIA, 25 January 1979 (UCA, CCIA, 88,088C, b.3, f.3, 2); emphasis in the original.

136 Wipprecht to Deanna Skeoch, 24 April 1979 (UCA, CCIA, 88,088C, b.3, f.3); emphasis in the original.

137 Wipprecht to D. Skeoch, 29 June 1979 (UCA, CCIA, 88,088C, b.3, f.3).

138 Wipprecht to the Israeli ambassador, 24 May 1979 (UCA, CCIA, 88,088C, b.3, f.3).

139 Deanna [Skeoch] to Mary and Clarke [MacDonald], n.d.; MacDonald to Wipprecht, 24 July 1979; Kenny to Wipprecht, 1 May 1979 (UCA, CCIA, 88,088C, b.3, f.3).

140 Clarke MacDonald to Shalev, 26 July 1979; Shalev to MacDonald, 3 August 1979 (UCA, CCIA, 88,088C, b.3, f.3).

141 L.M. Kenny, convener, Middle East Working Group, CCIA, "Human Rights in the Middle East," 20 December 1979 (UCA, CCIA, 88,088C, b.3, f.3); UC, *Record of Proceedings of the Twenty Eighth General Council, 1980,* 418–19.

142 "A Statement re the Middle East Situation by the United Church of Canada," 14 June 1982 (UCA, CCIA, 88,088C, b.6, f.5).

143 UC, *Yearbook, 1975,* 21.

144 UC, *Record of Proceedings of the Thirtieth General Council, August 1984,* 452.

145 UC, *Record of the Proceedings of the Thirty Fourth General Council, August 1992,* 148. However, the council called on the government to protest about discrimination against Jews in the Soviet Union and to relax Canadian immigration regulations in order to enable Jewish family reunification; see ibid., 632.

146 George Morrison to the author, 24 June 1995.

CHAPTER SEVEN: THE *OBSERVER* AND ISRAEL

1 Slonim, *Family Quarrel,* 21–3.

2 Plaut, *Unfinished Business,* 279.

3 Slonim, *Family Quarrel,* 23.

4 Interview with Gunther Plaut, 11 May 1995.

5 N. Bruce McLeod to the author, 29 May 1995.

6 Alan T. Davies to the author, 29 May 1999.

7 See chapter 2; also Prince, "The Global War."

8 Editorial, "Palestine," *United Church Observer,* 15 March 1947, 4.

9 Editorial, "The World Scene," *United Church Observer,* 15 December 1947, 8; editorial, "Palestine," ibid., 1 April 1948, 4; see also chapter 2 above. Predicting the trouble spots in 1948, the editor briefly mentioned in a non-committal manner the increasing civil strife in Palestine; see editorial, "The Year Ahead," ibid., 1 January 1948, 4.

10 W.E.L.S., Review of *The Story of the Arab Legion,* by Brig. John Glabb, *United Church Observer,* 15 December 1948, 20.

11 See Slonim, *Family Quarrel,* 47.

12 Ages, "The *United Church Observer* and the State of Israel," 2.

13 Graham Rockingham, "Alfred Clinton Forrest" (uca, acf, 86,104c, Finding aid 159, "Introduction"). *Globe and Mail,* 28 December 1978; *Toronto Star,* 28 December 1978.

14 Ages, "The *United Church Observer* and the State of Israel," 1.

15 Ibid., 2. David Taras argued the same vein; see Taras, "A Church Divided," 89.

16 Slonim, *Family Quarrel,* 47–8.

17 Editorial, "Egypt-Israel: Two Sides of It," *United Church Observer,* 15 December 1955, 6.

18 uc, ccia, Minutes, 5 January 1956 (uca, ccia, 88,088c, b.1, f.1); uc, *Record of Proceedings of the Seventeenth General Council, 1956,* 141. See also chapter 5 above.

19 uc, ccia, Minutes, 25 September 1956 (uca, ccia, 88,088c, b.1, f.1).

20 As to the discussion of this issue, see later in this chapter.

21 uc, ccia, Minutes, 5 January 1956 (uca, ccia, 88,088c, b.1, f.1). For Silcox's anti-Israeli attitude, see chapter 5 above.

22 "Observations," *United Church Observer,* 15 February 1956, 3.

23 Silcox, "The Crisis in the Middle East."

24 Editorial, "Observations," *United Church Observer,* July 1956, 5; Abraham L. Feinberg, "Christians and Arab Israel Peace," ibid., 13–14.

25 E.L. Homewood, "Where Christ Was Born," *United Church Observer,* 15 December 1958, 10–12; Homewood, "Palestine's Refugees: Scar of the Near East," ibid., 1 January 1959, 8–10, 24, 30; Homewood, "The Divided Holy Land," ibid., 15 February 1959, 12–14, 20; Homewood, "The New Testament Scene

Today," ibid., 15 May 1959, 10–13; Homewood, "The New Israel," ibid., 1 November 1959, 8–10, 18.

26 G.W. Goth, "Letters to the Editor: A Brain-Washed Editor," *United Church Observer*, 15 December 1959, 2; L.E. Smith, "Letters to the Editor: Not a Brain-Washed Editor," ibid., February 1960, 2.

27 Stuart E. Rosenberg, "Jews in the Soviet Union," *United Church Observer*, July 1961, 16–17, 29.

28 Grant, *The Church in the Canadian Era*, 186.

29 Mathers, *The Word and the Way*, 61–2; also 95, 150. See also Palin, "The United Church and the Jews," 6–7.

30 Editorial, "WASPS," *United Church Observer*, 1 June 1964, 11.

31 "Rabbi Rosenberg Replies," *United Church Observer*, July 1964, 17, 30.

32 Slonim, *Family Quarrel*, 51–2.

33 UC, CCIA, Minutes, 28 March 1957 (UCA, CCIA, 88,088C, b.1, f.1); Forrest, "The Holy Land," *United Church Observer*, 15 December 1964, 37; see also 12–15, 24.

CHAPTER EIGHT: A.C. FORREST

1 Editorial, "Christians Must Be Free to Criticize Jews," *United Church Observer*, 1 August 1967, 8.

2 Editorial, "What Can the Churches Do?" *United Church Observer*, 15 September 1967, 10.

3 Gershon Avner "To Whom It May Concern," 20 July 1967; Forrest to Avner, 25 August 1967; Forrest to G.J. Maloney, n.d. (UCA, ACF, 86,104C, b.18, f.2).

4 "Aftermath in the Middle East," *United Church Observer*, 1 October 1967.

5 Ages, "The *United Church Observer* and the State of Israel," 2.

6 Slonim, *Family Quarrel*, 52–3.

7 Ibid., 56; Ages, "The *United Church Observer*, and the State Israel," 11.

8 Editorial, "Editor Anti-Israel," *United Church Observer*, 15 November 1967, 2; Forrest to Gershon Avner, 4 October 1967 (UCA, ACF, 86,104C, b.18, f.3).

9 Ages, "The *United Church Observer* and the State Israel," 6.

10 Slonim, *Family Quarrel*, 55.

11 Avner to Editor of *United Church Observer*, 29 September 1967 (UCA, ACF, 86,104C, b.18, f.3).

12 Forrest to Avner, 4, 19 October 1967 (UCA, ACF, 86,104C, b.18, f.3). "I've had most astonishing mail from the Israeli ambassador," wrote Forrest to Paul J. Martin, the Canadian secretary of state for external affairs on 13 October 1967 (ibid.). W. Gunther Plaut's rejoinder appeared in the *United Church Observer*, 15 November 1967, 21–3.

13 Plaut, *Unfinished Business*, 281.

14 Plaut, "Israel Wants Justice Too."

15 Forrest to Harold B. Attin, 12 October 1967 (UCA, ACF, 86,104C, b.18, f.3); see also Forrest, "What Happened When I Criticized Israel," 27.

16 Woodside, "The Reluctant Conquerors," 38–9.

17 H.W. Silverman to Forrest, 24 September 1967 (UCA, ACF, 86,104C, b.18, f.3).

18 Alan Rose, Editorial, *Canadian Zionist Special Report*, December 1967, 16b.

19 Mrs R.G. Nicholls to Forrest, 27 October 1967; see also Forrest to Nicholls, 3 November 1967 (UCA, ACF, 86,104C, b.18, f.3).

20 Plaut, *Unfinished Business*, 278.

21 Quoted in H.E. Young to Forrest, Memo, 13 November 1967 (UCA, ACF, 86,104C, b.18, f.4).

22 R.W. Stephenson, "Letter to the Editor," *United Church Observer*, 15 December 1967, 2; see also Dorothy Henderson to the editor, ibid.

23 MacDonald to Forrest, 19 October 1967 (UCA, ACF, 86,104C, b.18, f.3).

24 Watkins to Forrest, 26 September 1967 (UCA, ACF, 86,104C, b.18, f.3).

25 Long to Forrest, 19 September 1967 (UCA, ACF, 86,104C, b.18, f.3).

26 Aba Gefen to Forrest, 4 July 1968 (UCA, ACF, 86,104C, b.18, f.6); *San Francisco Chronicle*, 24 May 1969.

27 Forrest to Sankri Suhak, October 1967; Shukri I. Saleh to Forrest, 5 November 1967; Forrest to inter-church feature editor, 30 November 1967; P.D. Dodd to Forrest, 16 October 1967; Moshe Menuhin to Forrest, 11 December 1967 (UCA, ACF, 86,104C, b.18, f.3–4).

28 Henry E. McCorkle to Forrest, 18 August 1968 (UCA, ACF, 86,104C, b.18, f.8).

29 Forrest to Yoon GuLee, 28 September 1967 (UCA, ACF, 86,104C, b.18, f.3); Forrest, Public address, 5 December 1967, 4–5 (ibid., b.5, f.1); Bruce McLeod to the author, 29 May 1995.

30 Forrest, "What Happened When I Criticized Israel."

31 Ernest M. Howse, "Racism Charge Can Be a Two Edged Sword," *Toronto Star*, 6 May 1971.

32 E.M. Howse, "Torrent of Abuse," *Toronto Star*, 12 January 1972; excerpts from this article were reprinted in the *United Church Observer*, March 1972, 12, 42.

33 MacDonald to Reuben Slonim, n.d. (UCA, CCIA, 82,250C, b.7, f.9).

34 Angus MacQueen to the author, 2 May 1995; see also MacQueen's MS. "Israel and the United Church of Canada" (1991).

35 N. Bruce McLeod to the author, 29 May 1995.

36 UC, *Record of Proceedings of the Twenty Third General Council, 1968*, 444.

37 Quoted in Plaut, *Unfinished Business*, 290.

38 Interview with Roland de Corneille, 20 July 1995.

39 Baum, "Salvation Is from the Jews."

40 Kenneth Bagnell, "Anti-Semitism" n.d. (UCA, ATD, 98,087v).

41 David Demson, "Criticizes Howse Defence," *Toronto Star*, 24 January 1972.

42 Davies, "Anti-Zionism, Anti-Semitism and the Christian Mind." "That is as succinct a statement of recent Jewish history as I have seen, and I was most excited when I ran into it because I had been using the symbol of crucifixion and resurrection rather hesitantly myself, when I saw that it hit you the same way, I took courage," wrote Franklin H. Littell, the American Shoah scholar, to Davies; Littell to Davies, 12 January 1972 (UCA, ATD, 98,087v).

43 Forrest to Harold B. Attin, 12 October 1967 (UCA, ACF, 86,104C, b.18, f.3).

44 Forrest to Gottlieb, 13 November 1967, 17 January 1968 (UCA, ACF, 86,104C, b.18, f.4, 5).

45 Gottlieb to Forrest, 12 January 1968 (UCA, ACF, 86,104C, b.18, f.5).

46 William Gottlieb, "An Anti-Zion Jew Tells: The Other Side of the Zionist Story," *United Church Observer*, 15 May 1968, 28–30.

47 Flannery, *A Christian View of Israel*, 3.

48 "Anti-Zionist Jewish Writers: *The Decadence of Judaism in Our Time*, by Moshe Menuhin," *United Church Observer*, November 1973, 9; Forrest to Pierre Luc Sequillon, 17 November 1970 (UCA, ACF, 86,104C, b.19, f.6).

49 "The Editor's Observations," *United Church Observer*, 1 February 1969, 9; Forrest, "The Middle East: It's Bad and It's Getting Worse and Here's Why It Matters So Much," ibid., 18–21.

50 Forrest to Norton Mezvinsky and Rabbi Everett Gendler, 28 January 1970 (UCA, ACF, 86,104C, b.19, f.1).

51 Forrest to Arab Information Office, 12 April 1972 (UCA, ACF, 86,104C, b.19, f.3).

52 Forrest to Fennell, 27 November 1972 (UCA, ACF, 86,104C, b.20, f.8).

53 Introductory sheet on A.C. Forrest, 1968/69 (UCA, ACF, 86,104C, b.18, f.8).

54 James E. Pierce to Forrest, 17 April 1968; Louis H. Benes to Forrest, 10 May 1968 (UCA, ACF, 86,104C, b.18, f.6).

55 Forrest, " 'You Don't Seem to Care About Us.' "

56 Plaut, "News and Views: Again Dr. Forrest."

57 Interview with David Demson, 30 March 1995; interview with Roland de Corneille, 20 July 1995.

58 Forrest to William Gottlieb, 13 November 1967 (UCA, ACF, 86,104C, b.18, f.4).

59 Interview with Ben Kayfetz, 12 March 1995.

60 Bruce McLeod to the author, 29 May 1995; A.B.B. Moore to the author, 10 May 1995; Angus MacQueen to the author, 2 May 1995.

61 McLeod to the author, 29 May 1995; UCA, ACF, 86,104C, b.20, f.3; see also Slonim, *Family Quarrel*, 57.

62 Plaut, *Unfinished Business*, 286–8.

63 Slonim, *Family Quarrel*, 57–8.

64 Alan Davies to Pierre Berton, 19 February 1970 (UCA, ACF, 86,104C, b.19, f.1).

65 Interview with Alan Davies, 10 March 1995; Pierre Barton to Alan Davies, 18 February 1970 (UCA, ATD, 98,087V).

66 Interview with Lou Ronson, 14 July 1995.

67 Booth, "How Zionists Manipulate Your News"; Salter,"He as God Sitteth in the Temple of God." The content of these articles and the reaction to them will be discussed in chapter 9.

68 Forrest to W. Gottlieb, 17 January 1968 (UCA, ACF, 86,104C, b.18, f.5).

69 P.C. [Patricia Clarke], editorial, "Dear Jews," *United Church Observer*, January 1969, 10.

70 Ernest Long to L.M. Azzaria, 11 March 1968 (UCA, ACF, 86,104C, b.18, f.6).

71 Plaut, *Unfinished Business*, 283.

72 Ibid., 284; UC, "The United Church and the Existence of the State of Israel: Text of Address to be Given by Dr. Robert B. McClure, Moderator, UCC, Toronto Zionist Council, 15 January 1969," UC, *News*, 15 January 1969, 1 (UCA, CCIA, 82,250C, b.13, f.3); hereafter cited as "McClure's Address."

73 Scott, *McClure*, 2: 234.

74 McClure's Address, 5.

75 Ibid., 5–7; *Religious News Service*, 20 January 1969.

76 Plaut, *Unfinished Business*, 286.

77 Sydney M. Harris to Robert McClure, n.d. (OJA, MG8/S, b.49, f.166).

78 Kelman to McClure, 7 January 1971 (OJA, MG8/S, b.53, f.161).

79 McClure to Kelman, 14 January 1971; Kelman to Ben [Kayfetz], 15 January 1971 (OJA, MG8/S, b.53, f.161).

80 Littman to N. Bruce McLeod and Don Stirling, 7 January 1971 (OJA, MG8/S, b.49, f.106). Despite Littman's remarks, Ben Kayfetz later stated that McClure was not antisemitic, only pro-Arab; interview with Kayfetz, 12 March 1995.

81 Long to all ministers, missionary and maintenance committee members, United Church women, and other lay leaders, including young people within reach of channels of the CBS-TV network, 11 December 1967 (UCA, ACF, 86,104C, b.18, f.4).

82 Jean Sadler to Ben Kayfetz, Re: meeting with UC, 10 November 1969 (OJA, MG8/S, b.41, f.88).

83 Ray to George I. Bernstein, 25 March 1971 (OJA, MG8/S, b.53, f.161).

84 Marcia Zucker to Littman, 1 April 1970 (OJA, MG8/S, b.45, f.168).

85 Shirley Geigen-Miller, "Media Has Pro-Israeli Bias, Editor Charges," *Don Mills Mirror*, 10 December 1969.

86 Rosenberg to Long, 26 December 1969 (OJA, MG8/S, b.41, f.88); emphasis in the original.

87 Long to Rosenberg, 23 December 1969 (OJA, MG8/S, b.41, f.88).

88 Pat [Patricia Clarke] to Bob, n.d. (UCA, ACF, 86,104C, b.19, f.1).

89 Long to de Corneille, 24 February 1970 (UCA, ACF, 86,104C, b.19, f.1).

90 Plaut, "News and Views: The Meeting with Dr. McClure."

91 "Editor's Observations," *United Church Observer,* 1 March 1970, 9; Plaut, "News and Views: The Irrepressible Mr. Forrest."

92 Plaut, *Unfinished Business,* 287; MacDonald to Slonim, n.d. (UCA, CCIA, 82,250C, b.7, f.9).

93 Forrest to I.M. Rabinowitch, 22 July 1970 (UCA, ACF, 86,104C, b.19, f.4).

94 Alan Davies to the author, 19 August 1999.

95 "Editor's Observations," *United Church Observer,* August 1970, 9.

96 Gefen, "A Vision of Peace Guides Israel."

97 Davies, "Why Critics of Israel Must Be Careful."

98 Plaut to Davies, 1 September 1970; Littman to Davies, 4 September 1970 (UCA, ATD, 98,087V).

99 David R. Wood, "Letters to the Editor," *United Church Observer,* October 1970, 2.

100 Shechter to Forrest, 31 July 1970; Forrest to Shechter, 19 August 1970 (UCA, ACF, 86,104C, b.19, f.4).

101 Forrest to Rabinowitch, 22 July 1970 (UCA, ACF, 86,104C, b.19, f.4).

102 Rosenberg to Forrest, 31 July 1970 (UCA, ACF, 86,104C, b.19, f.4).

103 Forrest to Frank Epp, 7 January 1972 (UCA, ACF, 86,104C, b.20, f.1).

104 Mrs J.E. Hiltz, "Letters to the Editor," *United Church Observer,* October 1970, 2.

105 Sienkiericz to J.R. Mutchmor, 20 January 1969 (UCA, CCIA, 82,250C, b.3, f.3).

106 Forrest to Harry Meadows, 30 March 1970 (UCA, ACF, 86,104C, b.19, f.2).

107 Davies to Pierre Berton, 19 February 1970 (UCA, ACF, 86,104C, b.19, f.1).

108 Plaut to Davies, 21 April 1971 (UCA, ATD, 98,087V).

109 Forrest, *The Unholy Land,* 151, 169, 172.

110 Ben G. Kayfetz to M.B. Spiegel, 5 February 1971 (OJA, MG8/S, b.49, f.166).

111 *Toronto Star,* 20 March 1971; "Editor's Observations," *United Church Observer,* December 1971, 6; "Letters to the Editor," *Telegram,* 30 March 1971.

112 "A Pulpit Conversation between A. Forrest, Editor of the *United Church Observer* and John Morgan, Minister, First Unitarian Congregation," *Unitarian Horizon,* 28 March 1971 (OJA, MG8/S, b.45, f.166).

113 Bahman (Beirut) to Forrest, 29 September 1971; Yehya Aboubakr to Forrest, 28 August 1972 (UCA, ACF, 86,104C, b.20, f.5).

114 Long to Ben G. Kayfetz, 26 February 1970 (OJA, MG8/S, b.45, f.168).

115 Moore to Freeman and Davies, 26 February 1971 (UCA, ATD, 98,087V).

116 Kayfetz to Spiegel, 23 December 1970 (OJA, MG8/S, b.45, f.168).

117 Littman, "United Church and Jews Must Seek Understanding."

118 Long and Moore, "United Church Outlines Stance on Middle East."

119 Forrest to senior secretaries, 4 November 1971 (UCA, ACF, 86,104C, b.19, f.14).

120 Editorial, "Russian Jews and Palestine Arabs," *United Church Observer*, August 1971, 11.

121 Forrest to John M. Sutton, 5 November 1970; Forrest to Pierre Luc Sequillon, 17 November 1970 (UCA, ACF, 86,104C, b.19, f.6); "Canadians for Middle East Understanding: Statement of Aims" (ibid., f.10).

122 Editorial, "For the War Record," *United Church Observer*, November 1971, 10–11.

123 Editorial, "Was This Editorial Anti-Semitic?" *United Church Observer*, March 1972, 11–12.

124 Slonim, *Family Quarrel*, 8; Plaut, *Unfinished Business*, 288. Forrest reprinted the editorial of November 1971, along with criticism of it, in the March 1972 issue (11) of the *Observer*.

125 Slonim, *Family Quarrel*, 8.

126 A.C. Forrest, "Draft of Proposed Statement on the Middle East," 11 May 1972 (UCA, ACF, 86,104C, b.23, f.5).

127 MacQueen to Donald Keating, 22 March 1972 (UCA, ACF, 86,104C, b.20, f.2).

128 Donald R. Keating, "An Open Letter" to A.B.B. Moore, moderator of the United Church; E.W. Scott, primate of the Anglican Church of Canada; the chairman, H.C. Hyman, and members of Halton Presbytery, Hamilton Conference, UC, 25 November 1971 (UCA, ACF, 86,104C, b.19, f.14).

129 Howse, "Torrent of Abuse"; excerpts from this article were reprinted in the *United Church Observer*, March 1972, 12, 42.

130 Hendry to Arthur B.B. Moore, 30 January 1972 (UCA, EMH, 87,043C, b.6, f.1).

131 *Canadian Jewish News*, 21 January 1972; see also a derogatory attack by a Jew, Arthur Rawet, written to Howse, 29 January 1972 (UCA, EMH, 87,043C, b.6, f.16).

132 David Demson, "Criticizes Howse Defence," *Toronto Star*, 24 January 1972. The editor of the *Star* shortened Demson's reply, emasculating his proof of Forrest's antisemitism; see the correspondence concerning this subject: Ben G. Kayfetz to Burnett Thall, 31 January 1972; Robert F. Nielson, to B.M. Thall, 3 February 1972; (OJA, MG8/S, b.53, f.161).

133 G. Douglas Young to editor of *Toronto Star*, 1 February 1972 (OJA, MG8/S, b.56, f.160a). It is not clear whether this letter appeared in print.

134 Cited in Plaut, *Unfinished Business*, 288.

135 Forrest to Peter Worthington, 4 February 1972 (UCA, ACF, 86,104C, b.20, f.1); Forrest to Gloria Keating, 8 June, 1973 (UCA, ACF, 86,104C, b.20, f.12).

136 Joy De Marsh, "Details of the Message Honouring Emil Fackenheim in Saskatoon," *Globe and Mail*, 6 May 1972.

137 Earl S. Leütenschlager to Forrest, 4 May 1972 (UCA, ACF, 86,104C, b.20, f.3); Forrest to J.N. Booth, 20 May 1972 (ibid., b.23, f.6).

138 Hayes to A.H. Krolik, 8 November 1972 (OJA, MG8/S, b.53, f.161).

139 Plaut, *Unfinished Business*, 289.

140 Cited in Slonim, *Family Quarrel*, 33–4.

141 Davies to the faculty and governing boards, St Andrew's College, Saskatoon, 12 May 1972 (UCA, ATD, 98,087v).

142 Smillie to Forrest, 15 May 1972; Forrest to Smillie, 5 June 1972 (UCA, ACF, 86,104C, b.20, f.4).

143 Sedwick to editor of *Globe and Mail*, 9 May 1972.

144 Leutenschlager to Forrest, 4 May 1972 (UCA, ACF, 86,104C, b.20, f.3).

145 Booth, "How Zionists Manipulate Your News"; A.J. MacQueen to Donald Keating, 22 March 1972 (UCA, ACF, 86,104C, b.20, f.2).

CHAPTER NINE: THE BOOTH ARTICLE

1 MacQueen to Donald Keating, 22 March 1972 (UCA, ACF, 86,104C, b.20, f.2).

2 Nielsen to B.M. Thall, 3 February 1972 (OJA, MG8/S, b.53, f.161).

3 Forrest to Booth, 13 September 1971 (UCA, ACF, 86,104C, b.23, f.2).

4 Booth to Forrest, 17 March 1972 (UCA, ACF, 86,104C, b.23, f.4).

5 Booth, "How Zionists Manipulate Your News."

6 Slonim, *Family Quarrel*, 9.

7 Forrest to P.B.C. Pepper, 24 February 1972 (UCA, ACF, 86,104C, b.23, f.3).

8 Kayfetz to Edell, 20 March 1972 (OJA, MG8/S, b.53, f.161).

9 Quoted in Plaut, *Unfinished Business*, 290.

10 Booth to Forrest, 17 March 1972; Morley S. Wolfe to Forrest, 24 March 1972 (UCA, ACF, 86,104C, b.23, f.4).

11 Kayfetz to Edell, 20 March 1972 (OJA, MG8/S, b.53, f.161).

12 "Father Gregory Baum Criticized Forrest for the Booth article," n.d. (UCA, ACF, 86,104C, b.20, f.8); editorial, "*Observer* Controversy: It's United Church's Dilemma," *Canadian Jewish News*, 21 April 1972.

13 Forrest to Roy DeMarsh, 12 May 1972 (UCA, ACF, 86,104C, b.20, f.3).

14 DeMarsh to Forrest, 10 May 1972 (UCA, ACF, 86,104C, b.20, f.3).

15 Brisbin to Forrest, Memo re: "Observer article about Zionism," 9 March 1972 (UCA, ACF, 86,104C, b.23, f.4).

16 MacQueen to Donald Keating, 22 March 1972 (UCA, ACF, 86,104C, b.20, f.2).

17 Moore to the author, 10 May 1995.

18 Morrison to the author, 24 June 1995.

19 Forrest to Booth, 6 April 1972 (UCA, ACF, 86,104C, b.23, f.5).

20 *United Church Observer*, May 1972, 9.

21 John Short, "Letters to the Editor," *Globe and Mail*, 10 May 1972; Forrest to Short, 10 May 1972 (UCA, ACF, 86,104C, b.20, f.3).

22 Cited in Forster and Epstein, *The New Anti-Semitism*, 83; Eckardt, *Your People, My People*, 106.

23 Kenny to Editor of *Toronto Star*, 24 May 1972 (UCA, ACF, 86,104C, b.20, f.4).

24 Whidden to Alan Davies, 17 February 1972 (UCA, ATD, 98,087V).

25 Wrixon to Forrest, 22 September 1972 (UCA, ACF, 86,104C, b.20, f.6).

26 Ben G. Kayfetz to Jordan Pearlson, 8 March 1972 (OJA, MG8/S, b.53, f.161).

27 Alfred Green, "The President's Message," *Digest* (UCA, ACF, 86,104C, b.23, f.3).

28 See Slonim, *Family Quarrel*, 6.

29 Ibid., 10.

30 Ibid.; Forrest to F.G. Brisbin, 15 February 1972; Forrest to F.R. Murgatroyd, 3 March 1972 (UCA, ACF, 86,104C, b.23, f.3–4).

31 A. McN. Austin to P.B.C. Pepper, 21 February 1972 (UCA, ACF, 86,104C, b.23, f.3); Herbert S. Levy to Harry J. Pachter, 5 April 1972 (OJA, MG8/S, b.53, f.161).

32 "Minutes of the action of the sub-executive of General Council," 15 March 1972, Donald G. Ray to Forrest, 20 March 1972 (UCA, ACF, 86,104C, b.23, f.4); *United Church of Canada Year Book, 1972*, 2: 1, 25, 32.

33 Brisbin to A.J. MacQueen, 27 March 1972 (UCA, ACF, 86,104C, b.20, f.2).

34 Murgatroyd to Forrest, 10 March 1972 (UCA, ACF, 86,104C, b.23, f.4).

35 Herbert S. Levy to Harry J. Pachter, 5 April 1972; Pachter to E.E. Long, 5 April 1972 (OJA, MG8/S, b.53, f.161).

36 Alan Davies dismissed Forrest's charge as "nonsense"; Davies to the author, 19 August 1999.

37 Howse to R.D. Keaye, 26 June 1972; Forrest to G.W. Goth, 19 June 1972 (UCA, ACF, 86,104C, b.20, f.4).

38 Forrest to William C. Heine, 12 April 1972 (UCA, ACF, 86,104C, b.20, f.3).

39 Forrest to Robert Bater, 11 April 1972 (UCA, ACF, 86,104C, b.20, f.3).

40 Forrest to E.E. Long, 13 April 1972 (UCA, ACF, 86,104C, b.20, f.3).

41 Brisbin to Forrest, 17 April 1972 (UCA, ACF, 86,104C, b.23, f.5).

42 Angus MacQueen to the author, 2 May 1995; Forrest to Ernest M. Howse, 29 June 1972 (UCA, ACF, 86,104C, b.20, f.4).

43 *United Church of Canada Year Book, 1972*, 2: 31.

44 Ibid.

45 Forrest to Robert Bater, 11 April 1972 (UCA, ACF, 86,104C, b.20, f.3).

46 Forrest to Booth, 5 May 1972 (UCA, ACF, b.23, f.6).

47 Ibid.

48 "APOLOGY," *United Church Observer,* June 1972, 17.

49 Ben G. Kayfetz to Herbert S. Levy, 4 June 1972 (OJA, MG8/S, b.53, f.161).

50 A. McN. Austin to Ernest Long, 13 June 1972 (UCA, ACF, 86,104C, b.23, f.7). "I recognize that you do not think the apology to be full enough; that is a different matter. The fact is that an apology was made," wrote Forrest's lawyer to the lawyer of B'nai Brith; P.B.C. Pepper to Mosley Wolfe, 20 June 1972 (ibid.).

51 Forrest to Pepper, 29 June 1972 (UCA, ACF, 86,104C, b.23, f.7).

52 "The Sub-Executive," *United Church of Canada Year Book, 1972,* 2: 13 June 1972.

53 Meeting, P.B.C. Pepper, A. McN. Austin, and M. S. Wolfe, 13 June 1972, minutes (UCA, ACF, 86,104C, b.23, f.7).

54 "The Sub-Executive," *United Church of Canada Year Book, 1972,* 2: 28 June 1972.

55 Memorandum of meeting with the Inter-Church and Inter-Faith Committee, UC, 8 January 1973, Alan Rose to Gunther Plaut, J.C. Horwitz, and B.G. Kayfetz, 11–12 (OJA, MG8/S, b.56, f.160b).

56 Angus J. MacQueen to the author, 2 May 1995.

57 P.B.C Pepper to Forrest, 7 December 1972 (UCA, ACF, 86,104C, b.23, f.10).

58 Forrest to Sutton, 23 August 1972 (UCA, ACF, 86,104C, b.20, f.5).

59 Bater to Forrest, 11 April 1972 (UCA, ACF, 86,104C, b.20, f.3).

60 Bagnell to Alan T. Davies, 7 January, 23 October 1972 (UCA, ATD, 98,087V).

61 *United Church Observer,* 1 October 1948, 27; 15 November 1948, 23.

62 McLeod to the author, 29 May 1995; White, *Voices and Visions,* 163.

63 Editorial, "Unofficial: Who Speaks Oficially for the United Church? The General Council," *United Church Observer,* 15 September 1968, 11.

64 Douglas Fisher, "What the Election Taught Me about the Observer," *United Church Observer,* 15 September 1968, 37.

65 Moore to the author, 10 May 1995.

66 Slonim, *Family Quarrel,* 30–1; White, *Voices and Visions,* 163.

67 Slonim, *Family Quarrel,* 30–4; Hayes to A.H. Crolik, 8 November 1972 (OJA, MG8/S, b.53, f.161).

68 Interview with Lou Ronson, 14 July 1995.

69 Forrest, "Draft of Proposed Statement on the Middle East," 11 May 1972 (UCA, ACF, 86,104C, b.23, f.5).

70 Forrest to Booth, 4 December 1972 (UCA, ACF, 86,104C, b.20, f.8); Forrest to Robert Bater, 11 April 1972 (ibid., f.3).

71 Slonim, *Family Quarrel,* 12–13.

72 Forrest to J. Richard Butler, 12 June 1972 (UCA, ACF, 86,104C, b.20, f.4).

73 UC, *News*, "For Release," 5 May 1972: "UC Executive issues statement on 'climate of alienation' and mistrust between it and a large portion of the Canadian Jewish community" (UCA, ACF, 86,104C, b.53, f.5).

74 W. Gunther Plaut editorial, *Canadian Jewish News*, 12 May 1972; "If they went on as before I would be disheartened," said Rabbi Plaut. See also Ben Kayfetz, memo, 7 May (CJCNA, ZA, 1972, b.3, f.28).

75 For a detailed discussion of the Saskatoon General Council, see chapter 6 above; See also Forrest to Yehia Abubaker, 31 August 1972; Forrest to John Sutton, 30 August 1972 (UCA, ACF, 86,104C, b.20, f.5).

76 Forrest to Booth, 19 September 1972 (UCA, ACF, 86,104C, b.23, f.8).

77 Plaut, *Unfinished Business*, 290.

78 Plaut, "United Church Assembly"; see also Editorial, "Observer Editor Masks His Bias in Role of an 'Abused Crusader,'" *Canadian Jewish News*, 1 September 1972. Forrest called the *CJN* piece a "complete fabrication" and a "distortion"; Forrest to P.B.C. Pepper, 15 September 1972 (UCA, ACF, 86,104C, b.23, f.7). See also his complaint that the *CJN* "has misrepresented me and distorted my viewpoint so seriously and so frequently that it has destroyed all confidence I have in it"; Forrest to Philip Slomovitz, 2 March 1973; Slomovitz to Forrest, 16 March 1973 (UCA, ACF, 86,104C, b.20, f.10).

79 McLeod, "Christian-Jewish Relations in Canada: A Statement by N. Bruce McLeod, Moderator of the United Church of Canada at the University of Windsor, 5 November 1973"; McLeod to the author, 29 May 1995.

80 Forrest to Sutton, 30 August 1972; Sutton to Forrest, 8 September 1972 (UCA, ACF, 86,104C, b.20, f.5).

81 *Globe and Mail*, 22 August 1972. Forrest reported that the new moderator had "made a very forthright statement, '100% backing'"; Forrest to Booth, 19 September 1972 (UCA, ACF, 86,104C, b.23, f.8).

82 Interview with Demson, 30 March 1995.

83 McLeod, "Windsor Statement," 5 November 1973.

84 "Anti-Semitism Roused by the New Testament Says UC Moderator," *St. John's Evening Telegram*, 12 October 1972; "Gospel Termed Unfair to Jews," *Evening Free Press* (London, Ont.), 9 February 1973.

85 Ben Kayfetz to George Promislow, 1 November 1972 (OJA, MG8/S, b.53, f.161).

86 Quoted in Slonim, *Family Quarrel*, 35.

87 Plaut, *Unfinished Business*, 291.

88 Ibid.

89 Morrison to the author, 24 June 1995.

90 Editorial, "Murder in Munich," *United Church Observer*, October 1972, 12; *Toronto Star*, 11 September 1972.

91 "Murder in Munich," *United Church Observer*, October 1972, 12; editorial, "Where Do Christians Stand on Violence?" ibid., January 1973, 8.

92 Plaut, *Unfinished Business*, 291–2; "Plaut Urges United Church to Phase Out Middle East Role: Jews Will Not Listen to Christians Moralizing," *Canadian Jewish News*, 27 October 1972.

93 Plaut, *Unfinished Business*, 292; McLeod, "Windsor Statement," 5 November 1973.

94 Plaut to Rose, 9 November 1972 (OJA, MG8/s, b.53, f.161).

95 Ibid.

96 Morrison to the author, 24 June 1995.

97 "Strictly Confidential and Not to Be Publicized in Any Form," Memorandum of meeting with the Inter-Church and Inter-Faith Committee, UC, 8 January 1973, Alan Rose to Gunther Plaut, J.R. Horwitz, and Ben G. Kayfetz (OJA, MG8/s, b.56, f.160b).

98 Morrison to Rose, 11 January 1973 (CJCNA, DA5, b.46, f.20).

99 Morrison to Plaut, 11 January 1973 (CJCNA, DA5, b.46, f.4).

100 J.C. Horwitz to S.M. Harris, 26 January 1973 (OJA, MG8/s, b.56, f.160b).

101 Plaut to Saul [Hayes], 11 May 1973 (CJCNA, ZA, 1973, b.2, f.21); Forrest to James Peters, 12 July 1973 (UCA, ACF, 86,104C, b.20, f.12).

102 "Toasts, Handshakes End United Church B'nai Brith Feud; United Church and B'nai Brith Sign Peace Pact on Refugee Issue," *Toronto Star*, 5 May 1973; Charles Lazarus, "Church and B'nai Brith Agree to Bury Hatchet, *Montreal Star*, 12 May 1973; Brian Stoneman, "Peace Pact Eases Hostility between Jews, United Church," *Canadian Jewish News*, 11 May 1973.

103 Kanee to Lou Ronson, 9 May 1973 (Ronson's private collection; I thank Mr Ronson for his kindness in showing me his collection); see also OJA, MG8/s, b.59, f.99a).

104 *Toronto Star*, 5 May 1973.

105 Editorial, "New Era of Understanding Seen in Peace Pact with United Church," *Canadian Jewish News*, 18 May 1973.

106 McLeod to Lou [Ronson], 17 August 1974; Morrison to Ronson, 8 November 1974; Sol Kanee to Ronson, 9 May 1973 (OJA, MG8/s, b.59, f.99a); see also Saul Hayes to Ronson, 15 May 1973 (Ronson 's private collection).

107 Brian Stoneman, "Peace Pact Eases Hostility between Jews, United Church," *Canadian Jewish News*, 11 May 1973.

108 Forrest to P.B.C. Pepper, 19 April 1973; Forrest to Gloria Keating, 8 June 1973 (UCA, ACF, 86,104C, b.23, f.12).

109 *United Church Observer*, June 1973, 11; "Statement Prepared for Press by A.C. Forrest," 4 May 1973 (UCA, ACF, 86,104C, b.23, f.13).

110 Forrest to McLeod and Morrison, 13 June 1973 (UCA, ACF, 86,104C, b.23, f.14).

111 P.B.C. Pepper to Forrest, 24 April 1973 (UCA, ACF, 86,104C, b.23, f.12); Forrest to Booth, 8 April 1974 (ibid., f.15).

112 Brisbin to Bruce McLeod and George Morrison, 3 May 1973 (UCA, ACF, 86,106C, b.23, f.13).

113 MacDonald to Bruce McLeod, 15 June 1973; McLeod to MacDonald, 2 July 1973 (UCA, ACF, 86,104C, b.23, f.14).

114 Hugh McCullum, editorial, "Freedom of the Press," *Canadian Churchman,* June 1973, 4.

115 "United Church Surrenders to Zionism, Arab Says," *Toronto Star,* 11 May 1973. McLeod answered that although the United Church was still committed to the survival of Israel, it did not abandon its concern for the plight of Arab refugees. "United Church and B'nai Brith Letter Didn't Mention Refugee Issue: Moderator," ibid., 18 May 1973.

116 Booth to McLeod, 12 May 1973; Booth to Forrest, 12 May 1973 (UCA, ACF, 86,104C, b.23, f.13). Replying to Booth, McLeod detailed the inaccuracies and insensitive phrases in the article; McLeod to Booth, 18 May 1973 (ibid.).

117 "Statement Prepared for Press by A.C. Forrest," 4 May 1973 (UCA, ACF, 86,104C, b.23, f.13); Forrest to Gloria Keating, 8 June 1973 (ibid., b.20, f.12).

118 Forrest to Booth, 24 May 1973 (UCA, ACF, 86,104C, b.23, f.13).

119 Kayfetz to Jordan Pearlson, 17, 19 April 1973 (OJA, MG8/S, b.56, f.160B); Bruce McLeod to the author, 29 May 1995.

120 Forrest to Booth, 26 April 1973 (UCA, ACF, 86,104C, b.23, f.12); Morrison to the author, 24 June 1995; see also Plaut, *Unfinished Business,* 293.

121 "Christians-Jews Plan Dialogue," *Toronto Star,* 7 June 1973; see also Plaut, *Unfinished Business,* 293.

122 *United Church of Canada Yearbook, 1974,* 9; UC, *Record of Proceedings of the Twenty Sixth General Council, 1974,* 174, 138.

123 Editorial, "New Era of Understanding Seen in Peace Pact with United Church," *Canadian Jewish News,* 18 May 1973.

CHAPTER TEN: THE TRUCE

1 Herbert L. Pottle, "Dear Sir: Zionization of Jerusalem," *United Church Observer,* May 1973, 4.

2 *United Church Observer,* May 1973, 13.

3 Brian Stoneman, "Observer Article Annoys B'nai Brith after Pact," *Canadian Jewish News,* 18 May 1973.

4 Rose to Morrison, 21 January 1974 (OJA, MG8/S, b.59, f.99b).

5 Salter, "He as God Sitteth in the Temple of God."

6 Kayfetz to Alan Rose, 10 March 1974 (OJA, MG8/S, b.59, f.99a).

7 Hablane to Forrest, 1 May 1974; Forrest to Hablane, 7 May 1974 (OJA, MG8/S, b.59, f.99b); Nicholls to George Morrison, 24 February 1974 (UCA, ACF, 86,104C, b.21, f.1); see also Charlotte McEwen to editor of *Ottawa Journal*, 17 June 1974 (ibid., f.4).

8 Editorial, *Globe and Mail*, 29 June 1974.

9 Forrest, "About Mr. Salter's Avertisement," *United Church Observer*, May 1974, 11.

10 McLeod to Horwitz, 19 April 1974 (OJA, MG8/S, b.59, f.99a).

11 Ibid.; Morrison to Rose, 1 April 1974 (OJA, MG8/S, b.59, f.99a).

12 Forrest, "About Mr. Salter's Advertisement," *United Church Observer*, May 1974, 11.

13 Wells to Dolores Nicholls, 5 March 1974 (UCA, ACF, 86,104C, b.21, f.1).

14 Horwitz to Bruce McLeod, 11 June 1974 (OJA, MG8/S, b.59, f.99a). David Rome, secretary of the Montreal Committee for Jewish-Catholic Relations, complained in the same vein. He was "deeply disturbed and dissatisfied" by the tone and content of Forrest's apology: while taking "full editorial responsibility," Forrest had reiterated the evil. Rome also criticized Forrest's reference to "bad taste," thus his failure to acknowledge the crime of antisemitism. See David Rome to Alan Rose, 15 June 1974 (CJCNA, DA5, b.14, f.20).

15 McLeod to Horwitz, 28 June 1974 (OJA, MG8/S, b.59, f.99a).

16 "Guarding Whose Christian Moral Values?" *United Church Observer*, June 1974, 22–4.

17 Confidential memorandum from Ronald de Corneille to Lou Ronson, Harvey Crestohl, Alan Rose, Jaycee Horwitz, Joel Pinsky, Ben Kayfetz, Gunther Plaut, Stan Beder, and Simon Gulden, 7 June 1974 (OJA, MG8/S, b.59, f.99a).

18 J.C. Horwitz to Bruce McLeod, 9 July 1974 (OJA, MG8/S, b.59, f.99a).

19 "The Question Box," *United Church Observer*, June 1974, 40.

20 "Israel and the Middle East Crisis," 9 December 1974 (UCA, ATD, 98,087v).

21 *Windsor Star*, 29 March 1975; Forrest to editor of *Windsor Star*, 24 April 1975 (UCA, ACF, 86,104C, b.21, f.7).

22 Forrest to Booth, 20 June 1975 (UCA, ACF, 86,104C, b.21, f.8).

23 Forrest to Judith A. Nagib, 5 September 1975 (UCA, ACF, 86,104C, b.21, f.9).

24 Editorial, "Hope for the Middle East Settlement," *United Church Observer*, May 1975, 8.

25 Editorial, "Let's Welcome the PLO," *United Church Observer*, August 1975, 8–9.

26 "Dear Sir," *United Church Observer*, October 1975, 2.

27 "For Information to *Observer* staff," 5 January 1976 (UCA, ACF, 86,104C, b.21, f.10).

28 Editorial, "Israel and the Bomb: Why Doesn't Somebody Scream?" *United Church Observer*, June 1976, 8.

29 Editorial, "In South Africa You Call It Apatheid," *United Church Observer*, October 1976, 11.

30 Demson to MacQueen, 9 February 1977; Nick Simmonds to Forrest, 22 October 1976; Forrest to Simmonds, 23 November 1976 (OJA, MG8/S, b.66, f.140) .

31 R. Emmett Tyrrell Jr, "Chimera in the Middle East: Against a Rational Interpretation of Arab-Israeli Relations," *Massadah* 9, no. 1, (1977): 1–3 (OJA, MG8/S, b.70, f.122).

32 Editorial, "Arabs and Muslims Libeled," *United Church Observer*, February 1978, 11.

33 Ronson to Clarke MacDonald, 9 February 1978; Jordan Pearlson to MacDonald, 20 February 1977; MacDonald to Ronson, 20 February 1978 (OJA, MG8/S, b.70, f.122).

34 Slonim, *Family Quarrel*, 139, 157.

35 Angus J. MacQueen, "*Family Quarrel*, by Reuben Slonim," in *Quill and Quire* (publication details unknown), MacQueen to the author, 2 May 1995.

36 Hugh McCullum, "Book Seeks Truth in Old Storms," *United Church Observer*, February 1977, 49.

37 Kenneth Bagnell, "Family Quarrel," *Globe and Mail*, 19 February 1977.

38 Ken Adachi, "Rabbi Searches for Cool Debate on Burning Issue," *Toronto Star*, 12 March 1977.

39 Editorial, "Bound to Divide," *Toronto Star*, 8 June 1978. For a detailed discussion of the petition and the responses, see chapter 5 above.

40 Editorial, "Can We Now Hope for Middle East Peace?" *United Church Observer* November 1978, 11.

41 UC, *Record of Proceedings of the Twenty Seventh General Council, August 1977*, 617; see, also chapter 6 above.

42 Angus MacQueen, "Israel and the United Church of Canada" (MS., 1991, MacQueen's private collection); Alan Davies to the author, 19 August 1999.

43 MacQueen, "Israel and the United Church."

44 *United Church Yearbook, 1979*, 16.

45 Ibid. McLeod to the author, 29 May 1995; see also "Al Forrest," *Toronto Star*, 28 December 1978; "Rev. A.C. Forrest: United Church Observer Editor, Often at Centre of Controversy," *Globe and Mail*, 28 December 1978.

46 Slonim, *Family Quarrel*, 32, 18.

47 Plaut, *Unfinished Business*, 29

48 John H. Berthrong, "Inter-Faith Dialogue," *United Church Yearbook, 1982*, 2: 142–3.

49 Moe Seidman to Milton E. Harris, 13 December 1983 (CJCNA, DQA, 15.1, b.3, f.60).

50 "A Statement re: the Middle East Situation by the United Church of Canada," 14 June 1982 (UCA, CCIA, 88,088C, b.6, f.5).

51 Berthrong to Tad Mitsui, 3 January 1983 (CCC, CWC, ME, 1983).

52 Standford Lucky, "Jerusalem on Earth, Heaven," *United Church Observer,* June 1982, 24–6.

53 UC, *Record of the Proceedings of the Thirty Third General Council, August* 1990, 289, 294; *Record of the Proceedings of the Thirty Fourth General Council, August 1992,* 351–2.

54 "Sober Hope for the Mideast," *United Church Observer,* November 1993, 47–8.

55 *United Church Observer,* June 1993, 31.

56 Baum, "The Churches, Israel and the Palestinians."

57 McLeod, "A Cry of Pain for Israel."

58 Michael McAteer, "United Church Conference Seeks Aid for Palestinians," *Toronto Star,* 31 May 1993.

59 Confidential memo from Research and Communication Departments to CIC Ad Hoc Media Committee, 31 May 1993, re: United Church Motion on Human Rights in the Territories (CJCNA, DA5, b.31, f.73).

60 Irving Abella to James Ritchie, 4 June 1993 (CJCNA, DA5, b.31, f.7b).

61 "Bearing Faithful Witness: United Church-Jewish Relations Today (For discussion, Prepared by the National Task Group on UC-Jewish Relations, February 1997)," 4, 24, 26 (in the possession of the author).

62 Breckenridge, "United Church Reaches Out to Jews."

63 Ibid.

64 White, *Voices and Visions,* 146–7.

65 Editorial, "Seeking an Honourable Peace: The Thirty Fourth General Council," *United Church Observer,* October 1992, 10–11.

66 *United Church Observer,* July 1992, 11–12; January 1993, 10–9.

67 *United Church Yearbook, 1991,* 37; see also *Presbyterian Record,* November 1991, 44–5.

68 White, *Voices and Visions,* 145.

CHAPTER ELEVEN: THE ANGLICAN CHURCH

1 "Anglicanism," *Canadian Encyclopedia* (1985), 1: 57; "Anglican Church of Canada," *Encyclopedia Canadiana,* 1: 164.

2 William Portman, "A Century of Changes, 1890–1993: The General Synod," *Anglican Journal* 119 (September 1993): 11.

3 C.B. Mortlock, "The Christian Revolution," *Canadian Churchman* 63 (3 December 1936): 691.

4 F.D.V. Narborough, "The Danger of Pharisaism," *Canadian Churchman* 70 (11 February 1943): 83.

5 "Report of Board of Management, Missionary Society of the Church of England in Canada," CEC, *Journal of the Proceedings of the General Synod*, 1946, 129–30; "Missions to Jews," Report of Board of Management, Missionary Society, ibid., 1943, 147–8.

6 "Nathanael Institute, Toronto," *Canadian Churchman* 76 (18 August 1949): 271–2; Morris Kaminsky, "The Liberal Jew and His Messianic Ideal," ibid., 76 (19 March 1949): 157.

7 Quoted in Davies and Nefsky, "The Church of England in Canada and the Jewish Plight," 2. For a detailed discussion of the attitude of the Church of England in Canada to the Holocaust, see ibid., 1–19; Davies and Nefsky, *How Silent Were the Churches?*; Nefsky, "The Shadow of Evil."

8 "Holy Church throughout the World," *Canadian Churchman* 60 (9 October 1933): 631.

9 CEC, *Journal of the Proceedings of the General Synod*, 1934, 13th Session, 117; "A Chat with the Editor," *Canadian Churchman*, 64 (23 January 1936): 50.

10 CEC, CSS, Executive Committee, Minutes, 17 November 1937; CSS, Annual Meeting, Minutes, 22 September 1938, 6 (ACCA, GS files, CSS, 75–106).

11 Davies and Nefsky, "The Church of England in Canada and the Jewish Plight," 10.

12 CEC, CSS, Executive Committee, Minutes, 5 May 1937 (ACCA, GS, files, 75–106).

13 CEC, CSS, *Bulletin* 104 (15 October 1941): 1.

14 CEC, CSS, Executive Committee, Minutes, 18 May 1938 (ACCA, GS files, CSS, 75–106).

15 CEC, CSS, Annual Meeting, Minutes, 22 September 1938, 51 (ACCA, GS files, CSS).

16 CEC, CSS, Executive Committee, Minutes, 14 December 1938 (ACCA, GS files, CSS, 75–106). For the history of the CNCR, see chapter 4 above.

17 CEC, CSS, 32; 26th Executive Committee, Minutes, 14 December 1938, Annual Report, 1941, 41–50; 27th Annual Report, 1942, 20; 28th Annual Report, 1943, 26–7; 29th Annual Report, 1944, 17–8, 40 (ACCA, GS files, CSS).

18 Prideaux to the author, 20 October 1995.

19 Davies and Nefsky, "The Church of England in Canada and the Jewish Plight," 16, see also Davies and Nefsky, *How Silent Were the Churches?* 47–56, 65–7.

20 Abella and Troper, *None Is Too Many*, 51, 284.

21 "The Real Meaning of the Dialogue Approach," 5 June 1961; see also Roland de Corneille, "A Specific Program for the 'Dialogue Approach,'" n.d.; "Recommendations by the Committee on the Christian Approach to the Jewish People," 7 November 1961; de Corneille to H.R. Hunt, 7 June 1961; Minutes of the Committee on the Christian Approach to the Jewish People, 1 October 1963 (ADTA, 87–15, b.16, f.12; b.3, f.4, 6; b.9, f.2).

22 J.M.N. Jackson, "To Obtain Information"; T.W. Hurley, "A Sense of Deep Concern"; Rabbi Albert Pappenheim, "Breaking Down Barriers"; Genya Intrader, "Why Are We Doing It?" *Canadian Churchman* 94 (March 1967): 12–14.

23 Interview with Lou Ronson, 14 July 1995. Israel's invitation is in Minutes of the Committee on the Christian Approach to the Jewish People, 1 October 1968 (ADTA, 87–15, b.3, f.5).

24 Scott to archbishops and bishops of ACC, 1 March 1979 (ACCA, GS files, GS, 97–10, b.3, Scott Pastoral Letters, 1979).

25 ACC, Inter-Church Inter-Faith Relations Committee, Minutes, 2–4 October 1987 (ACCA, GS files, GS); ACC, "Niagara Report: Jewish-Anglican Relations," ACC, *Journal of the Fifteenth General Synod 1989*, 9; "General Synod Daily Report," 22 June 1992, no. 4; "Middle East Problems Preoccupied Delegates," *Anglican Journal* 118 (September 1992): 8A.

26 "Statement of Key '73 by the Anglican Primate of Canada," 4 May 1973; see also the letter of appreciation by Sol Kanee of the CJC to Archbishop Scott, 8 May 1973 (CJCNA, DA5, b.14, f.24). For a detailed discussion of Key '73, see chapter 6 above.

27 "Advertisement of Jews' Conversion Leads to Protests," *Canadian Churchman* 98 (October 1972): 14; Mrs W.R. Symons, "Letterbasket: Christian Jews," ibid., 98 (December 1972): 26.

28 J.B. Boyles to Fleming, 3 June 1981 (CJCNA, DA 15,1, b.2, f.25).

29 Seidman to Jordan Pearlson, 4 December 1981 (CJCNA, DA 15,1, b.2, f.25).

30 Brian Prideaux to Ian Kagedan, 28 August 1986; Ian Kagedan to H. St. C. Hilchey, 18 July 1986 (ACCA, GS files, GS, 90–10, b.3).

31 Scott to Alan Rose, 6 February 1985 (ACCA, GS files, GS, 90–10, b.3). See Rose's appreciation of Scott's letter: "We have noted the constant re-affirmation of these position taken by the Anglican Church, which are a source of comfort to the CJC"; Rose to Scott, 19 February 1985 (ibid.).

32 ACC, *Journal of the Thirteenth General Synod, June 1983*, 40.

33 Ibid.

34 ACC, Jewish-Anglican Dialogue: Sub-Committee on Anglican-Jewish Relations, 1 September 1987; Inter-Church, Inter-Faith Relations Committee, Minutes, 22–4 October 1989; *Journal of Fifteenth General Synod, 1989*, 9 (ACCA, GS files); CCC, Christian-Jewish Dialogue, Montreal, Minutes, 22 September 1984 (CCC, Jewish-Christian Dialogue).

35 Editorial, "Came Out from Behind These Castle Walls," *Canadian Churchman* 100 (May 1974): 4.

36 ACC, CSS, Annual Report, 1963, 4–5. (ACCA, GS files, CSS).

37 ACC, CSS, Annual Report, 1945, 36–7. (ACCA, GS files, CSS).

38 The organizations that represented the Anglican Church were the World Alliance for the Promotion of Friendship through the Churches, the World Council of Churches, and the UN Association in Canada; see ACC, CSS, An-

nual Report, 1947, 37 (ACCA, GS files, CSS). In 1972 Archbishop Scott reiterated the Christian need to intervene on behalf of justice, "even though in some places this means opposing established governments. In doing this they are only doing what our forefathers did"; see "The Primate Responds," *Canadian Churchman* 98 (January 1972): 13.

39 ACC, CSS, Annual Report, 1957, 134; L.H. Hatfield to K.H. Tufts, 3 February 1958 (ACCA, GS files, CSS, GS 75–106, b.11, CIA, Correspondence, Report, General Synod, 1959, 38).

40 "Suggested Topics for Study – Proposed, International Affairs Committee of Diocesan Councils for Social Service," n.d. (ACCA, GS files, CSS, GS 75–106, b.11, IAC, Correspondence).

41 ACC, International Affairs Unit, Minutes, 18 January, 26 November 1968 (ACCA, GS files, GS, International Affairs, 1968–69).

42 Excerpts from the Minutes of the Program Committee, 1 October 1969 (ACCA, GS files, CSS, GS, 75–106, b.11, IAC, Correspondence).

43 Editorial, "Palestine," *Canadian Churchman* 75 (2 July 1948): 5.

44 Palestine was mentioned in the report of the Missionary Society, which asked for continuation of the annual support of the hospital grant in Jerusalem; see ACC, *Journal of the General Synod, 1949,* 120.

45 See Roland de Corneille, "Development of Christian Attitudes toward the Middle East," n.d. (ACCA, GS files).

46 ACC, *Journal of the General Synod, August 1967,* 207.

47 Ibid.

48 J.B. Boyles to E.D. Fleming, 3 June 1981 (CJCNA, DA 15,1, b.2, f.25).

49 Davison to Clarke MacDonald, 21 July 1971 (UCA, CCIA, 86,250C, b.4, f.9).

50 Lambeth Conference, 1968, Resolution re: Middle East, ACC, *Journal of the General Synod, 1969,* 205.

51 ACC, IAU, Minutes, 16 April 1969 (ACCA, GS files, CSS, GS 75–106, b.11).

52 ACC, IAU, Minutes, 13 February 1969 (ACCA, GS files, CSS, GS 75–106, b.11); *Journal of the General Synod, August 1969,* 83.

53 Anne M. Davison to Clarke MacDonald, 21 July 1971 (UCA, CCIA, 86,250C, b.4, f.9).

54 Editorial, "Our Editorial Policy," *Canadian Churchman* 105 (May 1979): 4.

55 J.E. Alsopp, "With the British Army in Palestine," *Canadian Churchman* 75 (February 1948): 9; "New Coins for Israel," ibid., 76 (17 March 1949): 88; M. Kaminsky, "The Orthodox Jew and His Messianic Ideal," ibid., 76 (5 May 1949): 141; J.R. Brown, "A Post Christian Date for the Scrolls," ibid., 85 (2 January 1958): 19; Gordon Baker, "Sunday in Jerusalem," ibid., 94 (April 1967): 20; "Galilean Boat Found," ibid., 112 (April 1986): 7; Margaret Mertens, "Holy Land Visits," *Anglican Journal* 115 (January 1989): 12.

56 R.L.T., editorial, "American Policy in the Middle East," *Canadian Churchman* 84 (7 February 1957): 51; see also the editorial "Russia's Role in the Near East," ibid., 83 (1 November 1956): 431.

57 Editorial, "1967," *Canadian Churchman* 95 (January 1968): 4.

58 A.C. Forrest, "A Christmas Story," *Canadian Churchman* 95 (December 1968): 1–2; Forrest, "You Don't Seem to Care about Us: Bethlehem 1968," *United Church Observer,* 15 December 1968, 28–9. For a detailed discussion of Forrest's article and the controversy about it, see chapter 8 above. See also Gunther Plaut's reaction, "News and Views: Again Dr. Forrest."

59 L.S. Garnsworthy and Roland de Corneille, "Letterbasket: Hate Literature," *Canadian Churchman* 66 (January 1969): 13.

60 "Letterbasket: Well Known Bias," *Canadian Churchman*, 96 (February 1969): 22. See also John M. Snoek, "The Refugee Problem," ibid., 96 (March 1969): 22; Forrest's reply, ibid., 96 (May 1969): 18; Snoek's reply, ibid., 96 (July–August 1969): 22; Forrest, "Christmas Watch in Bethlehem Hills," ibid., 96 (December 1969): 2–3.

61 "Christians in Middle East Crisis," *Canadian Churchman*, 96 (April 1969): 6;. Plaut, "Letterbasket: Rabbi Replies," ibid., 96 (June 1969): 22.

62 G.K. Watts, "Letterbasket: The Arab Plight," *Canadian Churchman* 96 (July–August 1969): 22.

63 F.L Elias, "Letterbasket: Anti-Zionist," *Canadian Churchman* 96 (September 1969): 26.

64 A.C. Forrest, "Church Neglect and the Middle East Strife," *Canadian Churchman* 99 (November 1973): 20. Floyd Honey replied to Forrest's attack in "Letterbasket: The Middle East," ibid., 99 (December 1973): 18.

65 Forrest, "Church Neglect," *Canadian Churchman* 99 (November 1973): 20.

66 Bishop H.R. Hunt, "Letterbasket: Unbalanced Reports," *Canadian Churchman* 97 (April 1970): 22; William J. Hulton, "Letterbasket," ibid., 100 (April 1974): 30; Florence S. McConney, "Letterbasket: Why Arab Land?" ibid., 96 (February 1969): 22.

67 Maurice Western, "International Aspect of Oil Crisis Largely Ignored," *Canadian Churchman* 100 (February 1974): 5.

68 Laurence Mullin, "Does the Bible Give Sanction to Israel's Territorial Claim?" *Canadian Churchman*, 104 (September 1978): 24; E.W. Abraham, "Letterbasket: Bible Does Not Sanction Israel's Territorial Claim," ibid., 104 (December 1978): 22.

69 Jerry Hames, "Israel: A Land Tortured by Conflict," *Canadian Churchman* 97 (April 1970): 18; P.F. Gilbert, "Letterbasket: Middle East Frustration," ibid., 98 (November 1972): 30.

70 Francie Miller, "The Haunting Beauty of Israel Now," *Canadian Churchman* 98 (June 1972): 27–8.

71 Ann Benedek, "Christians Meet Jews and Arabs in Holy Land," *Canadian Churchman* 103 (May 1977): 8–10; Margaret J. Howell, "Letterbasket," ibid., 103 (July–August 1977): 14.

72 Michael E. Marmura, "Letterbasket," *Canadian Churchman* 102 (October 1977): 26; see also Bishop H.R. Hunt, "Letterbasket," ibid., 104 (January 1978): 18.

73 "History in the Making," *Canadian Churchman* 105 (May 1979): 3.

74 Editorial, "Sadat: Daring the Improbable," *Canadian Churchman* 107 (November 1981): 4.

75 Editorial, "Israelis Should Have No Role in Palestine Transition," *Canadian Churchman* 108 (October 1982): 4.

76 "Israel, South Africa Locked in 'Unholy Embrace,'" *Canadian Churchman,* 108 (October 1982): 5, 8.

77 Dean Jon Donald, "Letters: Article Was Biased," *Canadian Churchman* 109 (February 1983): 5.

78 Editorial, "Silence over Massacres Deafening," *Canadian Churchman* 108 (November 1982): 4; T.W. Wilkinson, "Letters: Silence Was Appropriate," ibid., 108 (Decembe 1982): 18.

79 CCC, "Statement on the Middle East," 1988 (CCC, CWC, MEWG, December 1987). For a detailed discussion of the CCC's Middle East statement and the various reactions, see chapter 2 above.

80 ACC, House of Bishops, November, 1988 (ACCA, GS files, GS 93N, Middle East).

81 METF to Michael Peers, primate, 5 April 1989 (ACCA, GS files, GS, 93–11, ME, 1989–91).

82 Prideaux to Primate Peers, John Rye, and Peter Slater re: METF, 1 May 1989 (ACCA, GS files, M520, ME, 1989–90).

83 Brian Prideaux to the author, 20 October 1995.

84 ACC, General Synod, June 1989, Act 53, *Journal of the General Synod,* 1989.

85 Resolution no. 25, "Palestine-Israel, Anglican Consultative Council," Episcopal Church, Diocesan Press Service, (17 March 1988), 5 (ACCA, GS files, GS, Jerusalem and ME, AC/J 830).

86 ACC, *Journal of the General Synod, 1992,* 2: 24.

87 Shafik Farah's address to the CCC's triennial assembly, 1990, "Where I Come From, Where I Need to Arrive, and the Inevitable Way of the Cross" (CCC, MEWG, 1990).

88 Farah to Michael Peers, 26 January 1988 (ACCA, GS files, ME and Jerusalem, AC/J, 830).

89 ACC, *Journal of the General Synod,* 1989, 47.

90 "Primate's Pastoral Letter to the Bishops, Priests …," 1988 (ACCA, Primate's Pastoral Letters, 1988).

91 Naji Farah, Shafik Farah, Farid Ohan, and Jousef Said to Archbishop Peers, 3 January 1990 (ACCA, GS files, ME, 1990–92).

92 Farah to Peers, 20 September 1988 (ACCA, GS files, ME and Jerusalem, AC/J, 830).

93　CCC, MEWG, Minutes, 7 December 1988; CCC, MEWG, "Submission to the Department of External Affairs," 6 January 1989 (CCC, MEWG, 1987–89); Robert Assaly, "Outline Proposal for 1990 Middle East Trip," in Marion Boulby, ed., "Whose Will Be Done: Report of a 1989 Study Tour to the Holy Land" (CCC, MEWG, 1989); Bess Durham to Brian Prideaux, 4 May 1990 (ACCA, GS files, GS 93–11, ME, 1989–91).

94　Interview with Shafik Farah, 23 June 1995.

95　ACC, AMEC, Minutes, 17 February, 26 June, 1989, 9 January, 23 March, 20 June 1990 (ACCA, GS files, GS 93–11, ME, 1989–91); Elsa Musa to John Barton, 11 May 1990 (ibid.).

96　ACC, AMEC, Minutes, 25 April 1990 (ACCA, GS files, ME, M520); Brian Prideaux to Bess Durham, 12 June 1990 (ACCA, GS files, GS 93–11, ME, 1989–91).

97　Prideaux to the author, 20 October 1995.

98　Peers to Shafik Farah, 1 September 1988 (ACCA, GS files, ME and Jerusalem, AC/J, 830).

99　Rose to Les Scheininger, 23 November 1989 (CJCNA, DA5, b.30, f.12).

100　DuCharme to Tad Mitsui, 20 March 1989 (CCC, MEWG, 1989, 183).

101　ACC, AMEC, Minutes, 25 April 1990 (ACCA, GS files, ME, M520); Peers, "Ember Letter," Lent 1990 (ACCA, Primate's Pastoral Letters, 1988).

102　Peers, "Ember Letter," 1990, (ACCA, Primate's Pastoral Letters, 1988).

103　ACC, AMEC, Minutes, 25 April 1990 (ACCA, GS files, ME, M520).

104　"Anglican Primate Responds to CJC Statement," 12 April 1990, Anglican News Service, "Press Release."

105　Michael Peers, "Israel and the Occupied Territories: The Role of the Churches in Promoting a Just Peace," 20 April 1990 (ACCA, GS files, ME, 1990–92).

106　Quoted in Boris G. Fresman to editor of *Canadian Jewish News*, 17 May 1990 (ACCA, GS files, ME).

107　Kafity to Peers, 17 April 1990 (ACCA, GS files, ME and Jerusalem, AC/J 830).

108　Brian Prideaux to James A. Graff, 2 March 1987 (ACCA, GS files, ME and Jerusalem, AC/J, 830, 1984–90).

109　"Archbishop Peers, Anglican Primate in UN North American Regional Seminar on the Question of Palestine," 25 June 1990 (ACCA, GS files, ME, 1990–92).

110　"New Autonomous Anglican Province in Middle East," *Canadian Churchman* 102 (March 1976): 10; see also "Archbishop George Appleton Praises Peace Talks," ibid., 104 (March 1978): 2. Although Rev. Canon Najib Cuba'in was consecrated in 1958 as the first Anglican bishop, before Bishop Haddad, the former's jurisdiction was over the diocese of Jordan, Lebanon, and Syria; see "Jerusalem," ibid., 58 (2 January 1958): 3.

111　Graham to Scott, 1 September 1982 (ACCA, GS files, GS, M560).

112 Marjorie Ross to Douglas duCharme, n.d. (CCC, CIDA, 1986, MEWG); see also "Arab Priest Arrested by Israel," *Canadian Churchman* 96 (May 1969): 16.

113 *Church Times* (London), 29 January 1988; "Anglican Leader in Middle East to Visit Connecticut," *Harcourt Courant* (Harcourt, Conn.), 30 January 1988; "Jerusalem Bishop Blasts Israeli 'Iron Fist,'" *The Hour*, 5 February 1988.

114 Douglas duCharme to Stuart Brown et. al., 9 October 1990 (CCC, MEWG, 1990).

115 Clark to Peers, 3 February 1987 (ACCA, GS files, ME and Church in Jerusalem, Past Correspondence).

116 Peers to Clark, 5 August 1989; 24 April 1990 (ACCA, GS files, ME and Jerusalem, AC/J, 830). The "Israeli attack" that Archbishop Peers referred to was a search that Israeli soldiers conducted for Palestinians who had fled to the hospital after they had committed a terrorist act against Israelis. See also Michael Peers to ambassador of Israel, Ottawa, 8 July 1990; Israel Gur-Aryeh to Peers, 23 July 1990 (ACCA, GS files, ME, 1990–92).

117 "Massacre in the Tomb of the Patriarchs in Hebron," Anglican News Service, "Press Release," 2 March 1994.

118 Editorial, "The Cupboard Is Bare!" *Canadian Churchman* 94 (September 1967): 2; see also "World Church News," ibid., 94 (July 1967): 3; "The Primate's World Relief Fund: The Middle East," ibid., 95 (January 1968): 18.

119 "Primate's Fund Projects, 1987," *Canadian Churchman* 114 (March 1988): 16–17.

120 ACC, "Grants to Africa, 1990" (ACCA, Grants, 1990); see also Jerry Hames, "Anglican College Needs Financial Support," *Canadian Churchman* 100 (June 1975): 21. The document "Christians for Peace in the Holy Land: Prayer from Jerusalem," Palm Sunday, 1990, was distributed by the primate among Anglican congregations; see Elliott Wright to all regional directors, 21 March 1990 (ACCA, GS files, ME and Jerusalem, ME, AC/J, 830).

121 Another controversial subject was the strong opposition by the clergy of Jerusalem to the ordination of women, an issue that the General Synod in Canada had approved several years before; see Samir Kafity to Michael Peers, 10 May 1990 (ACCA, GS files, ME, 1990–92).

122 "A Day of Prayer for Peace in the Middle East," Anglican News Service, "Press Release," 10 January 1991. See also Stuart Brown to Brian Mulroney, 28 November 1990 (ACCA, GS files, GS 93–11, ME, 1989–91).

123 "Anglican Archbishop Rejects 'Just War' in Gulf," Anglican News Service, "Press Release," 17 January 1991; editorial, "Defining the Just Cause," *Anglican Journal* (the successor of the *Canadian Churchman*), 120 (November 1994): 15.

124 "Address, Bishop Samir Kafity to the U.S. Episcopal House of Bishops," *Anglican Journal* 116 (November 1990): 9.

125 ACC, "General Synod Daily Report," 21 June 1992, no. 3; "Forum on the Middle East: Address by the Right Reverend Samir Kafity," *Journal of the Twenty Third General Synod, June 1992*, 2: 56–7.

126 "Middle East Problems Preoccupied Delegates," *Anglican Journal* 118 (September 1992): 8A.

127 Rose to Douglas Parrett, 12 August 1992 (CJCNA, DA5, b.31, f.7c).

128 Edith W. Land to Alan Rose, 24 June 1992 (CJCNA, DA5, b.31, f.7e).

CHAPTER TWELVE: THE PRESBYTERIAN CHURCH

1 To the group of denominations that the Presbyterians and Baptists represent in this study also belong the Lutherans and the Mennonites, among others. Both the latter two followed conservative Christian teaching, and the Lutherans, in particular, had strong cultural, religious, and personal ties with Germany. They supported the Nazi regime and disregarded the fate of Jewish refugees. They also did not show great interest in the Middle East crisis.

2 Grant, *The Canadian Experience of Church Union*, 50–5; Grant estimated the opposition at "one-third" of the church (ibid., 51). According to the *Encyclopedia Canadiana* "some 60 to 65 percent of the church's 380,000 members passed into the United Church of Canada"; see "Presbyterian Church," *Encyclopedia Canadiana* (1977), 8: 297. See also Davies and Nefsky, *How Silent Were the Churches?* 22.

3 Grant, *The Canadian Experience of Church Union*, 51.

4 Ibid., 73; see also 70–3.

5 In 1925 approximately one-third of 380,000 members rejected the union; see "Presbyterian Church," *Encyclopedia Canadiana*, 8: 297; PCC, *Acts and Proceedings of the One Hundred and Twentieth General Assembly, 1994*, 730.

6 Davies and Nefsky, *How Silent Were the Churches?* 22–5.

7 Grant, *The Canadian Experience of Church Union*, 78; see also 74–8.

8 PCC, *Acts and Proceedings of the Sixty Second General Assembly, 1936*, 140, 22.

9 Morris Zeidman, "The Jews," *Presbyterian Record*, February 1938, 39–40.

10 M. Zeidman, "Scott Institute," PCC, *Acts and Proceedings of the General Assembly, 1941*, 30–3.

11 "Presbyterian Mission to Jews," PCC, *Acts and Proceedings of the General Assembly, 1942*, 25–6. See also "Christian-Jewish Relations: A Historical Review," PCC, *Acts and Proceedings of the One Hundred and Sixteenth General Assembly, 1990*, Appendix: History Committee.

12 Calvin H. Chambers, "The Modern State of Israel," *Presbyterian Record*, September 1961, 15.

13 Editorial, "Are Missionaries Sent to Convert Others?" *Presbyterian Record*, April 1988, 31, 4.

14 "Statement of Key '73 by the Anglican Primate of Canada," 4 May 1973 (CJCNA, DA5, b.14, f.2).

15 "Address, General Council Alliance of Reformed Churches, by His Excellency, Lord Tweedsmuir, Governor General of Canada," *Presbyterian Record*, January 1938, 12.

16 Davies and Nefsky, *How Silent Were the Churches?* 65.

17 Ibid., 76–7. For a detailed discussion of Mackenzie King's role in the closing of Canada to Jewish refugees from Nazism, see Abella and Troper, *None Is Too Many*.

18 Davies and Nefsky, *How Silent Were the Churches?* 65.

19 Ibid., 79; PCC, *Acts and Proceedings of the One Hundred and Fifteenth General Assembly, 1989*, 63.

20 Davies and Nefsky, *How Silent Were the Churches?* 79.

21 For a detailed treatment of the CNCR, see Craft, "Canada's Righteous."

22 "Christian-Jewish Relations," PCC, *Acts and Proceedings of the One Hundred and Sixteenth General Assembly, 1990*, 383.

23 PCC, *Acts and Proceedings of the General Assembly, 1943*, 147.

24 PCC, Board of Evangelism and Church Life and Work, "Open Canada to Refugees," *Presbyterian Record*, February 1944, 41.

25 "Christian-Jewish Relations: A Historical Review," PCC, *Acts and Proceedings of the One Hundred and Sixteenth General Assembly, 1990*, 383.

26 Davies and Nefsky, *How Silent Were the Churches?* 78.

27 PCC, *Acts and Proceedings of the One Hundred and Fifteenth General Assembly, 1989*, 63.

28 PCC, General Board of Missions, "Recommendation to General Assembly: Re: International Affairs," n.d. (PCCA, GBW, BWM, Overseas Missions, CIA, 1988-1003-42-15).

29 PCC, *Acts and Proceedings of the Eighty Fifth General Assembly, 1959*, Resolution "Re: International Affairs," 89.

30 E.H. Johnson to G. Deane Johnston, 4 January 1965 (PCCA, GBW, BWM, 1988-1003, 42-15).

31 PCC, *Acts and Proceedings of the Ninety Fifth General Assembly, 1967*, 354–5.

32 D.C. McLelland to E.H. Johnson, 18 February 1966; Johnson to McLelland, 1 March 1966 (PCCA, GBW, BWM, 1988-1003, 42-15).

33 PCC, *Acts and Proceedings of the Ninety Second General Assembly, 1966*, 339.

34 E.H. Johnson to Allison E. Mundle, 20 June 1972 (PCCA, GBW, BWM, 1988-1003, 52-21).

35 PCC, *Acts and Proceedings of the Ninety Eighth General Assembly, 1972*, 269. For a detailed discussion of the CCC's *Search for Understanding in the Middle East*, see chapter 2 above.

36 Mildred McAfee, "Suffering among Arab Refugees," *Presbyterian Record*, February 1953, 6–7; see also Wifred C. Smith, "Refugee Arabs from Palestine," ibid., January 1949, 9–10; Francis B. Sayre, "Refugees: A Challenge to Christianity," ibid., March 1956, 18–20.

37 "O Come Ye … to Bethlehem," *Presbyterian Record*, December 1953, 19–20; Helen E. Bricker, "Journey to Jerusalem," ibid., April 1954, 4–6; K.M. Glazier, "The Land Where Jesus Was Born," ibid., December 1955, 18–9, 30; De Courcy H. Rayner, "Digging in Jerusalem," ibid., December 1962, 4–6; "In Nazareth," ibid., December 1966, 13.

38 "Views of the Holy Land," *Presbyterian Record*, March 1964, 22–3.

39 Alexander Ferguson, "The Unholy War in the Holy Land," *Presbyterian Record*, March 1959, 11–13, 25.

40 "Inter-Church Aid and Refugee Relief," PCC, *Acts and Proceedings of the Eighty Second General Assembly, 1956*, 33–4; "Inter-Church Aid and Refugee Relief," PCC, *Acts and Proceedings of the General Assembly*, 1959, 11–13, 25.

41 PCC, *Acts and Proceedings of the Ninety Third General Assembly, June 1967*, 70–1.

42 For details of the Heraklion conference, see chapter 1.

43 Editorials, "The Churches and the Middle East" and "What Can We Do?" *Presbyterian Record*, October 1967, 4.

44 A.C. Forrest, "Tragedy in Jerusalem," *Presbyterian Record*, October 1967, 5; Forrest, "The Refugee Crisis in the Middle East," ibid., 10–13.

45 G. Douglas Young, "Peace in Jerusalem," *Presbyterian Record*, April 1969, 14–17; see also Alan Rose to Meyer Bick, 1 October 1971 (CJCNA, DA5, b.46, f.9).

46 DeCourcy H. Rayner, "Roses from Israel," *Presbyterian Record*, May 1976, 15; see also Valerie M. Dunn, "The Gardens of Israel," ibid., October 1977, 2–3. Rayner, who was the author of several pro-Israeli articles in the *Presbyterian Record*, wrote the eulogy for Forrest. He regarded Forrest as "one of our great Christian leaders."Although Rayner "sometimes disagreed with the stand he took, I respected his conviction and his courage." See De-Courcy H. Rayner, editorial, "A Tribute to A.C. Forrest," *Presbyterian Record*, February 1979, 4.

47 James E. Solheim, "The Middle East: Everyone Wants Peace," *Presbyterian Record*, April 1971, 13.

48 Editorial, "Middle East Refugees," *Presbyterian Record*, March 1969, 4. The editorial printed the telegram without comment.

49 PCC, *Acts and Proceedings of the Ninety Eighth General Assembly, 1972*, 61–2.

50 T. Meron to E.H. Johnson, 15 August 1972 (PCCA, GBW, BWM, 1988–1003, 52–21).

51 In 1974 the 100th assembly noted in one sentence its satisfaction about the current Geneva peace conference, and it expressed the hope that "a constructive and creative peace settlement may be achieved"; see PCC, *Acts and Proceedings of the One Hundredth General Assembly, 1974*, 285.

52 "Towards a Just Solution for Israel and the Palestinians," n.d. (PCCA, GBW, BWM, 1988–1003, 52–21); PCC, *Acts and Proceedings of the One Hundred and Second General Assembly, 1976*, 258.

53 For a detailed discussion of the CCC's involvement in the Middle East and Douglas duCharme's role in it, see chapter 2 above.

54 "International Affairs in 1982–3" (PCCA, BWM, General correspondence, CIA, 1982–85, 1989–1009, 3–5).

55 "Middle East," PCC, *Acts and Proceedings of the One Hundred and Ninth General Assembly, 1983*, 374.

56 "Middle East," PCC, *Acts and Proceedings of the One Hundred and Tenth General Assembly, 1984*, 389–90.

57 Interview with Hodgson, 13 June 1995.

58 "The Israeli-Palestinian Conflict," PCC, *Acts and Proceedings of the 115th General Assembly, 1989*, 367.

59 Ghassan Rubeiz, "Christians in Israel," PCC, *Acts and Proceedings of the 113th General Assembly, 1987*, 340–1.

60 Ibid., 341.

61 PCC, *Acts and Proceedings of the 114th General Assembly, 1988*, 481, 283.

62 Ibid., 366–7.

63 PCC, *Acts and Proceedings of the 115th General Assembly, 1989*, 468–9.

64 Ibid., 367–9, 63; see also Earl F. Roberts to Joe Clark, 15 July 1989 (CCC, CWC, MEWG, 1989).

65 PCC, *Acts and Proceedings of the 115th General Assembly, 1989*, 63. For a detailed discussion of the CCC's "Position Paper on the Middle East", see above chapter 2 above.

66 PCC, *Acts and Proceedings of the 116th General Assembly, 1990*, 384; History Committee, "Christian-Jewish Relations: A Historical Review," appendix A, 378–84.

67 "Moderator among Church Leaders to visit the Middle East," *Presbyterian Record*, April 1990, 43.

68 "Middle East," PCC, *Acts and Proceedings of the 116th General Assembly, 1990*, 394–400, 63.

69 Ibid., 301.

70 Ibid., 304.

71 "Middle East Problems Preoccupied Delegates," *Anglican Journal* 118 (September 1992): 8A.

72 Douglas duCharme, "The Middle East: Where Peace Is Broken and Where There Are Signs of Hope," PCC, 30 March 1992; "The Middle East: Where Peace Is Broken," "Signs of Hope – the Middle East," PCC, *Acts and Proceedings of the 118th General Assembly, 1992*, 342–4, 358–9.

73 PCC, *Acts and Proceedings of the 118th General Assembly, 1992*, 359.

74 PCC, *Acts and Proceedings of the 120th General Assembly, 1994*, 314; *Acts and Proceedings of the 119th General Assembly, 1993*, 253.

75 Interview with Hodgson, 13 June 1995.

CHAPTER THIRTEEN: THE BAPTISTS

1 The two major Baptist bodies are the Canadian Baptist Federation and the Fellowship of Evangelical Baptist Churches in Canada; see R.J. Preston, "Baptists," *Canadian Encyclopedia* (2d ed., 1988), 1: 176–7.
2 Davies and Nefsky, *How Silent Were the Churches?* 24–5.
3 Ibid., 80.
4 "Our Bible School Lesson," *Canadian Baptist*, 19 January 1933, 12; 3 March 1934, 12; W.S. Edgar, "Christ and Real Religion," ibid., 1 August 1935, 6; "The Three Crowns," ibid., 15 August 1945, 1.
5 "Berlin, 1934," *Canadian Baptist*, 6 September 1934, 3.
6 Hans Luckey, "Freedom of Religion in Germany," *Canadian Baptist*, 15 September 1938, 4.
7 Watson Kirkconnell, "The Price of Christian Liberty," *Canadian Baptist*, 17–24 August 1939, 5.
8 "Germany and the Jew," *Canadian Baptist*, 6 April 1933, 3.
9 "Ill Treatment of Jews," *Canadian Baptist*, 27 April 1933, 5.
10 "If I Were A Jew … ?" *Canadian Baptist*, 8 March 1934, 4.
11 Editor, "I See in the Paper," *Canadian Baptist*, 1 December 1938, 2; "Moose Jaw and the Jews," ibid., 12.
12 Editor, "More Settlers," *Canadian Baptist*, 11 April 1935, 2.
13 "The Convention Resolutions: European Refugees," *Canadian Baptist*, 29 June 1939, 11.
14 "Moose Jaw and the Jews," *Canadian Baptist*, 1 December 1938, 12.
15 C. Abraham Woodstock, "The Editor's Mail Bag: Munich and After," *Canadian Baptist* 25 May 1939, 13.
16 "Books," *Canadian Baptist*, 1 May 1939, 2.
17 T.N.T. Tattersall, "War and God's Judgment," *Canadian Baptist*, 1 February 1940, 7; see also "The Baptist Youth," ibid., 15 February 1940, 11.
18 "Our War Aims," *Canadian Baptist*, 15 June 1940, 1.
19 "Christmas while Cannons Roar across the Battle Fields," *Canadian Baptist*, 15 December 1939, 3; "War's Dilemmas," ibid., 1 January 1941, 3; "Bombing Policy," ibid., 16 August 1943, 11; "Thanks Be to God!" ibid., 15 May 1945, 3.
20 "European Church and German Nazism," *Canadian Baptist*, 1 October 1945, 8.
21 "Out of the Ashes – What?" *Canadian Baptist*, 15 June 1945, 3.
22 Editorial, "Three History-Making Events," *Canadian Baptist*, 15 April 1949, 3; editorial, "A Fateful Assembly," ibid., 15 October 1948, 3.
23 Editorial, "Israel," *Canadian Baptist*, 15 January 1949, 3.
24 Editorial, "Three History-Making Events," *Canadian Baptist*, 15 April 1949, 3.

25 Duke McCall, "Israel-Arab: Two Sides to the Problem," *Canadian Baptist*, 15 November 1950, 2, 10.

26 Baptist Convention of Ontario and Quebec, *Baptist Year Book, 1954–7*, 57–61; *Canadian Baptist*, May-June 1984; "Unity and Dissent Feature in Baptist Convention of Ontario and Quebec," ibid., September-October, 1992, 55.

27 William H. Jones, editorial and comment, "Structures for Mutual Work," *Canadian Baptist*, February 1984, 3.

28 Ibid., 3–4; J.K. Zeman, "Interfaith, Interface," *Canadian Baptist*, October 1984, 15.

29 "Reports of the Eighth Assembly of the Baptist Federation of Canada, 1967," 37–8; "Resolution Passed at June Assembly of Ontario and Quebec Convention, 1968," *Canadian Baptist*, 1 August 1968, 25.

30 "Reports of the Ninth Assembly of the Baptist Federation of Canada, 1967–70," 104; Olive M. Evans, "The Sharing Way: The Baptist Federation of Canada Relief and Development Committee," *Canadian Baptist*, February 1981, 4–5.

31 William R. Wood, "Evangelism and Mission," *Canadian Baptist*, April 1982, 6; see also editorial, "A Statement of Purpose in Evangelism," ibid., 1 February 1969, 3; editorial, "Evangelism – Concern," ibid., November 1969, 3; "Developments in Overseas Missions of Canadian Baptists in India, Bolivia and Africa," ibid., 15 September 1968, 11; Convention of Ontario and Quebec, *Baptist Year Book, 1986–7*, 171–2; Clark Pinnock, "Can the Un-Evangelized be Saved?" *Canadian Baptist*, November 1981, 5–9.

32 William H. Jones, editorial and comment, "Are They Free to Worship?" *Canadian Baptist*, September 1987, 3.

33 Editorial and comment, "What Is The Holy Land Like Today," *Canadian Baptist*, May 1972, 3.

34 J. Gordon Jones, "Lands of the Bible: Nazareth," *Canadian Baptist*, 15 February 1968, 16; "Bethlehem," ibid., 1 February 1968, 16, 20–1; "Galilee," ibid., 1 March 1968, 16, 20–1; "Jericho," ibid., 15 March 1968, 16, 20–1; "Jerusalem," ibid., 1 April 1968, 16, 20, 25. See also William H. Jones's articles on Jerusalem: "Why Should They Find Much Water," ibid., September 1977, 6–7; "Jerusalem," ibid., November 1979, 4–7; "Jesus' Last Days in Jerusalem," ibid., April 1982, 19–22; "Where Was the Easter Event?" ibid., 26–7.

35 R. Lindsay, "Thirty Christmases in Jerusalem," *Canadian Baptist*, December 1981, 14–15.

36 Michael Lipe, "Come to the Manger," *Canadian Baptist*, December 1986, 8–9.

37 "Women's Missionary Auxiliary Panel Discussion on Rhodesia, Czechoslovakia, Middle East and Canada," *Canadian Baptist*, 1 March 1969, 10.

38 R.M. Bennett, "A Journey in Israel," *Canadian Baptist*, February 1970, 7.

39 R.M. Bennett, "Israel – Sorrow, Injustice, Distrust," *United Church Observer,* 1 December 1969, 36–7.

40 Editorial and comment, "The Israel Idea," *Canadian Baptist,* November 1979, 3.

41 Richard C. Coffin and William H. Jones, editorial & comment, "Tearing Down Hatred's Walls," *Canadian Baptist,* March 1988, 3.

42 J. Martin Bailey, "The Hopes and Fears of All the Years," *Canadian Baptist,* December 1994, 9–11.

43 To be sure, there were several courageous leaders, including T.T. Shields and Watson Kirkconnell, but they were exceptions. See Davies and Nefsky, *How Silent Were the Churches?* 97.

CONCLUSION

1 Alan Davies to the author, 27 December 1999.

2 Interview with Raymond Hodgson, 13 June 1995.

3 Baum, "Salvation Is from the Jews," 777.

4 Exile meant that Jews were living on sufferance in countries which were not their own. See Plaut, *Israel, Jews and Canadian Churches,* 7.

5 Ibid., 11.

Bibliography

ARCHIVAL SOURCES

ANGLICAN CHURCH OF CANADA ARCHIVES (TORONTO)
Committee on International Affairs files
Correspondence files
Council for Social Service files
General Synod files
Middle East–Jerusalem files
Primate's Pastoral Letters files

CANADIAN BAPTIST ARCHIVES (MCMASTER DIVINITY COLLEGE,
    HAMILTON, ONTARIO)

CANADIAN COUNCIL OF CHURCHES ARCHIVES (TORONTO)
Canadian International Development Agency files
Commission on Justice and Peace files
Commission on World Concerns files
Dialogue files
Middle East Council of Churches files
Middle East Working Group files
Position Paper on the Middle East files
Responses to Position Paper files

CANADIAN JEWISH CONGRESS, NATIONAL ARCHIVES
    (MONTREAL)

EVANGELICAL LUTHERAN CHURCH IN CANADA, EASTERN
    SYNOD ARCHIVES (WILFRID LAURIER UNIVERSITY LIBRARY,
    WATERLOO, ONTARIO)

HOLY BLOSSOM TEMPLE ARCHIVES (TORONTO)

ONTARIO JEWISH ARCHIVES (TORONTO)
Canadian Conference of Christians and Jews files
Canadian Jewish Congress files
Jewish Community Relations Committee files
Religious Education files
United Church files

PRESBYTERIAN CHURCH IN CANADA ARCHIVES (TORONTO)
General Board World Mission files

LOU RONSON PRIVATE COLLECTION (TORONTO)

UNITED CHURCH OF CANADA ARCHIVES (VICTORIA
    UNIVERSITY, TORONTO)
Board of Evangelism and Social Service files
Commission on the Church, Nation and World Order files
Committee on the Church and International Affairs files
Committee on Overseas Relief files
Alan T. Davies Papers
A.C. Forrest Papers
Ernest Marshall Howse Papers
John R. Mutchmor Papers
Claris E. Silcox Papers

INTERVIEWS

Irving Abella (Canadian Jewish Congress), 10 June 1994
Alan T. Davies (United Church), 9 February, 10 March, 1995, 28 July 1999
Roland de Corneille (Anglican), 20 July 1995
David Demson (United Church), 30 May 1995
Douglas duCharme (Canadian Council of Churches), 5 June 1995
Shafik Farah (Anglican), 23 June 1995
Raymond Hodgson (Presbyterian), 13 June 1995
Joseph Kage (Jewish Immigrant Aid Society), 19 May 1995
Ben G. Kayfetz (Canadian Jewish Congress), 12 May 1995
W. Gunther Plaut (Canadian Jewish Congress), 11 May 1995
David Rome (Canadian Jewish Congress), 20 May 1995

Lou Ronson (B'nai Brith), 14 July 1995
John Rye (Anglican), 22 June 1995
Reuben Slonim, 12 May 1995

CORRESPONDENCE

Alan T. Davies (United Church), 19 August, 27 December 1999
Angus J. MacQueen (United Church), 2 May 1995
N. Bruce McLeod (United Church), 29 May 1995
A.B.B. Moore (United Church),10 May 1995
George Morrison (United Church), 24 June 1995
Brian Prideaux (Anglican), 20 October 1995

PAMPHLETS, BULLETINS, AND REPORTS
ISSUED BY CHURCH ORGANIZATIONS

Anglican Church of Canada. *From Darkness to Dawn: Rethinking Christian Attitudes toward Jews and Judaism.* 1989.
– *Journal of the General Synod.*
– Council for Social Service. *Annual Report.*
Baptist Year Book.
Canadian Council of Churches. *Old Patterns, New Possibilities.* 1988.
– *Peace, Justice and Reconciliation.* 1979.
– *Search for Understanding.* 1970.
– *Statement on the Middle East.* 1989.
Presbyterian Church in Canada. *Acts and Proceedings of the General Assembly.*
United Church of Canada. *Bearing Faithful Witness: United Church–Jewish Relations Today.* 1997.
– *Record of the Proceedings of the General Council of the United Church.*
– *United Church of Canada Year Book.*
– Board of Evangelism and Social Service. *Annual Report.*
World Council of Churches. *Collection of Statements made by the* WCC *and Representative Bodies of Its Member Churches.* Geneva, 1964.
– *The First Assembly of the World Council of Churches: Official Report.* New York, 1949.
– *Palestine Refugees: Aid with Justice.* Geneva, 1970.
– *The Theology of the Churches and the Jewish People: Statements by the* WCC *and Its Member Churches.* Geneva, 1983.

RELIGIOUS PRESS

Anglican Church of Canada. Council for Social Service. *Bulletin*
Anglican Journal

Anglican News Service
Canada Lutheran (Evangelical Lutheran Church in Canada, Eastern Synod)
Canadian Baptist (Baptist Convention of Ontario and Quebec and the Baptist Union of Western Canada)
Canadian Churchman (Anglican)
Canadian Council of Churches. News Service
Canadian Jewish News (Canadian Jewish Congress)
Ecumenical Press Service (World Council of Churches)
Fellowship (Canadian Conference of Christians and Jews)
Holy Blossom Temple Bulletin (Toronto)
New Outlook (United Church)
Presbyterian Record
Social Welfare (Council for Social Service of Canada, Anglican Church)
United Church Observer
United Church of Canada, *News*

OTHER NEWSPAPERS AND PERIODICALS

Canadian Jewish Historical Society Journal
Christian Century (U.S.)
Christianity and Crisis (U.S.)
Globe and Mail (Toronto)
Toronto Star

BOOKS, ARTICLES, AND UNPUBLISHED PAPERS

Abella, Irving, and Harold Troper. *None Is Too Many: Canada and the Jews of Europe, 1933–48*. Toronto: Lester Publishing Ltd, 1983.

Ages, Arnold. "*The United Church Observer* and the State of Israel." Toronto: B'nai Brith Anti-Defamation League, Basic Documents, 1969. (mimeographed, 13 pages; copy in OJA, MG8/S, b.53, f.161).

Baum, Gregory. "Catholic Dogma after Auschwitz." In *Antisemitism and the Foundations of Christianity*, ed. A.T. Davies (1979), 137–50.

– "The Churches, Israel and the Palestinians." *Catholic New Times* 8 (January 1989): 8–9.

– "Salvation Is from the Jews: A Story of Prejudice." *Christian Century* 89 (19 July 1972): 775–7.

– et al. "Peace, Justice and Reconciliation in the Arab-Israeli Conflict: A Christian and Canadian Perspective." Report of a study group established by the Ecumenical Forum of Canada, March 1978. (Copy in UCA, CCIA, 82, 250C, b.7, f.10).

Bennett, R.H. "Israel, Sorrow, Injustice, Distrust." *United Church Observer*, 1 December 1969, 36–7.

Bentall, Shirley. *From Sea to Sea: The Canadian Baptist Federation, 1944–94.* Mississauga, Ont.: Canadian Baptist Federation, 1994.

Bercuson, David J. *Canada and the Birth of Israel: A Study in Canadian Foreign Policy.* Toronto: University of Toronto Press, 1985.

Betcherman, Lita-Rose. *The Swastika and the Maple Leaf: Fascist Movements in Canada in the Thirties.* Toronto: Fitzhenry and Whiteside, 1975.

Booth, John Nicholls. "How Zionists Manipulate Your News." *United Church Observer,* March 1972, 24–6.

Breckenridge, Joan. "United Church Reaches Out to Jews." *Globe and Mail,* 23 May 1998.

Brockway, Alan R. "World Council of Churches and the Jewish People." *Ecumenical Trends,* October 1983, 134–6.

Cargas, Harry James. *Reflections of a Post-Auschwitz Christian.* Detroit: Wayne State University Press, 1989.

Chambers, Steven *This Is Your Church: A Guide to Beliefs, Policies and Positions to the United Church of Canada.* Toronto: United Church of Canada, 1982.

Cohen, Arthur. *The Tremendum: Theological Interpretation of the Holocaust.* New York: Crossroad, 1981.

Conway, John S. "Canada and the Holocaust." In *Remembering for the Future: Jews and Christians during and after the Holocaust.* papers presented at an International Scholars' Conference, Oxford, July 1988. Theme I, 296–305.

– "The Founding of the State of Israel and the Responses of the Christian Churches." Unpublished paper, March 1998.

Craft, Kenneth F.P. "Canada's Righteous: A History of the Canadian National Committee on Refugees and Victims of Political Persecution." MA thesis, Carleton University, 1987.

Crysdale, Stewart. *The Changing Church in Canada: Beliefs and Social Attitudes of United Church People.* Toronto: United Church of Canada, 1965.

Davies, Alan T. *Antisemitism and the Christian Mind.* New York: Herder and Herder, 1969.

– "Anti-Zionism, Anti-Semitism and the Christian Mind." *Christian Century,* 87 (19 August 1970): 987–9.

– "Why Critics of Israel Must Be Careful." *United Church Observer,* August 1970, 18, 26, 30, 36, 38.

– ed. *Antisemitism and the Foundations of Christianity.* New York: Ramsey; Toronto: Paulist Press, 1979.

– ed. *Antisemitism in Canada: A History and Interpretation.* Waterloo, Ont.: Wilfrid Laurier University Press, 1992.

– and Marilyn F. Nefsky. "The Church of England in Canada and the Jewish Plight during the Nazi Era." *Canadian Jewish Historical Society Journal* 10 (fall 1988): 1–19.

– *How Silent Were the Churches? Canadian Protestantism and the Jewish Plight during the Nazi Era.* Waterloo, Ont.: Wilfrid Laurier University Press, 1997.

– "The United Church and the Jewish Plight during the Nazi Era." *Canadian Jewish Historical Society Journal* 8 (fall 1984): 55–71.

Dekar, Paul R. "Canadian Christians and the Restoration of Jews to the Holy Land." *McMaster Journal of Theology* 3 (spring 1993): 161–82.

Dirks, Gerald E. *Canada's Refugee Policy: Indifference or Opportunism?* Montreal and London: McGill-Queen's University Press, 1977.

Domaki, Robert P. "While Millions Cried: Canada and the Refugee Question, 1938–1941." MA thesis, Carleton University, 1975.

Draper, Paula J. "The Accidental Immigrants: Canada and the Interned Refugees." *Canadian Jewish Historical Society Journal* 2 (1978): 1–38, 80–112.

– "Accidental Immigrants: Canada and the Interned Refugees." PhD thesis, University of Toronto, 1983.

duCharme, Douglas, "Learning to Live with the Enemies: The Churches and the Middle East." In *Canadian Churches and Foreign Policy*, ed. Bonnie Greene, (1989), 47–59.

Eckardt, A. Roy. *Elder and Younger Brothers: The Encounter of Jews and Christians.* New York: Scribner, 1967.

– *Your People, My People: The Meeting of Christians and Jews.* New York: Quadrangle, 1974.

Eisendrath, M.N. *Can Faith Survive?* Toronto: McGraw-Hill, 1964.

Emerson, J.A. "The World Council of Churches and the PLO." *Midstream,* 19 November 1984, 3–9.

Fackenheim, Emil. *The Jewish Return into History.* New York: Schoken Books, 1978.

– "The People of Israel Lives." In *Disputation and Dialogue*, ed. Frank Talmage (1975), 296–308.

– "Why I've Changed My Mind about Christians." *Ferment* 69 (1969): 8–11.

Feldblum, Esther. *The American Catholic Press and the Jewish State, 1917–1959.* New York: Ktav Publishing House, 1977.

Fisher, Douglas. "What the Election Taught Me about the *Observer.*" *United Church Observer,* 15 September 1968, 37.

Fisher, Eugene J. "Anti-Semitism: A Contemporary Christian Perspective." *Judaism,* summer 1981, 276–82.

– ed. *Visions of the Other: Jewish and Christian Theologians Assess the Dialogue.* New York: Paulist Press, 1994.

Fishman, Hertzel. *American Protestantism and a Jewish State.* Detroit: Wayne State University Press, 1973.

Flannery, Edward H. *The Anguish of the Jews: Twenty-Three Centuries of Anti-Semitism.* New York: Macmillan, 1965.

– "Anti-Zionism and the Christian Psyche." *Journal of Ecumenical Studies* 6 (spring 1969): 174–81.

– *A Christian View of Israel.* South Orange, NJ: Seton Hall University, 1970.

Forrest, A.C. "About Mr. Salter's Advertisement." *United Church Observer,* May 1974, 11.

–"APOLOGY." *United Church Observer,* June 1972, 17.

– "Church Neglect and the Middle East Strife." *Canadian Churchman,* 99 (November 1973): 20.

– "Five Years After: Another Side of the 1967 War." *United Church Observer,* February 1973, 25.

– "The Middle East: It's Bad and It's Getting Worse and Here's Why It Matters So Much." *United Church Observer,* 15 February 1969, 18–21.

– "The Other Side of Jordan." *United Church Observer,* 1 April 1967, 12–15.

– *The Unholy Land.* Toronto: McClelland and Stewart, 1971.

– "What Happened When I Criticized Israel," *United Church Observer,* 1 April 1968, 27–8.

– "You Don't Seem to Care about Us: Bethlehem, 1968." *United Church Observer,* 15 December 1968, 28–9.

Foster, Arnold, and Benjamin R. Epstein. *The New Anti-Semitism.* Toronto: McGraw-Hill Book, 1973.

Gaudin, Gary A. "Protestant Church, Jewish State: The United Church of Canada, Israel and the Palestinian Refugees Revisited." *Studies in Religion: A Canadian Journal* 24 (1995): 179–91.

Gefen, Aba. "A Vision of Peace Guides Israel." *United Church Observer,* August 1970, 14–17, 30.

Genizi, Haim. *American Apathy: The Plight of Christian Refugees from Nazism, 1933–45.* Ramat Gan: Bar Ilan University Press, 1983.

– *America's Fair Share: The Admission and Resettlement of Displaced Persons, 1945–52.* Detroit: Wayne State University Press, 1993.

– "The United Church of Canada and the State of Israel: The Impact of the Holocaust." In *Remembering for the Future: The Holocaust in an Age of Genocide,* editors in chief, John K. Roth and Elisabeth Maxwell, 2: 561–74. Basingstoke, Hants; New York: Palgrave, 2001.

Gilbert, Peter F. "Exploring Christian-Jewish Relations." *Presbyterian Record,* October 1975, 10–11.

Grant, John Webster. *The Canadian Experience of Church Union.* Richmond, Va: John Knox Press, 1967.

– *The Church in the Canadian Era.* Updated and expanded. Burlington, Ont.: Welch Publishing Co., 1988.

– "What's Past Is Prologue." In *Voices and Visions: Sixty Five Years of the United Church,* ed. Peter G. White (1990), 125–49.

Greenberg, Irving. "The Voluntary Covenant." In *Perspectives,* 3. New York: National Jewish Resource Center, 1982.

Greene, Bonnie, ed. *Canadian Churches and Foreign Policy.* Toronto: Lorimer Press, 1989.

Howse, Ernest Marshall. "The Rabbi Is Wrong." *Globe and Mail,* 17 July 1967.

– "Reject That Hate Law." *United Church Observer,* 15 January 1967, 22–3.

– "Torrent of Abuse." *Toronto Star,* 12 January 1972.

– "We Can Lead the Way to Greater Religious Understanding." *Toronto Star*, 27 April 1972.

– "The World: Racism Charge Can Be a Two-Edged Sword." *Toronto Star*, 6 May 1971.

Kirkconnell, Watson. *Canada, Europe and Hitler*. Toronto: Oxford University Press, 1939.

– *A Slice of Canada: Memoirs*. Toronto: University of Toronto Press, 1967.

– *Twilight of Liberty*. London: Oxford University Press, 1941.

Kirton, John, and Peyton Lyon. "Perceptions of the Middle East in the Department of External Affairs and Mulroney's Policy, 1984–88." In *Domestic Battleground: Canada and the Arab-Israeli Conflict*, ed. David Taras and David H. Goldberg (1989), 186–203.

Lappin, Ben W. *The Redeemed Children: The Story of the Rescue of War Orphans by the Jewish Community of Canada*. Toronto: University of Toronto Press, 1963.

Littman, Sol I. "United Church and Jews Must Seek Understanding." *Toronto Star*, 13 May 1971.

Long, E.E., and A.B.B. Moore. "United Church Outlines Stance on Middle East." *Toronto Star*, 26 May 1971.

Longley, Clifford. "Can World Council of Churches Grants to Guerilla Movements Be Defended?" *Canadian Churchman* 104 (November 1978): 8.

McLeod, N. Bruce. "Christian-Jewish Relations in Canada. A Statement by N. Bruce McLeod, Moderator of the United Church of Canada, at the University of Windsor, 5 November 1973." Unpublished MS. (Copy in author's possession).

– "Christians Reject the Unholy View of Judaism." *Toronto Star*, 25 March 1986.

– "A Cry of Pain for Israel." *Toronto Star*, 19 July 1988.

MacQueen, Angus J. "Israel and the United Church of Canada" Unpublished MS., 1991.

Maduro, O. *Judaism, Christianity and Liberation: An Agenda for Dialogue*. Maryknoll: Orbis, 1991.

Mathers, Donald N. *The Word and the Way*. Toronto: United Church Publishing House, 1962.

Matthews, Robert O. "The Christian Churches and Foreign Policy: An Assessment." In *Canadian Churches and Foreign Policy*, ed. Bonnie Greene (1989), 161–79.

– "Lobbyist or Prophet: The Christian Churches and Canadian Foreign Policy in Human Rights." Prepared for the CIIA Conference on Domestic Groups and Foreign Policy, Carleton University, June 1982.

– and Cranford Pratt, eds. *Church and State: The Christian Churches and Canadian Foreign Policy*. Toronto: Canadian Institute of International Affairs, 1982.

Nawyn, William E. *American Protestantism's Response to Germany's Jews and Refugees, 1933–41*. Ann Arbor, Mich.: UMI Research Press, 1980.

Neatby, H. Blair. *Politics of Chaos: Canada in the Thirties.* Toronto: McMillan, 1972.

Nefsky, Marilyn F. "The Shadow of Evil: Nazism and Canadian Protestantism." In *Antisemitism in Canada,* ed. Alan Davies (1992), 197–225.

Neuhaus, Richard John. "What the Fundamentalists Want?" *Commentary,* May 1985, 44–5.

Niebuhr, Reinhold. "Jews after the War." *Nation,* 21 February 1942, 214–16; 28 February 1942, 253–5.

– "The Relations of Christians and Jews in Western Civilization." *Central Conference of American Rabbis Journal,* April 1958, 18–32.

Palin, Jennifer. "The United Church and the Jews." History essay, Victoria College, University of Toronto, April 1995.

Palmer, Howard. *Patterns of Prejudice: A History of Nativism in Alberta.* Toronto: McClelland and Stewart, 1982.

Parkes, James. *History of Palestine from 135 AD to Modern Times.* Oxford University Press, 1949.

Petuchowski, Jakob J. "Israel as a Theological Problem in the Christian Church." *Journal of Ecumenical Studies* 6 (summer 1969): 329–53.

Plaut, W. Gunther. *Israel, Jews and Canadian Churches.* Montreal: Canada-Israel Committee, 1974.

– "Israel Wants Justice Too." *United Church Observer,* 15 November 1967, 21–3.

– "News and Views: Again Dr. Forrest." *Holy Blossom Temple Bulletin* 44, no. 19 (6 January 1969): 2.

– "News and Views: Dr. Forrest, Howse, et al." *Holy Blossom Temple Bulletin,* 17, no. 14 (31 January 1972): 2.

– "News and Views: The Irrepressible Mr. Forrest." *Holy Blossom Temple Bulletin* 46, no. 29 (9 March 1970): 2.

– "News and Views: *Judenrat.*" *Holy Blossom Temple Bulletin* 65, no. 15 (1 December 1969): 2.

– "News and Views: The Meeting with Dr. McClure." *Holy Blossom Temple Bulletin* 44, no. 22 (27 (January 1969): 2.

– *Unfinished Business: An Autobiography.* Toronto: Lester and Orpen Dennys, 1981.

– "United Church Assembly." *Holy Blossom Temple Bulletin* 68 (5 September 1972): 9–10.

Portman, William. "A Century of Changes, 1890–1993: The General Synod." *Anglican Journal* 119 (September 1993): 11.

Prince, A.E. "The Global War: Is Zionism a Denial of the Best Judaic Tradition?" *United Church Observer,* 15 December 1945, 4, 25, 28; 1 January 1946, 28; 15 January 1946, 25.

Rabinowitz, A.H. *Israel: The Christian Dilemma.* Jerusalem: Gefen Publishing House, 1985.

Rausch, David A. "The Evangelicals as Zionists." *Midstream,* January 1985, 13–16.

Renfree, Harry A. *Heritage and Horizon: The Baptist Story in Canada*. Missassauga, Ont.: Canadian Baptist Federation, 1988.

Rome, David. *Clouds in the Thirties: On Antisemitism in Canada, 1929–1939: A Chapter on Canadian Jewish History*. 6 vols. Montreal, 1977–81.

Rosenberg, Stuart, E. *The Christian Problem: A Jewish View*. New York: Deneau Publication, 1986.

Rosenthal, Judah. *The State of Israel and the Christian Church* (Hebrew). Jerusalem: Reuben Mass, 1966.

Rubinstein, Richard. *After Auschwitz*. Indianapolis: Bobbs-Merrill, 1966.

– "Some Perspectives on Religious Faith after Auschwitz." In *The German Church Struggle*, ed. Franklin H. Littell and Hubert G. Locke (Detroit: Wayne State University Press, 1970), 256–68.

Rudin, James A. *Israel for Christians*. Philadelphia: Fortress Press, 1983.

Ruether, Rosemary. *Faith and Fratricide*. New York: Seabury Press, 1974.

Salter, J.G. "He as God Sitteth in the Temple of God." *United Church Observer*, March 1974, 38.

Scott, Munroe. *McClure: A Biography*. 2 vols. Toronto: Canec Publishing and Supply House, 1977.

Silcox, Claris E. *Church Union in Canada: Its Causes and Consequences*. 1933.

– "The Crisis in the Middle East." *United Church Observer*, 15 February 1956, 5, 24–6.

– "The Desanctification of the Holy Land." *Presbyterian Register*, July 1948, 189–90.

– "Impasse in the Holy Land." *University of Toronto Quarterly* 16 (July 1947): 128–32.

– "The United Nations Should Reconsider Palestine." *Globe and Mail*, 28 February 1948.

– "Weizmann on Zionist Struggle." *Saturday Night* (Toronto), 16 August 1949, 10.

Slonim, Reuben, *Family Quarrel: The United Church and the Jews*. Toronto: Clarke, Irwin, 1977.

Smith, Donald. "The World Council of Churches and Its Critics." *Presbyterian Record*, June 1980, 23; July–August 1980, 21–2.

"Statement of Christian Concern about the Middle East." *Globe and Mail*, 19 October 1973.

Swindler, Leonard. "Catholic Statements on Jews: A Revolution in Progress." *Judaism*, summer 1978, 299–307.

– "A New Stage in Jewish-Christian Dialogue." *Judaism*, 1982, 363–4.

Talmage, Frank E., ed. *Disputation and Dialogue: Readings in the Jewish-Christian Encounter*. New York: Ktav Publishing House and Anti Defamation League, 1975.

Taras, David. "A Church Divided: A.C. Forrest and the United Church's Middle East Policy." In *The Domestic Battleground*, David Taras and David H. Goldberg (1989), 86–101.

– and David H. Goldberg, eds. *The Domestic Battleground: Canada and the Arab-Israeli Conflict.* Kingston: McGill-Queen's University Press, 1989.

"To Bigotry No Sanction." *Canadian Baptist* 15 August 1946, 4.

Tyrrell, R. Emmett, Jr. "Chimera in the Middle East: Against a Rational Interpretation of Arab-Israeli Relations." *Massada* 9, no. 1 (1977): 1–3.

Van Buren, Paul M. "When Christians Meet Jews." In *Visions of the Other,* ed. Eugene J. Fisher (1994), 55–66.

van Stempvoort, Mark. "Search for Social Unity: The Career of Claris E. Silcox, 1888–1940." Major research paper, Toronto, 1982. (UCA, Doc. BX 9883 s5v5).

Weinfeld, M., W Shaffir, and L. Cotler, eds. *Canadian Jewish Mosaic.* Toronto: John Wiley and Sons, 1981.

White, Peter G., ed. *Voices and Visions: 65 Years of United the Church of Canada.* Toronto: United Church Publishing House, 1990.

Willis, Robert E. "A Perennial Outrage: Anti-Semitism in the New Testament." *Christian Century* 87 (19 August 1970): 990–2.

Wollaston, Isabel L., "A Comparative Study of Jewish and Christian Responses to the Holocaust." PhD thesis, University of Durham, UK, 1991.

Woodside, Wilson. "The Reluctant Conquerors." *United Church Observer,* 15 December 1967, 38–9.

Index